BROOKLANDS BOOKS

LOTUS ELAN
Gold Portfolio
1962-1974

Compiled by
R.M. Clarke

ISBN 1 870642 627

Distributed by
Brooklands Book Distribution Ltd.
'Holmerise', Seven Hills Road,
Cobham, Surrey, England
Printed in Hong Kong

BROOKLANDS BOOKS

BROOKLANDS BOOKS SERIES
AC Ace & Aceca 1953-1983
AC Cobra 1962-1969
Alfa Romeo Alfasud 1972-1984
Alfa Romeo Alfetta Coupes GT.GTV.GTV6 1974-1987
Alfa Romeo Guilias Berlinettas
Alfa Romeo Giulia Berlinas 1962-1976
Alfa Romeo Giulia Coupés 1963-1976
Alfa Romeo Spider 1966-1987
Allard Gold Portfolio 1937-1958
Aston Martin Gold Portfolio 1972-1985
Austin Seven 1922-1982
Austin A30 & A35 1951-1962
Austin Healey 100 1952-1959
Austin Healey 3000 1959-1967
Austin Healey 100 & 3000 Collection No. 1
Austin Healey 'Frogeye' Sprite Collection No. 1
Austin Healey Sprite 1958-1971
Avanti 1962 1983
BMW Six Cylinder Coupés 1969-1975
BMW 1600 Collection No. 1
BMW 2002 1968-1976
Bristol Cars Gold Portfolio 1946-1985
Buick Automobiles 1946-1960
Buick Automobiles 1947-1960
Buick Riviera 1963-1978
Cadillac Automobiles 1949-1959
Cadillac Automobiles 1960-1969
Cadillac Eldorado 1967-1978
Camaro 1966-1970
Chevrolet Camaro & Z-28 1973-1981
High Performance Camaros 1982-1988
Chevrolet Camaro Collection No. 1
Chevrolet 1955-1957
Chevrolet Impala & SS 1958-1971
Chevrolet & SS 1964-1972
Chevy II Nova & SS 1962-1973
Chrysler 300 1955-1970
Citroen Traction Avant 1934-1957
Citroen DS & ID 1955-1875
Citroen 2CV 1949-1982
Cobras & Replicas 1962-1983
Cortina 1600E & GT 1967-1970
Corvair 1959-1968
Daimler Dart & V-8 250 1959-1969
Datsun 240z 1970-1973
Datsun 280Z & ZX 1975-1983
De Tomaso Collection No. 1
Dodge Charger 1966-1974
Excalibur Collection No. 1
Ferrari Cars 1946-1956
Ferrari Cars 1962-1966
Ferrari Cars 1969-1973
Ferrari Dino 1965-1974
Ferrari Dino 308 1974-1979
Ferrari 308 & Mondial 1980-1984
Ferrari Collection No. 1
Fiat Bertone X1/9 1973-1988
Fiat Pininfarina 124+2000 Spider 1968-1985
Ford Falcon 1960-1970
Ford Mustang 1964-1967
Ford Mustang 1967-1973
High Performance Mustangs 1982-1988
Ford RS Escort 1968-1980
Honda CRX 1983-1987
High Performance Escorts MkI 1968-1974
High Performance Escorts MkII 1975-1980
Hudson & Railton Cars 1936-1940
Jaguar Cars 1957-1961
Jaguar Cars 1961-1964
Jaguar Cars 1964-1968
Jaguar XK120 XK140 XK150 Gold Portfolio 1948-1960
Jaguar MK2 1959-1969
Jaguar E-Type 1961-1966
Jaguar E-Type 1966-1971
Jaguar E-Type V12 1971-1975
Jaguar XKE Collection No. 1
Jaguar XJ6 1968-1972
Jaguar XJ6 Series II 1973-1979
Jaguar XJ6 & XJ12 Series III 1979-1985
Jaguar XJ12 1972-1980
Jaguar XJS Gold Portfolio 1975-1988
Jensen Cars 1946-1967
Jensen Cars 1967-1979
Jensen Interceptor Gold Portfolio 1966-1986
Lamborghini Cars 1964-1970
Lamborghini Cars 1970-1975
Lamborghini Countach Collection No. 1
Lamborghini Countach & Urraco 1974-1980
Lamborghini Countach & Jalpa 1980-1985
Lancia Stratos 1972-1985
Land Rover 1948-1973
Land Rover Series II & IIa 1958-1971
Land Rover Series III 1971-1985
Lotus Cortina 1963-1970
Lotus Elan Gold Portfolio 1962-1973
Lotus Elan Gold Portfolio 1962-1974
Lotus Elan Collection No. 2
Lotus Elite 1957-1964
Lotus Elite & Eclat 1974-1981
Lotus Turbo Esprit 1980-1986
Lotus Europa 1966-1975
Lotus Europa Collection No. 1
Lotus Seven 1957-1980
Lotus Seven Collection No. 1
Maserati 1965-1970
Maserati 1970-1975
Marcos Cars 1960-1988
Mazda RX-7 Collection No. 1
Mercedes 190 & 300SL 1954-1963
Mercedes 230/250/280SL 1963-1971
Mercedes 350/450SL & SLC 1971-1980
Mercedes Benz Cars 1949-1954
Mercedes Benz Cars 1954-1957

Mercedes Benz Cars 1957-1961
Mercedes Benz Competition Cars 1950-1957
Metropolitan 1954-1962
MG Cars 1929-1934
MG TC 1945-1949
MG TD 1949-1953
MG TF 1953-1955
MG Cars 1957-1959
MG Cars 1959-1962
MG Midget 1961-1980
MGA Collection No. 1
MGA Roadsters 1955-1962
MGB Roadsters 1962-1980
MGB GT 1965-1980
Mini Cooper 1961-1971
Morgan Cars 1960-1970
Morgan Cars 1969-1979
Morris Minor Collection No. 1
Old's Cutlass & 4-4-2 1964-1972
Oldsmobile Toronado 1966-1978
Opel GT 1968-1973
Packard Gold Portfolio 1946-1958
Pantera 1970-1973
Pantera & Mangusta 1969-1974
Plymouth Barracuda 1964-1974
Pontiac Fiero 1984-1988
Pontiac GTO 1964-1970
Pontiac Firebird 1967-1973
Pontiac Firebird and Trans-Am 1973-1981
High Performance Firebirds 1982-1988
Pontiac Tempest & GTO 1961-1965
Porsche Cars 1960-1964
Porsche Cars 1964-1968
Porsche Cars 1968-1972
Porsche Cars in the Sixties
Porsche Cars 1972-1975
Porsche 356 1952-1965
Porsche 911 Collection No. 1
Porsche 911 Collection No. 2
Porsche 911 1965-1969
Porsche 911 1970-1972
Porsche 911 1973-1977
Porsche 911 Carrera 1973-1977
Porsche 911 SC 1978-1983
Porsche 911 Turbo 1975-1984
Porsche 914 Collection No. 1
Porsche 924 1975-1981
Porsche 928 Collection No. 1
Porsche 944 1981-1985
Porsche Turbo Collection No. 1
Reliant Scimitar 1964-1986
Riley 1½ & 2½ Litre Gold Portfolio 1945-1955
Rolls Royce Silver Cloud 1955-1965
Rolls Royce Silver Shadow 1965-1980
Range Rover Gold Portfolio 1980-1988
Rover P4 1949-1959
Rover P4 1955-1964
Rover 2000 + 2200 1963-1977
Rover 3500 1968-1977
Rover 3500 & Vitesse 1976-1986
Saab Sonett Collection No. 1
Saab Turbo 1976-1983
Studebaker Hawks & Larks 1956-1963
Sunbeam Tiger And Alpine Gold Portfolio 1959-1967
Thunderbird 1955-1957
Thunderbird 1958-1963
Thunderbird 1964-1976
Toyota MR2 1984-1988
Triumph 2000-2.5-2500 1963-1977
Triumph Spitfire 1962-1980
Triumph Spitfire Collection No. 1
Triumph Stag 1970-1980
Triumph Stag Collection No. 1
Triumph TR2 & TR3 1952-1960
Triumph TR4.TR5.TR250 1961-1968
Triumph TR6 1969-1976
Triumph TR6 Collection No. 1
Triumph TR7 & TR8 1975-1982
Triumph GT6 1966-1974
Triumph Vitesse & Herald 1959-1971
TVR Gold Portfolio 1959-1988
Volkswagen Cars 1936-1956
VW Beetle 1956-1977
VW Beetle Collection No. 1
VW Golf GTi 1976-1986
VW Karmann Ghia 1955-1982
VW Scirocco 1974-1981
VW Bus-Camper-Van 1954-1967
VW Bus-Camper-Van 1968-1979
Volvo 1800 1960-1973
Volvo 120 Series 1956-1970

BROOKLANDS MUSCLE CARS SERIES
American Motors Muscle Cars 1966-1970
Buick Muscle Cars 1965-1970
Camaro Muscle Cars 1966-1972
Capri Muscle Cars 1969-1983
Chevrolet Muscle Cars 1966-1972
Dodge Muscle Cars 1967-1970
Mercury Muscle Cars 1966-1971
Mini Muscle Cars 1961-1979
Mopar Muscle Cars 1964-1967
Mopar Muscle Cars 1968-1971
Mustang Muscle Cars 1967-1971
Shelby Mustang Muscle Cars 1965-1970
Oldsmobile Muscle Cars 1964-1970
Plymouth Muscle Cars 1966-1971
Pontiac Muscle Cars 1966-1972
Muscle Cars Compared 1966-1971
Muscle Cars Compared Book 2 1965-1971

BROOKLANDS ROAD & TRACK SERIES
Road & Track on Alfa Romeo 1949-1963
Road & Track on Alfa Romeo 1964-1970

Road & Track on Alfa Romeo 1971-1976
Road & Track on Alfa Romeo 1977-1984
Road & Track on Aston Martin 1962-1984
Road & Track on Auburn Cord & Duesenberg 1952-1984
Road & Track on Audi 1952-1980
Road & Track on Audi 1980-1986
Road & Track on Austin Healey 1953-1970
Road & Track on BMW Cars 1966-1974
Road & Track on BMW Cars 1975-1978
Road & Track on BMW Cars 1979-1983
Road & Track on Cobra, Shelby &
  Ford GT40 1962-1983
Road & Track on Corvette 1953-1967
Road & Track on Corvette 1968-1982
Road & Track on Corvette 1982-1986
Road & Track on Datsun Z 1970-1983
Road & Track on Ferrari 1950-1968
Road & Track on Ferrari 1968-1974
Road & Track on Ferrari 1975-1981
Road & Track on Ferrari 1981-1984
Road & Track on Fiat Sports Cars 1968-1987
Road & Track on Jaguar 1950-1960
Road & Track on Jaguar 1961-1968
Road & Track on Jaguar 1968-1974
Road & Track on Jaguar 1974-1982
Road & Track on Lamborghini 1964-1985
Road & Track on Lotus 1972-1981
Road & Track on Maserati 1952-1974
Road & Track on Maserati 1975-1983
Road & Track on Mazda RX7 1978-1986
Road & Track on Mercedes 1952-1962
Road & Track on Mercedes 1963-1970
Road & Track on Mercedes 1971-1979
Road & Track on Mercedes 1980-1987
Road & Track on MG Sports Cars 1949-1961
Road & Track on MG Sports Cars 1962-1980
Road & Track on Mustang 1964-1977
Road & Track on Peugeot 1955-1986
Road & Track on Pontiac 1960-1983
Road & Track on Porsche 1951-1967
Road & Track on Porsche 1968-1971
Road & Track on Porsche 1972-1975
Road & Track on Porsche 1975-1978
Road & Track on Porsche 1979-1982
Road & Track on Porsche 1982-1985
Road & Track on Rolls Royce & Bentley 1950-1965
Road & Track on Rolls Royce & Bentley 1966-1984
Road & Track on Saab 1955-1985
Road & Track on Toyota Sports & GT Cars 1966-1986
Road & Track on Triumph Sports Cars 1953-1967
Road & Track on Triumph Sports Cars 1967-1974
Road & Track on Triumph Sports Cars 1974-1982
Road & Track on Volkswagen 1951-1968
Road & Track on Volkswagen 1968-1978
Road & Track on Volkswagen 1978-1985
Road & Track on Volvo 1957-1974
Road & Track on Volvo 1975-1985
Road & Track Henry Manney Atlarce & Abroad

BROOKLANDS CAR AND DRIVER SERIES
Car and Driver on BMW 1955-1977
Car and Driver on BMW 1977-1985
Car and Driver on Cobra, Shelby & Ford GT40
  1963-1984
Car and Driver on Datsun Z 1600 & 2000
  1966-1984
Car and Driver on Corvette 1956-1967
Car and Driver on Corvette 1968-1977
Car and Driver on Corvette 1978-1982
Car and Driver on Corvette 1983-1988
Car and Driver on Ferrari 1955-1962
Car and Driver on Ferrari 1963-1975
Car and Driver on Ferrari 1976-1983
Car and Driver on Mopar 1956-1967
Car and Driver on Mopar 1968-1975
Car and Driver on Pontiac 1961-1975
Car and Driver on Porsche 1955-1962
Car and Driver on Porsche 1963-1970
Car and Driver on Porsche 1970-1976
Car and Driver on Porsche 1977-1981
Car and Driver on Porsche 1982-1986
Car and Driver on Saab 1956-1985
Car and Driver on Volvo 1955-1986

BROOKLANDS MOTOR & THOROUGHBRED & CLASSIC CAR SERIES
Motor & T & CC on Ferrari 1966-1976
Motor & T & CC on Ferrari 1976-1984
Motor & T & CC on Lotus 1979-1983
Motor & T & CC on Morris Minor 1948-1983

BROOKLANDS PRACTICAL CLASSICS SERIES
Practical Classics on Austin A 40 Restoration
Practical Classics on Henry Manney At Large & Abroad
Practical Classics on Land Rover Restoration
Practical Classics on Metalworking in Restoration
Practical Classics on Midget/Sprite Restoration
Practical Classics on Mini Cooper Restoration
Practical Classics on MGB Restoration
Practical Classics on Morris Minor Restoration
Practical Classics on Triumph Herald/Vitesse
Practical Classics on Triumph Spitfire Restoration
Practical Classics on VW Beetle Restoration
Practical Classics on 1930S Car Restoration

BROOKLANDS MILITARY VEHICLES SERIES
Allied Military Vehicles Collection No. 1
Allied Military Vehicles Collection No. 2
Dodge Military Vehicles Collection No. 1
Military Jeeps 1941-1945
Off Road Jeeps 1944-1971
V W Kubelwagen 1940-1975

CONTENTS

5	Lotus Elan Technical Report	Sports Car Graphic	Jan.	1963
8	The Lotus Elan 1500	Motor	Oct. 10	1962
11	The Lotus Elan	Autosport	March 8	1963
13	Lotus Elan 1600 Road Research Report	Car and Driver	Feb.	1964
19	The Lotus Elan Road Test	Autosport	April 3	1964
21	Lotus Elan 1600 Road Test	Cars Illustrated	Aug.	1964
24	With a Little Elan Road Test	Sports Car World	April	1964
28	Lotus Elan Road Test	Motor	Sept.	1964
33	Journey to Sicily	Motor Sport	May	1965
36	Lotus Elan S2 Coupé Road Test	Sports Car Graphic	June	1966
39	Lotus Elan S2 Road Test	Car and Driver	Aug.	1966
43	The IWR Lotus Elan Modified Test	Sporting Motorist	Sept.	1966
44	A Critical Look at the Lotus Elan	Motor Sport	Oct.	1966
50	The Lotus Elan BRM Road Test	Autosport	April 14	1967
52	If I said I Liked the Lotus Elan Would I be Lying? . . . No	Motor World	April 21	1967
55	Lotus Elan Coupé S/E Road Test	Autocar	June 1	1967
59	Lotus Elan – 12,000 Mile Report	Motor	Aug. 12	1967
65	Lotus Elan +2	Autocar	Sept. 7	1967
69	The Lotus Elan Plus 2	Autosport	Sept. 1	1967
70	Lotus Elan Plus-Two Road Test	Sports Car Graphic	Nov.	1967
74	Lotus Elan S/E Road Test	Road & Track	Nov.	1967
79	Better Than Best Road Test	Motor	Jan. 13	1968
81	Exhilarating, Satisfying — Elan Road Test	Autosport	April 5	1968
84	Elation is an Elan Road Test	Sports Car World	July	1968
88	Lotus Elan +2 Road Test	Car and Car Conversions	Nov.	1968
92	1965 Lotus Elan Used Car Test	Autocar	Feb. 20	1969
94	An Open Letter to the Geoghegans Road Test	Sports Car World	March	1969
97	2,000 Miles by Elan +2	Motor Sport	May	1969
99	Lotusland Revisited	Sports Car Graphic	July	1969
102	Lotus Elan Plus 2 Viewpoint	Car and Driver	April	1969
106	Unequalled Roadholding, Performance and Economy Road Test	Autosport	Oct. 23	1969
108	Elan Road Test	Wheels	Oct.	1969
113	Elan avec élan Road Test	Motor	April 18	1970
119	The First Lotus Luxury Car	Autosport	April 23	1970
121	Lotus Elan +2S Road Test	Motor Sport	March	1971
124	Lotus Elan Owner Survey	Road & Track	April	1971
127	Lotus Elan Sprint Road Test	Autocar	June 3	1971
131	Lotus 130 – Big Valve, Big Value	Modern Motor	June	1971
134	Lotus Plus 2S 130 Brief Test	Motor	July 31	1971
137	Lotus Elan Sprint Road Impressions	Motor Sport	July	1971
138	Elan Sprint: The Latest Lotus Position Road Test	Motor Trend	Jan.	1972
143	Lotus Elan Sprint Road Test	Road & Track	March	1972
146	An Elan with a Difference Tuning Topics	Motor Sport	May	1972
148	Lotus Elan Plus 2S 130 Road Test	Road & Track	June	1972
152	Lotus Elan +2S 130 Road Test	Car and Driver	June	1972
155	Refined Lotus Elan +2S with Five Speed Gearbox Road Test	Autosport	Oct. 26	1972
157	Lotus Elan Sprint Road Test	Car and Driver	Jan.	1973
162	Lotus Elan Sprint: Ideal for England Road Test	Autosport	Feb. 8	1973
164	Non-Stop to the Sun	Autocar	May 17	1973
166	Six Years of Sensible Refinement	What Car?	Jan.	1974
169	Added Elan Track Test	Classic and Sportscar	May 11	1985
171	Buying an Elan Buying Feature	Practical Classics	April	1981
175	Road Racers Super Profile	Classic and Sportscar	April	1987

BROOKLANDS BOOKS

ACKNOWLEDGEMENTS

Brooklands books are works of reference for owners and others that have a feel for interesting cars. Our aim has always been to cover marques that are sought out, kept, restored and cherished by enthusiasts and a glance at page 2 will show that the spectrum is indeed wide.

Our first book on the Elan appeared over ten years ago. Due to the enormous interest in the model we were forced on two occasions to search out further material which meant at one period we had three separate titles on a vehicle had had a production run of less that fifteen thousand. Colin Chapman designed a remarkably likeable car.

With two of these books now unavailable we thought it would be sensible to start afresh and compile one volume that would do justice to this clasic British sportscar. We have endeavoured to make it as international as possible and combine stories on racing, tuning and touring in amongst the inevitable road tests.

It would be impossible for us to produce books such as this if we did not enjoy the support of the worlds leading motoring journals. They for many years have understood our motives and have generously allowed us to include their informative and copyright stories. Our thanks in this instance go specifically to the publishers of Autocar, Autosport, Car and Car Conversions, Car and Driver, Cars Illustrated, Classic and Sportscar, Modern Motor, Motor, Motor Sport, Motor Trend, Motor World, Practical Classics, Road & Track, Sporting Motorist, Sports Car Graphic, Sports Car World, What Car? and Wheels for their ongoing help.

R.M. Clarke

TECHNICAL REPORT
LOTUS ELAN

"...surely the smoothest-running and safest handling sports car ever to have been produced by a British factory."

BY JOHN BLUNSDEN

Dubbed "the most important sports car of 1962," the sleek Elan is loaded with unique features.

FROM BOTH COMMERCIAL AND TECHNICAL STANDPOINTS, the Lotus Elan is the most important production car to be designed and marketed by Colin Chapman's Cheshunt-based factory.

It is the first British volume-produced sports car to feature a twin-overhead-camshaft engine, all-independent suspension, and rubber-cushioned drive, and certainly the first model with such an exciting specification to be offered at so attractive a price. In Britain, its price tag, in assembled form, of $4200 (£1,499), compared with the Elite at $5450 (£1,948), an 'E' type Jaguar at $5700 (£2,036), a Daimler SP 250 at $4050 (£1,451), an Alfa Giulietta Spyder at $4750 (£1,695) or a Porsche 1600 at $6100 (£2,163). Also, it can be bought in component form (thereby avoiding the burden of England's purchase tax) for an attractive $3050 (£1,095).

It is easy to talk about the backbone of the Elan, for its chassis is just that — a 11½-inches deep 18-gauge steel double backbone, with appendages which act as attachment points for the front-mounted engine, clutch and gearbox units, the rear-mounted differential, and the suspension units. The glass-fiber body molded in five pieces, is an entirely separate unit, and is bolted to the chassis at sixteen points.

The engine is a production development of the unit used in Jim Clark's Lotus 23 at Nurburgring in May 1962 for the 1,000 Kilometers race. It is basically the 1,498 cc four-cylinder Ford unit, with five-bearing crankshaft, as fitted to the Consul 315 and Capri, but with a special twin-overhead-camshaft cylinder head developed by Lotus from a design by Harry Mundy.

The end product is a superbly smooth power unit, running on a 9.5 to 1 compression and giving 100 horsepower at 5,700 rpm. This, of course, is nothing approaching the limit of power development on this engine (readings of 140 horsepower and more have already been achieved with reliability). In this case emphasis has been put on torque characteristics; a maximum of 102 pounds feet is given at 4,500 rpm, with 85 pounds feet at 2,500 rpm, 90 pounds feet at 3,100 rpm, 95 pounds feet at 3,500 rpm, and 100 pounds feet or more between 3,900 and 5,100 rpm.

There is an almost constant build-up of power throughout the rev range, the following figures having been seen on the brake:

2,000 rpm	32 horsepower
2,500 rpm	41 horsepower
3,000 rpm	51 horsepower
3,500 rpm	63 horsepower
4,000 rpm	76 horsepower
4,500 rpm	87 horsepower
5,000 rpm	96 horsepower
5,500 rpm	99 horsepower
6,000 rpm	97 horsepower

The cylinder dimensions remain unaltered from the standard Ford specification of 80.96 mm bore, and 72.75 mm stroke, which gives the 1,498 cc displacement. The firing order is 1-3-4-2, and the twin overhead camshafts are driven by a single-stage roller chain.

Separate inlet and exhaust ports, of course, are provided for each cylinder, and the inlet manifolds are cast integrally with the cylinder head. There is a 12-volt ignition system, and 14 mm long-reach spark plugs are used.

The rotor-type oil pump is mounted externally, and main-

5

LOTUS ELAN

tains full pressure to the main, big-end and camshaft bearings. There is a full-flow filter, and the system has a capacity of 7½ U.S. pints.

The dual twin-choke Weber 40 DCOE carburetors, equipped with replaceable-element air cleaners, are fed by mechanical pump from a 12 U.S. gallon fuel tank. The pressurized water cooling system has a capacity of just under 17 U.S. pints.

The transmission units are Ford throughout, being taken, like the bottom half of the engine, from the Consul 315. This means there is synchromesh of the Porsche type on all forward gears, and a really slick shift mechanism.

There is an interesting story behind the development of the backbone chassis of the Elan. The prototype frame was built up three years ago, and when tested it was found to have no less than six times the stiffness of the then current multi-tube frame of the Lotus Formula 1 car. It was this discovery which first set Colin Chapman thinking about monocoque construction for racing cars, for there was obviously little to choose between the two types of construction in terms of net weight!

Some interesting detail work has gone into the design of the frame, which was the work of Mike Costin, before he resigned from Lotus to rejoin Keith Duckworth in the company he helped to form — Cosworth Engineering. The base of the frame, for example, is an elongated 'U' section member, the recess of which acts as a neat housing for the exhaust pipe, which is thereby kept well clear of the ground, and largely out of sight.

There is also a novel arrangement for supporting the final drive unit. This is attached to a transverse beam, which in turn is rubber-jointed to the rear crossmember of the chassis by means of vertical studs. Fore and aft location of the axle is by a pair of radius rods running forwards from the unit and pinned laterally into the sides of the backbone. The axle housing is also rubber mounted to the 'U' section bottom frame member, and carries the inner bearings of the final drive.

This is perhaps the most interesting part of the transmission. The hollow drive shafts carry three-prong forgings at either end, coupling them to rubber units, similar to, but slightly smaller than those used in the final drive of the Formula 1 Lotuses. The Elan, therefore, has four of these units, one on each side of the final drive unit, and one at the outer end of each drive shaft.

Immediately outboard of the outer rubber units are the Lotus-designed 10-inch disc brakes, these in turn being placed well inboard of the alloy hub carriers.

The rear suspension is of the strut type, incorporating high-mounted Armstrong telescopic shock absorbers within coil springs, and fitted with rubber buffers at the top end. The base of the hub carriers are attached to extremely wide-based wishbones, with double fore-and-aft bracing, which in turn are linked to the chassis through Metalastic metal-and-rubber bushes. The very small variation in lateral

The four-cylinder, five-main-bearing Ford, at left, is fitted here with a DOHC cylinder head, develops 100 strong horses.

Tasteful and compact, the fibreglass body, below, contributes to the rigidity of the central-beam frame shown at right. A departure that led to Chapman-built monocoque car, this unit has little weight advantage but is extremely high in strength.

movement of the wheels caused through suspension movement is absorbed by the four rubber units.

The front suspension, by means of compact wishbones and small-diameter coil springs encircling telescopic shocks, is a refinement of the system used on the Lotus Elite. The outboard front disc brakes are 9½ inches in diameter, and are recessed into the wheel rims. Once again the Triumph rack and pinion is used, in modified form, for the steering giving 2½ turns of the 15-inch wood-rimmed wheel, lock to lock. Lotus have designed special high-speed steel wheels, with four-stud fixing, and these are shod with 5.20 x 13 Goodyear tires.

The five-piece body consists of the body, trunk lid, engine hood, and the doors — and the body section is probably the most elaborate one-piece moulding yet to have been achieved for car production. One of the most interesting detail features concerns the headlamp arrangement, the lights being recessed under swivelling covers when not in use. Double dashboard switching is provided to raise or retract the headlamps, which are coupled to vacuum cylinders, which in turn are coupled to a vacuum reservoir, the whole system being operated by manifold vacuum. When locked in the raised position, the lamps comply with the regulation distance from ground level to the center of the glass, and a finger-tip flashing control is built in. The lamps cannot be left on in the retracted position, or remain off when they are raised.

Another unusual feature is the use of foam-filled glass-fiber bumper bars, which are said not to crack, dent, or bend under minor impact. The weatherproofing arrangement is also unconventional, in that it includes a PVC fabric soft top, and separate clip-on glass-fiber cant rails, which surround the side window apertures, and carry the support rails for the top. A PVC strip along the front of the soft top is recessed into the top of the windshield, and a solid rail below the rear window panels secures the top to lugs on the body. Finally, there are the usual clip-on fasteners to seal the minor gaps.

(continued on page **105***)*

Left: This view gives some idea of the economy of structural metal which connects the mechanical components into a single self-contained chassis.

Right: A long narrow air intake is tucked away below the glass fibre front bumper and registration numbers are attached directly to the grille mesh. Retractable headlights have made it possible to use a particularly low and attractive nose shape.

Below: Wide-rimmed 15 in. pressed steel wheels are pierced with cut-outs the shape of the Lotus emblem. A backbone chassis places few restrictions on body design and the doors extend far enough forward to make entry easy.

the LOTUS Elan 1500

ALL INDEPENDENT FULLY EQUIPPED 2-SEATER WITH TWIN CAM ENGINE AND 170 b.h.p./ton

BEFORE the monocoque Lotus 25 G.P. car first appeared several months ago, Colin Chapman remarked that his thoughts had turned to this form of structure because of his experience with a new sports car prototype. He said that when they discovered that they had built a sports car chassis that was as light as the space frame of the Lotus F.1. car and six times stiffer they were a bit shaken. He was referring, of course, to the steel backbone structure of the new Lotus Elan, which has just been unveiled; amongst other features, the specification of this advanced and ingenious two-seater includes a 1½-litre twin o.h.c. engine with all synchromesh gearbox, independent suspension and disc brakes on all four wheels, rack and pinion steering and a glass fibre body with retractable headlamps.

Although the Elan 1500 has mechanical features which derive very obviously from past or present racing Lotuses, it is probably the first car from this factory that has been designed entirely as a practical and comfortable road car with no overriding concern for its competition future; its appeal, therefore, is likely to be wider and its potential market much greater than that of any previous Lotus. Both the much cheaper Lotus 7 and the rather more expensive Lotus Elite will remain in production to satisfy more specialized markets.

Lotus success is founded on weight consciousness; proprietary components inevitably form such a large part of any production

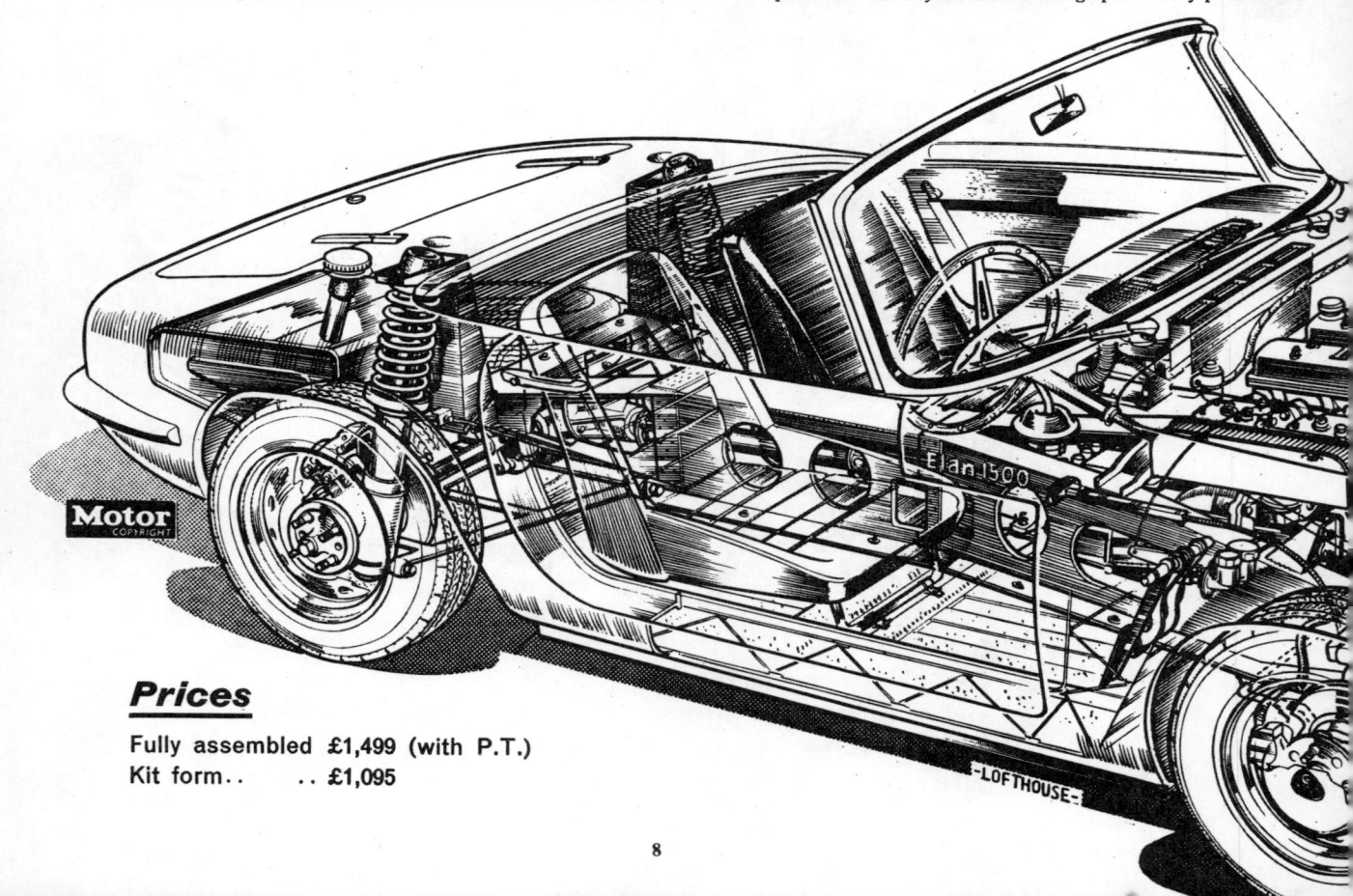

Prices

Fully assembled £1,499 (with P.T.)
Kit form.. .. £1,095

THE MOTOR
October 10 1962

car that they are fortunate in their close collaboration with the most weight conscious of the large manufacturers—the Ford Motor Company. Engine, gearbox and final drive units are all based on current Ford parts and so are some of the minor components.

The Lotus engine has a special light alloy twin o.h.c. cylinder head with valves inclined at 27° on either side of the vertical and twin double-choke Weber 40 DCOE carburetters. The camshafts are driven directly from a crankshaft sprocket by a single roller chain inside a special timing case but the rest of the engine is the new five-bearing 1,500 c.c. Ford Classic unit. When we described the Lotus engine in our issue of May 23 we were naturally unable to reveal this fact but a full account of this light, compact and remarkably smooth 116E unit was published on August 29. The cylinder block is 0.6 in. taller than that of a Ford Anglia engine but otherwise it is no bigger and not a great deal heavier. Since the twin-cam head, even with its present mild valve timing, raises the power output to 100 b.h.p. at 5,700 r.p.m., this engine has outstanding power/weight and power/size ratios. The inlet extension tubes of the Weber carburetters, which are necessary to reduce petrol spit-back, are now surrounded by a one-piece air cleaner with a paper element which helps to reduce power roar.

The standard Ford gearbox now has synchromesh on all forward gears and, although the ratios are rather widely spaced for a sports car, the outstandingly pleasant gearchange should be further improved by the shorter Lotus lever.

Although used by several manufacturers before the war, the steel backbone frame is a type of structure which has been largely neglected recently; it has conspicuous advantages for a practical open car in which a large central tunnel is no great handicap. It combines enormous rigidity and strength with light weight, it can be made without the tremendously expensive dies and press tools which are only appropriate to large scale production and it leaves the designer free to employ any suitable material and manufacturing process for the entirely separate body.

The central part of this frame is a 16 gauge mild steel rectangular box approximately 10½ in. x 6 in. and only about 25 in. long. Further forward the tube bifurcates, running each side of the engine and gearbox unit to a cross member which joins the front suspension mounting points; a similar but shorter fork at the back encloses the final drive and provides mounting points for the rear springs and wishbones. Large flanged holes facilitate assembly of components as well as lightening the structure.

The complete frame weighs 75 lb. and its stiffness is given as greater than 4,500 lb.ft./degree twist between the wheel planes. The true figure may well be nearer 6,000, which is about twice that of the Lotus Elite and very much more than one could hope to attain with a practical multi-tube frame of reasonable weight.

Familiar Pattern

Generally speaking, suspension follows familiar Lotus lines. At the front pressed steel wishbones of unequal length are pivoted to the frame on rubber bushes and sprung on Armstrong coil spring/damper units; the camber angle is zero to 1° positive and both castor and king-pin angles are high at 7° and 9° respectively. An Alford and Alder rack and pinion, as used on the Triumph Vitesse, is rubber mounted to absorb shock and kickback and a Herald telescopic steering column allows for individual adjustment.

The rear suspension may well be described as a mixture of Lotus Elite and current G.P. Lotus. As on the former, Armstrong suspension struts, using coil springs from the front of a Ford Classic, spigot at their bottom ends into cast light alloy hub carriers, but by offsetting the centre line of these units so that they pass down in front of the drive shafts, they have been lowered by several inches so that it is possible to accommodate a much longer spring travel without raising the conical rubber upper mounting points excessively. The articulated half shafts, however, no longer act as lateral radius arms; this job is done by wide-based lower wishbones which also control the steering angle of rear wheels which are set with zero to 1/8 in. toe-in in the static position. Progressive spring stiffening towards the full-bump position is provided by Aeon hollow bump cushions incorporated in the strut.

The geometry is so arranged that very little variation of drive shaft length is needed to accommodate suspension movement and this is obtained, without the use of splines, from the axial flexibility of the two Metalastik rubber couplings in each shaft which replace ordinary universal joints. Their torsional flexi-

The Elan is a properly finished and furnished production car with full provision for radio and heater and ample room for extra instruments or switches on the oiled teak dashboard.

LOTUS Elan

Tapered vertical columns support the rear suspension struts. This view also shows the Lotus light alloy differential housing and wide-based lower wishbones.

bility helps to cushion the drive but also makes the use of inboard brakes impracticable; 10 in. diameter Girling rear discs are therefore mounted on the inboard side of the hub carriers. Similar brakes at the front are of slightly smaller (9½ in.) diameter to fit inside the rims.

A Ford Anglia/Classic type nose piece, with special 3.9 to 1 hypoid bevel gears, bolts into a light-alloy housing which is fixed to the rear cross-member by rubber mountings above and below the housing, the upper ones being very widely spread and the lower ones having soft rubber washers which permit some fore and aft flexibility. In this way the unit has a limited freedom to pivot about the top mountings, a movement which simulates the rotation of a normal back axle on semi-elliptic springs and helps to cushion driving shock loads.

The moulded glass fibre plastic body, which is built by S. Bourne of Nottingham, drops down over the chassis tubes to sit on flanges along their bottom edges. It is bolted down at 14 points along the entire length of this frame, the bolts threading into die-cast Mazak bobbins which are moulded into the plastic. The whole body is designed as a stressed structure, double skinning being used in parts where strength or good finish is important. Although it is not intended to stiffen the chassis appreciably, it supports most of the auxiliary loads such as seats, occupants, petrol tank, spare wheel, luggage, etc. A 10-gallon tank, spare wheel and transverse silencer all live under the floor of a fairly small but useful boot. Luggage accommodation is considerably increased by the space in the cockpit behind the seats which has been designed to take a carry-cot or a child sitting astride the central tube.

Specially made seats give a typically Lotus long-arm driving position and the fore and aft adjustment mechanism is so arranged that the rear mounting rises as it moves forward so that short drivers can still command a satisfactory view over the scuttle. Sliding glass side windows push up and down and the doors hinge on fully adjustable projecting nylon studs which seat in Mazak cups.

Since so many small low-built cars have had both their frontal appearance and their aerodynamic lines spoiled by the legal requirement that headlamps must be mounted with centres not less than 24 in. from the ground, Lotus decided that the complication of retractable lights was essential. The drawing shows how these are pivoted and energized by inlet manifold suction through a vacuum cylinder which raises the lamps to fixed factory pre-set stops; final beam setting is by means of the usual screws round the rim. This mechanism is very rapid and powerful and the lights can be raised in little more than 1 second for signal flashing.

An oiled teak facia forms a structural bracing member between the central tube and the scuttle. The bonnet opening is characteristically ingenious; when two separate catches (for safety) are released inside the cockpit the lid opens automatically under the action of two large tension springs, the front end sliding on nylon headed screws in curved guides which are shown in the drawing. When the springs are unhooked it can be lifted off altogether. Front and rear bumpers are made from very flexible resilient glass fibre plastic and filled with expanded polyurethene foam.

Apart from routine checking of the usual oil levels, servicing has been virtually eliminated and there are no chassis greasing points. The car is some 2-3 in. shorter, narrower and lower than a Lotus Elite and, if the estimated weight of 11½ cwt. proves to be correct, about 1½ cwt. lighter. On the standard axle ratio maximum speed will probably be limited to about 110 m.p.h. (about 6,200 r.p.m. in top), but with a 100 b.h.p. engine of notably high torque, acceleration should be impressive in the extreme.

Specification

Engine
Cylinders .. .. .. 4 in line with 5-bearing crankshaft
Bore and stroke .. .. 80.96 mm. × 72.75 mm. (3.19 in. × 2.86 in.)
Cubic capacity .. .. 1,498 c.c. (91.5 cu. in.)
Piston area .. .. 31.92 sq. in.
Compression ratio 9.5/1
Valvegear: Inclined overhead valves operated directly through inverted piston tappets from chain driven double overhead camshafts.
Carburation: 2 double choke 40 DCOE Weber carburetters, fed by AC mechanical pump, from 10-gallon tank.
Ignition: 12-volt coil, with centrifugal timing control, 14 mm. Lodge long reach sparking plugs.
Lubrication .. .. Full-flow filter and 5¼-pint sump (+1 pint for filter).
Cooling: Water cooling with pump, fan and thermostat; 14-pint water capacity.
Electrical system: 38 amp hour, 12-volt battery charged by 300 watt generator.
Maximum power: 100 b.h.p. (net) at 5,700 r.p.m., equivalent to 151 lb./sq. in. b.m.e.p. at 2,740 ft./min. piston speed and 3.13 b.h.p. per sq. in. of piston area.
Maximum torque: 102 lb.ft. at 4,500 r.p.m., equivalent to 168 lb./sq. in. b.m.e.p. at 2,150 ft./min. piston speed.

Transmission
Clutch: .. .. 7¼ in. single dry plate with hydraulic operation.
Gearbox: 4-speed all-synchromesh with direct drive on top gear.
Overall ratios .. .. 3.90, 5.51, 9.34, 13.82; rev. 15.45
Propeller shaft .. .. B.R.D. single-piece open
Final drive .. .. Hypoid bevel

Chassis
Brakes .. .. Girling discs all round
Brake dimensions .. .. .. Front 9½ in. dia.; rear 10 in. dia.
Brake areas: 26 sq. in. of lining (13 sq. in. front plus 13 sq. in. rear) working on 320 sq. in. rubbed area.
Front suspension: Independent by Armstrong coil spring/damper units, unequal length transverse wishbones and anti-roll bar.
Rear suspension: Independent by Armstrong coil spring/damper struts and lower wishbones.
Wheels and tyres: Slotted pressed steel wheels with 4½J rims and 5.20-15 Goodyear tyres.
Steering .. .. .. Rack and pinion, 2½ turns lock to lock

Dimensions
Length .. .. .. Overall 12 ft. 1¼ in.; wheelbase 7 ft.
Width .. .. Overall 4 ft. 8 in.; track 3 ft. 11 in. at front and rear
Height: (to top of screen) 3 ft. 8 in.; ground clearance 6 in.; (to top of hood) 3 ft. 9 in.
Turning circle.. .. .. 29¾ ft.
Kerb weight: Estimated 11½ cwt. (without fuel but with oil, water, tools, spare wheel, etc.).

Effective Gearing
Top gear ratio: 17.8 m.p.h. at 1,000 r.p.m. and 37.3 m.p.h. at 1,000 ft./min. piston speed.
Maximum torque 4,500 r.p.m. corresponds to approx. 80 m.p.h. in top
Maximum power 5,700 r.p.m. corresponds to approx. 101 m.p.h. in top gear.

JOHN BOLSTER tries

The Lotus Elan

In a very short time I am hoping to carry out a full road test of the Lotus Elan, which I am expecting from the manufacturers. However, I am getting so many letters from readers about this car that I have taken the opportunity of having a short preliminary canter. Please note that the car I used was below standard, because it had only the wide-ratio Ford gearbox and the engine was not stretched to run in the 1,600 c.c. class. Nevertheless, its performance was so outstanding that I can hardly wait for the "works" car to turn up.

The Elan which I tried was built from a kit of parts by a customer of The Chequered Flag. He wanted them to check the car to see if it was buttoned together properly, and Alan Foster suggested that my road test routine would do just that. That was how I unexpectedly found myself at the wheel of one of the most outstanding cars I have driven.

The Elan has a steel backbone chassis with independent suspension and disc brakes all round. Over this a plastic 2-seater body fits like a saddle. The car is propelled by a five-bearing Ford engine with a twin overhead camshaft Lotus light-alloy head and two twin-choke Weber carburetters. It has many brilliant design features, which will be discussed in full detail when the official road test car arrives.

I do not know whether to enthuse most about the acceleration, roadholding, silence, smooth running, or braking. Let me say at once that in all these departments the Elan is fantastic.

The engine is flexible right down to the lowest speeds, and the acceleration in the middle ranges is so potent that there is no real need to change out of top gear for overtaking or hill climbing. Above 30 m.p.h. the car simply rushes forward in top, the acceleration feeling almost constant right up to 100 m.p.h. Above that speed, the pressure from the back of the seat begins to be less pronounced and a maximum speed of 109.7 m.p.h. is eventually reached. It must be emphasized that even more startling figures would be available with the close-ratio gearbox, but the results which I obtained were sufficiently dramatic.

The standing quarter-mile occupied 16.4 secs., and the acceleration took 2.8 secs. for the 0-30 m.p.h. range and 6.2 secs. for 0-50 m.p.h., which included two gear changes with this box. 0-60 m.p.h. was achieved in 8.4 secs., and 0-80 m.p.h. in a staggering 14 secs. dead. The 0-100 m.p.h. time was 21.6 secs., and the fuel consumption was approximately 20 m.p.g., including the performance testing.

Once upon a time the four-wheel drift was reserved for Grand Prix drivers. I think that even a beginner, with L-plates up, would soon learn to drift the Elan! It is probably the fastest sports car through a corner, but the breakaway is so gradual that there is no lack of warning, as is sometimes the case with cars of high cornering power. The braking, with large discs all round, is very powerful with no tendency to lock the wheels.

The sound insulation is excellent, the absence of road noise being reminiscent of a very costly limousine. The engine is also remarkably quiet, an expansion chamber close up to the manifold no doubt playing its part. Complete insulation of the final drive has also been achieved, the metalastic universal joints possibly assisting

Lotus Elan 1500

here, and they certainly avoid any jerk in the transmission. It is in these respects that the Elan is such an advance on any previous Lotus.

I am tired of moaning about driving seats that do not locate the driver. The bucket seats of the Elan give absolute lateral stability, but they are also very, very comfortable. The driving position is ideal, with a wooden steering wheel and gear-lever knob, the central remote control working nicely and the pedals being arranged for heel-and-toe. The retractable headlamps are rather fun, a touch of the switch bringing them up already flashing if some clot gets in the way. The size of the boot is quite outstanding for a 2-seater sports car.

The Lotus Elan is a sports car which handles like a racing car. Yet, it has many of the virtues of an expensive touring car, while its small size renders it very suitable for London traffic. With the hood up, it is as cosy as any saloon, the heater being particularly effective, and the quiet running encouraged me to use the radio. When an engine developing 100 b.h.p. is placed in a car weighing 11½ cwt. something pretty dramatic is going to happen. If you add silence and flexibility to that sort of performance, the result is a car that will have a tremendous popularity, especially as it can be bought in component form for £1,095.

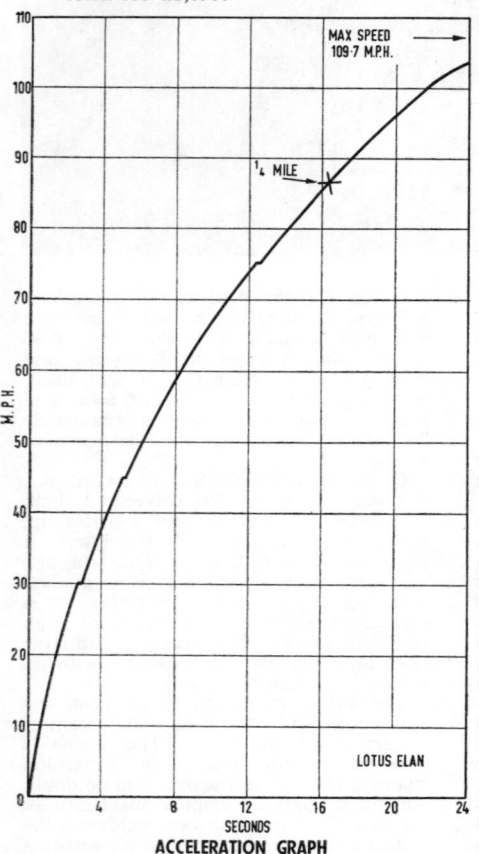

The retractable headlamps are rather fun . . .

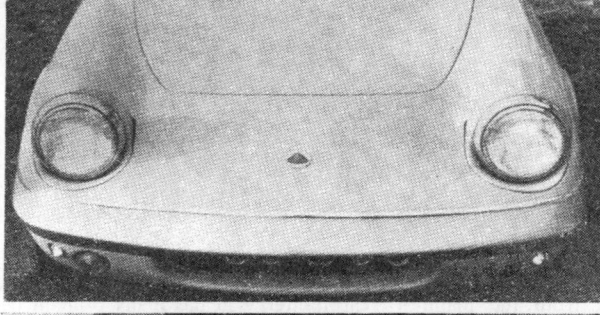

. . . a touch of the switch brings them up already flashing

ACCELERATION GRAPH

Road Research Report:

LOTUS ELAN 1600

Sophistication comes to the sports car—in a truly modern design

One of the daily office bull sessions, a few months ago, got off on the nature of enthusiasm and other similarly esoteric subjects, and we were wondering what the 1963 enthusiast drives. Fifteen years ago, he was in an MG-TC with no windscreen, or some kind of bellowing Allard. Nowadays, we decided, a true enthusiast, a real purist, ought to have a Lotus 23 to drive on the streets, since that fantastic car is about as extreme—and pure—an example of sporting automobile as there is around.

That was before we'd driven the Elan. Now, blanching at the prospect of trying to protect a 23 in modern traffic on one hand, and having sampled the joys of the Elan on the other, we'd like to make a substitution. The Elan very simply represents the sports car developed in tune with the state of the art. It comes closer than anything else on the market to providing a Formula

LOTUS ELAN

car for ordinary street use. And it fits like a Sprite, goes like a Corvette, and handles like a Formula Junior.

Driving it is very simply another sort of automotive experience altogether. Most people tend to come back from their first ride a little bit glassy-eyed; the knowledgeable usually remark that the car reminds them of nothing so much as a Formula Junior. What you *will* get from a Lotus Elan that you aren't apt to be able to experience in a Junior, is the absolute joy of *charging*—under all sorts of conditions and in all kinds of circumstances. A combination of the very tiny exterior dimensions of the car, the great acceleration and stopping power, and the complete, reliable *safety* of it, makes hurrying into a pretty good sport in itself.

That safety aspect is perhaps the strongest impression the car makes. Underway, it seems less a car than a *system*, with its elements complementing each other well enough to pretty well wipe out previous notions of how a car should go. Safety comes in other forms than massive padding—a well-balanced, positive, and predictable chassis, as in this case, will do.

Almost everything about the Elan seems to represent a complete reversal of Colin Chapman's design philosophy, as exemplified by the unit-construction fiberglass-bodied Elite and the monocoque Lotus 25 Grand Prix car. The Elan is built up on a deep box-section steel backbone frame with something like six times greater torsional stiffness than the structure of the Formula One vehicle. Chapman also breaks with past Lotus practice in the Elan suspension, and relies on Ford for the complete engine and drive train.

Backbone frames have almost disappeared since unit-construction came into vogue, but they were quite popular in pre-war days. The original backbone frame was designed by Edmund W. Lewis and used on the 1904 Rover, but the design which the Elan chassis brings to mind is the R-Type MG of 1935, designed by H.N. Charles. The similarity of concept and execution between these two cars is so striking that one is tempted to conclude that Chapman took his inspiration for the Elan from the single-seater MG. The R-Type had a backbone steel frame of immense structural strength, and wishbone-type independent suspension front and rear, but used torsion bars rather than coil springs as on the Elan.

The Elan frame forks out at both ends to resemble a cruciform structure, with the front triangle providing room for the engine and gearbox and attachment points for the front suspension, while the rear triangle provides a base for the rear suspension and final drive. The frame is made of 18-gauge steel (0.048-in. thickness) with 16-gauge (0.064-in. thickness) reinforcements. The center section, which makes up the console between the two seats, has a width of six inches and a depth of 11½ inches. The frame is drilled for lightness and weighs only 75 lbs.

The body is a fiberglass shell with metal reinforcements for the doors and windshield. It is itself a unit structure and does not rely on the backbone frame for stiffness. The same theory has been applied with steel bodywork on the Triumph Spitfire, which also has a very rigid frame. The Elan body rests on the frame midriff and has 14 additional mountings—10 on the lower edge of the frame and 4 on the suspension pillars. The fiberglass structure is manufactured by S. Bourne of Nottingham and shipped to Lotus at Cheshunt in Hertfordshire for assembly and finishing.

Front suspension on the Elan follows the main principles laid down in the Elite, with unequal-length

The tastefully simple dash layout puts all the controls within

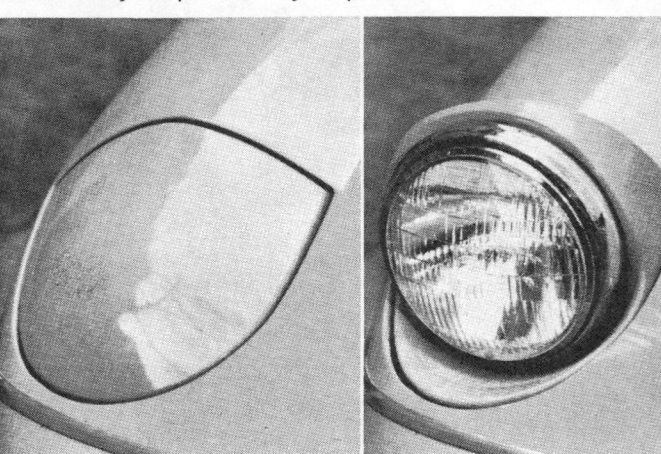

Pop-up lights are vacuum operated, work faster than electrics.

The very small overall size of the Elan isn't evident in photos

easy reach, but interior dimensions are all a wee bit cramped.

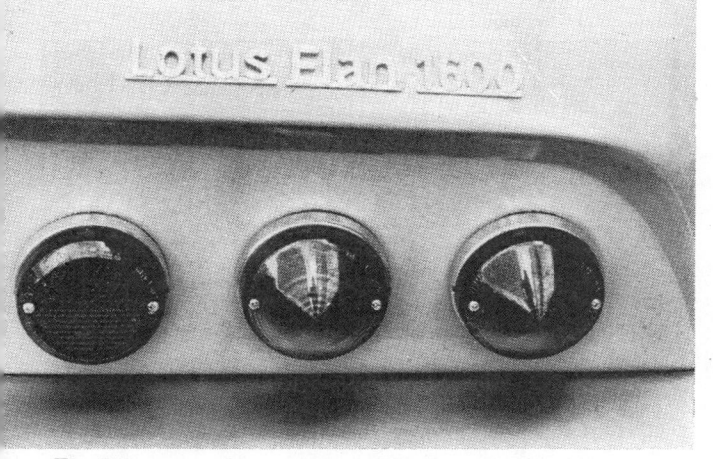

The Elan rear end resembles the Elite's semi-chopped after-half.

but driving it, it seems smaller than just about anything else.

wishbones and narrow-diameter coil spring-and-shock absorber struts. The normal setting for the front wheels of the Elan gives one degree of positive camber.

While the rear end of the Elite has a lower transverse link and uses the half-shafts as upper locating members, the Elan has lower wishbones only and positive top location via the Chapman suspension struts, relieving the half-shaft of all location duties. The shafts still have fixed length, but some flexibility is provided by the Metalastik universal joints. Like Lotus racing designs, spring rates on the Elan are as low as possible, keeping the wheels in constant contact with the road and giving a ride comfort far superior to any other sports cars—if not better than many luxury sedans!

As befits a Chapman design, the Elan's cornering power is simply phenomenal. It's a considerable improvement on the 1955 Lotus 11, which first established modern standards for high-speed small-displacement sports cars. Going through a corner progressively faster with the Elan, it first drifts, then slides and makes a low cat-like growl when the limit of propriety is approached. It then crouches and goes still faster. But there is never anything untoward or unexpected—everything merely happens faster than with other cars because this one can be cornered faster.

The car has absolutely neutral handling characteristics, and wonderfully quick steering response with all the accuracy of a racing machine. And just like the old Lotus 11, the car won't do anything funny if the driver uses the brakes well into a corner—it will stay right on the intended line. Changes in throttle opening affect its course so slightly as to be of no moment.

Our test car was fitted with Goodyear Tubeless tires, a mistake that the importer was happy to acknowledge. Later cars will be fitted with a more suitable Dunlop tire, and the car will undoubtedly be more controllable in the wet and quieter during cornering on the dry.

For a large driver, the Lotus Elan borders on being too small. Pedal placement is as good as possible, but the narrow tunnel just doesn't give enough space for really good location. As a result, heeling-and-toeing is possible for the big-footed, but you ought to wear nice tight shoes to try it. The brake foot tends to catch a bit of the gas pedal when you don't want it to, and you have to slide your clutch foot under the clutch pedal to rest it—or to dim the lights. We found ourselves lifting only our toe to get off the accelerator pedal, and thinking the throttle was stuck; it was just that we were still holding the gas pedal down with the arch of our foot. Detail changes are planned.

The result of all this is that a larger driver will feel unnaturally clumsy in the tiny car, as a first impression. The evidence of a quick and vital kind of response is so apparent that he'll blame himself, feeling guilty for manhandling a thoroughbred. Then, as miles accumulate, things start falling into place, and the driving procedure becomes a kind of whirling tapdance, with only a touch needed here and there, a soft, light, effortless controllability. But it is truer of the Elan than of most cars that you need to put some time in before the car begins to work properly for you.

The seats of the Elan are less extreme in the angle of reclining than on any other Lotus, including the Elite. The backrests are not adjustable, but the fixed angle will suit most drivers who prefer a straight-arm position. Short drivers are aided in their efforts to see out by the fact that the seat moves upward as it is moved forward.

Attractive is unquestionably the word for the interior, which is nice but not terribly practical. There's

Road Research Report: Lotus Elan

Importer: Cox & Pulver, Inc.
233 East 70th Street, New York 21, N.Y.

PRICES:
Basic price........................$4295.00 POE East Coast

ENGINE:
Water-cooled four-in-line, cast-iron block, 5 main bearings.
Bore x stroke............................3.25 x 2.86 in, 82.55 x 72.75 mm
Displacement...95 cu in, 1558 cc
Compression ratio...9.5 to one
Carburetion..2 Weber side-draft DCOE/2
Valve Gear...............................Twin chain-driven overhead camshafts
Valve diameter......................Intake 1.62 in, exhaust 1.46 in
Valve timing
   Intake opens..22° BTC
   Intake closes..62° ABC
   Exhaust opens...62° BBC
   Exhaust closes..22° ATC
Valve lift...0.35 in
Power (SAE)...105 bhp @ 5500 rpm
Torque..108 lb-ft @ 4000 rpm
Specific power output............1.1 bhp per cu in, 67.5 bhp per liter
Usable range of engine speeds.......................................1500-7000 rpm
Electrical system.................12-Volt, 57-amp-hr battery, 300 W generator
Fuel recommended...Premium
Mileage..22-28 mpg
Range on 12-gallon tank...265-335 miles

DRIVE TRAIN:
Clutch: 8½-inch single dry plate
Transmission: 4-speed all-synchro gearbox

Gear	Ratio	Overall	mph/1000 rpm	Max mph
Rev	2.92	11.38	-5.9	-41
1st	2.51	9.78	6.8	47.5
2nd	1.70	6.63	10.2	71
3rd	1.23	4.80	13.9	97
4th	1.00	3.90	17.1	112

Final drive ratio..3.90 to one

CHASSIS:
Backbone steel frame and monocoque fiberglass body.
Wheelbase..84 in
Track..47 in
Length..145 in
Width..56 in
Height...45 in
Ground clearance..6.0 in
Dry weight..1420 lbs
Curb weight...1485 lbs
Test weight...1715 lbs
Weight distribution front/rear.....................................48/52
Pounds per bhp (test weight).......................................16.5
Suspension: F: Ind., wishbones and coil springs, anti-roll bar.
          R: Ind., lower wishbones and coil springs on Chapman struts.
Brakes...Girling 9½-in discs front, 10-in discs rear, 358 sq in swept area
Steering..Rack and pinion
Turns lock to lock..2½
Turning circle...30 ft
Tires..5.20 x 13
Revs per mile...896

MAINTENANCE:
Crankcase capacity...3.75 quarts
Oil change interval..5000 miles
Number of grease fittings..3

ACCELERATION:

Zero to	Seconds
30 mph	2.2
40 mph	3.3
50 mph	5.0
60 mph	7.1
70 mph	9.8
80 mph	12.9
90 mph	17.0
100 mph	22.1

Standing quarter-mile..15.7 @ 87 mph

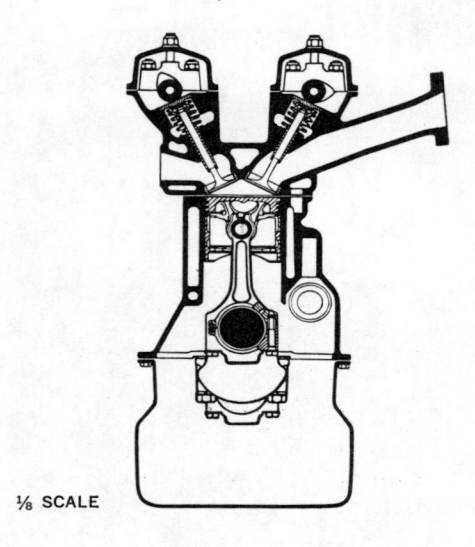

⅛ SCALE

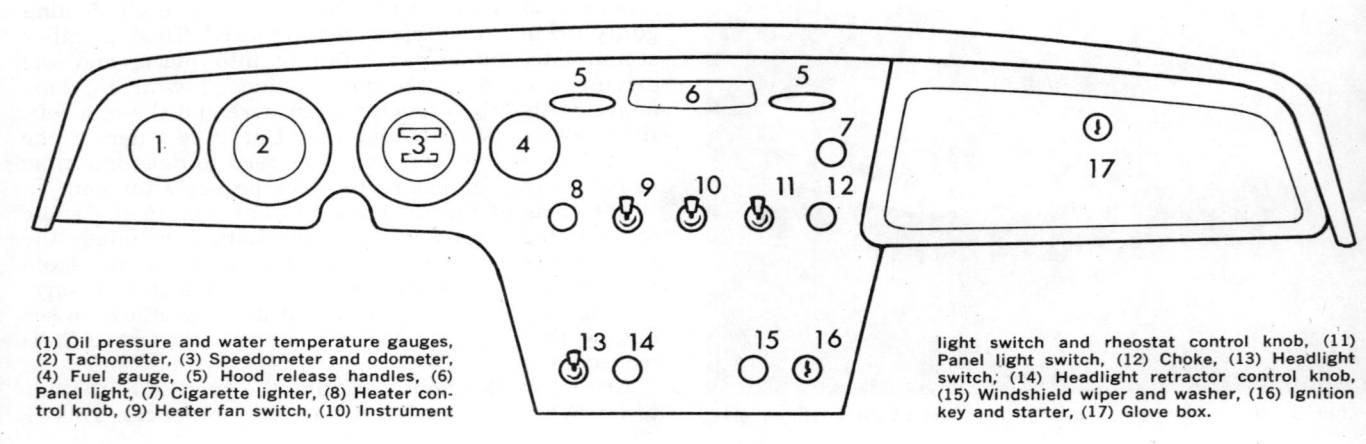

(1) Oil pressure and water temperature gauges, (2) Tachometer, (3) Speedometer and odometer, (4) Fuel gauge, (5) Hood release handles, (6) Panel light, (7) Cigarette lighter, (8) Heater control knob, (9) Heater fan switch, (10) Instrument light switch and rheostat control knob, (11) Panel light switch, (12) Choke, (13) Headlight switch, (14) Headlight retractor control knob, (15) Windshield wiper and washer, (16) Ignition key and starter, (17) Glove box.

16

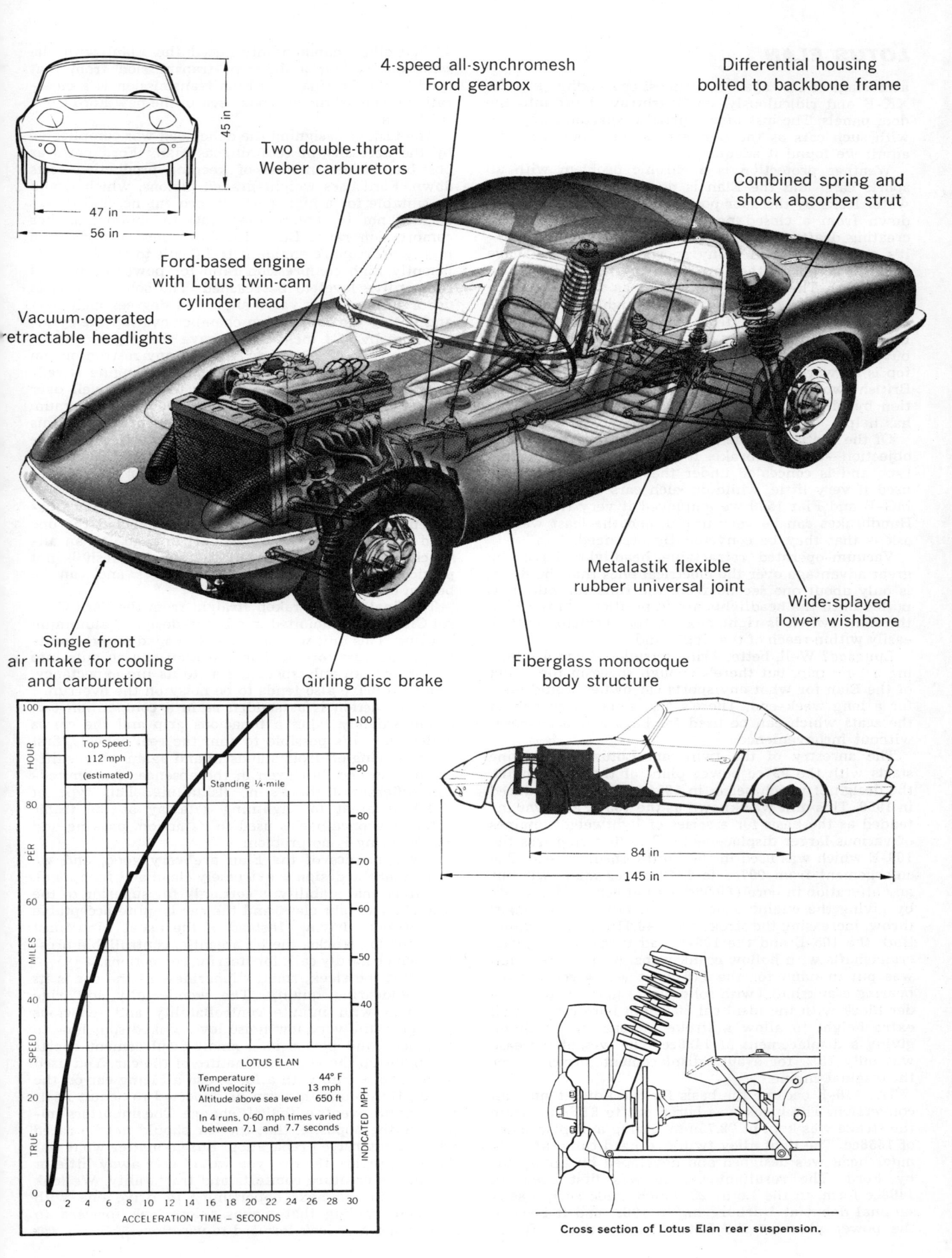

- 4-speed all-synchromesh Ford gearbox
- Differential housing bolted to backbone frame
- Two double-throat Weber carburetors
- Combined spring and shock absorber strut
- Ford-based engine with Lotus twin-cam cylinder head
- Vacuum-operated retractable headlights
- Single front air intake for cooling and carburetion
- Girling disc brake
- Fiberglass monocoque body structure
- Metalastik flexible rubber universal joint
- Wide-splayed lower wishbone

Dimensions: 45 in height, 47 in, 56 in width; 84 in, 145 in length

LOTUS ELAN
Top Speed: 112 mph (estimated)
Standing ¼-mile
Temperature 44° F
Wind velocity 13 mph
Altitude above sea level 650 ft
In 4 runs, 0-60 mph times varied between 7.1 and 7.7 seconds

Cross section of Lotus Elan rear suspension.

LOTUS ELAN

a shortage of stowage space almost as striking as in the XK-E and ridiculously small ashtrays built into the door panels. The instrument panel is spartan compared with such cars as the Sunbeam Alpine, but we must admit we found it adequate.

Weather protection is a chronic problem with all sports cars, and the Elan is no exception. There are water leaks by the door posts, and the windows juggle down from a closed position as the car progresses, creating drafts and leaks galore. But what the hell—it's still better than many sports cars that we have come to accept as they are (and try to drive only on nice days). The floor of the Elan is as tight as a space suit, so the car can be driven through sizeable pools and puddles without fear of getting wet feet. The Elan's soft top fits nicely and does not flap in the wind, but does create some noise at speed. Removal of the top is no worse or no better than average for an open British two-seater. One man can complete the operation by himself, but if he's in a hurry, it's nice if he has help.

Of the controls in the Elan we have only one strong objection—the handbrake. It's of the umbrella-handle type and is concealed under the dash. We found we used it very little, while on such cars as the Spitfire, MG-B and Fiat 1500 we employed it very frequently. Handbrakes can be very useful, and the least we can ask is that they be conveniently arranged.

Vacuum-operated retractable headlights have the great advantage over the electrical ones that the delay is only about one second from the time the button is pulled until the headlights are in position. On the Elan the light switch is right next to the retractor button, easily within reach of the right hand.

Luggage? Well, better bring a trailer if you are taking a long trip, but there's enough space in the trunk of the Elan for what any sports car owner would need for a long week-end. There's also some space behind the seats which can be used for bags and brief-cases without inconvenience.

The ancestry of the twin-cam Lotus-Ford engine starts with the 997cc power plant of the new Anglia, the design of which began in 1954 and was introduced in 1958. This unit was known as the 105-E and was intended as the basis for a series of lightweight engines of various larger displacements. The first step was the 109-E which was used in the Ford Consul Classic. The enlargement from 997cc to 1340cc was made without any alteration in bore (80.96mm) but achieved entirely by giving the engine a new crankshaft with a longer throw, increasing the stroke from 48.41mm to 65.09mm. Both the 105-E and the 109-E had three-bearing cast crankshafts with hollow crank webs. A major redesign was put in hand for the 116-E; it was given a five-bearing crankshaft (with solid webs) and a new cylinder block with the identical 80.96mm bore but enough extra height to allow a stroke increase to 72.75mm, giving a displacement of 1498cc. The weight increase was only 15% for a 50% displacement increase over the original engine.

The 116-E became the basis for the Lotus twin-cam conversion. The block was bored out to 81.6mm while the stroke was kept at 72.75mm, giving a displacement of 1558cc. The light alloy twin overhead camshaft cylinder head was designed and developed by Lotus, not by Ford. The resultant engine was first used, in 1498cc form, in the Lotus 23 which made such a sensational debut at Nürburgring in 1962, and it became the power plant of the Lotus-Cortina that autumn. Then Colin Chapman introduced the Elan, with the same engine but a different transmission from that used in the Cortina. The Elan transmission is a close-ratio version of the gearbox used in the new Ford Consul Corsair.

The task of designing the dohc head was complicated by the necessity of retaining as many Ford parts as possible, in the interest of keeping production costs down. Ford uses weight-graded pistons, which would be suitable for a high-performance engine, and it was decided not to replace them just to obtain a higher compression ratio. But with flat-topped pistons in a highly oversquare engine it is difficult to obtain a sufficiently high compression ratio for power outputs of competitive level to be reached. The solution was to use a quite narrow valve angle (54 degrees included) and letting the combustion chamber overlap the cylinder bore by 0.34 inches. This gave the engine a compression ratio of 9.5 to one, without any restrictions on valve size, gas flow or turbulence. The engine is redlined at 6500 rpm but is willing to rev to well over 7000. Peak power is developed at 5500 and maximum torque at 4000, but what is most surprising in this high-speed unit is that brake mean effective pressure never falls below 134 psi between 2000 and 6000 rpm. It is a unique combination of racing car and tractor engine and remarkably silent at all speeds.

Apart from the closer ratios, the only difference between the standard Corsair transmission and the one used in the Elan is the Lotus shift linkage. It's an all-synchromesh four-speed but the synchromesh is not particularly effective on rapid changes and can be beaten on all gears.

The final drive is taken straight from the Ford Consul Classic and mounted in a Lotus-designed aluminum housing. This unit was of course intended for transmitting much less torque than the Elan engine puts into it, and we can only speculate as to its life expectancy. The final drive also tends to be noisy on the overrun.

Clutch action is as sudden as in a competition car. It immediately takes a tenacious grip and the car is under way. It's possible to spin the rear wheels, first when moving off from standstill and again when shifting into second, but even in the absence of a limited-slip differential there's no fishtailing. This type of clutch is great for lightning getaway at the traffic lights, and once one is used to its action, parking and maneuvering is no problem.

Aerodynamics of the Elan are very good, and we agree that the design is extremely clean and functional. Its directional stability is certainly far superior to the rest of its weight class, and the car is quite acceptable for turnpike driving. Instead of the usual wind blast from the big trucks, there's a gentle, controllable pressure which hardly calls for steering corrections.

In fact the sleek, small slipperiness of the car is its most endearing quality. The wonderfully soft ride combined with infinite controllability and tenacious road grip, the very low noise level linked somehow to so much solid power in a small displacement sports car, point up the very dual nature of the car. You used to have to put up with a lot to use a racing car on the street. Here's one that can be expected to acquit itself well in club events with little change. The importers emphasize the opposite, that the car should not be raced without extensive preparation. But no matter what was done to prepare the car, you would give away little or nothing in creature comforts and tractability. We look forward to the next opportunity to drive one with the same feeling that makes skiers look forward to winter and kids look forward to vacations.

C/D

fairly leaping forward at a touch of the accelerator, irrespective of the gear engaged. To reach 60 m.p.h. in 7 secs. or 100 m.p.h. in 20.2 secs. is a delightful experience, especially when the car is so compact that it can nip through any hole in the traffic.

The ride is flat and by no means hard, in spite of the proper bucket seats, which have no excessive padding. The engine and transmission are generally quiet, though the power unit vibrates fairly strongly as the maximum revolutions are approached. Wind noise does not trouble the occupants. The heating is effective, though one could do with more ventilation, as the windows are not easy to set for the supply of fresh air without a gale.

One can use the performance all the time because the roadholding is so remarkable. The car can be "flicked" into position with no effort and it corners very fast indeed under perfect balance. Bumps do not disturb its course, and I must again emphasize the fundamental safety of such controllability, with powerful brakes to match.

For British roads the Elan approaches the ideal, except that it is very much under-

JOHN BOLSTER tests

The Lotus Elan

The typical small sports car at a competitive price is better than ever before. Yet it is obvious to the enthusiast, as he watches racing single-seaters in action, that modern suspension techniques can give roadholding which is not approached by conventional cars.

The Lotus Elan makes single-seater roadholding available for everyday use. We know that the theoretical advantages of all-round independent suspension are seldom realized at the present stage of the art. In the case of the Elan, however, the exceptional cornering power of a racing car is quite certainly available. On the road this means that the car can make high averages with great ease, and that it is, above all, phenomenally safe.

A steel backbone frame, suitably protected against rust, forms the main structure. Unequal length wishbones in front, and upper struts with wide-based lower wishbones at the rear, work in conjunction with helical springs and telescopic dampers. The rack and pinion steering has a collapsible telescopic column, Girling disc brakes being used all round. At the rear they are mounted on the inner side of the bearing housings instead of on the wheel hubs. The articulated half shafts have rubber universal joints at both ends.

The final drive-hypoid unit is mounted on the backbone and, like the suspension pivots, it is sound insulated. The propeller shaft is contained in the chassis, which spreads out to embrace the engine. This is basically a five-bearing Ford unit of 1,558 c.c. with a Lotus twin-cam head. The camshafts are driven by roller chains and operate directly upon the valves through inverted pistons. Two twin-choke horizontal Weber carburetters supply the mixture. The diaphragm clutch drives a four-speed, all-synchromesh gearbox with exceptionally close ratios and a short, central lever.

This simple but brilliantly executed chassis is carried on pressed-steel wheels with 5.20 × 13 ins. tyres. The body, of glassfibre construction, fits on to the backbone like a saddle. The doors contain sliding windows, which are raised directly by hand, without winding mechanism. The seats have ample adjustment, taking up a more reclining position of the squab in the case of the long-legged driver. Small luggage can be placed behind the seats and a useful boot is in the tail. A neat hard top was fitted to the test car.

My first surprise, on driving off, was the remarkable flexibility of the engine. In the Cortina the same unit objects strongly to slow-speed pulling, but the Elan is a top-gear car. This is entirely due to the shock-absorbing qualities of the rubber universal joints. Naturally, such easy running on the higher gears renders the machine an untiring means of transport on overcrowded roads.

When the Elan is given its head the acceleration can only be described as tremendous, particularly in such a small package. The car is delightfully lively, geared for motorway cruising. One should be able to run all day at 100 m.p.h. in such a car, but at this speed the engine is turning at over 6,000 r.p.m., which is not a smooth process. An overdrive or a fifth speed are indicated, especially when SP tyres are used, which have a reduced diameter compared with some other makes.

With this equipment the maximum speed is 107.1 m.p.h. if the governor is used on the ignition. We were given permission to remove this safety device for the maximum speed runs, but we did not wish to over-rev. unduly so we dispensed with the excellent SP tyres. The speed of 115.3 m.p.h. was then obtained under adverse

19

conditions. With a higher gear the Elan would be a 120 m.p.h. car, no doubt. The gear ratio fitted would suit short British racing circuits and it is admirable for winding country roads which do not permit sustained driving at maximum speed.

Having wide shoulders I sometimes find little cars too narrow for me, but the Lotus Elan has just enough room to allow me full arm movement with an overcoat on. The controls are well placed, with the exception of the hand brake, which I soon forgot because I didn't use it. All the dials one wants, except an ammeter, are conveniently located on the instrument panel. The optional radio could be enjoyed at quite high speeds, emphasizing the quiet running. Praise must be given to the silencing of the exhaust, which avoids unwelcome attention from you-know-whom.

Having driven through rain and the mud thrown up by lorries, it is such an advantage to have clean headlamps that pop up only when required. The vacuum servo snaps them into position quickly, and they arrive already flashing if the button is touched during daylight. No doubt they contribute to the aerodynamic qualities of the body,

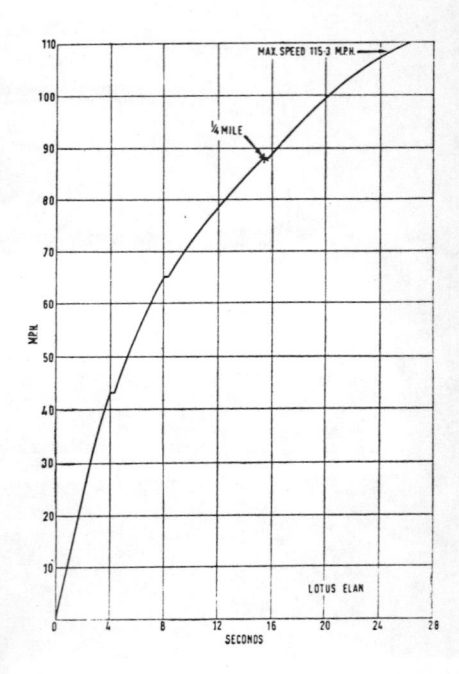

ACCELERATION GRAPH

which assist the Elan to run straight and true with a complete disregard of side winds.

The machine is not spectacular in appearance but it is completely functional. There is no unnecessary chromium plating or useless decoration, which adds greatly to the attraction of the car in the eyes of the true enthusiast. The foam-filled glassfibre bumpers will avoid the unsightly rust and dents which parking in London tends to inflict.

The Lotus Elan is a small sports car with a very big performance. It shows just how much has been learnt recently from independently sprung racing cars. It is almost unique in having no handling vices whatsoever, and its roadholding cannot be caught out, irrespective of the surface.

SPECIFICATION AND PERFORMANCE DATA

Car Tested: Lotus Elan sports two-seater, price £1,387 14s. 7d. including P.T. Hard top £68 including fitting and P.T.
Engine: Four-cylinders 82.55 mm. × 72.75 mm. (1,558 c.c.). Twin chain-drive overhead camshafts. Compression ratio 9.5 to 1. 105 b.h.p. at 5,500 r.p.m. Two twin-choke Weber carburetters. Lucas coil and distributor.
Transmission: Single dry plate diaphragm clutch. 4-speed all-synchromesh gearbox with central lever, ratios 3.9, 4.8, 6.63 and 9.78 to 1. Hypoid differential unit. Articulated half shafts with rubber joints.
Chassis: Steel backbone frame. Independent front suspension with wishbones, helical springs and telescopic dampers. Rack and pinion steering. Independent rear suspension on strut and lower wishbone system, with helical springs and telescopic dampers. Girling disc brakes all round. Bolt-on disc wheels, fitted 5.20 × 13 ins. tyres.
Equipment: 12-volt lighting and starting. Speedometer. Rev counter. Oil pressure, water temperature and fuel gauges. Retractable headlamps. Flashing direction indicators. Windscreen wipers and washers. Heating, de-misting, and ventilation system. Radio (extra).
Dimensions: Wheelbase, 7 ft.; track (front), 3 ft. 11 ins. (rear) 4 ft. 1¼ ins.; Overall length, 12 ft. 1 in.; width, 4 ft. 8 ins.; turning circle, 29 ft. 6 ins.; weight, 11½ cwts.
Performance: Maximum speed, 115.3 m.p.h.; speeds in gears: 3rd, 88 m.p.h.; 2nd, 65 m.p.h.; 1st, 43 m.p.h. Standing quarter-mile, 15.4 secs. Acceleration: 0-30 m.p.h., 2.6 secs.; 0-50 m.p.h., 5.8 secs.; 0-60 m.p.h., 7 secs.; 0-80 m.p.h., 12.4 secs.; 0-100 m.p.h., 20.2 secs.
Fuel Consumption: 26 m.p.g.

CARS ON TEST

LOTUS ELAN 1600

COLIN CHAPMAN'S LOTUS ELITE, which set the motoring world by the ears when it was first presented, undoubtedly represented a major advance in the category of small Grand Touring cars. As, perhaps, our road test shows, however, in some respects the car now falls short of 1964 requirements, and it is thus that we find, in the Elan 1600, the logical development of the Elite's conception. It is small, compact and is powered by a small-capacity engine: in road manner it is very close to the modern racing car—it is, in fact, a refined, very sophisticated Seven. Not in any way outstandingly beautiful, the car nevertheless has particularly clean lines and a pleasing absence of unnecessary ornamentation: the interior is far from stark—the equipment even includes a cigar lighter—yet it is functional and in every way practical. Its performance is well above average, and its passenger accommodation achieves high standards of comfort: above all, it is fast and phenomenally safe, factors which combine with a competitive price to make the Elan one of the most desirable small sports cars currently available.

The chassis represents a departure from the construction arrangements of the Elite, and in fact is similar to that of the sports-racing Twenty-three. A steel backbone frame forms the main structure on which is mounted the glass-fibre body: earlier problems in the matter of finish have now been overcome, and little criticism is possible on this point. The power unit is the Lotus twin-overhead camshaft development of the Ford 1½-litre four-cylinder unit, with five bearing crankshaft. The camshafts are chain driven and the mixture is admitted to the combustion chambers by means of two twin-choke Weber carburetters. Bore and stroke of 82.55 mm. 72.75 mm. give increased dimensions of 1,558 c.c., and with a compression ratio of 9.5 : 1 the engine develops 105 b.h.p. at 5,500 r.p.m.: maximum torque of 102 lb. ft. is produced at around 4,000 r.p.m., giving the engine a useful middle-range performance. Indeed, the degree of flexibility with which the Elan has been endowed is remarkable, and while a willing engine and a delightful gearbox, with very close ratios, encourage the driver to make full use of it, the Elan can be driven as a top-gear car, and top gear will allow smooth, easy acceleration away from speeds as low as 20 m.p.h. without fuss or unpleasantness. The five-bearing crankshaft imparts considerable smoothness, although some roughness was apparent on the test car at crankshaft speeds in excess of 6,000 r.p.m. A reasonable degree of silence is achieved from a mechanical point of view: at tickover speeds there was occasional rattling from the crankshaft chain-drive. Whether hot or cold the engine was always easy to start, and pulled well from cold: the warm-up period is short.

The power unit is mated through a diaphragm-spring clutch to a four-speed and reverse gearbox, with a short, central gearlever. Synchromesh is provided on all four

Eyes Down . . .

forward gears and is powerful and difficult to beat. The gearbox is quiet in operation, and the ratios could scarcely have been better placed: their closeness permits really thrilling acceleration through the gears and, at the same time, the ratios take full advantage of the engine power characteristics. The clutch is extremely light and, in fact, rather disconcertingly quick until one grows used to it: it grips well, with no sign of slip—even during the full-power take-offs employed during the performance testing. This, combined with a light, "notchy" gearlever permits the changes to be put through extremely quickly.

The hypoid final drive unit is mounted on the chassis backbone, and, like the articulated half-shafts, is rubber-mounted and well insulated against noise, which enhances the Elan's properties of smooth, silent running.

It is the suspension which imparts racing-car road-holding to the Elan. In front, unequal length wishbones, and wide-based lower wishbones and "Chapman struts" at the rear, work in conjunction with coil springs and telescopic shock absorbers. Spring and damper settings have been arranged to provide an extremely level ride, and the occupants are not conscious of any lean during hard cornering. The ride is firm, yet at the same time there is no harshness, and irregularities in the road surface are smoothed out with complete efficiency. Due largely to the liberal use of insulating material, little road noise penetrates the cockpit, and the overall impression is one of an extremely refined machine for long-distance motoring. The handling characteristics are, to all intents and purposes, neutral; there is just sufficient understeer to impart a feeling of steadiness under all circumstances. Under normal conditions the car is reluctant to slide, and to reach the limit of adhesion it is necessary to be travelling very fast indeed through the corners. When it does slide, it does so controllably with all four wheels, and intelligent use of the gearbox enables the driver to find sufficient power in reserve to maintain the attitude to suit his requirements. Gusty side-winds affect the car to a negligible degree, and the Elan will run straight and true "hands-off" at all speeds up to its maximum. It is safe to assume that the Elan

Bright Eyes . . .

Cars on Test

LOTUS ELAN 1600

Engine: Four cylinders, 82.55 mm. × 72.75 mm. (1,558 c.c.) Compression ratio 9.5 : 1; twin overhead camshafts; twin Weber twin-choke carburetters; 105 b.h.p. at 5,500 r.p.m.

Transmission: Diaphragm spring clutch; four-speed and reverse gearbox, with synchromesh on all four forward ratios and central gear-lever.

Suspension: Front, independent with wishbones and coil springs; rear, independent with strut and lower wishbone, coil springs. Tyres: 5.20 × 13.

Brakes: Front and rear, Girling disc brakes.

Dimensions: Overall length, 12 ft. 1 in.; overall width, 4 ft. 8 ins.; turning circle, 29 ft. 6 ins.; weight, 11¼ cwt.

PERFORMANCE

	m.p.h.		secs.
MAXIMUM SPEED	— 118.5	ACCELERATION 0–30	— 2.7
		0–40	— 3.9
(Mean of 2 ways)	— 117.3	0–50	— 5.8
		0–60	— 7.6
		0–70	— 9.6
SPEEDS IN GEARS First	— 49.0	0–80	— 13.0
		0–90	— 16.5
Second	— 75.0	0–100	— 25.2
		0–110	— 34.3
Third	— 94.0	Standing quarter mile	— 16.0

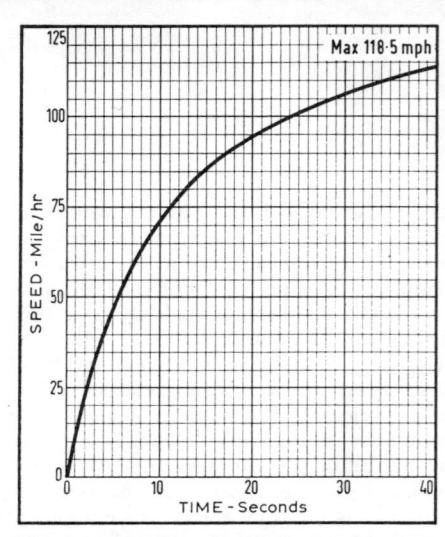

Manufacturers: Lotus Cars Ltd., Delamare Road, Cheshunt, Herts.
Price: £1,387 14s. 7d., including purchase tax.

approaches ideal handling properties, and it is difficult to conceive higher standards of road behaviour.

Excellent brakes assist in the safe maintenance of high average speeds. Girling disc brakes, of generous dimensions, are fitted all round, and are powerful in operation in exchange for pleasantly light pedal pressure: on the test car, the pedal had a rather "soft" feeling, but the brakes themselves proved admirable and well up to dealing with the car's performance. The handbrake is powerful and fully effective, but is operated by an umbrella-handle located beneath the dashboard—a long and awkward reach from the driving seat. The interior of the car is well-equipped and surprisingly roomy. Very comfortable bucket seats, with generous adjustment for tall drivers, have built-up sides to the cushions and backrests and provide positive location for driver and passenger alike: additional prevention from sideways movement when cornering hard is provided by the chassis backbone, through which the prop-shaft runs, and its top is padded. A tray for small oddments is fitted around the base of the gear-lever, ash-trays and door-pulls are fitted in the arm-rests in the doors and there is a lockable glove compartment in the attractive wooden facia. The doors contain sliding windows, which are raised by hand without winding mechanism: the glass moves freely and remains in any intermediate position. The instruments are well laid-out and easy to read: a matching rev.-counter and 140 m.p.h. speedometer are flanked by oil-pressure, water temperature and fuel contents gauges: all the instruments have steady needles. Hand controls are equally well-placed on a central facia panel and are easily identified: particularly handy is the headlamp control which operates a vacuum-servo mechanism raising and lowering the headlamps. In daylight, or with sidelights only in operation, the lamps come up flashing: with headlights on, an over-riding dip-switch is provided through a stalk on the steering column. Apart from the obvious advantages of improved aerodynamics in keeping the headlamp projection out of the way, there are ancillary benefits through maintaining clean glasses in wet weather. The reluctance of the light units to return to the closed position at high speeds experienced on early Elans has now been overcome, and their action is precise and rapid.

The driving position is extremely "straight-arm" in the modern manner, and the driver's control is absolute. The steering is feather-light and absolutely precise, the wheel providing good "feel" of the road, while corners are negotiated by a mere flexing of the wrists. The bonnet is released by two dashboard-mounted handles and the lid is counter-balanced, operation of the release handles permitting it to swing automatically into the raised position. Engine accessibility is good. Contact with a small bird while travelling fast caused the mesh intake grille with its attached number-plate numerals to be dislodged from its mounting on the nose of the car, but even so it was the work of a few minutes to remove the grille from where it had been flung back against the radiator and refit it. Nevertheless, one feels that stouter attachments for the number-plate would be an advantage, since we managed nearly two hundred miles with no apparent front number-plate, fortunately without attracting the attention of the men in blue. A useful boot, with a spring-stayed lid, is provided at the rear of the car.

The performance is, of course, absolutely outstanding for a car of only 1,600 c.c. capacity. Somewhere around seven seconds is sufficient to reach 60 m.p.h. from a standstill, and the car will reach 70 m.p.h. in a time which is impressive in much larger cars reaching a lower speed! Our maximum speed in one direction of 118.5 m.p.h. was achieved at slightly higher r.p.m. than the tachometer's red mark, at 6,500 r.p.m., would normally permit, although the engine appeared to be far from overstressed: we were given permission to employ 7,000 r.p.m. in the gears for acceleration purposes, at this speed first gear will encompass almost 50 m.p.h. In such a small car the acceleration is stupendous, and 100 m.p.h. comes up on the speedometer with astonishing frequency on even quite short straights. This combined with the outstanding road-holding permits astonishingly high average speeds to be achieved without fatigue, and the little car can be shot through gaps in the traffic which, for larger cars, simply do not exist.

Driven hard throughout the test, the car returned an overall fuel consumption figure of 26 m.p.g., while the fuel tank, containing ten gallons, provides a useful cruising range. It is, in fact, extremely difficult to find fault with the Elan: the standard of finish is high, and the tremendous performance is achieved at more than moderate economy. It is a car which demonstrates in every way the true meaning of the words "race-bred".

SPORTS CAR WORLD ROAD TEST

Not everybody's pleasure is 1600 cc, twin overhead camshafts, independent suspension and remarkable handling.

YOU walk out and find it there in the parking lot, headlights hooded in patient resignation and asking almost audibly to be taken out on the open road where it belongs. The Lotus Elan is patently unhappy sitting still.

We remember it best slicing through a series of opening and closing corners in the half-light of a summer morning, putting on and taking off lock with the fingertips, the distant thunder of the exhaust deflecting off rock walls and trees, 6500 rpm in the indirects and calling in the discs at that last-moment, tippy-toe second deep into the heart of a corner.

Almost 70 mph in second gear and zero to 100 mph in less than 30 seconds is always invigorating. The Elan did all this so quickly and well that we often found ourselves in the classic situation of almost running right over the top of someone with 50 mph speed differential. It is a marvellous little car, slightly larger outside than a Sprite with twice as much performance and price. Best of all, you point it at a line and say "Go There", and it does. In an Elan, understeer and oversteer are dirty words.

At the time, ours was the first set of performance figures done on the car, which itself was the first to be assembled in Australia from the box of tricks in which Elans arrive. Lotus distributor Leo Geoghegan kept the red car for his own use; we took it at 1600 miles and returned it some 350 miles later.

The most immediate reaction to the car is that this is the sports car among sports cars. It gets its urge from rpm and close-ratio gears instead of cubic centimetres, and has far more than 1600 cc's worth of performance. It rides, handles, and stops better than most, is infinitely more flexible in all gears, and is always worn like a second pair of trousers. It feels right to sit in, and does the right things always. Its only real vice, in fact, is the clutch, which has limited throw and very little sensitivity.

The Elan is a peculiar car to us, because we are

BILL TUCKEY DRIVES... WITH A

Handling superb, steering direct, performance astonishing.

accustomed to mass-production sports cars from large factories, with all their compromises away from purity. We had expected that a small-volume, almost hand-built cars like this would reveal many deficiencies which just do not occur in large-production cars because they come from factories which long ago sorted out things like the placement of door handles and the best hood-fixing studs. But the Elan has only a few of these faults, probably because the Lotus factory has made extensive use of existing components from sub-contracting suppliers to big factories. The floor rubber, for instance, obviously comes from the people who supply BMC with the Mini coverings, and, unless we miss our guess, the glovebox, trafficator arm, and headlight dimmer arm are Triumph Herald parts.

The Elan was first released, in October, 1962, in 1499 cc form. It then developed 100 bhp, but with the 1600 engine the output is 105. In its use of glass-fibre it owes a little to the far more unorthodox Lotus Elite, which was actually a moulded hull, with a few metal reinforcements, but with no separate chassis frame. The engine, suspension and steering were mounted direct to the glass-fibre. The main disadvantage of this system proved to be that it limited desirable design changes and needed a long period of development.

The Elite is still in production in Britain. The

Seats offer excellent lateral support and are very comfortable.

LITTLE ELAN

Exterior is neat and aerodynamic. Headlights are vacuum-actuated.

25

Elan, however, is far more orthodox in construction. It has a separate backbone chassis frame to which the body — actually glass-fibre-reinforced plastic — is mounted. The frame has outstanding strength and torsional rigidity, although it weighs only 75 lb, for all the joints are electric or arc-welded and the metal thickness averages less than 0.050 in. The centre section, which passes through the cockpit, is in box section, and then branches into channel section members front and rear which form into box-section cross-members at their ends. It is from these cross-members and pillars that the suspension and steering components are hung. Bare, it resembles an "X" with elongated centre piece.

The floor area of the body is formed as one piece to pass over the top of the frame unit and includes the side sills, the luggage compartment section, and the scuttle, so that it has enormous rigidity. The body has few separate moulded parts — again for rigidity and inserted metal reinforcements at strategic places like the screen pillars.

From any angle, but particularly from the front, it is an exceptionally pretty car. Small at just over 12 ft overall and just over 3 ft to the top of the windscreen, it is nonetheless beautifully proportioned. Apart from general outline, this is almost entirely due to the use of front and rear "bumper" ribs made of glass-fibre packed with polythene. The park and turn lights are concealed from upper view below this rail, and it forms a nice frame for the recessed rear. A clean bonnet line has been gained by fitting retractable headlights that are covered by flush-fitting lids when not in use. The biggest problem is where to hang the front number-plate.

The front suspension is by wishbones and integral coil/damper units, with an Alford and Alder rack and pinion steering. At the rear, the final drive unit — a standard Ford Cortina in Lotus casing — is mounted on rubber to the chassis with two torque stays. The driveshafts

Twin camshafts, Lotus, 1600 cc and dual Webers constitute 105 bhp.

have rubber couplings at each end. Rear suspension is by a tubular lower wishbone and upper Chapman-type strut comprising a damper/coil spring unit again. There are alloy hub carriers which also mount the Girling disc brakes. Wheels are drilled disc, with plain nave plates.

Perhaps the most expensive part of the entire car is the twin overhead camshaft engine based on the five-bearing 1500 cc Cortina unit that has seen so much competition work. It has been well described before; mainly, the Lotus parts are the cylinder head assembly, water pump, timing cover and pushrods. The same engine is used in the Lotus-Cortina. The standard Ford pistons are retained, but the problem of getting a high compression ratio with flat-top pistons in a spherical head and with opposed valves is dealt with by modifying the valve angles.

The head is of cast aluminium, with shrunk austenitic valve seats, double valve springs and two twin-choke 40 DCOE Weber carburettors sitting on extensions from the integral inlet ports. Lotus has retained the standard Ford four-speed all-synchromesh gearbox and the ratios; and final drive ratio is 3.9 to 1 as in the Cortina GT and Corsair 1500.

This collection of material alone is a fine basis for a fine sports car. Chapman has tried hard to make the physical equipment of the same standard, and has succeeded to a certain extent. The pvc hood fits neatly over two detachable glass-fibre window frames and two detachable centre stays. It takes about five minutes to erect or collapse, and its main trouble is in the location of four press-studs too close to the drip rail in the window frames. The hood equipment is stowed in the boot without any covering of its own, and the hood sticks do annoy by rattling around loose. The boot has a pvc covering over a platform that conceals the spare wheel. The jack and a small set of tools live in a recess in the right wheel arch.

The cockpit is a mixture of good and bad. All of our drivers liked the seats, which show the benefit of competition experience in the correct reclining angle of the fixed backrests and their

SPECIFICATIONS

CHASSIS AND BODY DIMENSIONS:

Wheelbase	7 ft 0 in
Track, front	3 ft 11 in
Track, rear	3 ft 11 in
Ground clearance	6.0 in
Turning circle	29 ft 3 in
Turns, lock to lock	2.5
Overall length	12 ft 1.2 in
Overall width	4 ft 8 in
Overall height	3 ft 7.5 in (hood erected)

CHASSIS:

Steering type	Alford and Alder rack and pinion
Brake type	Girling non-servo discs front and rear
Swept area	358 sq in
Suspension, front	coils, wishbones, anti-roll bar
Suspension, rear	independent, Chapman strut, lower wishbones
Shock absorbers	telescopic
Tyre size	5.20 by 13
Weight	11.5 cwt
Fuel tank capacity	10 gals
Approx cruising range	300 miles

Invitation to exhilaration: A mixture of good and bad.

Below these are a cigar lighter and heater control (marked, appropriately, with a red flame), then a row of three unlabelled tumbler switches for heater fan, instrument lighting, and interior light. The instrument light switch is rheostated — the first such tumbler switch we have found so treated.

Other controls are for choke — which we never had to use — ignition, wipers, park and headlight switch, and the pull-knob to elevate the headlamps. The ignition switch is on the passenger's side of the facia and the choke on the driver's side, so that the ergonomics of the thing are all wrong. The headlamp elevator is a vacuum electric system that gets its boost from inlet manifold pressure. Thus if the switch is used four or five times without the engine running it becomes inoperative. However, it flicks the headlights up neatly into a firmly locked position, and simultaneously the left light starts flashing audibly. This is the headlight flasher commonly used in Britain, and while it is overriden by the main headlight switch it does have the effect of making the driver keep his lights locked down except when actually in use.

In front of the passenger is the Triumph Herald glovebox, which allowed everything put in it to slide out under heavy acceleration or cornering. The turn and dip levers on the column, again Herald units, look cheap and out of place in a £2000 sports car. On the central tunnel is mounted a five-inch gearlever in a flexible rubber boot, which had already split on the test Elan. It is topped with a wood knob carrying the same green and yellow Lotus emblem as in the steering wheel boss.

The rear vision mirror is tinted, and the passenger's door can be locked from the inside, while

relation to the spring-alloy spoked, wood-rimmed wheel, which is itself adjustable. The seats have padded raised lips on all edges, and are deeply pleated horizontally.

The facia is of heavy ply veneered with oil teak and fixed to the floor tunnel. Nevertheless, there is marked scuttle shake over lumpy bitumen roads. The facia carries, in front of the driver from right to left, a combined water temperature and oil pressure gauge, Smiths speedometer, Smiths electric tachometer segmented from 6500 to 8000, warning lights for high beam ignition and trafficators, and the fuel gauge. In the centre of the panel is the interior light, which also works off both doors, and two pull-handle bonnet locks. One of these jammed solidly during our test.

(Continued on page 35)

ENGINE:
Cylinders	4, in line, water cooled
Bore and stroke	82.6 mm by 72.70 mm
Cubic capacity	1558 cc
Compression ratio	9.5 to 1
Fuel requirement	98 octane
Valves	opposed, by twin overhead camshafts
Maximum power	105 bhp at 5500 rpm
Maximum torque	108 ft/lbs at 4000 rpm

TRANSMISSION:
Overall ratios
First (synchro)	13.81
Second (synchro)	9.34
Third (synchro)	5.51
Fourth (synchro)	3.90
Final drive	3.9 to 1

PERFORMANCE

Top speed average	112.15 mph
Fastest run	113.2 mph
Maximum, first	48 mph
Maximum, second	69 mph
Maximum, third	84 mph
Maximum, fourth	113 mph
Standing quarter mile average	18.1 seconds
Fastest run	18.0 seconds
0 to 30 mph	4.1 seconds
0 to 40 mph	4.8 seconds
0 to 50 mph	6.0 seconds
0 to 60 mph	10.0 seconds
0 to 70 mph	12.5 seconds
0 to 80 mph	17.1 seconds
0 to 90 mph	20.4 seconds
0 to 100 mph	25.5 seconds
0 to 60 mph to 0	12.3 seconds

	Top	Third
40 to 60 mph	6.8 secs	5.5 seconds
50 to 70 mph	6.8 secs	6.3 seconds
60 to 80 mph	7.1 secs	5.6 seconds

Brake fade resistance on test hill	98 percent
Fuel Consumption, overall	32 mpg
Fuel Consumption, cruising	36 mpg

... the ultimate in its chosen field ... a true, practical "fun car"

Number 38
MOTOR TESTED
2665 MILES

PRICE
£1,148 plus £239 14s. 7d. purchase tax equals £1,387 14s. 7d.

Lotus Elan

How they run ...

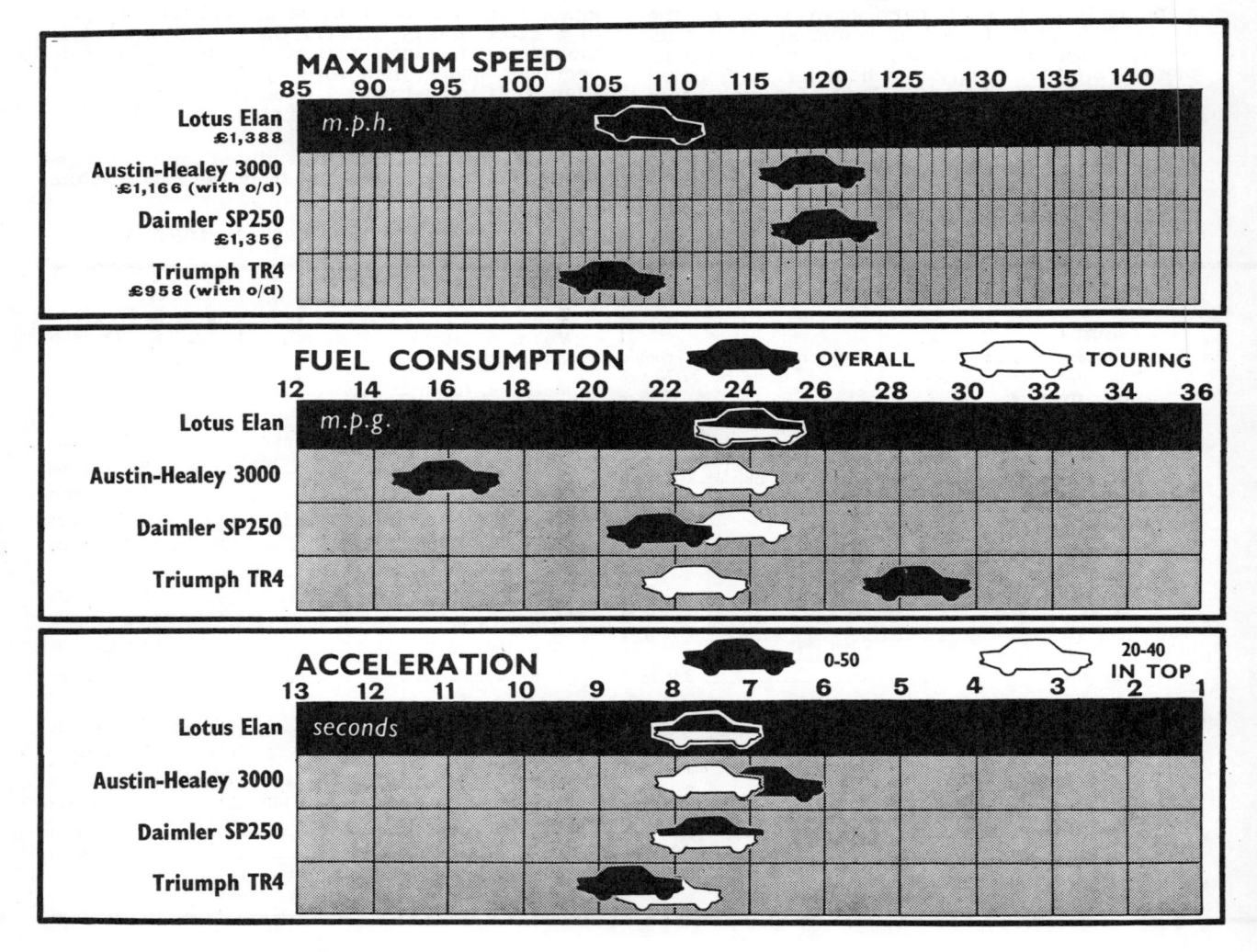

MAXIMUM SPEED (m.p.h.)

Car	Speed
Lotus Elan £1,388	~110
Austin-Healey 3000 £1,166 (with o/d)	~118
Daimler SP250 £1,356	~120
Triumph TR4 £958 (with o/d)	~103

FUEL CONSUMPTION (m.p.g.) — ● OVERALL ○ TOURING

Car	Overall	Touring
Lotus Elan	24	26
Austin-Healey 3000	16	24
Daimler SP250	21	23
Triumph TR4	23	28

ACCELERATION (seconds) — ● 0-50 ○ 20-40 IN TOP

Car	0-50	20-40 in top
Lotus Elan	7	7
Austin-Healey 3000	7	6
Daimler SP250	7	7
Triumph TR4	8	8

28

JUST occasionally one comes across the car which is the ultimate in its chosen field; the Elan, in performance and driveability, is way ahead of all opposition in its class—the field of the true, practical "fun car". As an ideal sports car, the Elan has surging, kicking acceleration—0-50 m.p.h. in 6·8 sec., 0-100 m.p.h. in 24·1 sec.—and it is tractable, pulling strongly and quietly from under 20 m.p.h. in top. It handles as it should with its thoroughbred ancestry, leech-like predictable and always controllable with an outstandingly good ride for a sports car. The driving position is relaxed and fashionable; you sit well back in seats that grip comfortably with all the controls appearing naturally to hand. A car which is already physically small shrinks round you and becomes part of you; it is just the right size for its performance to be really useful on crowded roads and you soon get used to being knee-high to a bus wheel.

At the same time it is practical with the boot taking at least a couple of reasonable weekend suitcases as well as the hood, its cross bars and side pieces. A 10-gallon fuel tank even with our overall consumption at 25·5 m.p.g. gives a really useful range which would normally approach 300 miles. You sit right down inside the cockpit and the curved screen and sliding glass windows give unusual protection from back-draughts and turbulence. Once up, the hood is rigid and water-proof and doesn't obstruct entry. Anyone who dislikes the very slight hood vibration (this is the sort of car where the hood is used as little as possible for enjoyment's sake) can buy a detachable hardtop for £68.

Perhaps the trim could be more beautiful, and the rubber coupled drive shafts cause some longitudinal surging unless the car is driven very smoothly, but there is little else on which to fault a car superbly designed for its job.

Like its forerunner the Elite, the Elan departs from conventional chassis design. A central boxed girder forks at either end towards suspension mountings which are on separate arms at the end of each prong. The engine and gearbox sit between the front arms with the prop shaft driving down the central tunnel. Conventional independent front suspension uses wishbones but the rear uses the Chapman strut independent layout with coil spring/damper unit and a lower wishbone as developed on early Formula Lotuses and used on the Elite; it has the advantages of double wishbones but saves space.

Power in plenty comes from the Lotus conversion of the Ford 116E engine with twin overhead camshafts, which is used in the Lotus Cortina as well as in many different types of racing cars, so reliability is now assured.

The separate glass fibre body is only lightly stressed and is well finished, although bare glass fibre in places inside is a little unsightly.

For such refinement one obviously has to pay more than for a mass produced car, but £1,388 is a fair price for a unique car which assembles so many virtues and so few vices.

Performance

THE PERFORMANCE is little short of phenomenal, not only through the gears and for tractability in high gears, but for its complete lack of temperament. The engine will fire first time in the morning after two dabs on the throttle to work the accelerator pumps, and the choke is unnecessary in warm weather; tickover is a little irregular but this smooths out in turbine fashion from 1,200 r.p.m. onwards to over 6,000 r.p.m., pulling strongly all the way. Towards 7,000 r.p.m. there is a trace of roughness but it can be over-revved so easily that production Elans, like the Lotus Cortina, have an ignition cut-out set for 6,500 r.p.m. to safeguard the thoughtless.

This Lotus conversion of the Ford five bearing engine is now well known, but the sight of the twin camboxes with their crackle-blue finish is still an exciting hint of power. Accessibility is not its strong point, although all fillers are easy, but the distributor is hidden beneath twin double choke Webers bolted to the cast-in manifold.

Not long ago 0–100–0 m.p.h. in under 30 seconds needed over three litres but the Elan manages it with 1½ litres giving 105 b.h.p. (unladen power-weight ratio of 158 b.h.p./ton)

Wooden facia with well placed instruments. The seats look a little hard, but give really comfortable support to thighs and back. Ashtrays are contained in each door.

Not the way Lotus intended, but the headlight treatment is neat. The glass-fibre bumper is filled with foam rubber.

Lotus Elan

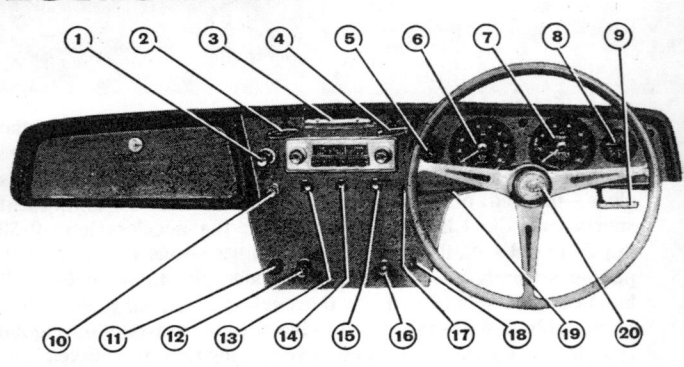

which is a tribute to its wind-cheating shape—it is slightly quicker with the hood up. Our standing start times could probably be improved with a little more practice, but letting the clutch in at around 3,500 to 4,000 r.p.m. produced a little wheelspinning squeak and the revs dropped to 2,000 r.p.m., rather below the best pulling point. But 0–60 m.p.h. in nine seconds is very much in the top performance bracket and 100 m.p.h. comes up in a further 15 seconds.

Its performance in top gear is particularly impressive with each 20 m.p.h. step from 20 to 80 m.p.h. taking between six and seven seconds; it's not really a top gear car but it can be one without complaining.

For performance one choke per cylinder is the ideal no-compromise carburation arrangement and it certainly works well on the Elan which returned 25·5 m.p.g. overall despite all our staff behaving like enthusiasts; this is also the calculated touring figure. At 50 m.p.h. it gave 46½ m.p.g., but it dropped sharply to 24 m.p.g. at 80 m.p.h. and 18 m.p.g. at 100 m.p.h.

We took performance figures with 100 octane petrol, but 97 octane is perfectly satisfactory. Oil consumption at 250 miles to the pint (2,000 m.p.g.) shows adequate lubrication of a hard working engine and is not excessive.

It would be ironical if a car capable of tackling a 1 in 5·8 hill in top gear were unable to start on 1 in 3, but it could easily.

1, cigar lighter. 2, and 4, bonnet catches. 3, interior light. 5, fuel gauge. 6, rev counter with main beam and ignition lights. 7, speedometer with trip and mileage recorders and indicator warning light. 8, water temp/oil pressure gauge. 9, handbrake. 10, heater temperature control. 11, ignition/starter key. 12, wiper/washer switch. 13, heater fan. 14, rheostat panel light. 15, interior light. 16, headlights. 17, choke. 18, lights. 19, dip-switch. 20, horn.

The bonnet can be completely removed by detaching the retaining springs. 1, oil filler. 2, starter solenoid. 3, washer reservoir. 4, distributor (almost invisible). 5, dipstick. 6, hydraulic reservoir. 7, radiator cap.

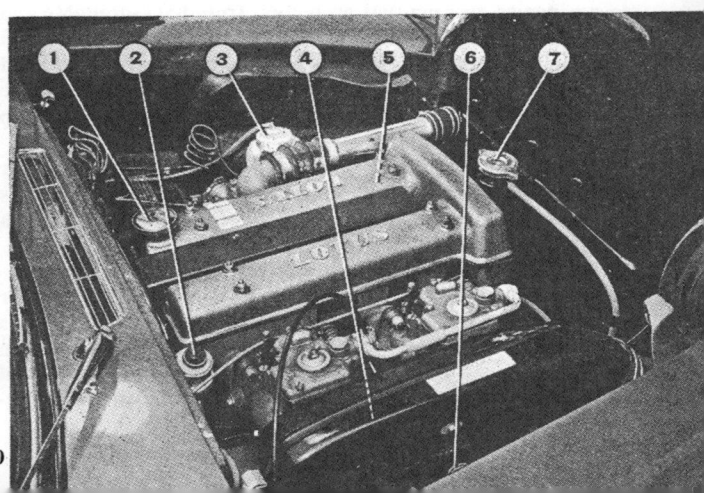

Transmission

IN SPECIFICATION the transmission side is as good a complement to the design as one could expect for a road car. The ratios feel ideally close and evenly spaced; in fact they get progressively closer towards top gear—as near to a true geometric progression as design will allow—without bottom gear being too high for traffic creeping.

A mixed blessing are the rubber "doughnuts"—the Metalastik couplings in each drive shaft—which take a lot of shock out of the drive and probably account for the Elan appearing more tractable than the Lotus Cortina. But they are also responsible for slight surging at constant low speeds in any gear and for some reversing judder. It may be that they cause the slight tendency to hang in gear, normally only noticed during fast changes under load. The clutch bites very quickly, almost too abruptly and can excite the doughnuts when starting off and during quick changes.

Once you get used to it there is little on which to fault the transmission either in noise or gearbox design. For American markets, the back axle ratio is ideal with very quick surging up to 70 m.p.h., but motorway cruising at 100 m.p.h. needs almost 6,000 r.p.m. and an overdrive, if it could be fitted, would be an advantage to anyone habitually doing this. The test car had the highest available Ford ratio (3·90 to 1) which allows the maximum speed at 7,000 r.p.m. to occur well over the power peak at 5,500 r.p.m.

Handling and brakes

THE ELAN is the ultimate denial of the fallacy that for good cornering ability you must have stiff suspension and damping and a hard ride. Vintage cars were always bolted up solid to limit roll and handle well on good roads, but on any but the best surfaces they leapt from ridge to bump and back again; some live-axled sports cars still do.

In contrast, the Elan gets the best of all worlds with sure-footed stability on all surfaces and yet still gives a ride comparable to better saloons, soft not overdamped. It really feels as though there is a well sprung wheel at each corner.

On fast corners, the handling remains neutral right up to a limit which most people will never even approach on ordinary roads; there is a little roll and a surprising amount of tyre squeal from the SP41s on smooth roads. On slower corners, power carelessly or deliberately applied can easily bring the tail round but it is always recoverable even from quite high attitude angles with quick movements of high geared steering; despite the gearing and a comfortably small wooden rimmed steering wheel, the steering is light and extremely sensitive, though with none of the kickback often associated with rack and pinion gears.

The three boxes on the right (3·1 cu. ft.) fit in the boot, the other two (2·1 cu. ft.) go behind the seats inside. Total, 5·2 cu. ft.

All corners are taken with the minimum of fuss and at speeds which unknowledgeable passengers find hard to believe ; the car goes just where it is pointed without any need to change steering angles with roll—you would have to be very foolish to get into trouble. In the wet extreme sensitivity keeps the driver fully aware of any loss of grip at either end; it is easy to provoke the back end but even on fast wet take-offs the SPs gripped very quickly.

With a car like this, brakes are vitally necessary for self defence as other road users seem to be quite unaware of the Elan's speed. They are outstandingly powerful and light and got extremely hard treatment. One pair of pads had to be replaced at 4,000 miles: a ten minute job for the owner.

Performance

Test Data: World copyright reserved: no unauthorized reproduction in whole or part.

Conditions: Weather: Dry with gusty breeze 5-20 m.p.h. (Temperature 66°-72° F, Barometer 29·65-29·60 in. Hg.). Surface: Dry tarmacadam. Fuel: Super premium 101 octane (R.M.).

MAXIMUM SPEEDS

Mean of opposite runs..	111·9 m.p.h.
Best one way ¼-mile	112·5
3rd gear	92·0
2nd gear	70·0
1st gear	46·0
"Maximile" Speed: (Timed quarter mile after 1 mile accelerating from rest)	
Mean	111·9
Best	112·5

ACCELERATION TIMES

0-30 m.p.h.	3·2 sec.
0-40	4·6
0-50	6·8
0-60	9·0
0-70	11·5
0-80	14·5
0-90	19·0
0-100	24·1
Standing quarter mile	16·5

m.p.h.	Top sec.	3rd sec.
10-30		
20-40	6·8	4·9
30-50	6·4	4·9
40-60	6·3	5·4
50-70	6·2	5·2
60-80	6·7	5·4
70-90	7·7	7·0
80-100	9·0	—

HILL CLIMBING

At steady speed — lb./ton
- Top .. 1 in 5·8 .. (Tapley 350)
- 3rd .. 1 in 4·6 .. (Tapley 430)
- 2nd .. 1 in 3·4 .. (Tapley 575)

FUEL CONSUMPTION

Touring (consumption midway between 30 m.p.h. and maximum less 5% allowance for acceleration) .. 25·5
Overall .. 25·5
Total test distance .. 2,228 miles
(25·5 m.p.g.=11·1 litres/100 km.)

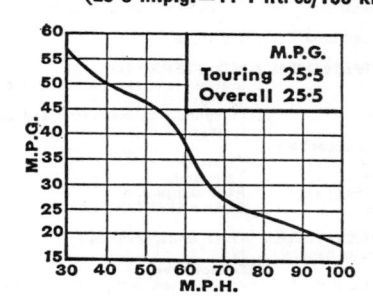

M.P.G. Touring 25·5 Overall 25·5

BRAKES

Pedal pressure, deceleration and equivalent stopping distance from 30 m.p.h.

lb.	g	ft.
25	0·30	100
50	0·62	48
75	0·90	33
100	1·00	30
Handbrake	0·40	75

STEERING

Turning circle between kerbs: ft.
- Left .. 30¼
- Right .. 30¼
- Turns of steering wheel from lock to lock .. 2½

SPEEDOMETER

30 m.p.h.	7% fast
60	6% fast
90	8% fast
Distance recorder	2% fast

WEIGHT

	cwt.
Kerb weight (unladen with fuel for approximately 50 miles)	13½
Front/rear distribution	51½/48½
Weight laden as tested	17

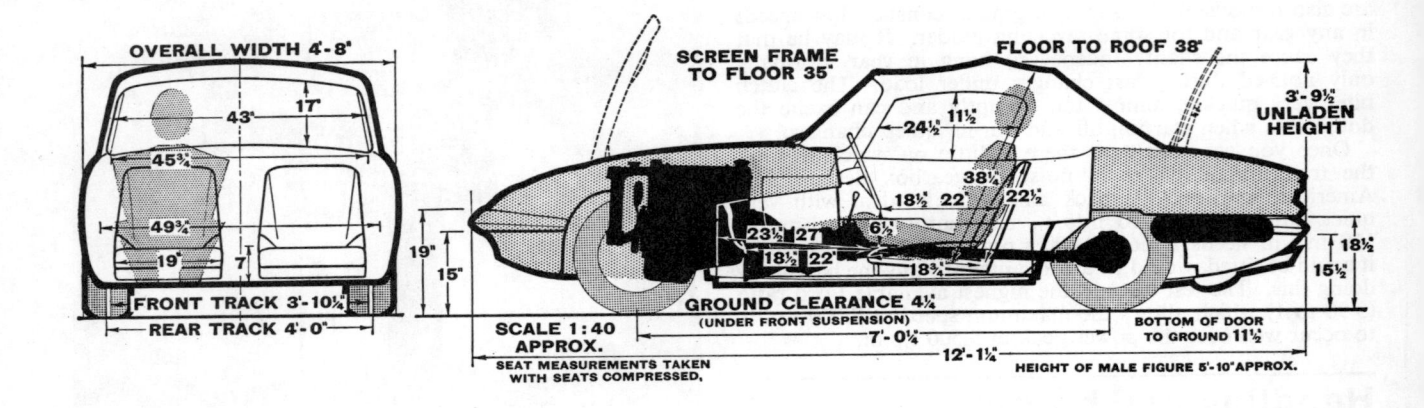

Lotus Elan

The handbrake under the facia needs only a two-finger pull and easily holds the car on a 1 in 3 hill as well as giving a 0·4g stop with rear wheels locked.

Comfort and control

SOME DRIVERS of heavy saloons will find the Elan driving position takes some getting used to, but leaning back is the most comfortable position for the job. Though the seats are narrow, people with vastly different hip sizes all felt that they gripped comfortably and that the backrests gave excellent support all the way up. Adjustment for leg lengths is adequate for people up to 6 ft. 4 in. although several complained that there was no resting place for the left foot. The pedals, slightly offset, are also ideally angled for heel and toe but big feet can hit the accelerator when braking.

Separate plastic frames fitting round the side windows and braced by two cross hoops give one of the most rigid hoods we have met. It is not as quick to put up as some but the result is worth the extra effort; it is rattlefree, draught- and water-proof and gives particularly good visibility. Above 75 m.p.h. the wireless gets a bit drowned whether the hood is up or not but in the latter case there is surprisingly little draught.

Hard acceleration produces intake roar and some exhaust noise but gentle town work is completely unobtrusive, except for slight resonance on the overrun.

The pop-up headlamps are now fairly well known but never fail to amuse strangers, particularly children in the car in front; the lights come up flashing when you pull the switch nearest the gear-lever but there is a slight delay while the vacuum system gets under way; a normal two-position switch holds them on for night work when they give very good vision.

A heater is standard, too, with a slightly noisy fan needed as a supplement only in traffic; two flaps control air to either leg compartment and temperature is adjusted on the facia. In summer the interior, with the hood up, can get very hot.

Fittings and furniture

FOR SO small a car the Elan has a surprising capacity for luggage and general oddments; its boot has a flat floor with the spare wheel underneath and there is room for quite large bags or suitcases in deep wells behind the front seats. Oddments and maps can go in the lockable glove box or in the moulded tray around the gear lever.

Some people think that the light wood facia looks out of character and bitty but all controls are well laid out and easily seen through the spokes of the special Lotus wheel.

All trim, including both the moulded rubber flooring and the p.v.c. door trim is easily scrubbable. When considering safety in the event of someone else's accident (the Elan itself is very safe) a traffic light-jumper could easily squash the Lotus's passenger up against the central backbone since there is little strength in the outrigged body mountings. Inside, the heater box with sharp corners at knee level and the window lifters at temple level could both cause injury but acceleration and general swervability are big safety features

---

MAKE Lotus • **TYPE** Elan 1600 • **MAKERS** Lotus Cars Ltd., Delamare Road, Cheshunt, Herts, England

ENGINE
Cylinders .. 4
Bore and stroke .. 82·55 mm. × 72·75 mm.
Cubic capacity .. 1,558 c.c.
Valves .. Twin overhead camshafts
Compression ratio 9·5 : 1
Carburetters .. Two twin-choke Weber 40 DCOE
Fuel pump .. AC mechanical
Oil filter .. Full flow, renewable element
Max. power (net) .. 105 b.h.p. at 5,500 r.p.m.
Max. torque (net) 108 lb. ft. at 4,000 r.p.m.

TRANSMISSION
Clutch .. 8 in. dia. s.d.p. diaphragm spring
Top gear (s/m) .. Direct
3rd gear (s/m) .. 1·23
2nd gear (s/m) .. 1·64
1st gear (s/m) .. 2·50
Reverse .. 2·79
Final drive .. Hypoid bevel 3·90 : 1
M.p.h. at 1,000 r.p.m.:—
Top gear .. 16·5
3rd gear .. 13·4
2nd gear .. 10·1
1st gear .. 6·6

CHASSIS
Construction .. Welded steel backbone. Glass fibre reinforced plastic body and bumpers

BRAKES
Type .. Girling hydraulic
Dimensions .. Front, 9½ in. disc; Rear ,10 in. dia. disc
Rubbed area .. 298 sq. in.

SUSPENSION AND STEERING
Front .. Independent, wishbones and coil springs
Rear .. Independent, wishbones and coil springs. (Chapman strut)
Shock absorbers:
Front .. Telescopic
Rear .. Telescopic
Steering gear .. Rack and pinion
Tyres .. Dunlop SP41 145—13

COACHWORK AND EQUIPMENT
Starting handle .. No
Jack .. Scissor type
Jacking points .. 4, under wishbone cross members
Battery .. 12-volt 57-amp.-hr.
No. of electrical fuses .. 2
Indicators .. Flashers
Screen wipers .. Variable speed, self-parking
Screen washers .. Manual plunger
Sun visors.. None
Locks:
  With ignition key Doors
  With other keys Boot
Interior heater .. Fresh air—standard
Extras .. Hard top; radio (Smiths
Upholstery .. P.v.c.
Floor covering .. Rubber
Alternative body types .. Detachable hardtop

MAINTENANCE
Sump .. 6¾ pints S.A.E. 20W/30
Gearbox .. 1¾ pints S.A.E. 80 EP
Rear axle .. 2 pints S.A.E. 90 EP
Steering gear .. S.A.E. 90
Cooling system .. 14 pints (2 drain taps)
Chassis lubrication Every 1,500 miles to 2 points
Ignition timing .. 14° b.t.d.c.
Contact breaker gap .. ·014—·016 in.
Sparking plug type Autolite AG32
Sparking plug gap ·023—·028 in.
Tappet clearances (hot/cold) .. Inlet ·005 in., Exhaust ·006 in.
Front wheel toe-in 1/16—1/8 in.
Castor angle .. 3°
Tyre pressures:
  Front 18—22 lb. sq. in.
  Rear 22—26 lb. sq. in.

Journey to Sicily

Further Impressions of the Lotus Elan

CALABRIA.—The Lotus Elan which the Continental Correspondent used to cover the Siracusa G.P. seen in a typical Southern Italian setting, not far from where the Team Lotus transporter broke down. In this impromptu road-test the car covered 3,807 high-speed Continental miles.

AT the end of last year MOTOR SPORT had a Lotus Elan for road-test and due to other commitments the Editor gave it to M. L. T., who used to be our Assistant Editor, and he did the test and write-up, this appearing in the February 1965 issue of MOTOR SPORT. I viewed this move with great displeasure, as the Elan was one road-test car I badly wanted to have a go in, not being very interested in the usual run of bread-and-butter stuff that the Editor road-tests himself. However, the Editor said " Don't fret, we will borrow it from the Assistant Editor for a time," and this we did, the time being the splendid traffic-free one of Christmas Day, just before the ice and snow appeared, and while most people were getting over Christmas dinner and watching television we thrashed the little Elan across and around Salisbury Plain, doing more 100-m.p.h. motoring than seemed reasonable in such a tiny car. We actually reached an all-time high of 6,900 r.p.m. in top, which was over 115 m.p.h., and it seemed to do 6,000 r.p.m. on any short straight. When we got back we agreed that the Elan was a real 2-seater sports car but wondered about its use for serious journeys, and as the Editor said in his article on his Year's Motoring, ". . . we did wonder how long this very enjoyable Elan would hold together . . . ," this thought being provoked after sitting at 6,500 r.p.m. for quite a long while on the Andover road. In the Elan brochure are the words " Colin Chapman says . . . we wanted to build you a ' fun car '," and with that remark we were in full agreement, though I doubted whether I could stand the noise, fuss and pandemonium for more than a 200-mile cross-country stretch.

We returned the Elan to the Assistant Editor full of admiration for the performance, handling and road-holding of this true sports car, and put the brief encounter as one of our memorable experiences, and I mentally said to myself, " that was the Elan, that was," and turned my attention to other cars and activities. However, this was not to be the end of my Elan motoring and it hadn't been the first, for I had short " flips up the road " in various Elans previous to the road-test car. In early February a friend rang up to say " I've just bought an Elan, do you want to try it and come with me to lunch with Eric Oliver; he's bringing his racing Elan along?" Needless to say, I went, both as a chance for another dice in an Elan and to meet my old sidecar driver, and over lunch it transpired that it was Eric in his Elan that had given the Editor trouble on the M1 when he was testing a 4.2-litre E-type Jaguar. As recorded in the January 1965 MOTOR SPORT, the Editor wrote, ". . . we caught up with a Lotus Elan on trade plates which proved able to hold the Jaguar on acceleration up to 135 m.p.h. . . ." After that trip the Editor asked " How fast is a really good Lotus Elan?" and I estimated 135/140 m.p.h. in racing trim and asked why, and he explained how this Elan had given chase on the M1. As it was on trade plates he thought it was probably a works car, but it turned out to be Eric Oliver's privately owned and privately tuned one, which shows what can be done without factory backing. He explained that he had spent many hours balancing everything, matching cylinder, piston and valve gear to each other, fitting 11-to-1 compression pistons, and being meticulous about assembly and adjustments and clearances, just as we used to be with Norton and Velocette engines in earlier days. If the standard Elan is a real sports car, then a highly-tuned one is a real racing car! I thought this was the finish to Elan motoring, but I was wrong again.

In the paddock at Brands Hatch I was approached by Rosemary Sears and Graham Arnold, who look after Lotus Press and Sales affairs, and they suggested that an afternoon with the road-test car wasn't really sufficient to appreciate an Elan. They suggested that as I was one of the few motoring correspondents who still motored long distances to race meetings, in preference to flying, perhaps I would like to take an Elan to Sicily when I went to the Siracusa Grand Prix. I did not take this suggestion very seriously, so promised to phone them about it later, thinking they were only joking and were just in a race-going mood. When I did ring Lotus, Rosemary said " It's all ready, when do you want to collect it?" so I was committed, and my friends were not exactly encouraging about my prospects of getting to Sicily, especially those that knew the last 300 miles through Calabria in Southern Italy. Team Lotus were competing at Siracusa, so I was told that if I had any trouble the mechanics would help me out, and just as a precaution there was a box of spares in the boot of the Elan.

The car in question was not a specially prepared road-test one, but Graham Arnold's own car, and though an early one basically it was brought up to S2 specification and fitted with a hard-top, and appeared to have done nearly 10,000 miles. Apart from a new set of Goodyear G800 tyres and an oil change, it was as he had been using it, even to some of his personal " rubbish " in the boot and glove-box. The remarkable thing about the Elan's cockpit is that in spite of the small overall size of the car it will accommodate the longest legs, and as my legs barely reached down to the ground I had to modify the seat mounting with some wood and a cushion before setting off. The rev.-limit on the twin-cam Lotus Ford engine is at 6,500 r.p.m., though you can go into the red up to 7,000 r.p.m. for short bursts, so as I had a 3,000-mile trip ahead of me I decided to keep to a maximum of 6,000 r.p.m. for gear-changes and 5,500 r.p.m. in top for cruising, and it did not need many miles across France to find that 5,500 r.p.m. (90 m.p.h.) was a very happy cruising speed, although strong side winds called for concentration at this speed. The brilliant ride characteristics of the Elan smoothed out the undulations on French roads in a most impressive manner and the miles went by very quickly indeed. In the Vosges mountains approaching Switzerland a " clonk " began to intrude every time I opened up out of corners, and I began composing my telegram to Lotus and making plans for getting to Sicily by public transport. Eventually I stopped to investigate and jacked the back end up and pulled and kicked everything but could find nothing wrong, so put the jack away and motored on, and the " clonk " had disappeared! Yes, it was the jack that had been flopping about in the boot, down in the well beside the petrol tank. I once had a similar " trouble " in my Porsche, with a thump on right-hand bends; it was a tin of oil rolling about in the nose, which I had forgotten about.

In Switzerland, along that splendid road towards Sion, I thought I ought to see just how fast this Elan went, and it wound itself up to 7,000 r.p.m. in top (116 m.p.h.) and, unlike the road-test car, this one had a very smooth engine right through the range, from 4,000 r.p.m. onwards it was sounding and running like a sewing machine. There was quite a gusty wind blowing, so it was a pretty busy 116 m.p.h., but this is an inevitable price to pay for having a very light and accelerative car; back at its cruising 90 m.p.h. it was quite happy. An over-night stop was being made at Modena, so the last leg of the journey was being run on the splendid Autostrada del Sole, and a continual eye had to be kept on the rev.-counter to keep it down to my pre-arranged limit of 5,500 r.p.m., even in the dark, until I began to notice that the headlamps were beginning to sag. The vacuum-operated "pop-up" headlamps on the Elan is one feature that I have never liked, for even though they have an automatic flasher unit incorporated for daylight use I find that by the time you have reached for the knob, and the lamps have come up and flashed, the incident you wanted to flash at is way behind you. Now another snag had appeared, for obviously the system had sprung a leak and with the throttles open there was not enough suction to hold the lamps up. As Modena was not far off I motored on in a series of bursts of acceleration into progressive inky darkness, and full headlamps beam on the over-run! I later found that a stone had split a T-pipe in the pipe-work for the vacuum system under the car, and some tape effected a temporary cure.

With 500 miles of non-stop *autostrada* motoring available the expression "it will cruise all day at 5,500 r.p.m." is now really true, and at a continuous cruising speed of 5,500 the Elan covered the *autostrada* down through Florence, Siena, Rome, Naples, Salerno, to where it finishes at the moment at Battipaglia. On this sort of motoring, which is getting more and more commonplace in this modern age, another tiresome fault in the design of the Elan appeared, a fault common to many British cars for I am sure the designers do not do serious motoring trips. The fault in question is the fuel-tank capacity, 10 gallons on the Lotus, and at 24 m.p.g. this gives 240 miles providing you get on to the *autostrada* with a full tank and there is a petrol station at the point where you run dry, two suppositions that are purely imaginary. Consequently you have to rely on the petrol gauge and the mileometer, and at 200 miles you get uneasy, especially as you can be more than a gallons-worth from the next pump. With no reserve tap the "peace-of-mind" range is 200 miles, which just isn't sufficient for modern motoring, for in spite of the noise and pandemonium in the Elan it is no hardship to put 500 miles into a day's motoring.

After Salerno you get into the Calabrian mountains, where you spend most of your time in 2nd and 3rd gears, and here the Elan really came into its own, for the handling and cornering are superb, and I liked the characteristics of the Goodyear G800 tyres very much, except that the right-front one rubbed on the body on left-hand hairpins, but this was a fault in the bodywork where it had been repaired at some time in its hard life. The way the Elan would squirt out of corners and "straight-line" cambered ess-bends was most impressive, the uneven and bumpy roads not worrying it at all, and though you feel the suspension working overtime it never showed signs of "bottoming." At first the Elan had seemed a fussy, tiresome little car, but it was definitely growing on me, and though its looks are too simple and plain to be endearing, its character as regards driving fun could not be questioned. By the time I got to Siracusa, which was 1,650 miles from my home, I had extended the Elan under almost all possible types of going and had found it to be absolutely vice-free. It may well be that the handling is so perfect that it appears unimaginative and that it needs sober reflection to realise just how good it really is. A lot of cars feel very nice, except for some little detail, so you think, "with slightly higher-geared steering this car would be terrific" or "with a little more adhesion on the rear wheels it would be ideal." With the Elan I was finding it hard to think of any improvements as regards ride, handling, steering and cornering, which is as it should be, for if Colin Chapman and Lotus cannot produce a perfect handling car, then I don't know who can.

When I met Team Lotus in the paddock they all cried "You've made it," and for a joke I said, "Yes, but I badly need a good Elan mechanic," to which they replied, "You should worry, we need a good Ford mechanic, our transporter broke down in the mountains." In fact there was nothing to do to the Elan, except to put in a second pint of Esso oil, in deference to Team Lotus who use Esso products, to bring the level of the sump up to the full mark, for there are no suspension greasing points and it needed no water. When I left the factory in Cheshunt they had said I would be all right when I got to Sicily because there would be some Lotus mechanics there, but as it turned out it was I who helped them. The two lads from Team Lotus, Doug. Bridge and Bill Cowe, had been driving the "Chapman Special Transporter," with one car on board with all the spares and towing a trailer carrying the second car. This high-speed transporter was a good idea that never really worked due to being over-stressed, for it was a lengthened Thames fitted with a Zephyr engine and its career has been one long series of mishaps. Doug. and Bill were as near as makes no odds halfway between Naples and Reggio Calabria, in the very centre of the Calabrian mountains, when the left-hand end of the rear axle broke clean off. They had found an Italian bandit who had spent 53 years in America and was now retired at Spettano Albenese and with his help on organising they had got the whole lorry and trailer dragged to the edge of town on a sort of huge roller-skate. Then they had hired two lorries and got the racing cars, spare engine, gearboxes and equipment down to Siracusa in a non-stop drive, in time for first practice.

You can imagine how pleased they were when Jim Clark won the race for Team Lotus, and justified all the efforts, but now came the job of getting home. The Team Walker lads took all the spares and equipment in their huge transporter, and while Doug. spent Monday morning organising two more lorries for the return trip to the centre of Calabria I took Bill in the Elan and we pressed on ahead. The idea was that he could start taking the broken axle off the Ford and get everything ready for bolting in a new one, for a phone call to Cheshunt had got Andrew Ferguson stirring everyone up and sending a complete axle out to Naples by air freight. At 6 p.m. I dropped Bill and his tools and luggage at the stricken transporter, still sitting by the roadside on blocks of wood, and I motored on to the next big town for the night, as I had an evening of Grand Prix report writing to get on with. While Bill was having a kip in the Ford's cab, Doug. arrived in the small hours of the morning with two lorries, two Sicilian drivers, and two Lotus Grand Prix cars, and they offloaded them and made plans for the next move. I had offered them the Elan to go to Naples, but we could not visualise it carrying a Ford commercial rear axle in the boot. It had uncomplainingly brought Bill and me with two suitcases, a bulky briefcase, a box of spares, Bill's great steel toolbox, overcoats and odds and ends, and there are people who complain about the lack of luggage-space in an Elan. I was fully prepared for it to ground and bottom the suspension with this load on board, but the only defect was that the tyre-rubbing on tight left-hand hairpins got worse. As we were pressing on through the mountains there were occasional smells of hot rubber and hot fibre-glass as we went a bit too quickly into some corners, but there were no ill-effects.

The original plan had been that Doug. and Bill would hire a small pick-up truck to drive the 200 miles to Naples airport to collect the axle, but they later changed their minds and decided to hitch-hike through Calabria and rent a Hertz hire car at the airport. By this time I was ahead of them, but they set out at dawn and got a lift in a Fiat 500, of the modern "clockwork" variety, and this slowly ground its way through the mountains. I set off pretty early next morning and as I came round a corner I saw the two mechanics by the roadside with the owner of the Fiat 500, having a rest and a smoke. Leaving Bill to follow on with the Italian, who spoke quite good English and was off to America at the end of the week, like so many Italians and Sicilians, I took Doug. in the Elan and we pressed on to Naples, with the idea of getting the freight and customs people stirred up, always assuming the axle had arrived. As always, there was no axle and no one knew anything about an axle, so after meeting two planes from London, neither carrying the Ford axle, I had to leave and press on to Modena, where I was due that night. Just as I was leaving, a happy and relieved-looking Bill found us, having successfully hitch-hiked his way along, so I left them hiring an estate-car and phoning Cheshunt to find out what had happened to the axle. This was well after lunchtime but, modern Italy being the impressive way it is, I was comfortably in Modena for supper that night. The *autostrada* is less than five minutes from the airport and it was then constant 5,500-r.p.m. cruising all the way to the Modena South turn-off and toll-gate. There was a brief interlude when a Giulia TI Alfa Romeo got in behind me, and stayed there at 6,000 and on to 6,500 on the Lotus rev.-counter. At 6,800 it began to drop back, and with the honour of Lotus at stake I felt forced to sit at 6,800 until the Alfa gave up, which it did after a few miles, and, rather relieved, I eased back to 6,000 and then reluctantly back to 5,500. This particular engine showed no signs of stress or roughness at these revs and felt as if it would go on for ever at that speed, but I was still 1,200 miles from home, with important consignments ahead.

After a day in Modena I set off for Le Mans, for the test week-end, and put a very easy 465 miles into the day, including traversing the Alps on the train, the passes still being closed. Feeling that I was on the last leg of the journey and the Elan

ELAN IMPRESSIONS—

having by now instilled an incredible amount of confidence in me I held it at 6,000 r.p.m. for 50 minutes on the *autostrada* from Milan to Turin, and really felt that the Lotus-Ford twin-cam engine was unburstable. After 700 miles of hard going in the mountains and on the undulating roads of Calabria and Sicily, I was convinced that bits were not going to fall off the Elan, as my friends prophesied, and brief spells of really heavy rain did not leave one saturated as other people suggested. On the final run to Le Mans I caught up with a DS19 Citroën that was cruising at 85 m.p.h. on a bumpy cambered road, so I sat behind for many miles comparing the ride of the Lotus with that of " the most advanced car in the World." It was not as good, but it was not far behind, and I have yet to find the equal of the DS19 for level-ride and controlled suspension. I thought that the Elan was showing up well, especially for its light weight and small size, and felt forced to overtake the DS just to let the driver see that Britain knows something about road-holding and ride. At 100 m.p.h. I was busy, but not out of control, for this was not a *Route Nationale*, it was one of those B-C roads that cross France, and as the couple in the Citroën had shown great interest when I came up behind them at first, we then ran in company for about 100 miles, taking turns at leading the way, until the French people turned off my route.

Le Mans was visited and then it was back to England and to Cheshunt to return the Elan to Graham Arnold, having covered 3,807 miles in the two weeks I was away. A third pint of oil had brought the level up to " Full " and the only breakage was that the Smiths water-temperature gauge had stopped working. The rather useless umbrella-type hand-brake still didn't work and the car was devoid of all its Lotus badges, for after Clark's win at Siracusa the local " enthusiasts " had got to work with penknives during the night. The two mechanics I had left at Naples were back at work, their friends considering the trip to Sicily a holiday, but their troubles had not been over when I left them on the Tuesday after the race. The axle did not arrive until Friday morning and they then had to drive the mountainous 200 miles back to Spettano Albenese, fit the axle, load the cars, and return the hire car to Naples and get back to England. On the *autostrada* the transporter suddenly shed a wheel, fortunately without serious consequence, and by driving in shifts non-stop they made Cheshunt by Sunday night, which was a pretty good marathon. In many papers the only mention of the race in Sicily was " Jim Clark won the Siracusa Grand Prix in a Lotus-Climax at record speed." Few people can imagine what it involved in effort, time, money and ingenuity to achieve that simple headline, but two Team Lotus mechanics won't forget in a hurry. I'm told the transporter is going to be put in the Lotus museum!

As Rosemary Sears and Arnold had said in the Brands Hatch paddock, an afternoon with an Elan was not sufficient, but two weeks' constant use gave me a much better idea, and I cannot praise the handling, road-holding, cornering and performance of the Elan highly enough, while my trip answered our original query about how long it would hold together. It is not perfect, for it is too fussy and noisy, and I still think it is a dull-looking car, lacking character in its shape. but all its character lies in the way it goes. It is an incredibly safe car, forgiving and vice-free, and so obviously comes from a parent-hood of racing knowledge; it is essentially a sports car, and as Colin Chapman says, it is a fun car. It is not cheap, but then nothing that is good is cheap, but to anyone contemplating buying a cheaper 2-seater sports car, and there are many of them, I would say " Sell the television set, the washing machine, the wife's car, give up smoking, even give up drinking, but scrimp and save and buy an Elan, you won't be disappointed."

It is a car that every young man should strive his utmost to acquire, and a lot of old men too. Why don't I have one myself? If it looked like the Marcos 1800 I think I would.—D. S. J.

WITH A LITTLE ELAN

(Continued from page 27)

the boot and driver's door lock with keys. The overall standard of finish is not good, particularly when one finds ill-fitted rubber sealing on the windscreen cowling, rattling door trim, and floor rubber that had already rubbed into a hole in only 1600 miles. However, the quality of the exterior paint is deep and lustrous — far better than one can expect from glass-fibre and better than most baked enamel finishes. Boot and bonnet lids — both very light — fit neatly.

There is good room around the engine for most tasks, particularly as the bonnet will stay in a number of positions through its lightness and inertia. There are studs for tonneau cover fixing, if needed.

But the disappointments in finish did not mar the enjoyment of this remarkable car. It fits a great size range of driver without any need for the fair range of seat adjustment. The pedals are beautifully placed for heel-toe work, the gear-lever is exactly the right length, the steering wheel in exactly the right place. If anything, one fault is that clutch and brake pedals are too close.

The clutch proved troublesome in city driving, although ideal for high-speed touring. It needed either a whole bagful of rpm or none at all. The engine idled smoothly at 700 rpm and became lumpy at 1000. Maximum torque comes in at 4000 rpm and maximum power at 5500; but there is no perceptible "cam" point. The engine just goes hard from nothing to peak. It is remarkably flexible. We customarily drove the car through heavy traffic at 1500 rpm in top gear without using the gearbox.

The ratios are quite close and well chosen, with second a marvellous gear for all work. We used a limit of 6500 rpm on our acceleration runs, purely out of respect for an expensive power plant, and even at that rate there was not much engine noise. Very little wind gets into the cockpit, going mostly across the top of the head.

There is little suspension noise, and while the Elan rides far better than live-axle sports cars it does shake and rattle a bit on bad bitumen surfaces. It may be that a kit car takes some bedding-down on assembly before being finally tightened up.

Handling is absolutely superb. One can add 2000 rpm instantly in a corner with no perceptible result. We suppose that the car is a final under-steerer, because it lifts an inside front wheel when pressed very hard in corners. But it is as neutral as all get-out. You sit there, flicking the wheel a millimetre this way and that, and the only sign that the car has deviated from the straight-ahead is an increase in moan rate of the tyres. Suburban right-angle intersections can be taken without shifting the hands from a quarter-to-three. Closing the throttle suddenly on a fast 90 mph sweeper produces, again, no marked result. It has no vices at all.

It stops well, as one would expect with discs all round, and pedal pressures are quite light, considering the lack of servo assistance. We managed to lock up one rear wheel at the last moment in crash stops from 60 mph. There was some friction noise whenever the front discs cooled, but this was doubtless caused by pad misalignment.

It proved possible to spin the rear wheels momentarily from a standing start in first gear, and again on the change to second. The acceleration in second is tremendous, but the car goes hardest over 4000 rpm in third and top. It ran to 6000 in top very quickly, and, again, with little engine thrash and only medium wind noise. The seats located both people exceptionally well in hard corners, despite some roll movement.

All in all, the Elan is best described as a delightful driver's car. It is far easier to drive on its limit than any sports car we know, and, pound for pound, one of the fastest point-to-point cars in existence. As a pure result of competition improving the breed, it made a remarkable impact on the staff of SPORTS CAR WORLD.   #

Road Test 6/66

Lotus Elan S2 Coupe

It may not sound reasonable
but you may not be a good enough driver
to be able to handle a Lotus Elan!

IF YOU ARE FAMILIAR WITH THE LOTUS ELITE, the quickest way to visualize the Elan is as a logical updating and improvement of nearly the same concept. To be blunt, the Elan is not everyone's "cup of tea." It is a car for the enthusiast's enthusiast. In many ways it's a very expensive toy...a toy to be enjoyed by very knowledgeable drivers, and those enamored enough with modern and somewhat exotic machinery to overlook its more practical shortcomings. As a Lotus representative allegedly put it, "If we sell one of these cars to Joe Average motorist, we're in big trouble!" For the price, there seems relatively little danger of this occurring. If it did, we'd have to agree.

There is no major difference between the first Elan and the S2 model, just detail improvements to make it quieter and more docile. It is an exceptionally light car (1282 pounds at the curb) with a 1.6-liter engine (the Cosworth-designed twin-cam head on the Ford 120E block) that develops 105 horsepower. The result is a horsepower/weight ratio of 12.2-to-1. Combine this with a first-rate sophisticated suspension system and a streamlined, low-frontal-area body, and it becomes apparent you are going to wind up with maximum roadability and performance. Then mix in the Lotus logic in driver packaging and controls-design (with the annoying exception, in this instance, of foot controls) to assure good comfort and driveability. We got the impression that Luxury — what there is of it — was an afterthought taken into consideration when they figured out what the retail price of the vehicle was going to be.

As our test unit was one of the first coupes to arrive on the West Coast (thus having zero mileage), we borrowed an S2 soft-top from Bill Young's La Cañada Sports Car Center to obtain performance figures. There's very little difference in body lines and the top, including the electric-operated windows, adds under 100 pounds to the weight, so the figures should be nearly identical. It was our first trip in an Elan (SCG's Blunsden did the initial test in England) excepting our test of Young's race car last year. A short time after we picked up his car we were on the phone to him: "You flake! You forgot to tighten the U-joints!" Ignoring our diplomacy, he countered that he had forgotten to tell us how to *drive* it. And we had some choice comments about THAT remark. What was under discussion was the "rubberband

PHOTOS: DARRYL NORENBERG

Cornering, as shown below, is the real forte of the Elan. Here it takes a tight, reverse-camber turn in stride. Both beautiful and business-like are the lines of the S2 coupe, shown in "living" red at right. Note the unusual door cutout that allows easy access to the semi-reclining seats.

effect" of the rubber donuts used as inner joints on the rear axles. Accelerate or stop at a rapid rate, and you can feel these joints compress and unload, transmitting a very discernible lurch. It requires extremely smooth clutch release and throttle application to control. By the second day of driving, this smoothness became pretty much automatic and we ceased to be annoyed by the wrap-up, but it remains a factor under very hard braking and, for around-town use, requires that the engine be in an excellent state of tune to enable the smooth take-offs. But Bill was right; you have to learn to *drive* it.

The 1548-cc engine is, as we stated earlier, a twin-cam conversion of the strong Ford 120E ex-pushrod four-cylinder. Despite a relatively high power peak, it has good torque on the lower end. Fed by two dual-throat Weber DCOE-40 carburetors, it is almost over-carbureted and requires delicate adjustment of idle and linkage settings. Once this is accomplished, however, the engine will tick over below 1000 rpm, and pull from 1500 rpm in high gear providing the throttle is reasonably feathered. It is a very quiet powerplant and has an almost timid exhaust note. Gas mileage is quite impressive with the light car; an average of 25 mpg, which also makes the relatively small fuel tank (12½ gallons) no bother.

Behind the engine is basically a Cortina close-ratio gearbox with special shift-linkage modifications. It's really great fun to shift, due to the extremely short lever and tight pattern. The lever is mounted on the high center tunnel (remember, the Elan frame is a huge, boxed sheet-metal "X"), close at hand, and shifts with an audible "click-click" of its detents. Full synchromesh, it's really beautiful.

Handling, of course, is the real forte of the Elan. Without a G-meter comparison with other machines, we'd venture that it has the best side-bite of any production car in existence. At one point we sailed through what would normally be an 85-mph banked sweeper and glanced down to see an indicated 105 mph on the speedometer. Slip-angles were barely discernible! This extremely good bite and light, rapid response is very much like a first-rate small Modified or Formula car. This could even be a dangerous trait in the hands of an unskilled driver, as the complete feeling of security at horrendous velocity could easily lead him into BIG trouble before he realized it. The attitude is light understeer at high cornering speeds, almost neutral. In tight corners, the understeer becomes stronger. The stopping power is very good and very stable, but not quite as quick as we expected in view

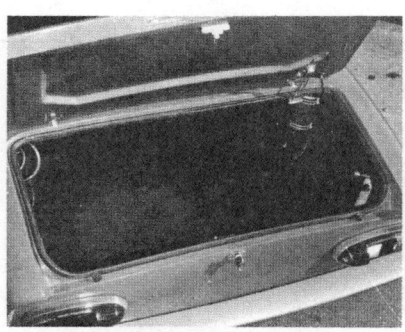

Trunk area is small, due to gas tank, spare tire, and battery being in this area, but access is good, and interior fully carpeted.

Instrumentation and controls are attractive, straight-forward, and efficient. Pedals were too small and close together for our liking.

Pop-up headlights are actuated by a vacuum cylinder and work very well. Wheels are pin-drive and knock-off.

Understeering through a tight corner, above, the Lotus indicates how good the tire-bite is by the amount of lean. A model of efficient engineering is the twin-cam conversion of the four-cylinder Ford, at right. Compartment is crowded, but general accessibility is good. Note the cold-air box.

37

of the sensational handling, and the fact that it has big, four-wheel disc brakes. Perhaps this is due to the relatively narrow-profile tires used, yet there is not an abnormal tendency to lock up the wheels on hard deceleration.

The body lines and general appearance of the Elan are very likable. To keep the sleekness, pop-out headlights are used. These are operated by vacuum cylinders that instantly open or close via a separate switch. If the headlights are not turned on when they are in the UP position, a relay automatically makes them blink until they are. Yet they can be turned to DOWN, with the sealed beams concealed within the bodywork and the light remains on. It seems like they should work just the opposite. The cockpit is very comfortable, with semi-reclining buckets and relatively easy entrance by virtue of a long forward cutout in the door shape. The small steering wheel is ideally positioned and, with 2½ turns lock-to-lock, the response is very positive. As we carped earlier, the pedals are both miniaturized and close together. There really is adequate room in the footwell, so the size and spacing appears illogical to us. It's not impossible to hit two pedals at once, even with our size 7½'s. Instrumentation is Smith's; nice, round, legible gauges. Most of the switches are toggle type, mounted on the polished-wood flat dash. Visibility is excellent, except that a side-view mirror is a must, due to the proximity of your head to the left side of the hardtop. A unique feature on the relatively spartan Elan coupe is electric windows. The soft-top has high-quality pull-up type windows, with a small latch to lock them in the desired position. The electrics really seem out of place.

Trunk room is pretty small. You can get one good-sized suitcase in, plus a couple of small kits, but that's about it. Below the trunk platform is the spare tire and tool kit. The gas tank and battery are also in this rear section.

Our total impression of the Elan coupe was quite enthusiastic. It has the looks, the roadability, and the ride qualities that make it an extremely pleasant car to own. It certainly fulfills the requirements of basic transportation while being an exotic, fully-independent-suspension, light, high-performance machine. Mainly, you describe the Elan with a three-letter word: FUN. You can rationalize much of its high cost in durability under abuse — which it certainly appears to have — the general low operating costs, and the high-quality engineering that went into it. As we said, though — it's a car for the connoisseur, not for the volks.

LOTUS ELAN S2 COUPE ROAD TEST 6/66

PERFORMANCE:
0-30	2.8 sec.	0-70	9.5 sec.
0-40	4.1 sec.	0-80	11.1 sec.
0-50	5.9 sec.	0-90	13.8 sec.
0-60	7.9 sec.	0-100	17.0 sec.

Standing ¼ mile .... n.a.
Top Speed (av. two-way run) .... 115 mph

Speed Error	30	40	50	60	70	80	90
Actual	30	40	50	60	69	79	88

Fuel Consumption
Test: .... 25 mpg   Average: .... 25 mpg
Recommended Shift Points   Max. 2nd .... 58 mph
Max. 1st .... 36 mph   Max. 3rd .... 86 mph
RPM Red-line .... 6,000 rpm
Speed Ranges in gears:
1st .... 0 to 38 mph   3rd .... 8 to 86 mph
2nd .... 5 to 60 mph   4th .... 15 to top mph
Brake Test: 70 Average % G, over 10 stops.
No fade encountered.

Vehicle .... Lotus Elan
Model .... S2 Coupe
Price (as tested) .... $5065.00 POE LA
Options .... Included, except radio

ENGINE:
Type .... Ford 120-E, 4-cylinder, in-line, water-cooled
Head .... Removable, alloy, hemispherical chambers
Valves .... Dohc, direct-acting
Max. BHP .... 105 @ 5500 rpm
Max. Torque .... 105 lbs. ft. @ 3200 rpm
Bore .... 3.25 in. 82.6 mm
Stroke .... 2.864 in. 72.8 mm
Displacement .... 95 cu. in. 1558 cc
Compression Ratio .... 10.5 to 1
Induction System .... Two 40 DCOE Webers
Exhaust System .... Steel headers
Electrical System .... 12 V. distributor ignition

CLUTCH:
Single disc, dry
Diameter: .... 8.25 in.
Actuation: .... Hydraulic

TRANSMISSION:
Four-speed, full-synchro
Ratios: 1st .... 3.543 to 1
         2nd .... 1.63 to 1
         3rd .... 1.23 to 1
         4th .... 1.0 to 1

DIFFERENTIAL: Sprung
Ratio: .... 3.55 to 1
Drive Axles (type): ... Open, 2-joint (rubber inner)

STEERING: Rack and pinion
Turns Lock to Lock: 2.25
Turn Circle: .... 30 ft.

BRAKES:
Disc Diameter .... Front 9.5 in.
                     Rear 10.0 in.
Swept Area .... n.a. sq. in.

CHASSIS:
Frame: .... Steel cruciform box
Body .... Fiberglass
Front Suspension: .... Unequal A's, coil/shocks
Rear Suspension: ... I.R.S. McPhearson-type strut with lower arm, coil springs
Tire Size & Type: .... Dunlop SP 13 x 4.5

WEIGHTS AND MEASURES:
Wheelbase: .... 85 in.   Ground Clearance .... 6 in.
Front Track: .... 56 in.   Curb Weight .... 1282 lbs.
Rear Track: .... 56 in.   Test Weight .... 1585 lbs.
Overall Height .... 46 in.   Crankcase .... 4 qts.
Overall Width .... 56.5 in.   Cooling System .... 9 qts.
Overall Length ...... 145 in.   Gas Tank .... 12.5 gals.

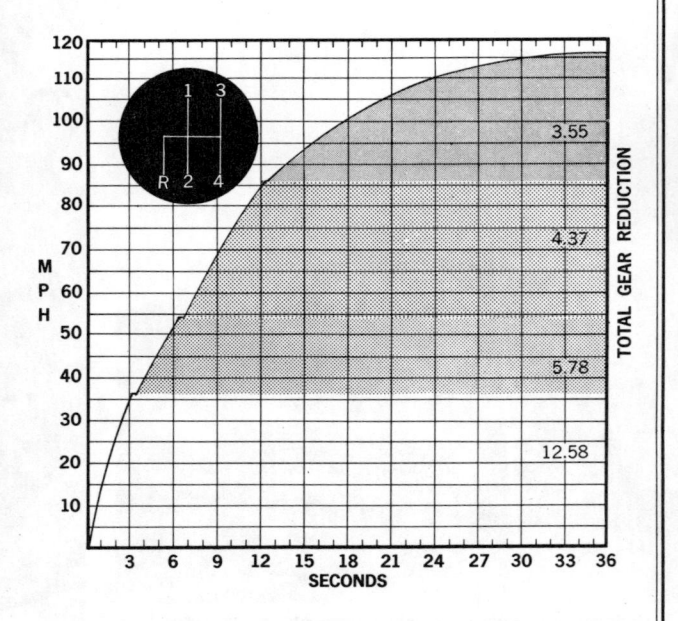

Gear ratios on chart: 3.55, 4.37, 5.78, 12.58 (TOTAL GEAR REDUCTION)

REFERENCE FACTORS:
1.11 bhp. per Cubic Inch   12.2 Lbs. per bhp.
Piston Speed @ Peak rpm .... 2622 ft./min.

CAR and DRIVER ROAD TEST

LOTUS ELAN S2

A purist's potpourri of sophisticated engineering features, the Lotus Elan Coupe deserves its pedigree

Back in our old purist days, it didn't matter whether a car was any good or not, as long as it had all the right *stuff* under the hood. The specifications had to *read* right. Double overhead camshafts—not pushrods. One carb choke per cylinder—not a big, dumb four-barrel, even if it wouldn't start on a cold morning. And a minimum of four gears—either all-synchro or a Big Boy crashbox. A *multitubular space frame!* (Who even knew what one looked like?) All-independent suspension, even if it meant wild camber changes and even wilder handling. No need to have actually seen a car like that—much less have ever driven one. If it had the right thing in fine print on the last page of the brochure, we were ready to buy it.

So along comes Ford and hurls their Mk. II into the crucible of racing. It's got pushrods and a big, dumb four-barrel, and it's maybe the most sophisticated piece of racing machinery ever assembled, with the possible exception of the fiberglass chassis, *automatic transmission* Chaparral. After a while, all we cared about a car's design specifications was whether or not the car got the job done.

Looking at the specifications of the Lotus Elan brought it all back. Gad! What a pedigree! Here is a car that should stoke the fires of desire in every fine-print-reading purist who ever breathed. It's got everything they hold sacred (except possibly the backbone chassis, which hasn't cut any ice with anybody since kindly old Dr. Ledwinka slid one under his Tatra three decades ago). But does all that exotica make any difference?

Stand easy, men; the answer is yes—a qualified yes. Given artificially imposed limitations, technology makes all the difference.

First and foremost, the Elan is a tiny car. It is also very much a sports car, in the best sense of the word. Starting with these criteria in mind, designer Colin Chapman has done a bang-on job. Over a dozen laps of, say, the Nürburgring, the Elan would probably get the job done faster and with less effort than any other production car in the

The handling is superlative. The Elan uses roadway very sparingly and lets go very gradually. Ride comfort is outstanding for such a light car.

world; certainly with more . . . élan, shall we say, than anything that ever came out of Detroit—which is, after all, what the whole purist bag is about.

But who does a dozen laps of the Nürburgring every morning before breakfast? Or every week? Or once in a lifetime? Not many of us. Sure, a sports car should be fun, but most prospective buyers want a healthy dose of day-in, day-out utilitarian value thrown in as well. Once the driver is ensconced in his Elan, it's as practical and enjoyable a means of transportation as any (it is, in fact, kind of a stylish, comfortable Mini-Cooper), but the car does have its limitations, mostly self-imposed.

To begin with, the Elan's size makes it difficult to get into or out of. Once inside, there's little hip room (due to the backbone frame), little headroom (styling and aerodynamic considerations), and it's also pretty tough trying to see *over* any object larger than a tall dog. And, for some insane reason, the traditionally miniscule foot pedals (a revered principle among British car designers) are huddled together in the middle of a passably wide space.

The drive train is an irritating conglomeration of disturbing sensations. The clutch engages so suddenly and so violently that the car invariably stalls. A clutch should be positive, yes, but why does it have to be feathered in over only a quarter-inch of pedal movement? The only sure way to move smartly off the line without a lot of sniggering from the bystanders is to rev the engine to the peg and drop the clutch like a bad habit. Okay, so the owner soon gets used to it; why should he have to bother?

Against this, the rest of the drive train is sloppy. The ultra-sophisticated Chapman-strut suspension demands a certain amount of lateral compliance. Ordinarily, this would be accommodated by splined half-shafts, but as the half-shafts are holding the Elan's rear wheels on, this movement is kept within limits by Metalastik rubber doughnuts surrounding the differential-mounted universal joints. This unit looks

LOTUS ELAN COUPE

Distributor: Lotus/East
Box 394
Salisbury, Conn.
Price as Tested: $4980.00

ACCELERATION
Zero To	Seconds
30 mph	2.4
40 mph	3.7
50 mph	5.6
60 mph	7.5
70 mph	10.3
80 mph	13.3
90 mph	16.9
100 mph	22.1
Standing ¼ mile	87.5 mph in 15.9

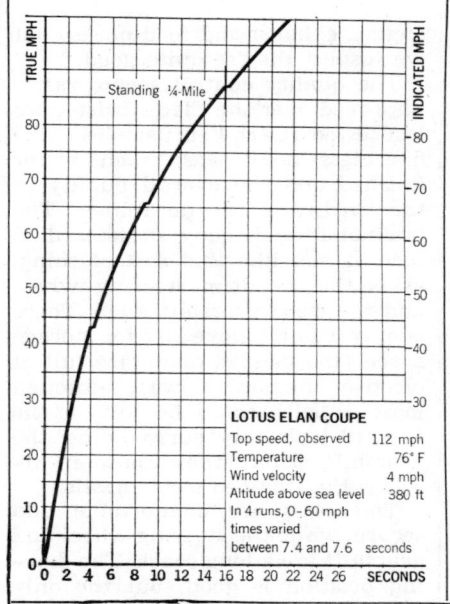

LOTUS ELAN COUPE
Top speed, observed 112 mph
Temperature 76°F
Wind velocity 4 mph
Altitude above sea level 380 ft
In 4 runs, 0–60 mph times varied between 7.4 and 7.6 seconds

ENGINE
Water-cooled four-in-line, cast iron block, aluminum head, 5 main bearings
Bore x stroke.................3.25 x 2.86 in, 82.6 x 72.8 mm
Displacement...............95 cu.in, 1588 cc
Compression ratio..................9.5 to one
Carburetion....2 x 2 Weber DCOE/2 sidedraft
Valve gear....Chain-driven double overhead camshafts
Power (SAE).............105 bhp @ 5500 rpm
Torque..............108 lbs-ft @ 4000 rpm
Specific power output....1.11 bhp per cu.in, 65.6 bhp per liter
Usable range of engine speeds
..............................1000–6500 rpm
Electrical system...12-volt, 57 amp-hr battery, 300W generator
Fuel recommended.................Premium
Mileage.....................22–28 mpg
Range on 12-gallon tank......264–336 miles

DRIVE TRAIN
Clutch...........8.5-inch single dry plate
Transmission.........4-speed manual, all synchromesh

Gear	Ratio	Overall	mph/1000 rpm	Max mph
Rev	2.92	11.38	–5.7	–37
1st	2.51	9.78	6.6	43
2nd	1.64	6.40	10.2	66
3rd	1.23	4.80	13.5	88
4th	1.00	3.90	16.6	109

Final drive ratio....................3.90 to one

CHASSIS
Steel backbone chassis, fiberglass body
Wheelbase........................84.0 in
Track.....................F 47.0 R 47.0 in
Length..........................145.0 in
Width............................56.0 in
Height...........................46.0 in
Ground Clearance..................6.0 in
Curb Weight.....................1560 lbs
Test Weight.....................1780 lbs
Weight distribution front/rear......48/52%
Pounds per bhp (test weight).........16.6
Suspension F: Ind., unequal length wishbones, coil springs, anti-sway bar
R: Ind., lower lateral links, halfshafts acting as upper links, coil springs
Brakes....Girling discs, 9.5 in F, 10 in R, 358 sq in swept area
Steering.....................Rack and pinion
Turns, lock to lock...................2.5
Turning circle.....................30.0 ft
Tires and wheels....5.20-13 Dunlop SP 41 on 4.5J rim, knock-off wheels

CHECK LIST

ENGINE
Starting...........................Fair
Response.......................Very Good
Noise..............................Fair
Vibration..........................Good

DRIVE TRAIN
Clutch Action......................Poor
Transmission Linkage..........Very Good
Synchromesh Action...........Very Good
Power-To-Ground
    Transmission................Excellent

BRAKES
Response........................Excellent
Pedal Pressure..................Excellent
Fade Resistance....................Good
Smoothness.....................Very Good
Directional Stability............Very Good

STEERING
Response........................Excellent
Accuracy........................Excellent
Feedback........................Excellent
Road Feel.......................Excellent

SUSPENSION
Harshness Control..............Very Good
Roll Stiffness.....................Fair
Tracking...........................Good
Pitch Control......................Good
Shock Damping......................Good

CONTROLS
Location...........................Good
Relationship.......................Fair
Small Controls.....................Fair

INTERIOR
Visibility.........................Good
Instrumentation....................Good
Lighting........................Very Good
Entry/Exit.........................Fair
Front Seating Comfort..........Very Good
Front Seating Room.................Fair
Rear Seating Comfort...............—
Rear Seating Room..................—
Storage Space......................Poor
Wind Noise.....................Excellent
Road Noise.....................Very Good

WEATHER PROTECTION
Heater.........................Very Good
Defroster..........................Good
Ventilation........................Fair
Weather Sealing....................Good
Windshield Wiper Action........Very Good

QUALITY CONTROL
Materials, Exterior................Good
Materials, Interior................Good
Exterior Finish....................Good
Interior Finish....................Good
Hardware and Trim..................Good

GENERAL
Service Accessibility..............Good
Luggage Space......................Poor
Bumper Protection..................Poor
Exterior Lighting..................Fair
Resistance to Crosswinds......Excellent

> A quarter-mile in less than 16 seconds is no mean accomplishment for a 95 cu. in. GT, but the tires seem to be the limiting factor in an 80-0 mph panic stop.

great on Formula One cars, and the fact that it allows some rubber-cushioned rotation looks—on paper—as if it might damp out torsional vibrations. In practice, it causes a disconcerting pitching oscillation every time the throttle is opened or closed—it's unpleasantly reminiscent of being rocked in a baby carriage. (Not all of us had happy childhoods.)

The only other reservations we have about recommending a Lotus center around the fact that Mr. Chapman has acquired a reputation for being a *very* shrewd businessman, in selling production cars as well as in racing. Deserved reputation or not, the Lotus retail operation in this country has been shaky from the beginning. There's a million-dollar lawsuit pending in California, filed by a former distributor who was disenfranchised. An impressive New York outlet, a swanky showroom on Madison Avenue, folded within the year. Although some of the dealerships seem literally to be here today and gone tomorrow, we obtained our test car from one of the longest-established Lotus dealers in the country. There are others, of course, and if we can't *promise* that the U.S. marketing and servicing organizations will get any better, they at least seem to have arrested the downward spiral of confidence that has plagued them in the past.

Finally, friends, five thousand bucks is a lot of money for a funny little foreign car.

Our test car is sort of a prototype of the new Elan coupe. It is identical with the ones now being imported, with the exception of the final drive ratios. Our car had the close-ratio gearbox and 3.90 rear axle used in the Elan roadsters, but current coupes will be equipped with a longer 3.55 final drive for faster cruising at less engine revs, a higher top speed, and better fuel economy, and also a wider-ratio gearbox that features a tighter overall first gear ratio (12.6 vs. 9.8 in the test car), which should make it much easier to get the car off the line.

The coupe, which costs about $650 more than the roadster, includes a more luxurious interior, electric windows, as well as the comfort and insulation of a fixed roof. The only option on our test car was a $30 Canadian-made Stebro exhaust system—with a bazooka-sized tailpipe—which increased the top end performance a little and the exhaust noise a whole lot. This made it difficult to estimate the normal level of engine, exhaust and road noises, but we suspect they're quite good.

The quality control seems vastly improved over the Elan roadster we last tested (*C/D,* February '64); the fiberglass body was much better finished and the overall quality of the hardware was far higher. The laminated mahogany dashboard is nice, if you like that sort of thing, as is the woodrim steering wheel and the wood gearshift knob. There is only a small glove box for storage space (the padded doors are full of electric motors now), although loose articles could be left in the 6 x 10-inch tray surrounding the gearshift lever—the "console" itself is the stamped steel chassis.

The seats are comfortable and secure, while the steering wheel and gearshift are a long reach. The driving position is good, but the only provision for adjustment is the fore-and-aft movement of the seat, and —as mentioned—the pedals are too small and too close together. Leg room is sensational—as much as the Porsche, but narrower.

The car performs as well as you'd hope it would, being the offspring of the same outfit that engineered wins in the World Driver's and Constructor's Championships, plus the Indianapolis 500, all in the same year. The handling is superlative. Very forgiving. At one point we thought we had the car extended to the limit of a fast turn when a turtle strayed into the path of the inside wheels. The only way to avoid *Clemmys insculpta* was to broadside the Elan, from which the car and the turtle recovered nicely, thank you.

There is a dollop of initial understeer, then a gentle slide into eventual oversteer through a broad working range of neutral steer. The Elan uses up roadway very sparingly, and lets go very gradually. There is a lot of body roll, which doesn't have any adverse effects; we tried, but failed, to pick up an inside wheel. We ran the whole test with low, touring-type tire pressures (22/24 psi) in the radial-ply tires, which squealed like Cagney's

continued on page 105

PHOTOGRAPHY: JOHN R. HEARST, JR.

0-70 mph in 10 secs...

The IWR Lotus Elan

QUITE a lot of people are on record as saying they would not own a sports car in England so long as the 70 mph speed limit exists, but they are perhaps losing sight of the real joys of owning one. The handling, acceleration and general feel of a sports car are every bit as important as the maximum speed anyway, and when Ian Walker lent us his IWR Lotus Elan for a test we thought he was nearing the ultimate in drag-sprint specials.

Regular readers will have gathered that we regard the Elan as one of the most desirable sports cars available, partly because it is so comfortable on the move, quiet and smooth in the engine department, and because it handles so well. If Ian Walker had produced a lumpy and noisy "special" he might never have been forgiven, but in fact his version is every bit as pleasant but accelerates considerably faster.

Any owner can carry out a simple modification to improve acceleration just by putting in a lower-geared axle, which costs £35. So long as he does not intend to exceed the speed limit (and what law-abiding citizen would consider doing that?) a 4.4 axle, for instance, will give an ordinary Elan something like 15 mph per 1000 rpm and a top speed—at the governed 6500 rpm—of 97 mph.

Going one better than this, Ian Walker installed in his new Coupé demonstrator a 135 bhp power unit governed to 6900 rpm, and the acceleration of this car was quite staggering! The driver can reach the 70 mph mark inside 10 seconds and if no one is looking go on to 100 mph in 18.4 seconds, reaching terminal velocity in 20 seconds. This is really exciting performance by any standards, the sort which sends oddments in the tunnel-mounted tray flying into the back during a tyre-smoking standing start. This is the instant transportation which today's motoring conditions really require.

The low axle ratio of the IWR Elan is a mixed blessing, and there will be customers who might prefer a 4.1, giving 16 mph/1000 rpm. As tested the Elan was distinctly fussy and to begin with we reached out several times to select top gear, finding of course that there were no more cogs to choose from. On the other hand, it accelerated in top gear like most Elans perform in third and had the feeling that it would climb the side of a house; frequently the governor on the rotor arm had the ignition cutting out on *uphill* gradients, and more often than not it was necessary to lift-off going along level roads. Anyway, this car does away, positively, with the argument that sports cars are a waste of time in England.

Apart from its straight-line performance the Elan has such beautifully balanced handling, steering and braking that even the proverbial Mini feels antique by comparison and one can put up really high averages without trying at all hard. Ian Walker reckons the Elan as a rally car, and so long as he sticks to tarmac-road events like the Tulip his optimism should be well justified.

The engine modifications have in no way spoilt the renowned smoothness of the twin-cam Ford unit, although the torque is not effective below 3000 rpm the gearing overcomes this. The modified Elan isn't happy below 40 mph in top gear, but once 3000 rpm shows up on the rev-counter it is pulling strongly, and then there is a surge of power all the way from 4000 to 7000 rpm when the ignition cuts. The cutout, incidentally, is desirable and for some drivers, necessary, because it would be all too easy to over-rev and break the engine in first and second gears. Four or eight seconds of enthusiasm could result in a bill for hundreds of pounds, but the governor removes all worries like this. Despite the remarkable traction of the Elan, it is possible on this gearing to keep the wheels spinning for a "grand prix" take-off, the close-ratio gearbox with its precise change helping to beat the stopwatch.

The Stage 3 conversion is fairly expensive, costing £146, but the owner does not need to have any work done to the braking or suspension in order to cope with higher performance. Modified camshafts are fitted and a lot of work is done on the cylinder head, especially around the inlet valves, to improve combustion and low-speed flexibility. To cope with a 30 per cent increase in power it is necessary to strip and balance the engine throughout, fitting stronger big-end and main bearing shells and modifying the pressure relief valve to give a higher oil pressure reading.

Comparative performance figures would be misleading, as the Elan is available with almost any gearing to give the owner the sort of performance that suits his everyday needs, but this one is almost the ultimate in fast-accelerating road cars. It is not noisy and the engine is entirely docile in traffic, so it rates highly as an all-purpose machine.

M.L.C.

PERFORMANCE

mph	secs
0 - 30	2.7
0 - 40	3.4
0 - 50	5.0
0 - 60	7.1
0 - 70	9.6
0 - 80	11.7
0 - 90	15.4
0 - 100	18.4

Speeds in gears	mph
1st	42
2nd	64
3rd	86
4th	104

Conversion by Ian Walker Ltd, 236 Woodhouse Road, Finchley, London, N12.

SPORTING MOTORIST MODIFIED TEST

A CRITICAL LOOK AT THE LOTUS ELAN

Sleek lines of the Elan Coupé are emphasised by Colin Chapman.

Colin Chapman's Lotus project has been a significant success story, from humble but enthusiastic beginnings up to World Championship Grand Prix winning and Indianapolis-victorious level. This is attributable to Chapman's genius and drive, allied to the fact that he was a genuine motoring enthusiast before he became a business tycoon—and still is. So far as the sort of Lotus cars you can buy and use on the road are concerned, what is more sporting than a Lotus 7, perhaps home-assembled from the kit, what was more covetable than the Lotus Elite, even if commercially it didn't quite come off, or more effective as a car which is very safely very fast than the current Lotus Elan?

The Elan can be likened to the better sports cars of the vintage years, inasmuch as it is race-bred, highly individualistic, built in a factory where enthusiasm is evident on all levels and, as a car, has quick high-geared steering, pulls high axle-ratios, has a twin-cam engine, a manual gear-change of a kind which should please the most blasé driver, centre-lock wheels, and can be equipped to suit individual tastes. There the comparison most certainly ends, because the backbone-chassis Lotus Elan is one of the lightest, fastest-for-its-size and finest " road-clingers " of all time, in the modern manner, a credit to the Ford components it uses so effectively. Moreover, it is a British-built sports car.

It is for this reason that we feature it fairly prominently in the articles below, in this rather special issue of MOTOR SPORT published during the month of the London Motor Show at Earls Court. The Lotus factory is at Cheshunt but is soon to move to Hethel—and Hertfordshire's loss will be Norfolk's gain!—THE EDITOR.

" *It's the nearest you can get to a racing car for everyday use on the road.*"—Sid Fox, Director, Motor Racing Stables.

" *The Elan is a fantastic road car, with a great racing record and background.*"—Jackie Oliver, Team Lotus driver.

" *It's all right—I like it.*"—John Miles, Willment team driver.

" *Why can't we all have Elans?* "—William Boddy, Editor, MOTOR SPORT.

* * *

THE Lotus Elan, or Lotus 26 as the purist might call it, is sufficiently well known by now to need little introduction. In our opinion it is the most sensitive and rewarding car available to the public, demanding in the sense that it won't tolerate bad driving, satisfying because of the way it responds to a modicum of skill. To reinforce this opinion we talked to three satisfied customers, quoted above, who probably demand far more from their cars than the average customer. Jackie Oliver and John Miles race Elans which are far from standard (we'll describe the modifications later) but, for the record, Motor Racing Stables have just announced that their three standard Elans purchased for tuition have now completed a total of 10,000 laps of the Brands Hatch short circuit with no mechanical failure whatsoever.

So much for what we think of the car. We regard it as an outstanding success and so do the Lotus people themselves, for when it was announced production was planned at 10 a week—at the moment production is running at 40 a week, and when the new factory at Hethel, Norfolk, opens its doors on November 28th the capacity will rise to at least 60, possibly 70, a week. So far the credit squeeze has not hit the company very hard, partly due to the strenuous export drive now resulting in a third of the output reaching America, another third going to Europe.

It is relevant to ask at this point how it has so succeeded. The entire history of car production is studded with lost causes, not all of them complete failures, and in this day of amalgamation and growth it is a little surprising to find a small but efficient organisation which is actually doing all it claims to be achieving. Even now there are perhaps half a dozen small enterprises which must be hanging on grimly by their fingernails in the face of the economic difficulties, all of them in a class which Colin Chapman's outfit was part of only five or six years ago. Clearly he has outpaced them, and will continue to do so judging by his future plans, and this can be traced to about six factors which reflect great credit to the organisation.

When Jim Clark's Lotus-Ford won at Indianapolis last year, John Eason-Gibson, Secretary of the B.R.D.C., wrote that this was just as much a reward for Chapman's pitwork as his design skill. His mind, if we understand it correctly, is constantly planning and scheming, always one jump ahead of the next man's. He is a constant nightmare to race organisers whose regulations have to be Chapman-proof, to suppliers who have to deliver the goods or suffer the sharp edge of his withering invective. Enormous success on circuits of the world must have greatly helped Lotus (Sales) Limited, but this wouldn't be enough if the Elan was no good, or terribly unreliable.

The Elan is renowned principally because it is a brilliant car, the product of a small team which has no use for committee work and the inevitable compromise. It is not strictly true, however, to give all the credit to Chapman himself, for working on his concept, and with his approval, is a development group led by South African-born Ron Hickman. This is the first success-factor. Second, surely, is Chapman's business acumen, which speaks for itself. Third, the competition record and the prestige which goes with it, especially in the export markets. Fourth, a most useful liaison with the Ford Motor Company which has supplied not only a remarkably useful power unit for the Elan, but the background for a good deal of the Team Lotus record. Fifth, and this is a master stroke, the Elan is so designed that it can be readily assembled by the home handiman with limited mechanical knowledge, thus avoiding purchase tax liability and making the Elan available at a most reasonable price. For the record, the great majority of these cars are sold in kit form, the actual number being a secret between Lotus and H.M. Customs and Excise!

Elite to Elan

To understand how the Elan was planned, developed and produced we must go back to the days of the Elite. The first spark of inspiration probably came from Peter Kirwan-Taylor, later a director of Lotus Cars, who wanted a ready-to-go GT car for racing and road use. He, John Frayling, and Ron Hickman, then a Ford designer at Dagenham, got together with Colin Chapman at the

Cramped assembly area for the Elan production line will be eased by the move to Norfolk.

Earls Court Show in 1956, put the idea of a car based on the Eleven, and without any delay the project was got under way. The Elite was a joint effort by Kirwan-Taylor, Chapman, John Frayling, Frank Costin, Hickman, with Peter Cambridge working on the interior. Only a year later, the Elite made its appearance at the Motor Show, and Lotus Cars were in business as a company retailing to the public at large, as opposed to the racing fraternity. The Fourteen, as the Elite was designated, was a pure glass-fibre monocoque powered by a 1,220-c.c. Coventry-Climax engine, absolutely perfect for GT racing though doubtful as a road car, unless you stayed near home! To quote Chapman : " We knew a lot about racing cars by then, but nothing about production. We got to know our customers pretty well; they were always calling on us to have their cars put right, but their attitude was always ' the Elite is fabulous while it's going.' We learned a lot."

The monocoque construction proved its point, though. It was immensely strong, as Graham Warner of the Chequered Flag proved when he rolled one at high speed at Zandvoort. Between 1957 and 1963 about 1,000 Elites were built and a great number of improvements were made, including complete revision of the A-bracket rear suspension on a Series 2 modification. From a production point of view the Elite was both difficult and expensive to produce, involving six major mouldings and a number of smaller ones with a back-to-back laminate process.

Ron Hickman had joined the company as Design and Development Engineer in 1958, acquiring the immense problems of glass-fibre moulding—also the experience, of course. It is not really possible to pin down the actual date when the Elan was first envisaged, but it was really meant to be a 2+2 replacement for the Elite, still using monocoque construction. It was, however, to be made in a single mould known to plastics engineers as monolithic, or to Hickman as a unimould—whatever you call it, it was going to simplify the production and reduce cost significantly.

Going through the history with us, Hickman says that designing open road cars is far more difficult than designing closed cars, "but we did not know that at the time." To which Chapman

Clay model of the Elan circa 1961 experiments with faired headlights.

added : " Designing road cars is ten times more difficult and expensive than designing racing cars—we quickly learned that!"

The Elite's replacement was taking shape on the drawing-board, claiming more and more of the development team's time. Chapman was raring to go with his ideas on suspension, and before the plans were finally decided about the body construction it was decided to try out the running gear. Without delay, Chapman sketched out a backbone chassis and this was made up, purely and simply to test the suspension and drive layout. It was quickly realised that this was just perfect as a road car, and remember that at this point the procedure had been exactly as in the design of a racing car. In other words, unencumbered with production problems, a most advanced form of chassis and suspension had been envisaged.

It was also realised that one-piece monocoque construction was going to be exceedingly difficult, for an open sports car, and it was with a mixture of glee and relief perhaps that it was realised the backbone chassis lent itself very nicely to the installation of a glass-fibre bodyshell. Not only that, but it was going to be cheap to produce, so economies would not have to be sought on the overall specification.

By this time, in 1961, Lotus were aware that Ford were busy on a 1,500-c.c. engine. With remarkable foresight Chapman asked Harry Mundy and Richard Ansdale to get busy designing a twin-cam head, and when this was done Cosworth Engineering constructed the unit. At 1,499 c.c. it gave a level 100 b.h.p.; in exactly this form it was installed in a Lotus 23 for Jim Clark to drive in the Nurburgring 1,000 km. in September 1962. It led on the first lap, to the chagrin of Scuderia Ferrari, the surprise of 100,000 spectators, the amazement of Jim Clark, Colin Chapman, and Keith Duckworth, to name but a few.

At which point the 2+2 project was set aside (but not forgotten) is not altogether clear but by the beginning of 1962 the Elan scheme was hardening. It was to be a two-seat sports car with fairly luxurious fittings, and above all else it was to be a nice, refined, practical model to sell to the public. Hickman says that where the Elite was 60% beautiful, 40% practical, the Elan was to be 60/40 practical and beautiful. Even now he sticks to this, believing that the Elan is not particularly graceful. Hickman intends that the next car will meet both ideals equally. Big motor manufacturers are quite prepared to let the Press visit their styling departments and view artists' impressions of possible future models, saying in guarded tones that they won't see the light of day. Likewise, Hickman's office is adorned with impressions of a 2+2 distinctly reminiscent of the Elite, but the usual disclaimer is made—for this year, anyway.

It is not quite true that the Elan has a one-piece body mould, since the floor and wheel-arch pressing is made on one mould and the upper part on another, the two parts being bonded and finished when curing is taking place. No less than 110 metal inserts are used to attach the body to the backbone, for attaching the doors, the seat mounting points and so on, each one requiring a special bobbin developed by Hickman (he wishes he had patented it). Even this small part of the design is an article in itself, but the bobbins have a shear strength exceeding a ton, which means that if you sit an elephant on an open door the bolt will break before the surrounding bodywork—but not under warranty! On this point, the Elan has the incidental but important advantage that it is much easier to repair than an Elite. We have heard pessimists say that an Elan is not a safe car in which to have an accident (what is ?), but this can be fairly countered by the known safety advantage inherent in glass-fibre, in that it breaks up at a uniform rate and spreads the shock and deformation rate over a relatively safe band.

By the middle of 1962 the Elan was taking shape, and finishing was mainly a matter of detail. For instance, Hickman was quite bothered about the headlights for, as the clay model picture shows, the Elan was fitted with lights which did not conform with the law on height, so retractable mechanism was designed. He wanted to avoid hydraulics or electricity for the operating mechanism, designing a manual lever to do the job from the driving seat. Probably a great many people on the M1 were surprised to see Colin Chapman's Jaguar 3.8 rushing up and down at top speed, with a pair of pop-up headlights mounted on an outrigger at the front. In this way the mechanical force required to raise the lights was calculated, a useful experiment which only days before the Motor Show of 1963 led to vacuum operation. When the car appeared on the stand the lights had never been operated on a test vehicle, but they didn't break down and by the end of the 10-day marathon they had undergone the equivalent of 15 years' use—point made!

A cheap replacement was designed for the Seven, based on

45

the Elan, and this is the car we illustrate. It was to have a very simple two-piece body with the top part bonded to the floor panel, the beading trimmed with brightwork. It was to be spartan, very cheap (up to £75 less than the Seven), and just about everything was to be an extra—even an automatic gearbox, it is interesting to note. An Anglia 105E engine (in standard form) was to be the basic power unit, a rigid axle was to be fitted, and the end product would, quoting Hickman's memorandum, " be inferior to an Austin Healey Sprite (or an M.2 Seven) only as regards comfort—seats, doors, weatherproofing—convenience, appearance, finish, noise level, road-holding and carrying capacity."

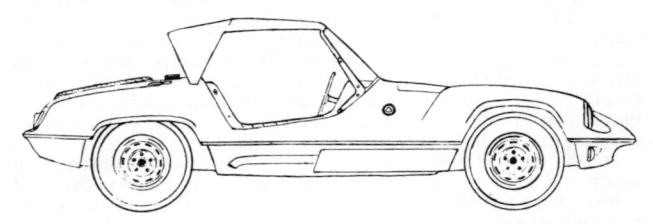

It is to his credit that Hickman did not blush when he allowed us to carry the drawing and memorandum out of his office! This car, of course, was never made, and we feel that when the Seven is replaced it will have none of the disadvantages mentioned.

The letters NVH won't mean much to the public, but have absorbed the minds of the design team. They stand for noise, vibration, harshness, and are the key to the difference between the Lotus Elan and other glass-fibre, do-it-yourself sports cars. An immense amount of work has gone into eliminating these factors and the 400 detail modifications that have been made since September 1962 are largely to do with the niceness of the car as it is today. Chapman says that regarding the production rate, his development costs are out of all proportion; an economist might think him a fool. His problem is balancing the economic feasibility of improvements with the cost, and in relation to what the big manufacturers can do his changes are vastly more expensive. But, as we said before, in limited production it is less of a problem to make a specification change, and no less than 200 further refinements are in mind for the future. The Elan will certainly be with us, much as it is now, for at least another five years. It is significant that, year by year, between 50 and 70% of the development team's time has been taken up with current models, this being an exceptionally high ratio by any standards.

Very few real modifications have been required in production; in fact since the first prototype was designed. The original prototype had inboard disc brakes at the rear, but torque effects produced a severe judder at the back if the brakes were applied between 40-50 m.p.h. Apart from that the car moved up to 10 inches against the hand-brake, due to take-up in the rubber doughnuts, so the discs were taken to the outboard end, with the consequent rise in unsprung weight. Ah well, Chapman can't win all the time! Larger callipers were fitted when the Series II was introduced, and the early doughnuts gave some drivers trouble (oddly enough, not always the fastest drivers).

A year ago the Coupé (type 36) was introduced, and it is entirely due to Ron Hickman's design team, notably Brian Luff, that the bodywork can be made on the same moulds as the new (type 45) open car. This, of course, means that it can be offered at virtually the same price with the triple advantage that it has increased the market, the sales, and the profit margin, also increasing production flexibility.

The problems that are involved in modifying the body shape are great. Since the cars are made with eight sets of tools, each set has to be altered, taking up a week at a time, with consequent slowing down and difficult phasing in production. We are breaking an embargo by a few days to mention that no less than 20 schemes were tried to get a satisfactory air extraction system working on the Coupé.

At one point it was thought that the Elan would lend itself nicely to special coachbuilding efforts, but this was a fallacy for three reasons. First, it was later realised that coachbuilders like to have an underpan to work on, building upwards. Only Frua, and Ian Walker for one Swiss customer, have really tried to tackle the matter of designing a complete, fully stressed bodyshell around the backbone. Second, upon a compact chassis there is no scope for extending the range beyond that of a two-seater. Third, customers really do pay for size rather than styling, and any special job could only be more expensive. Any attempt to produce a

Backbone chassis ready equipped with diff. and suspension shows off the layout.

cheaper version would founder, just as the Mark 7 replacement did, upon the high cost of the chassis equipped with running gear. By introducing the Coupé, appealing to older and more discriminating customers, Lotus really solved this problem for themselves. Even now the sales of the Coupé haven't stabilised sufficiently to quote a definite ratio compared with the Convertible.

Competition Cars

As Chapman said, the Elite was designed as a track car, and they found out afterwards how to make it work as a road machine. Conversely, the Elan was primarily for road use, and just as happened with the E-type Jaguar, customers got their hands on it and rushed straight out to the circuits to meet with varying success. Of course the potential was there, but quite a fair amount of sorting out was needed.

First thing to remember is that the engine was not meant as a competition unit, either. That is what we are told, anyway. Jim Clark's Nurburgring epic was simply a trial, but Ford got very interested and only a few months later the Lotus-Cortina made its debut. That's another story, too. The first 50 power units made were 1,499 c.c., but a very early decision was made to increase the bore by $\frac{1}{16}$ in., taking the capacity to 1,558 c.c. in production. Thus a 1 mm. increase in bore, permitted by the F.I.A. regulations, would take the engine conveniently to the limit of the 1,600-c.c. class; very handy. The power went up to 105 b.h.p. also.

Keith Duckworth was asked to develop a competition version of this unit, the early Cosworth unit appearing with stronger pistons, new camshafts, bigger counterbalance weights on the crankshaft, and a bigger clutch. At the factory Steve Sanville and his engine and transmission staff had been developing the engine and running gear for road use, and quite a number of improvements have taken place.

So you puts the body on the chassis and away you goes. . . .

46

One of the rare special-bodied Elans, prepared by Ian Walker for a Swiss customer.

Engine development becomes complicated at this stage. The Cosworth units as just described gave 140 b.h.p., but all such engines were quickly modified to Phase II which gave the same power *reliably*, with the help of stronger rods, better gudgeon-pins and different pistons. Due to production difficulties B.R.M. were asked in 1965 to prepare some of the competition engines, and now, with dry-sump lubrication, the engines from Bourne are giving 155-160 b.h.p. Equipped with fuel injection they are giving up to 185 b.h.p., as raced in the Team Lotus-Cortinas recently, while a carburetter version with fuel injection cams and inlets has given 168 b.h.p. so far. For the future, the new F.2 Cosworth unit with a 4-valve head, giving in excess of 200 b.h.p., will be very convenient.

Oddly these super engines have been used mainly in the saloons, no-one having progressed beyond 160 brake in an Elan as yet. That must be next on the agenda.

If you say it costs £1,200 to knock four seconds off the short circuit at Brands Hatch, it sounds an awful lot of money. A lot of work is done, though, to take the price up to £2,450, the price of a Competition Elan available from Lotus (Components) Ltd.; this is about the same price as a new Formula Three car.

Explained by John Joyce, the development manager, the chassis is modified at the rear with the pick-ups raised to lower the (strengthened) diff. carrier, thus lowering the suspension. The backbone is strengthened at the front and rear, but not to any great extent. Bottom wishbones at the rear, and the top wishbones at the front, are rose-jointed to facilitate camber adjustments; Armstrong racing struts are fitted, different springs, dampers and anti-roll bar adopted. The rack-and-pinion steering assembly is rigid-mounted. Magnesium hub carriers replace alloy at the rear, while magnesium is also used for wheel construction and the diff. carrier, all to save weight. Incidentally, the 13-in. knock-on wheels pioneer another development, having a special type of cone fitting.

The intermediate driveshaft incorporates a B.R.D. roller spline, and the outboard driveshaft assembly carries smaller discs to alter the braking ratio. An oil cooler replaces the scoop on the diff., partly because of the extra heat generated in racing conditions and partly because a limited slip unit is fitted, naturally running hotter. The gearbox is not modified, apart for ratios, but alloy replaces steel for the bell-housing and tailpiece.

Twin master cylinders with an adjustable balance bar are fitted in the braking system. An aluminium radiator, an oil cooler, Perspex headlight fairings, and a safety rollover bar make up the equipment side. By the time all this has been done, a special lightweight body having wider wheel arches is needed to keep the weight approximately the same as on the road cars, at just under 13 cwt. Special seats, seat belts to choice, extra instruments, and a leather-rimmed steering wheel are all included in the specification. Joyce thinks it is the only competition car equipped with a cigar-lighter, but he's not sure.

Under development at the moment is a rally version, which has been entered a couple of times under Ian Walker colours, but confidence that it would last a rough and tough event like the R.A.C. Rally sounds tentative.

Following their normal policy of racing one car of each type made, Team Lotus had a great deal of success last year with a competition Elan in the hands of Ray Parsons.

Assembly and Sales

At the time of our visit the bodies, constructed in Norfolk, were being brought to Cheshunt for final assembly, but by December the whole operation will take place under one roof in a new factory. The offices will also be located at Hethel, so that as far as motoring is concerned Cheshunt will disappear from the map. In keeping with the organisation's outlook, the office suite will be completely open plan with plants, trees and fountains to break up the office atmosphere.

The power units are delivered by the J.A.P.-Villiers Company, Wolverhampton, who take the basic parts from Ford at Dagenham and do the assembly with special parts, starting with a special crankshaft and working upwards. Blue cylinder heads are fitted on the standard 105-b.h.p. engines, and green heads on the 115-b.h.p. Special Equipment engines also developed by Steve Sanville's staff, having special cams, chokes, jets and exhaust system. These represent 25% of the output. All the engines are bench run for an hour before installation, helping to build up a marvellous reputation for reliability.

Assembly is a pretty straightforward job, especially since most cars are sold in kit form. In an unguarded moment, Graham Arnold, the Sales Director, admitted that glue techniques have improved considerably since the early days when customers came back from Spain complaining that their Elans had reverted to kit form. Customers who do build the cars themselves are invited to take the completed job back to the factory to have their handiwork checked over.

It is surprising, but not altogether out of character, to realise that every Elan made now has electric windows. This actually avoids the problem of having a bulky winder mechanism in the doors and is a cheap comfort factor regarded as a sound investment.

Over 500 people are employed at Cheshunt, and many of them will be moving up to Norfolk. Lotus directors are very confident that locally recruited labour will be of high quality in any case.

To sell the cars, Lotus have 39 main dealers in Britain, four in America with 200 agents, and with European outlets there are about 350 dealers altogether. Graham Arnold spends much of his time chasing about the overseas markets fighting a personal crusade against Porsche, even going to the trouble of entering local events when there is time in order to take on the Stuttgart company on a neutral battleground.

An interesting aside to the Elan story is the development of a Cortina with independent rear suspension. Two have been made—Jim Clark runs one of them, Colin Chapman the other, but so far Ford have declined to take any special interest. Notable customers for the Elan have included Prince William of Gloucester, Lady Sarah Curzon, Viscount Gormeston, Stirling Moss, The Yardbirds, and the Jordanian Ambassador.

Through the Elite, the public were first able to get first-hand experience of Lotus design. It may have been a salutary experience for some of the customers, but roughly in line with the company's racing record of the time. As the racing record improved, so did the product, and the two facts may be allied, for Chapman learned the hard way that to win a race the car must cross the finishing line. By now, we need no convincing that the lesson has been thoroughly assimilated in all departments.—M. L. C.

ROAD IMPRESSIONS OF THE LOTUS ELAN

MOTOR SPORT has not been neglectful of the Elan—we have written of its road behaviour previously and the Continental Correspondent, after driving one to Monza and back, commented very favourably on this highly-desirable Lotus. The remarks which follow are based on recent experience of the latest version on the constipated roads of England and less congested by-roads of Wales.

After lunch with Colin Chapman and his executives at Cheshunt, when all manner of motor racing topics were aired, I was handed over a dazzlingly yellow-hued coupé, its colour enabling this small low vehicle to be easily seen by other, perhaps more pedestrian, road users and, I hope, being in some way radar-repellant. It was the newest of the range, a fixed-head coupé with electrically-operated windows, in Special Equipment guise, developing 115 b.h.p. by reason of high-lift camshafts, special Weber carburetters, and a 4-branch exhaust manifold, and pulling a 3.5 to 1 axle ratio in conjunction with semi close-ratio gears.

47

Apart from being told not to use the choke and warned that, though light, the clutch is fierce, there were no special driving instructions issued to me as Graham Arnold, Lotus' Sales Director, sent me on my way. The Elan was, however, turned out for test in a manner of which the great Daimler-Benz Press organisation would not have been ashamed. In the boot were a gasket-set, a spares-kit containing hoses, plugs, brake pads, rotor arm, decoke set, etc. and a workshop manual, apart from which I had also been issued with an instruction book, sales literature, servicing vouchers, a Lotus tie-pin and day and night telephone numbers in case of emergencies. All of this was most reassuring, although I only intended to go a few hundred miles, and it effectively emphasises the progress made in Messrs. Lotus' affairs within a comparatively short space of time.

It was, too, intriguing to drive one of the fastest A-to-B coupés out of a factory where racing cars from 250 c.c. to Indianapolis-size are prepared and saloon racing Lotus-Cortina Fords made ready for battle.

One's first surprise about the Elan is its quite astonishing docility. Although I had the S/E coupé capable of some 120 m.p.h. or more, the twin-cam 1,558-c.c. Ford power unit is quite happy idling along in top gear at around 1,500 r.p.m., which is comfortably below the town speed-limit of 30 m.p.h. This was just as well, because it wasn't until some 45 miles after leaving Cheshunt, and then only for very brief occasions, that I was able to exceed about 50 m.p.h., so choc-a-bloc with mimsers were our infernally narrow roads. So the Elan's docility didn't come amiss, and I was also pleased to discover how quietly it runs with the windows shut. Engine and exhaust noise certainly belie the vivid performance that is released when it is possible to depress the right foot.

The new electric windows are extremely worthwhile. Lotus will tell you that they are a good sales gimmick and almost as cheap to install as manually-wound window glasses. Maybe. But this little coupé gets infernally hot within and as the driver is apt to be pretty fully occupied if he is enjoying himself as he should be, to be able to get some fresh air on tap merely by pressing a conveniently-placed flick-switch is indeed a blessing. Admittedly this sudden exposure to blasts of outside atmosphere on the face and neck of a perspiring driver may well give rise to new ailments, in the category of " Lotus elbow " known to owners of open Lotus 7s, but this problem will have been resolved by new ventilating arrangements in time for the Motor Show. Under-scuttle air inlet doors are already provided but tend to promote chilly feet.

In addition to the convenience of windows which go up or down, slowly but surely, under electric control, with separate switches for driver and passenger, the adjustable racing type bucket seats are effectively supporting and comfortable. Forward visibility is good due to thin screen pillars, even if the small steering wheel is a trifle high-set for the low seating position (but it is adjustable to individual requirements), nor do I think I walk with a permanent kink through driving the Elan with my legs biased to the right in the foot-well containing the close-set but conveniently located pendant pedals; a wide transmission tunnel necessitates this off-set to the off-side, and divorces passenger from driver. It does, however, enable a lipped tray to be formed on top of the tunnel, from which the very stubby gear lever protrudes, and if the rearward extension restricts movement of the left elbow to a greater extent than the padded door limits movement of the right elbow, I found no cause for serious complaint.

The interior of the fixed-head Elan is quite luxurious. The facia and its extension downwards to join the aforesaid transmission tunnel is in dark polished wood and it abounds in un-labelled flick-switches and knobs, all sensibly situated for quick manipulation. The Smiths dials are confined to a small 140 m.p.h. speedometer with trip and total odometers, a matching electronic tachometer reading to 8,000 r.p.m., with the red sector commencing at 6,500 r.p.m., a fuel gauge, and a combined oil-pressure and cylinder head temperature gauge, this last-named normally registering 40-45 lb./sq. in. and 85°C. or 96°C. in heavy traffic.

The pull-out handbrake is invisible under the scuttle on the right, but is perfectly easy to feel for and operate. There are three interior lamps (one for map-reading) with courtesy action, and the headlamps, normally recessed, pop up and flash a warning if a knob convenient to the left-hand is pulled out—although this occupies perhaps a whole second longer than conventional flashing of normal lamps it is a small penalty to pay for aerodynamic efficiency, clean glasses, and the *panache* of being able to retract one's lights, especially as the Elan has Italian Stibel high-note horns of great penetrating power !

Two toggles on the facia release the bonnet panel (which can be infernally difficult to open with the fingers and the panel of which has to be lifted off as it doesn't stay up, also a tricky operation for one person), stalk-levers look after lamps dipping and the twin indicators, which have Carello repeater units on the front wings, there is a facia pull-out ash-tray, and provision for a radio (£40 extra, Radiomobile on the test car), the screen-wipers' control is combined with the washer's control, and there is a wooden-lidded, unlockable lined cubby-hole in front of the passenger. A warning light remains on until the handbrake is released.

This Lotus Elan is a genuine two-seater coupé, by which I mean that although there is very useful upholstered stowage space behind the seats, by no manner of means could a passenger be carried therein. There is a coat hook on each side, suitable for hanging a mini-skirt on. And there is a useful shelf ahead of the big back window. The upholstered boot, with lockable, self-supporting lid, enables far more luggage to be accommodated therein than the external size of the car suggests—plenty in addition to a full-size suitcase, the spare wheel being under the floor and the Exide battery tucked in the n/s rear corner. To

The Lotus Elan, as tested, in Special Equipment coupé form, with electrically-controlled windows, which sells for £1,711 5s. 2d. inclusive of purchase tax.

The Elan's boot is far more roomy than it looks and the lid is lockable and self-supporting.

THE LOTUS ELAN FIXED-HEAD SPECIAL EQUIPMENT COUPE

Engine: Four cylinders, 82.5 × 72.7 mm. (1,558 c.c.). Inclined overhead valves operated by twin chain-driven overhead camshafts. 9.95 to 1 c.r. 115 (gross) b.h.p. at 6,000 r.p.m.
Gear ratios: 1st, 8.9 to 1; 2nd, 5.8 to 1; 3rd, 4.37 to 1; top, 3.55 to 1.
Tyres: 5.20 × 13 Dunlop SP41 on centre-lock steel disc wheels.
Weight: 13 cwt. 3 qr. 21 lb. (without passengers, but ready for the road, with approx. one gallon of petrol).
Steering ratio: 2½-turns, lock-to-lock.
Fuel capacity: 10 gallons (Range approx. 288 miles).
Wheelbase: 7 ft.
Track: Front, 3 ft. 11 3/32 in.; rear, 4 ft. 0 7/16 in.
Dimensions: 12 ft. 1 in. × 4 ft. 8 in. × 3 ft. 9¼ in. (high).
Price: £1,420 (£1,711 5s. 2d. inclusive of p.t.). (£1,391 in kit form).
Makers: Lotus Ltd., Delamare Road, Cheshunt, Hertfordshire, England.

---

say that driving the Elan is immense fun is almost an understatement. The 15 in. steering wheel with its three drilled metal spokes is very small and its rubber rim is cased in a lace-up leather gaiter. The tiny central gear lever with its polished wooden knob bearing a tiny Lotus badge is right where it should be and clicks from slot to slot in a precise but very notchy "mechanical" manner, unimpeded by spring-loading, except for that which safeguards reverse. There is considerable gear lever "fizz."

Normally it is unnecessary to use more than about 5,500 r.p.m. to not only keep the Elan at the head of the queue but to leave the opposition out of sight. The car I drove didn't have the ignition cut-out and 7,000 r.p.m. was perfectly permissible. Using considerably less than this, maxima of 40, 60, 85 m.p.h. and 120 m.p.h. are available in the respective gears of the Lotus-Ford gearbox. "The ton" comes up along the average short straight—on private test tracks, of course! There was no time to take performance figures, although the go-ahead Lotus organisation did suggest flying the car over to Jabbeke for a day's timing! I have, therefore, to be content with their claim of 0-60 m.p.h. in 6.8 sec. Acceleration continues to be impressive beyond 80 m.p.h., so the Elan is a match for all but the big-engined GT cars in this respect.

All this performance is achieved without any feeling that the 1.6-litre Ford engine is working at all hard. The exhaust note is unobtrusive, the noise within the car entirely tolerable. As for road-holding, the Elan goes round corners, in the wet as in the dry, faster than any normally-skilled fast road driver will have an opportunity to exploit and does this in a pleasantly neutral manner, with neither oversteer nor understeer bias. Very rarely indeed is it possible to make the Dunlop SP41 tyres protest, and if the car does get out of line, mere wrist movement of the light steering, which is geared 2½-turns lock-to-lock with not an atom of lost motion on the Alford and Alder rack-and-pinion mechanism, serves to flick it back where it belongs. The whole question of road-holding can best be summed up by saying this is undoubtedly one of the very safest very fast road cars it is possible to experience.

The suspension is firm but definitely not soggy. So the ride is good, while the wheels remain glued to the ground; roll is a word associated with jam and undergarments but not with Elans....

The backbone chassis is so rigid that the coil spring and wishbone i.f.s. and Chapman coil strut i.r.s. have to do all the shock absorption. This does give rise to some thump and transmission of movement, while the steering kicks back at times but the glass-fibre body naturally remains free from mechanical rattles. The ride becomes choppy over undulating surfaces.

Ground clearance (normally 6 in.) is not the Elan's best point; it is one of the very few cars which bottomed on the road that I am pleased to call my drive, although not after passenger and luggage had been removed, and did so over main-road bumps of the more severe kind even when lightly loaded. However, I am assured this has now been cured, by fitting stiffer rear shock absorbers. Another weakness was lack of guttering on the doors, so that they deposited rain on the seats when opened after a spell of wet-weather parking.

To light steering and a light clutch must be added light pedal pressure when applying the Girling 9½ in./10 in. disc brakes, which are splendidly progressive in action, very powerful, and free from the squeal sometimes experienced with disc anchors. The hand-brake holds quite effectively in spite of being applied to the rear discs.

The test car had Teleflex reel-type safety belts, there is generous crash-padding and the glass-fibre body is a further safety factor in the event of impact.

The engine picks up speed very smoothly (5-bearing crankshaft) and cleanly (twin 32 mm. Weber 40 DCOE18 carburetters) a rather violent flat-spot only being experienced very low down in the rev. range. There is, admittedly, transmission snatch accompanied by subdued squeaking due to the use of Rotoflex rubber couplings in the rear-wheel drive-shafts but I did not find this sufficiently noticeable to merit criticism.

Reverting to the interior appointments of the Elan, the black upholstery contrasts nicely with the plated door cappings, which incorporate built-in "pulls," and the pile carpeting. There is even a vanity mirror in the n/s vizor, for the benefit of girls who go out in Elans. The doors shut properly, lock easily, and have effective "keeps." They open sufficiently far for any normally agile person to enter and leave easily—anyone who cannot cope is probably too old to want an Elan anyway, although I believe the customers are aged from 18 to over 80....

The name LOTUS is set across the boot lid, the familiar Lotus badge is on the nose, the "Coupé S/E" wording on the body sides, and the badges proclaiming Lotus to have been the World Champion Car Constructors in 1963 and 1965 and Indianapolis winner in 1965 are proudly displayed on the body. The screen is of Triplex non-craze laminated glass. The coupé top cuts off the view at oblique road junctions and the close proximity of the pedals makes it necessary to rest the left foot under the clutch pedal. The dipstick and oil-filler are extremely accessible, and cold starting was instantaneous.

The engine, having a c.r. of 9.95 to 1, naturally deserves the best petrol, which it consumed at the rate of 28.8 m.p.g. in mixed traffic and open-road driving. Just over a pint of oil was needed at the end of 800 miles of highly enjoyable motoring. The tank, filled through a good quick-action filler, holds 10 gallons.

To sum up, only by driving a Lotus Elan fast and far can you appreciate the subtle fascination exerted by this very fast, compact, extremely safe-handling sports car. It is a car which keeps young men young and makes old men younger and is one of the few cars which can average 69 without exceeding 70....—W. B.

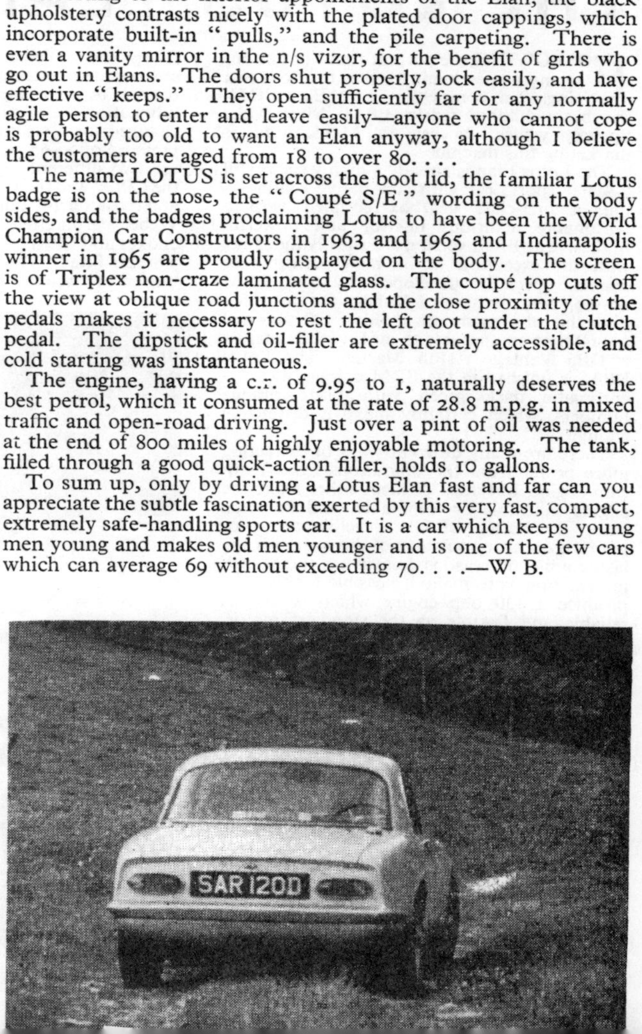

Road Test by
PATRICK McNALLY

THE LOTUS ELAN BRM

FOLLOWING the current trend of famous racing names joining forces to produce a single car comes the Lotus Elan BRM, the brain-child of works BRM driver Mike Spence, whose concern in Maidenhead is marketing this machine.

The Lotus Elan is already a highly successful 2-seater sports car with superlative roadholding, a first-class gearbox coupled with a reasonably luxurious interior and powerful brakes. The BRM version is basically the same, with the exception of its high performance engine, specially developed by the BRM development division of Rubery Owen, which gives the car a maximum speed of 130 mph and a 0-60 time comparable to an E-type Jaguar or a DB6 Vantage Aston Martin. The Lotus BRM is finished in the BRM colours of polychromatic dark green with blaze orange bumpers, which certainly make it distinctive enough.

There are many different ways of extracting more power from the ubiquitous Ford twin-cam engine, but most of them either make the engine inflexible or unreliable, and in some cases do both. BRM's development programme on racing versions of this unit over the last couple of seasons has given them such information as to make it possible for them to produce a 130 bhp engine which is just as reliable and flexible as the standard motor. Every engine is completely dismantled at the BRM works in Bourne, and the following modifications are made: the cylinder head has 0.010 ins removed from its face and the inlet and exhaust ports are extensively modified to increase the air-flow. The inlet valves are replaced by BRM units with 1.55 ins diameter heads, the standard exhaust valves being retained. The cylinder block has 0.020 ins machined from its top face to give 0.014 ins squish deck height to the piston—trueing the cylinder block also ensures a perfect seal between the block and head. The crankshaft is dynamically balanced and the flywheel and clutch assembly are assured of constant union by being double dowelled. As the latest versions of the Ford twin-cam engine are fitted with C-type rods which are good for 7000 rpm, these are retained but are balanced along with the pistons to very fine limits. To ensure good lubrication the oil pressure relief valve spring is changed for a stronger one which gives an oil pressure of 55-65 psi at running speeds. There are two different types of camshaft available, the CPL 2 and the L1; the former gives 130 bhp, and the latter 140 bhp. The standard 40 DCOE Weber carburetters are retained, but 33 mm chokes and 130 main jets and 170 air correction jets are fitted. The exhaust system, which is one of the weakest points of a standard Elan, as it restricts the engine breathing considerably, is changed for a fabricated four-branch manifold with a large diameter pipe and a "special equipment" silencer—a straight-through muffler can be specified at no extra cost. Before every engine leaves the factory after being meticulously assembled, it is bench-tested to ensure it produces the correct number of horses. If the engine's power curve falls short by more than 2.5 bhp it is not released.

When I was asked to road-test the car prior to its announcement I was far from convinced that the character of the Elan would be changed in any major way. But the effect of 130 bhp changes the whole nature of the car. The fully independent suspension of the Lotus Elan can cope ably with the standard engine, but when the extra horsepower is added, so is a great deal of excitement. The roadholding is still first-class, but much more fun can be experienced as the car can be driven far more on the throttle, and requires more skill and handling.

Starting the car from cold is no problem, but when the engine is hot, as with all Weber carburetted cars, it is better for the throttle to be depressed fully to provide a leaner mixture. Pumping the throttle will result in wet plugs. When the engine bursts into life it settles back to idle at 750 rpm without the least sign of lumpiness. The particular car I drove had no cut-out fitted to the distributor, and I was told I could use 7000 rpm in the gears and what I could get in top. The engine was as clean as a whistle all the way through the rev range, with not a flat spot anywhere—a remarkable achievement.

In far from ideal conditions and with limited time the performance figures were taken, and to add to our troubles the engine was still relatively tight, having covered only 200 miles. Nevertheless the performance figures were little short of incredible: 0-60 mph was reached in 6.8 secs, with 80 mph coming up in 11.4 secs. The 0-100 figure started off at 18.2 secs, but towards the end of the test some better times were recorded. However in the interests of consistency all the acceleration figures quoted, with the exception of the quarter-mile, were taken during the initial part of the test and not towards the end, when the engine became noticeably more free. The real telltale is of course the quarter-mile which was covered in the mean time of 15.1 secs. Maximum speed recorded was 128.63 mph at 7000 rpm, but this was not a true indication of the absolute maximum of the car as a strong cross wind was having an adverse effect, and I have no hesitation at all in describing this as a true 130 mph car. In fact, in coupé form with a different axle ratio one could expect a speed well in excess of this. The speeds in the gears were 42 mph, 63 mph and 95 mph, for the car was fitted with the standard four-speed close-ratio Ford gearbox with ratios of 2.97, 2.01 and 1.40 to 1, with a final drive ratio of 3.55 to 1. An ultra-close-ratio gearbox is available.

Apart from the obvious performance advantages of the extra horsepower, the BRM-tuned power unit also encouraged the most enthusiastic cornering techniques, as there is sufficient power available to sort out any difficulties encountered. The test car had the optional straight-through silencer, but even so was not aggressively noisy, and there was certainly no increase of mechanical noise in the engine itself.

As the rest of the car, with the exception of the exterior finish, is standard we will not dwell too much on this subject. All Elans have first-class gearboxes, suspension systems and steering, and the increased horsepower was no problem for the servo four-wheel disc-brakes which stood up remarkably well to the test, though they did suffer a slight tendency to pull to the right towards the end of the test. Oil consumption would appear to be approximately a quart for 600 miles, but this figure may be slightly pessimistic as the engine was not fully run-in, and with piston rings well bedded-in it could be expected to drop to half this. Fuel consumption is about 25 mpg, but this depends very much on how the car is driven.

The BRM polychromatic green, much to my surprise, looks very attractive, especially when emphasized against the blaze orange bumpers. The whole effect is remarkably sophisticated for what might appear to the layman to be a rather jazzy scheme. The tasteful BRM insignia below the Lotus badge on the front of the car is the final touch, though it does rather give the game away. This fact was rather surprisingly drawn to my attention by a small boy in a Buckinghamshire village who turned to his mother and said with great aplomb "That, Mum, is a Lotus BRM."

The car is available both in coupé and hardtop form, either special equipment (£1,650) or standard (£1,525). Though the car tested was the 130 bhp version, the 140 bhp with the L1 camshafts is exactly the same price. Further details may be obtained from Mike Spence Ltd, Eland House, 11 High Street, Maidenhead, Berks, who are the sole distributors.

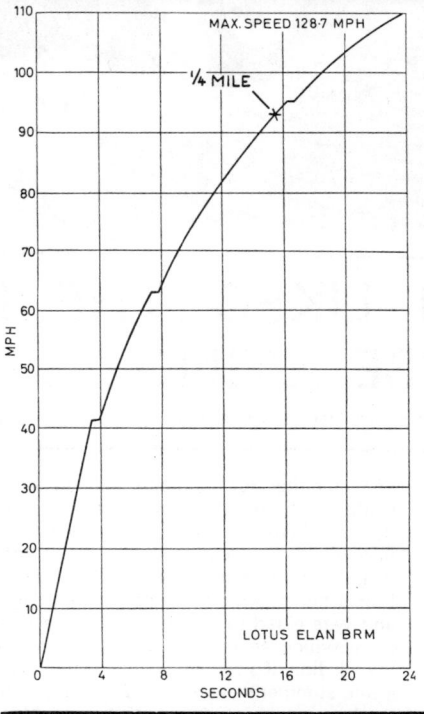

SPECIFICATION AND PERFORMANCE DATA

Car Tested: Lotus Elan BRM Special Equipment, price £1,650 in component form.

Engine: Four cylinders, 82.55 mm x 72.75 mm (1558 cc). Twin chain-driven overhead camshafts. Compression ratio 9·5 to 1. 130 bhp at 6500 rpm. Two twin choke Weber carburetters. Lucas coil and distributor.

Transmission: Single dry plate clutch. Four-speed all-synchromesh gearbox ratios 1, 1.40, 2.01, 2.97 to 1. Chassis-mounted Hypoid final drive unit, ratio 3.55 to 1.

Chassis: Steel central backbone chassis. Independent front suspension by wishbones and helical springs. Rack and pinion steering. Independent rear suspension by bottom wishbones and struts with helical springs. Telescopic dampers all round. Disc brakes front and rear with servo assistance. Centre-locking disc wheels with three-eared caps, fitted 145 x 13 SP41 tyres.

Equipment: 12-volt lighting and starting. Speedometer. Rev counter. Ammeter. Oil pressure, water temperature, and fuel gauges. Heating and demisting. Variable speed windscreen wipers and washers. Electrically controlled windows. Flashing direction indicators. Radio (extra).

Dimensions: Wheelbase 7 ft. Track 4 ft. Overall length 12 ft 1½ ins. Width 4 ft 8 ins. Turning circle 29 ft 9 ins. Weight 13 cwt (dry).

Performance: Maximum speed 128.63 mph at 7000 rpm. Speeds in gears: 3rd, 95 mph; 2nd, 63 mph; 1st, 42 mph. Standing quarter-mile, 15.1 secs, terminal velocity, 93 mph. 0-30 mph, 2.65 secs. 0-50 mph, 5.2 secs. 0-60 mph, 6.8 secs. 0-80 mph, 11.4 secs. 0-100 mph, 18.1 secs.

Fuel Consumption: 25 mpg.

IF I SAID I LIKED THE LOTUS ELAN WOULD I BE LYING?... NO!

The Editor unscrambles his childhood in sports cars and eventually gets round to telling us how much he likes the Lotus Elan

I often wish the word "sportscar" had never been invented. It causes more trouble than all the other collective words in the automobilistic lexicon. They've been asking what sports cars are for years and everyone has a different answer. I'm not going to try and define one because I tend to be too literal in my translations. A sports car to me is a car for sport, whether on the track or in the alley, with more emphasis on the former than the latter. Many of my friends would disagree, however, and put the cart before the horse; if you understand. When used for amatory pursuits the cars known in the past as Sportscars have often resulted in odd situations and even injury to the person because sports cars were made for one man, the driver, and not as stamping grounds for all-in wrestling. Back in my day—groan—the sports car was the lure, the family saloon the spider's web. So let's dispense with the sports car as an end and consider it as a pleasurable driving machine.

My first introduction to sports car motoring—by that I mean really open car motoring—was an illicit drive at the tender age of 17 on the public highway in a car uninsured and with no driving licence. I may add that the owner, my friend and buddy, had no insurance and no driving licence either but had been allowed by his slightly dotty mother to buy the thing from the proceeds of lucre accrued by the passing of his dear father. The "thing" was a front wheel drive B.S.A. Scout four-wheeler which steered, but only just, and was aided in the pursuit by the front drive which seemed to do more steering than I did. If I remember correctly it was a fine summer's evening in Edinburgh, the roads were quiet, for in the early fifties cars were still hard to find, and after about three hours of pushing we managed to get the beast to come alive. Elated we drove off and being offered the wheel after a few miles I agreed, jumped into the seat, with not one idea how to drive the thing, and proceeded to defy all mechanical means at my disposal and actually get it moving. I didn't know what the pedals were for and totally dispensed with the clutch for I felt if man was meant to use three pedals he would have been born with three feet; all I needed was a go-er and a stopper. Once on the road I thought I was doing well until my friend's white face told me that the bump back there had been me riding up on a shallow pavement on a twisty road up to Currie near Edinburgh. He decided by the simple expedient of switching off the ignition, that I'd had my first and last driving experience and within a few months we were both yanked off to the Royal Air Force for two years hard labour—abroad in my case, in Belfast, fighting the Irish. My next meeting with sports cars came at Compton Bassett camp in Wiltshire in the shadow of one of these White Horses they keep talking about in guide books. The car was a brand new M.G. TD and the driver a young recruit called Tommy Bridger. He spent all his time on the Chippenham road burning up the asphalt telling everyone he was going to be a racing driver. Imagine my surprise when he actually became a racing driver in the old formula III and did very well at it too; his father was something to do with H.P. sauce if I remember correctly.

Once in Ireland came stage three in my, up to then, unexciting life with sports cars. It started with a pal I met who made gravestones for a living and between taps of his little hammer he dreamt about being Ireland's answer to Geoff Duke. The day he bought his Porcupine A.J.S. I went with him round the old Ards racing circuit and found the experience frightening to a point where I've never really trusted motor cycles or bike racers ever since. This was further underlined when, on a fine Saturday evening riding down Lagganbank Road at about 60 m.p.h. (it was a 30 m.p.h. limit by the way) we chanced upon a pile of refuse left by a horse and spent the next few minutes in a welter of arms, legs and hot metal. The evening was ruined, my suit was ruined; and the smell! Later Paddy bought himself a Morgan three wheeler and this saw the end of our friendship. It was thoroughly lethal on the cobbles and shown a wet road would spin without asking. I often wonder what Paddy is doing now, if he is still chiselling out grave stones or maybe lying under one!

It strikes me this is a long round about way of getting into a story about the Lotus Elan but until I can think of another way it will have to do! For you see the Elan always brings back memories of these days to me. To me it is a classic sports car in modern guise, the perfect answer to an enthusiast's prayer. It is true I don't like Fibreglass bodied cars but then I also don't like butter and can maintain about as strong an argument about disliking either as I can on the subject of why flies take-off backwards from a wall. Maybe the first ride I had in an Elite many years ago put me off. It was a pre-production model, it is true, but these old memories stick with one. It is sufficient to say however I was less conscious of the Fibreglass when I drove two of the latest Elans recently than I have been in the past. Maybe I'm mellowing. To me, and I say this honestly, I find the Elan "right". It is civilised to appeal to the civilisation trend that is going on in the sportscar world but at the same time it has something of the animal about it.

It has a chassis which is different from most cars and is shaped like a tuning fork at one end and a bottle opener at the rear. Between the prongs of the tuning fork lies the neat twin-cam engine and within the rear triangle the differential unit and drive shafts. It is a good chassis with no whip and the body unit almost appears to be moulded on to it making a neat fit. To keep the shape low the driver and passenger sit on either side of the main central "I" frame and behind them there are the two supports for the rear coil springs. Suspension at the front is by wishbones and coil springs with an anti-roll bar.

Power comes from a 1558 c.c. engine derived from the five bearing crankshaft Ford engine which has proved to be so reliable. Despite the or maybe even because of, the good design work by Keith Duckworth this engine produces some 105 b.h.p. on a 9.5:1 compression. The head is worked in light alloy, the crank case remains, however, in cast iron. Twin Weber carburettors supply the fuel and with a fairly light all up weight the Elan is very good on petrol.

The original Elans had a funny dashboard layout really but this along with a number of other things has been cleaned up considerably. Part reason for this is that Jim Clark at one time had a car done up by Radford and the ideas incorporated proved to be very successful and were grafted on to the production Elan. From the instrumentation standpoint then the Elan is a much improved car. To give a run down there are now electric window winders controlled individually from the dash. On one of the Elans with a good few miles on the clock these worked perfectly but on the car that Steele Sport had just put on the road one of the windows was sticky but as the car had not had its proper first check out at 500 miles and was only being hustled in for photographs, this could hardly be put down as representative. The wood trim on the dash is much more subdued now but there are still a number of switches and levers screwed into it such as the two pulls for opening the bonnet. This I'm not too sure about for I always get a bit leery when I open the bonnet of an Elan and never know whether I should take it off altogether or prop it up to check things in the engine compartment. I'd like to see it better supported. Back on the dash you have a heater switch, a two speed blower and buckets of hot air for running with the hood down on chilly mornings. No complaint in that department and warmthwise it is a most civilised car. The steering wheel is woodrimmed in the tradition of the marque and you can see more of the detail work put into the car in the doors where the arm rests are comfortable. Obviously someone with a lot of taste, like Jim Clark, has been responsible for tidying up the car. You have a hand brake warning light to tell you that you haven't quite put the hand brake off which is not surprising when you have to really reach for it under the dash. But there doesn't seem to be anywhere else for it but there. The gear lever is short, stubby and "falls easily to hand" (they sang in unison!).

Faced with your first Elan you admire the little plaque which announces "Lotus, World Champion Constructors 1963/1965" which is a good talking point for a start and helps the image. Its door handles are better than they were and you slip into the hip hugging seats. These are designed by someone who knows something about sports cars and the Elan in particular. They have a good recline angle and once you have gingerly tip-toed away from the owner's view and begin to relax maybe you'll let yourself fall into the shape that Colin Chapman has provided.

You've turned the key starter and the engine has muttered into life. It surprises you that it doesn't growl like an Alfa, bark like a Ferrari or twitter like a 2C.V. Citroen. It just seems to sit there and hum. A dab of the clutch, a slow and steady release of the pedal, it grips and you're off. No drama, no squeak as you leave two black marks where the clutch bites; it's all very smooth. You are burbling along in top gear around 20 m.p.h. now. Wait a minute, 20 m.p.h. in top! After you get over the surprise of the smoothness of the thing you leave the limit, change down to second and then open up the main jets in those Webers. There is a microscopic pause in your progress then the engine bursts into life and you are off. Acceleration when pressed in anger is tremendous. Thanks to a fairly smooth climbing torque curve it clambers up through 2,000 r.p.m. to 3, then 4 then 5 when you nick into the next gear with the satisfaction of a quick change and off you go on that roller coaster ride up the torque curve. This must surely be one of the most exciting cars to drive in the world. Again there isn't the noise and fury of a Ferrari flaying its twelve cylinders about, or the smooth woofle of a Vee 8 Mustang running out of steam at about 105 m.p.h. but just a lot of action which vibrates right through the car. Handling is superb and it is a car designed for braced tread tyres—in this case Dunlop SP 41's. It fits in with the fairly soft springing and suspension of the Elan to give a kind of fluid cornering. The car grips the road but it is flexible. You feel its lightness and the direct steering makes twisty roads a delight. An Elan on the Loch Long road from Whistlefield to Arrochar is ecstasy. It is hard to imagine anyone getting into trouble with an Elan but obviously a car of this performance and handling has to be given a degree of respect.

A couple of years ago with a wet and slippery airfield to play with and at the wheel of an Elan I determined to find the breakaway point. When it did go you could get it back fairly easily and then when going hard through the gearbox I had to make a sudden swerve at about 70 m.p.h. and before I could blink I was round once and the car expended all its energy in the space of about 50 yards and one violent spin. In moments like these you say thank goodness for good suspension design, a low centre of gravity and steering which offered a great deal of control even in these few seconds. Related to a road width the whole operation could have been done on one side of a dual carriageway without touching the kerbs but I'd rather not do it thank you. So the car needs a degree of respect but I am convinced that even in the ultimate it is a forgiving motor car.

Both the Coupe version and the roadster have air vents on either end of the dashboard. This is a good idea in the Coupe where on a hot day you could do with some cool air on your face but of less use in the roadster where you would probably have the hood down anyway. This isn't a criticism more an observation.

In conclusion then we have in the Elan a real man's car which gives the kind of thrill to drive that was the province of the Bugatti and the Frazer-Nash only the Elan is much more civilised in its comfort. As with the rites of the African tribes where a youth is sent out to kill a lion with his bare hands—or something like that—before he becomes a man so every youth should be required to drive an Elan and learn what a real sportscar feels like before doomed to family car motoring for most of his life.

I still don't have an alternative to that word sportscar; I'll work on it. (G.G.)

Autocar road test number 2134
Make: Lotus Elan Coupé S/E 1,558 c.c.

TEST CONDITIONS
Weather: Fine. Wind: 5-10 m.p.h.
Temperature: 16·5 deg. C. (62 deg. F.)
Barometer: 29·63in. Hg.
Humidity: 35 per cent
Surfaces: Dry concrete and asphalt

Figures taken at 3,500 miles by our own staff at the Motor Industry Research Association proving ground at Nuneaton.

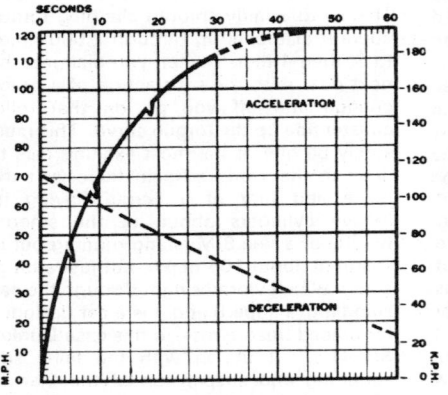

WEIGHT
Kerb weight: 14·1 cwt (1,574lb-715kg) (with oil, water and half-full fuel tank)
Distribution, per cent: F, 47·6; R, 52·4
Laden as tested: 17·8cwt (1,996lb-906kg)

MAXIMUM SPEEDS

Gear	m.p.h.	k.p.h.	r.p.m.
Top (mean)	122	196	6,950
(best)	123	198	7,000
3rd	94	151	7,500
2nd	66	106	7,500
1st	44	71	7,500

Standing ¼-Mile 15·7 sec 90 m.p.h.
Standing Kilometre 29·0 sec 112 m.p.h.

TIME IN SECONDS	3·0	4·2	6·0	7·6	10·0	12·7	15·8	20·9	27·7
TRUE SPEED M.P.H.	30	40	50	60	70	80	90	100	110	120
INDICATED SPEED	31	39	50	60	70	80	93	104	116	127

Mileage recorder 0·9 per cent over-reading. Test distance, 1,852 miles.

Speed range, gear ratios and time in seconds

m.p.h.	Top (3·55)	Third (5·28)	Second (7·57)	First (2·97)
10— 30	—	—	3·5	2·3
20— 40	—	5·0	3·3	2·3
30— 50	7·7	4·8	3·1	—
40— 60	7·4	4·7	3·1	—
50— 70	7·4	4·4	—	—
60— 80	7·5	5·2	—	—
70— 90	7·5	7·1	—	—
80—100	8·5	—	—	—
90—110	12·0	—	—	—

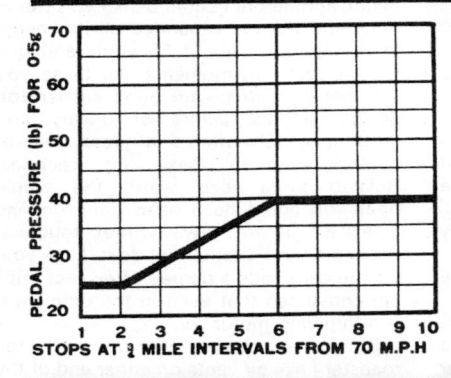

FUEL CONSUMPTION
(At constant speeds—m.p.g.)
30 m.p.h. 59·7
40 54·0
50 48·2
60 39·2
70 34·5
80 30·5
90 27·8
100 22·8

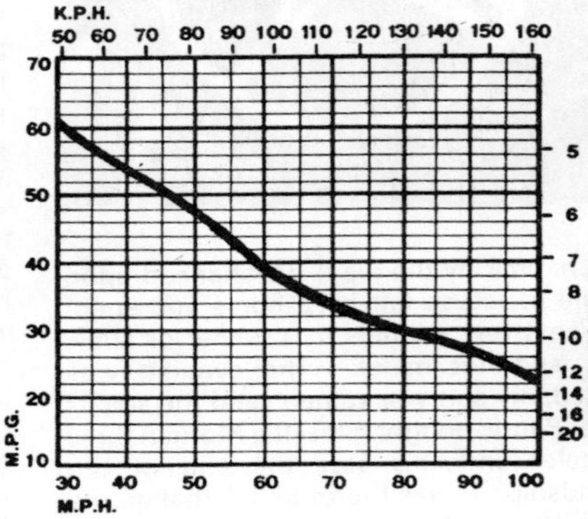

Typical m.p.g. 28 (10·1 litres/100km)
Calculated (DIN) m.p.g. 31·4 (9·0 litres/100km)
Overall m.p.g. 26·0 (10·9 litres/100km)
Grade of fuel, Super Premium, 5-star (min. 100RM)

OIL CONSUMPTION
Miles per pint (SAE 20/50) .. 350

BRAKES (from 30 m.p.h. in neutral)

Load	g	Distance
25 lb	0·40	75 ft
50 "	0·88	34·2 "
75 "	1·05	28·7 "
Handbrake	0·38	79

Max. Gradient, 1 in 3
Clutch Pedal: 35lb and 3·5in.

TURNING CIRCLES
Between kerbs L, 30ft 8·5in.; R, 32ft 5·5in
Between walls L, 32ft 1·5in.; R, 33ft 7·5in
Steering wheel turns, lock to lock .. 2·6

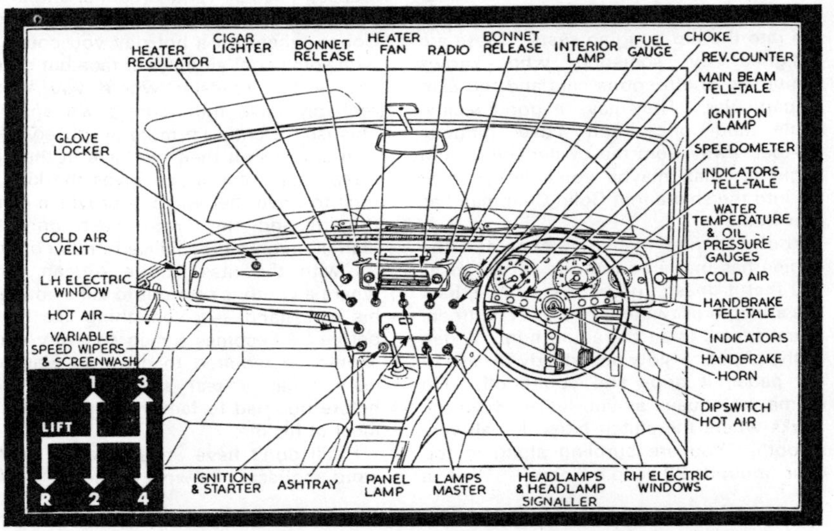

HOW THE CAR COMPARES:
MAXIMUM SPEED (mean) M.P.H.
Lotus Elan Fixed Head Coupe SE
Alfa Romeo Giulia Sprint GTV
Jaguar E-type — 153
Reliant Scimitar
Sunbeam Tiger 260 Tourer

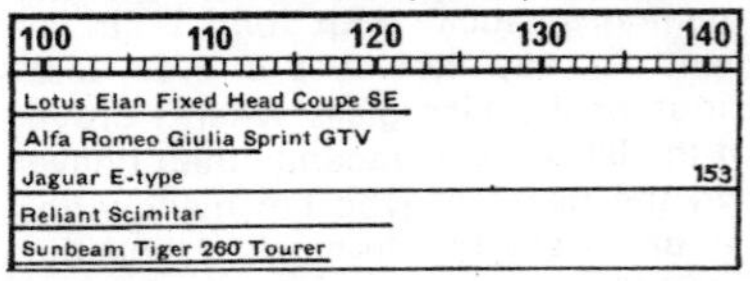

0-60 M.P.H. (sec.)
Lotus Elan Fixed Head Coupe SE
Alfa Romeo Giulia Sprint GTV
Jaguar E-type
Reliant Scimitar
Sunbeam Tiger 260 Tourer

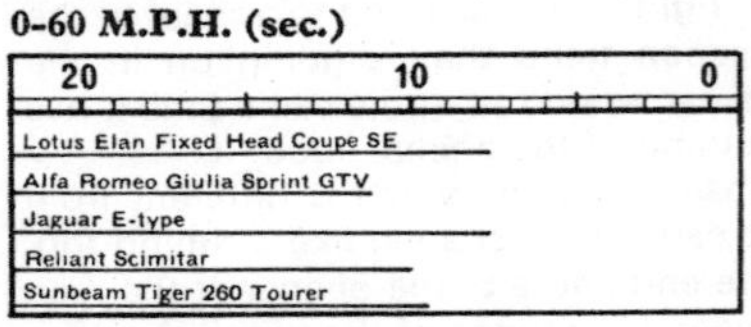

STANDING START ¼-MILE (sec.)
Lotus Elan Fixed Head Coupe SE
Alfa Romeo Giulia Sprint GTV
Jaguar E-type
Reliant Scimitar
Sunbeam Tiger 260 Tourer

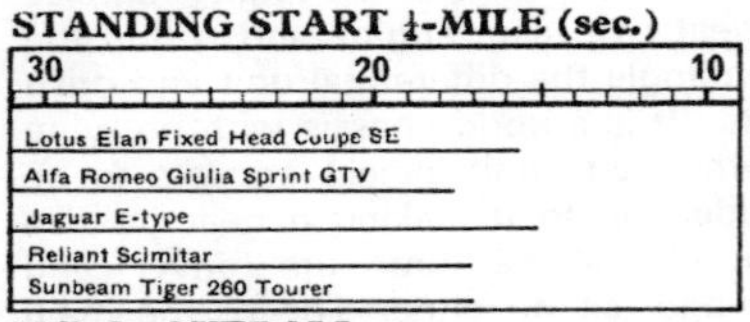

M.P.G. OVERALL
Lotus Elan Fixed Head Coupe SE
Alfa Romeo Giulia Sprint GTV
Jaguar E-type
Reliant Scimitar
Sunbeam Tiger 260 Tourer

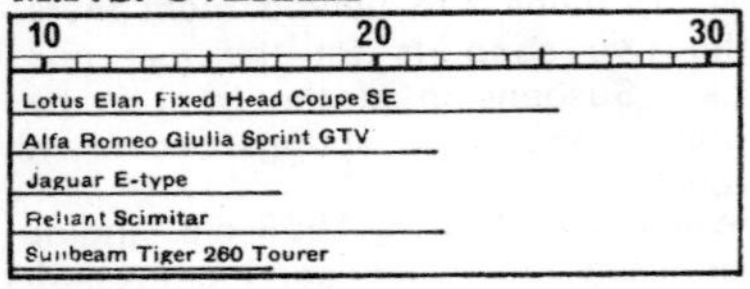

PRICES

Lotus Elan Fixed Head Coupé SE	£1,762
Alfa Romeo Giulia Sprint GTV	£1,950
Jaguar E-Type	£2,068
Reliant Scimitar	£1,516
Sunbeam Tiger 260 Tourer	£1,471

Autocar ROAD TEST NUMBER 2134

Lotus Elan Coupé S/E 1,558 c.c.

AT A GLANCE: Very fast fixed head coupé with competition-bred 1·6-litre twin-cam engine. Vivid acceleration to 120 m.p.h. Good fuel consumption for its performance. Very high cornering power easily controlled. First class rack and pinion steering. Excellent brakes. Expensive but well finished.

MANUFACTURER
Lotus Cars Ltd., Norwich, Norfolk (NOR 92W), England.

PRICES
Basic	..	£1,432 0s 0d
Purchase Tax	..	£329 19s 3d
Total (in G.B.)	..	£1,761 19s 3d

EXTRAS (inc. P.T.)
Radio	..	£40 0s 0d

PERFORMANCE SUMMARY
Mean maximum speed	122 m.p.h.
Standing start ¼-mile	15·7 sec
0-60 m.p.h.	7·6 sec
30-70 m.p.h. (through gears)	7·0 sec
Fuel consumption	28 m.p.g.
Miles per tankful	280

IT is now five years since the Lotus Elan was introduced, and in that time nearly 5,000 have been built in the factory or sent out as kits of parts for the owner to assemble. The reputation of the car exceeds even the output, and the performance of the competition versions on the track is always spectacular. As a sports car it is unique, not just in the way it is constructed but in the way it behaves on the road.

As it is almost three years since we tested an Elan, a brief look at the specification seems appropriate. Structurally the car is based on a deep, box-section backbone with forks at each end to carry the all-independent, all coil-spring, all-wishbone suspensions. Between the arms of the front fork is the twin-cam Lotus-Ford 4-cylinder engine mated to a Ford Cortina GT gearbox and driving the rear wheels through Rotoflex couplings at each end of each of the short drive shafts. The body is a separate glass fibre moulding painted with cellulose.

Key features of the Elan, like all Lotuses, are low weight (14 cwt), high gearing and a very low body drag. These qualities, combined with the really beefy Ford engine, give a performance quite out of the 1½-litre class and several above it. A mean maximum speed of 122 m.p.h. and acceleration from rest to 100 m.p.h. in only 20·9sec are truly breath-taking and have never before been combined with a fuel consumption as outstanding as 26·0 m.p.g.

If this were all the Lotus had to offer, it would be impressive enough, but these are only incidentals to its greater qualities of supreme road-holding and perfectly balanced handling. All the years of successful Lotus racing can be felt in one's finger tips on the steering wheel, and we can even boast that we sent our g-meter off its scale (above 1·0g) *laterally* on a flat 60-m.p.h. bend at MIRA.

Returning to technicalities, but only for a moment, the version in this test is the special equipment fixed-head coupé. All Elans now are coupés, either drophead or fixed-head, but the special equipment models have very neat knock-on wheels, a servo for the brakes (with harder pads), 115 b.h.p. instead of 105 and a slightly higher final drive ratio (3·55 instead of 3·77 to 1). Fitted carpets throughout the cockpit and boot, inertia reel seat belts, and a soft leather-covered 14in. dia. steering wheel also form part of the S/E package, which adds £163 to the total-with-tax price.

Left: The big cutaway at the front of the door opening makes getting in and out quite easy; switches for the electric window winders are on the lower part of the facia. Right: Some of the useful space behind the seats is taken up by the seat belt reels. Interior lamps and coat hooks are fitted on both rear quarter pillars

Compared with the open Elan we tested in August 1964, the latest S/E version is a lot quicker. That car had a 3·9-to-1 final drive and we said then how much faster than 114 m.p.h. it would have run if a higher ratio were fitted. The message got through and all Elans have had a 3·77 axle for some time now. With the 3·55 and the extra 10 b.h.p. we were able to reach almost 7,000 r.p.m. in top in opposite directions very quickly, so the car could be made to go even faster. But for road work the gearing is quite high enough, and 100 m.p.h. cruising at about 5,700 r.p.m. is smooth, quiet and fuss-free.

Another difference between this one and the previous car tested is the gearbox. It is still the same excellent Ford unit, with a very positive, notchy shift and completely unbeatable synchromesh on all ratios, but instead of the ultra-close ratio gears, this time we had the standard box. In conjunction with the higher axle the speeds in the indirect gears are not that different from before, so acceleration has improved considerably.

Getting Away

Too much adhesion can be a problem in getting a car with a sporty engine away from rest in the quickest possible time. On the Lotus we eventually found at least 6,000 r.p.m. were needed to get a "clean" take-off, whereupon the little bullet screeched away with a minimum of wheelspin to reach the quarter-mile post in only 15·7sec and to pass the kilometre at about 112 m.p.h.

Apparently the latest crankshafts are safe for 7,500 r.p.m. for short bursts so the distributor cutout at 6,600 r.p.m. is no longer fitted. We used about 7,200 for maximum acceleration, but found 6,000 plenty for normal road use. The wide torque band of the twin-cam Ford is one of its greatest features, and it was only surge in the Rotoflex couplings that prevented us from recording top gear acceleration from 20 or even 10 m.p.h. The whole set of 20 m.p.h. increments in top from 30 to 90 m.p.h. are between 7·4 and 7·7sec, which shows well how flat the torque curve must be.

Going back to the 1964 car, its top gear times were a little quicker (because of the axle difference), but from rest that car took 6sec longer to reach 100 m.p.h. and 12sec longer to reach 110 m.p.h.

Starting the engine either hot or cold is the same; just turn the key with the accelerator half-way to the floor. When cold it may be necessary to pump the pedal a few times to enrich the mixture, but the engine runs evenly straight away and stays running while the garage doors are closed. There is a choke fitted for abnormal conditions, but we never used it. When hot the exhaust puffs out a cloud of blue smoke as the engine fires up, and we saw the same thing in the mirror when we pulled away after a period of idling in traffic. Oil consumption at 300 miles per pint is not excessive for an engine built to near-racing tolerances for free-running.

Clutch movement is very short with only 3½in. total and probably about 1½in. effective take-up, so a delicate touch is needed. Insensitive footwork gives rise to the characteristic surges in the Rotoflex couplings, but one learns how to prevent these. Some of the time, when driving hard and changing gear fast, the carburation causes the occasional surge to slip in, but this is welcome cushioning from the jerk that would certainly stress the transmission violently.

With the benefit of a large vacuum servo the brakes are extremely light and nicely progressive. Less than 75lb caused all four wheels to lock together on dry tarmac—no slewing—and just before this point we achieved a maximum retardation of well over 1·0g. There was some slight fade as the discs warmed up, but they stabilized at a low 35lb for repeated stops at 0·5g from 70 m.p.h. The

The two big twin-choke Weber carburettors have to be removed to get at the distributor. Air horns are standard, with the compressor just behind the screenwasher bottle on the right

Extractor vents in the rear quarter pillars help interior ventilation. There are indicator repeaters on both front wings

Lotus Elan Coupé S/E

handbrake is tucked away under the right of the facia where one must lean forward to use it, but it held facing both ways on the 1-in-3. Starting again was possible, but not at all easy as the driver had to pull himself forward against the gradient to let the handle off, and at the same time delicately balance the clutch and throttle.

The seating compartments each side of the backbone are narrow, with just enough room for an average bottom to sink down into the well-shaped seat. The elbows then lie naturally on the padded armrest in the door and on the similarly padded cover to the high central tunnel. It feels right to lie back and drive at arms' length, but the seat can be set to different positions and angles by means of its swinging-link adjustment and alternative mountings for the front frame. Padding is only thin, but the frame supports elastic webbing or a diaphragm underneath so comfort is first class. The backrest gives lateral support right up to the shoulders, which helps tremendously when throwing the car about.

Steering is ultra-high geared with only 2·6 turns from lock to lock on a 31ft turning circle. It is perfectly positive yet free from violent kickback. In towns no more than half a turn ever seems to be needed and on motorways barely an inch of movement is sufficient to change lanes at speed. The response at the front wheels is absolutely immediate.

Steering

The Elan neither understeers nor oversteers—it just steers. We tried a steering pad test on a fixed diameter and found the nose turned in towards the centre progressively with the throttle opening (and hence power at the wheels), but we stayed on line. We tried cornering on a dry track as fast as we dared. Up to a certain speed (which was already above the limit for many cars) the Elan just ran round the corner wherever one chose to steer it without even squealing its tyres. At faster speeds more of the road width was needed as the tyres began to drift, but it still seemed much too easy to calculate just where to clip the apex and just where on the outside edge the car would straighten its angle. Eventually we were flying into the corners at apparently impossible speeds with plenty of steering control still, a huge angle of tail drift, deafening tyre squeal and a tremendous boost of ego.

The Mintex manometer was mounted laterally for these tests, but the column of fluid disappeared into the instrument with the sideways g.

On the road the Elan can be tossed at any corner and it steers round flat on the road with no drama. This is how one manages to put up such outstanding journey times, and we found ourselves taking bends a good 20 to 30 m.p.h. faster than in other cars. The extremely compact size of the coupé, plus its very brisk acceleration enable great streams of traffic to be overtaken in one manoeuvre, usually when the "first man to go" is still trying to make up his mind. No one seems to mind as the Elan is so soon out of their way, but very keen reactions and some experience of fast cars is needed to make sure one's presence has been noticed. Here we found the white colour of the test car a great asset and would strongly recommend all buyers to choose a light colour. The automatic flip-up-and-flash headlamp control is extremely useful, but seems slow to operate when needed quickly. Often one manages only a bleary blink just in time.

The ride in the latest test car is a lot firmer than in the earlier one, because stiffer rear dampers are used to improve the high-speed stability with the S/E engine. If one thinks

A good deal of luggage can be packed into the carpeted boot, which has the spare wheel stored under the floor; the wire keep is none too strong and the lid is easily blown shut

about it, all kinds of vertical jogs can be felt as the car goes along, but compared with other small sports cars the ride is still much softer and much more absorbent. There is no pitch or float and surprisingly little dive and squat under the extremes of braking and acceleration.

Visibility is good, although one tends to lose the bonnet line if one lies back in the seat too far. At first one feels "blind," not being able to see ahead through other cars' back windows, but the trick is to edge slightly to one side or other for a quick peep round at regular intervals. At night the headlamp adjustment is more critical than with most cars because of their proximity to the ground.

Because the twin-cam head is a conversion on the Cortina block, all the accessories like fuel pump, distributor and hydraulic reservoirs are buried underneath the two big Weber carburettors. During servicing, therefore, these would need to be removed first (an added expense); it took many minutes and a burnt and grazed fore-arm before we could fit our petrol meter in the fuel line between pump and carburettors.

There can be few faster ways of A-to-B motoring than in a Lotus Elan and we found there are even fewer ways in which we can enjoy ourselves so much in the process. With its minimum overtaking time, supreme cornering power and sure-foot braking, the all-important primary safety factor must be among the highest as well. ∎

SPECIFICATION: LOTUS ELAN COUPE S/E (FRONT ENGINE, REAR-WHEEL DRIVE)

ENGINE
- Cylinders .. 4, in line
- Cooling system .. Water; pump, fan and thermostat
- Bore .. 82.6mm (3.25in.)
- Stroke .. 72.8mm (2.86in.)
- Displacement .. 1,558 c.c. (95.19 cu. in.)
- Valve gear .. Twin overhead camshafts
- Compression ratio 9.5-to-1; octane requirement 100
- Carburettors .. Two Weber 40DCOE18
- Fuel pump .. AC mechanical
- Oil filter .. Full flow
- Max. power .. 115 b.h.p. (net) at 6,000 r.p.m.
- Max. torque .. 108 lb ft (net) at 4,000 r.p.m.

TRANSMISSION
- Clutch .. Borg and Beck diaphragm spring, 8in. dia.
- Gearbox .. Four-speed, all-synchromesh
- Gear ratios .. Top 1.0; Third 1.40; Second 2.01; First 2.97; Reverse 3.32
- Final drive .. Hypoid bevel, 3.55-to-1

CHASSIS and BODY
- Construction .. Welded steel backbone with glass fibre reinforced plastic body

SUSPENSION
- Front .. Independent, wishbones, coil springs, telescopic dampers
- Rear .. Independent, wishbones, coil springs, telescopic dampers

STEERING
- Type .. Alford and Alder rack and pinion
- Wheel dia. .. 14in.

BRAKES
- Make and type .. Girling discs front and rear
- Servo .. Girling vacuum
- Dimensions .. F, 9.5in. dia.; R, 10.0in. dia.
- Swept area .. F, 139 sq. in.; R, 159 sq. in. Total 298 sq. in. (334.5 sq. in. per ton laden)

WHEELS
- Type .. Pressed steel disc, five stud knock-on type, 4.5in. wide rim
- Tyres—make .. Dunlop
- —type .. SP41 radial-ply tubed
- —size .. 145—13in.

EQUIPMENT
- Battery .. 12-volt 57-amp. hr.
- Generator .. Lucas C40, 42 amp.
- Headlamps .. Lucas F700, 120/90-watt
- Reversing lamp .. Extra
- Electric fuses .. 2
- Screen wipers .. Variable speed, self-parking
- Screen washer .. Standard, manual plunger
- Interior heater .. Standard, water valve type
- Safety belts .. Standard
- Interior trim .. Leathercloth seats, pvc headlining

- Floor covering .. Carpet
- Starting handle .. No provision
- Jack .. Screw scissor type
- Jacking points .. Along undertray
- Windscreen .. Laminated
- Underbody protection .. Non-corroding glass fibre plastic body
- Other bodies .. Drophead coupé

MAINTENANCE
- Fuel tank .. 10 Imp. gallons (no reserve) (45 litres)
- Cooling system .. 14 pints (including heater) (8 litres)
- Engine sump .. 7.5 pints (4 litres) SAE 20/50. Change oil every 3,000 miles; Change filter element every 6,000 miles
- Gearbox .. 1.75 pints SAE 80EP. Change oil every 6,000 miles
- Final drive .. 2 pints SAE 90EP. Change oil every 10,000 miles
- Grease .. 2 points every 1,500 miles
- Tyre pressures .. F, 18; R, 20 p.s.i. (normal driving). F, 22; R, 26 p.s.i. (fast driving)

PERFORMANCE
- Top gear m.p.h. per 1,000 r.p.m. 17.62
- Mean piston speed at max. power 2,864 f.p.m.
- B.h.p. per ton laden 129

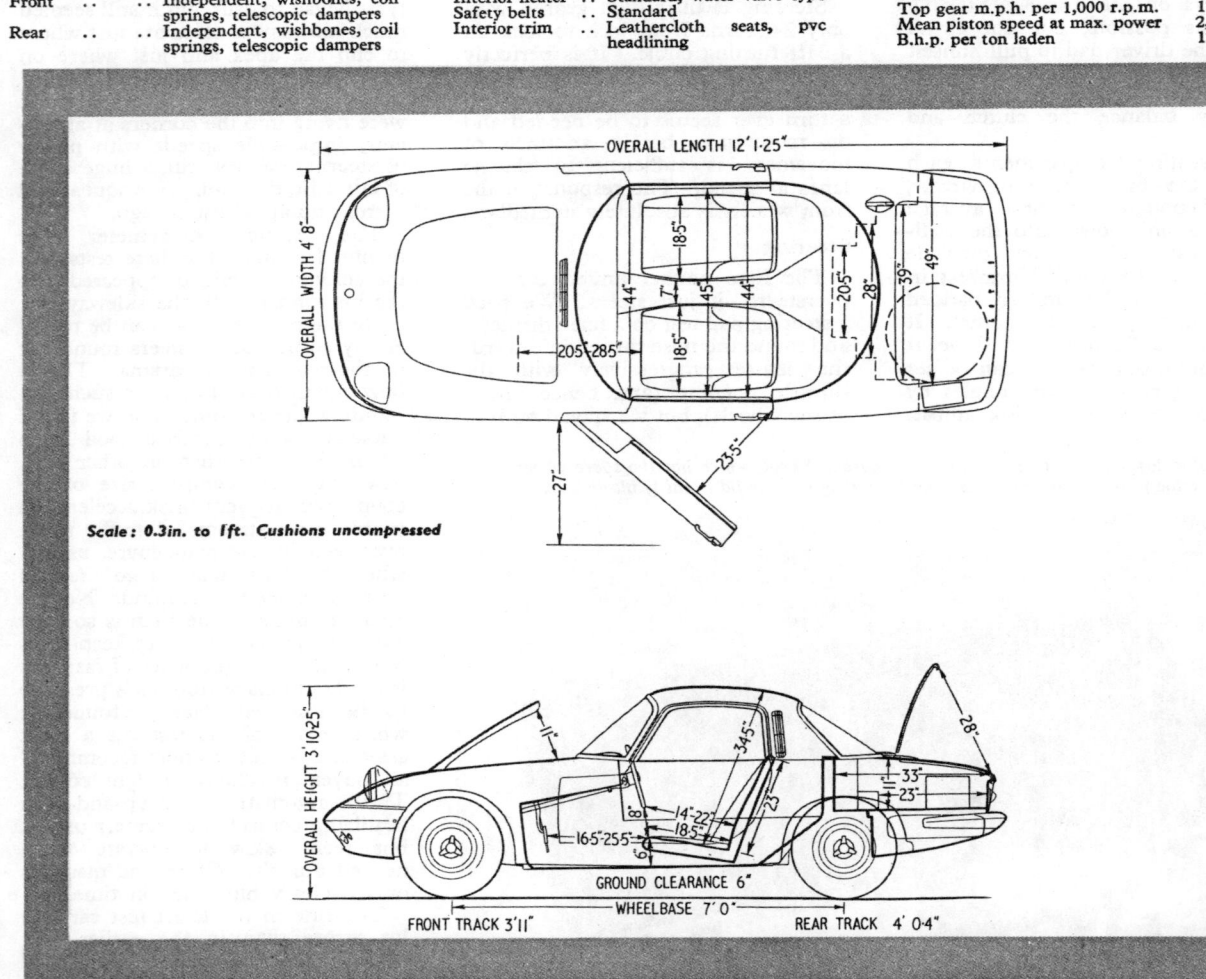

Scale: 0.3in. to 1ft. Cushions uncompressed

Lotus Elan

by the editor

12,000 mile staff car report

". . . probably the most reliable car I have ever owned and certainly the most enjoyable to drive."

IT was about 15 months ago that we published the pre-natal section of this report—the description of how KGH765D was assembled from kit form to running order. This account (April 30, 1966) started with a query, or rather a string of queries: "Would it be reliable, waterproof, easy to maintain and service? Would it do 3,000-mile Continental journeys without attention and, on the other hand, would it object to motoring just in and out of London for week after week?" Well, 18,000 miles later I can say that the answer is "no" to the last question and "yes" to all the others. It has been probably the most reliable car I have ever owned and certainly the most enjoyable to drive.

Now let's go back to the beginning and start with the "delivery" faults built into the kit of parts.

1. Headlights flickered on and off with a fluttering noise from a relay behind the facia.
2. Indicator warning light didn't work.
3. Loud rattle inside the nearside door.
4. Wind whistle from nearside door.

Since I hadn't assembled any of these components I didn't feel responsible for them. But on the other hand I thought that a little probing might be less trouble than setting up the rather elaborate organization you always need for getting your car to the nearest agent (11 miles away) and back again. And so it proved: the headlamp trouble succumbed at once to pure deduction from the wiring diagram—a little more spring tension was needed for the earthing microswitch. The door was more difficult; it wasn't hard to re-set the hinges so that the top of the window frame made proper contact with the rubber seals, and this cured the wind whistle, but the rattle was caused by the door handle operating link hitting the window glass, which involved a lot of stripping-down to bend the link a little.

At **300 miles** I rang the Lotus Service Department at Cheshunt to book the free 500-mile service. They said they could do nothing for a fortnight but reminded me that a compulsory works inspection of kit-built cars (taking three days) was essential to validate the warranty. Meanwhile, they said, I could have the 500-mile service done at any agents and it was done a few days later by Len Street Motors of Bayswater who found loose rear differential mounting bolts and tightened them, and found and replaced the indicator warning light bulb which I had forgotten to mention. In fact this free service cost £1 18s. 11d. for engine oil, gear oil, a new bulb and new cam cover gaskets (after checking the valve clearances).

The only thing that was not done satisfactorily was the carburetter adjustment and this has been a source of complaint after nearly every occasion on which the car has been serviced. If the idling mixture screws of the two double choke Webers are set too rich the idling gets lumpier and lumpier as the engine gets

OUR TEST CARS

Motor 12,000-mile tests are carried out on staff cars which have been purchased through normal retail trade channels. They are serviced only by independent garages according to the manufacturers' instructions and are given absolutely no special treatment of any kind.

Lotus Elan

hot, leading eventually to stalling in traffic and, finally, to plug oiling. It is essential to get the engine really hot and then to adjust to the weakest limit of even firing by moving the set screws downwards (clockwise) until they are only about three-quarters to one turn off their seatings at 800 r.p.m. With a little practice I found that I could re-set the whole adjustment by ear (including throttle balance) in about five minutes and that it would then stay in adjustment for thousands of miles and idle happily in traffic jams for half an hour at a time. I should perhaps make one reservation here—prolonged idling in hot summer weather brings the water temperature up to boiling point eventually—in all other circumstances the cooling is entirely adequate.

The only fault which arose in the next few miles was that the chromed plastic strip which separates the front bumper from the bonnet started to rise out of its slot and flap about in mid-air at speeds over 50 m.p.h. This was fixed by the factory when the car went back to get its "certificate of roadworthiness" at **765 miles.** They also adjusted the bonnet catch cables, sought but failed to

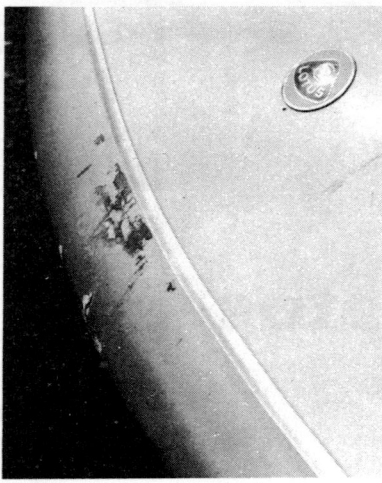

After more than a year's hard use the bodywork is virtually unmarked, free from cracks and, of course, immune from rust.

The glass fibre front bumper however, suffers badly from people who use it as a stop during parking manoeuvres

What it cost

Running costs	£	s.	d.
Road Fund Licence	17	10	0
Initial inspection		18	6
Service at 500 miles	1	13	11
Service at 1,500 miles	3	0	0
Service at 6,000 miles	11	14	10
Service at 12,000 miles	26	18	8
Tyre wear (53% of 5 tyres)		19	11	0
Petrol: 473 gallons at 5s. 8d. a gallon	119	7	0
Oil: 28 pints	3	14	8
Running costs total: £204	8	7
Insurance AOA Group 7, Class A*	100	0	0
Price of new car (with tax)	1,646	0	0
Price of new car (as kit but including delivery and building costs)	1,364	0	0
Second-hand value (approximately)	1,100	0	0
Cost/mile (excluding depreciation and insurance)			4.09d.
Cost/mile of kit car including depreciation and insurance			11.37d.
Cost/mile of fully built car including depreciation and insurance			17.01d.

*This insurance figure is a rough approximation. For different circumstances and individuals it may vary widely in either direction and can be considerably reduced by a no-claims bonus.

Performance Comparisons

	KGH 765D (at 7,000 miles)	KGH 765D (at 17,000 miles)	Road Test (26/9/64)
Maximum speed	120 m.p.h. approx.	(See text)	111.9 m.p.h.
Maximile	112.2 m.p.h.	115.0 m.p.h.	111.9 m.p.h.

Acceleration in upper ratios	Top	3rd	Top	3rd	Top	3rd
20-40 m.p.h.	7.8	5.6	7.4	5.5	6.8	4.9
30-50 m.p.h.	7.5	5.8	7.7	5.6	6.4	4.9
40-60 m.p.h.	6.9	5.4	7.1	5.5	6.3	5.4
50-70 m.p.h.	6.7	5.7	7.1	6.1	6.2	5.2
60-80 m.p.h.	8.4	6.6	8.1	6.8	6.7	5.4
70-90 m.p.h.	11.8	—	9.2	9.5	7.7	7.0
80-100 m.p.h.	13.4	—	10.2	—	9.0	—

Fuel consumption			
at 30 m.p.h.	59.0 m.p.g.	57.5 m.p.g.	57.0 m.p.g.
at 40 m.p.h.	50.0 m.p.g.	51.0 m.p.g.	50.0 m.p.g.
at 50 m.p.h.	45.5 m.p.g.	47.0 m.p.g.	46.5 m.p.g.
at 60 m.p.h.	37.5 m.p.g.	37.5 m.p.g.	38.0 m.p.g.
at 70 m.p.h.	27.5 m.p.g.	30.0 m.p.g.	27.0 m.p.g.
at 80 m.p.h.	26.5 m.p.g.	26.0 m.p.g.	24.0 m.p.g.
at 90 m.p.h.	25.0 m.p.g.	25.0 m.p.g.	22.5 m.p.g.
at 100 m.p.h.	22.0 m.p.g.	24.0 m.p.g.	18.0 m.p.g.
Overall	27.4 m.p.g.	28.3 m.p.g.	25.5 m.p.g.

Speedometer error									
Indicated	30	40	50	60	70	80	90	100	110
True	29	38	48	57	66	75	83	92	101

Distance recorder accurate

find a squeak from underneath and, at my request, bled the brake and clutch circuits which felt spongy. The last cost 18s. 6d., the rest was free and the whole operation wasn't quite completed when I took the car away after six days so it had to go back again later.

There followed a thousand miles of uneventful running-in which revealed one most irritating characteristic—a tendency for the gear lever to vibrate at various engine speeds and particularly with a loud waspish buzz at about 4,000 r.p.m., which represents a cruising speed just over 70 m.p.h. I discovered that you could reduce the noise to reasonable proportions by removing the gear knob altogether or you could magnify it to an intolerable level by using certain proprietary decorative knobs. Finally I compromised with a small piece of rubber tube over the end to cushion the sharp edges of the screw thread. The factory confessed themselves baffled at the time although Graham Arnold of Lotus proffered the hopeful thought that a similar noise on his car had disappeared at about 7,000 miles. Although I received this information with the scepticism which I felt it deserved, the fact remains that the noise diminished gradually until, at 7,000 miles, I was able to screw the official knob back on again and since then there has barely been any sound.

At **1,600 miles** the speedometer started to fluctuate more and more wildly and at **1,790 miles** it was replaced under guarantee when the car went back to the factory for the completion of its initial inspection and a 1,500 mile service. This marked the end of the first phase of its life—it was now fit for hard work and the following day it left Southampton on a hurried journey to Spain which was my first real opportunity to assess the car properly.

Motoring abroad

In one respect KGH765D is non-standard; it has both the highest available final drive gears (3.55:1) and the very close ratio gearbox. This combination was ordered (at an extra cost of £25) because I thought it would be the best for road use and experience hasn't changed this opinion. It gives you maxima in the lower gears of 50, 70 and 95 m.p.h. (in very round figures) and a top gear which allows 90 m.p.h. cruising at 5,000 r.p.m. or 100 m.p.h. at the power peak of 5,500; anything lower geared than this is, in my opinion, too fussy for long runs.

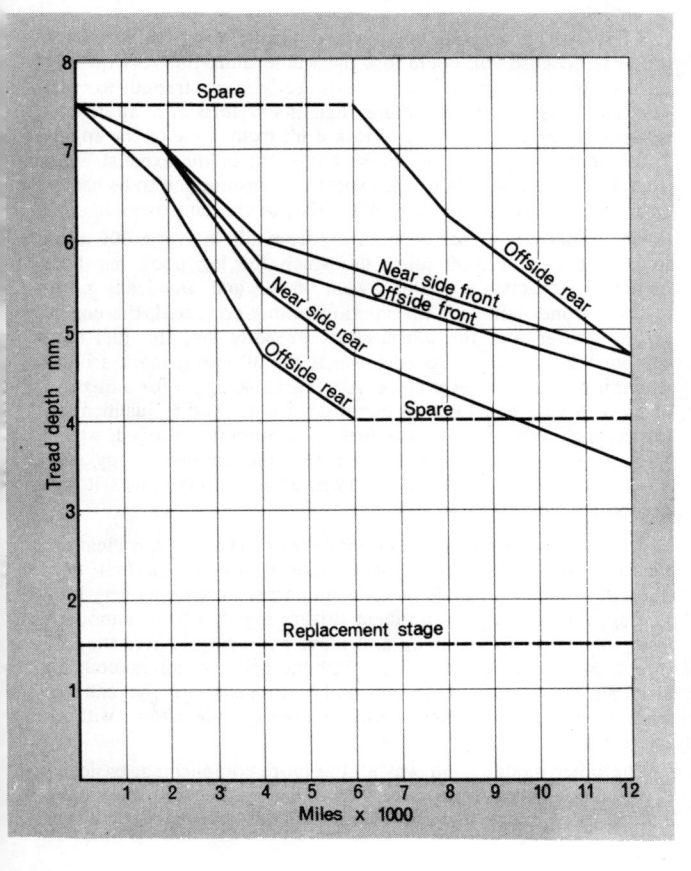

But heading southwards from Le Havre across the wavy roads of Northern France we found the first (and only) disappointment. With two people aboard, a full load of luggage for a fortnight and a full tank we couldn't maintain much more than 80 m.p.h. without grounding the exhaust system occasionally. It can't have done it much harm, since the same components are still in use a year later, but it is certainly a design fault which needs correction. Probably a small extra clearance—half to three quarters of an inch—would be enough to bring the bump stops into play first.

Further south, the French roads seem to lose their long wavelength irregularities and the Elan was able to resume its normal comfortable cruising speed in the nineties. It is, of course, an unusually comfortable sports car—at very low speeds the softness of the suspension is masked by heavy damping and a certain amount of road harshness but as the speed rises so does the ride flatten out. The Elan is the only car I have owned which didn't need any modification to the seats—they are hard but well-shaped, they give you proper side support and they recline at the fairly considerable angle which I find most comfortable.

The steering column has a telescopic adjustment and this I had previously set to have the wheel as far away as possible; this is a job you want to get right first time—it took me a large part of one morning to find and loosen the various invisible nuts which allow it to move. I found it well worth doing because the final result is an armslength driving position which I can occupy quite comfortably all day. In fact on this occasion we put well over 600 miles into 12 hours in spite of a rather lengthy lunch stop.

I have always thought that for light, responsive, balanced handling, sheer cornering power and driver rapport, this car stands by itself amongst production sports cars. It is also quite remarkably safe and vice-free because you can approach your corners any way you like—with or without heavy braking into the apex—and *take* them any way you like although you get the best results by driving round under considerable power.

This period of exploring the car's potentialities on roads eminently suitable for the purpose was expensive in fuel and tyres. By **4,000 miles** the tyre wear looked alarming, particularly at the back (see graph). In fact one must put this down only partly to joie de vivre and partly to the rather rapid scuffing which occurs during the period when the tyres are wearing into a shape which conforms with suspension movement. Far from having to replace one SP41 at 7,000 miles, which seemed likely, they practically stopped wearing at around 4,000-6,000 miles and I doubt whether all five covers will be gone at 24,000 miles—we shall see. It is noticeable that the rear tyres wear half as quickly again as the front ones and, being strongly opposed to the interchanging of front and rear wheels (although this is recommended in the handbook), I have brought the spare into play by rotating three wheels round the two rear positions.

A trip to Holland just before **5,000 miles** gave an opportunity

By disconnecting two springs and joining two wires together the automatic lamp flashing system can be disconnected so that the headlights can be left up but illuminated only when needed. With this arrangement, of course, they can also be left on when folded away.

Lotus Elan

to measure maximum speed but the attempt was thwarted by persistent misfiring over 6,000 r.p.m. A rattle developed inside the driver's door, probing fingers (not mine) pushed the radio blanking panel through its hole in the facia and the boot lock seized. When I took the car to Puttocks of Guildford for its 6,000 miles service I told them to fix these things and also to check the compression of No. 1 cylinder because if you listened at the carburettor intakes it always sounded different from the other three.

For the first and last time it returned with carburetters properly tuned; the rest of the work was satisfactory except for two things —the oil filler cap was not tight and the timing chain was much too tight so that it produced a loud whine. When the engine was new I found that this rather long chain needed adjustment every 1,500 miles or the engine would begin to sound very loose and rattly, particularly at tickover. Officially, the proper way to tension the chain is to remove the cam covers and adjust the tensioner until there is a maximum lift of $\frac{1}{2}$ inch in the horizontal chain run between the camshaft sprockets. In fact, however, I used to screw it in until the clatter stopped and the whine hadn't quite started. Since the tensioning set-screw is perfectly accessible at the front of the engine the whole operation takes less than a minute. Now that the stretch rate has diminished, it will last the 6,000 miles between major services.

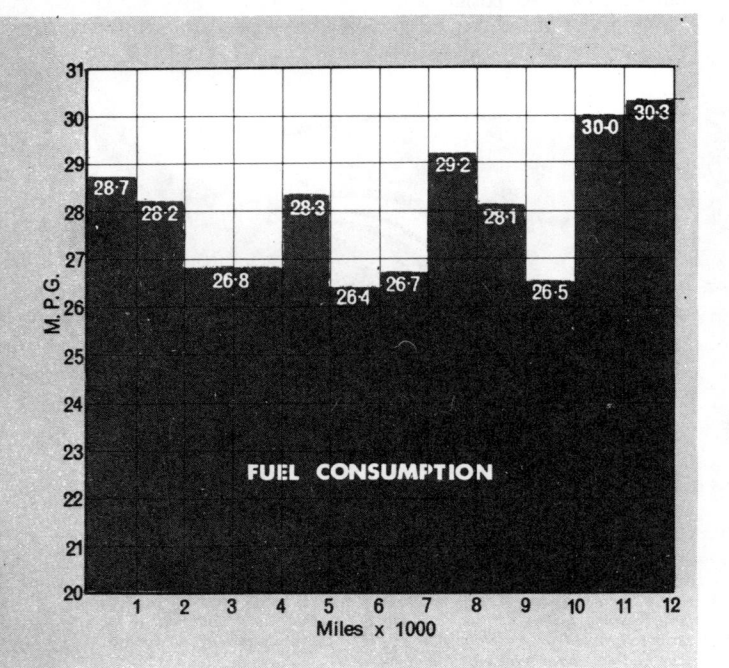

The following week a thorough Crypton check was arranged which showed that the ignition timing was 9° retarded. Although this was the only serious fault revealed, a number of rather interesting points came to light during the test. I have already mentioned that I had harboured unjustified doubts about the compression of No. 1 cylinder; the Crypton gauge, in fact, showed that all the compressions were extremely high—between 200 and 210 lb./sq. in. This meant that a plug voltage of about 13 kv. was demanded during full throttle acceleration and with a maximum available coil voltage of 16 kv. (at low r.p.m.) the margin was not adequate at high speeds. Re-setting the plug gaps to 0.025 in. and trimming the electrodes reduced the voltage demand to 10 kv. on the oscilloscope; obviously Elan plugs have to be maintained meticulously to avoid a misfire at high r.p.m.

This situation is probably worsened by the centrifugal governor type rotor arm fitted to these engines; as the plug voltage rises it is probable that this will start to flash over at a lower speed than the 6,500 r.p.m. limit it is intended to enforce. On the grounds that I could trust myself not to over-rev, I replaced it with a standard rotor (No. 400051). This engine has such outstandingly good low and middle range torque that there is little point in exceeding an indicated 6,500 r.p.m. in the lower gears. As the performance tests later showed, this is really about 6,000 r.p.m. because the rev counter is some 8-10% fast on my car and so is the speedometer (see performance panel); it strikes me that this is a quite excessive degree of flatter.

While the car was undergoing a final full power run on the Crypton "Rolling Road" chassis dynamometer, I noticed that the oil filler cap was loose and that oil was streaming out in large quantities. A moment later it came off and in the few seconds before the engine was stopped the whole windscreen, roof and rear window were covered in oil. At 6,000 r.p.m. and over oil seems to build up under considerable pressure in the cam boxes which suggests (a) that breathing could be improved (b) that bigger oil return passages to the sump or a restricted camshaft feed might be desirable and (c) that heavy oil consumption at very high cruising speeds may be accentuated by flooding of the valve guides.

Above all it emphasizes that you must put the cap back properly because you could lose the whole sump-full very quickly on a motorway. On my car the cap needs great strength to twist into its locked position—more than many forecourt attendants possess. Since oil does tend to leak a bit from some of the engine joints and since clouds of smoke come out of the exhaust when you blip the engine, one would expect oil consumption to be heavy. In fact it has averaged about 400 miles to the pint overall.

There followed a spell of motoring from a little over **6,000 miles** to a little over **12,000 miles** on which the log book has little comment—practically nothing went wrong and practically nothing was done, but with the ignition timing corrected, the engine getting looser and the carburetters properly set, the fuel consumption gradually improved towards the 30 m.p.g. mark around which it has hovered ever since. A remarkable figure for a mixture of hard driving and London commuting and another justification for the high axle ratio. As the fuel consumption improved, so did the octane requirement increase; at first the car was happy with 97/98 octane fuel (4 star) but from about 10,000 miles it has needed the best to avoid pinking.

Only two changes have been made from standard specification. One of them, which was actually made before the car first went abroad, was the fitting of Fiamm wind horns. I use horns very little in England but on the Continent drivers expect you to announce your intention of overtaking and move accordingly; here they fly into a rage and obstruct you. Without being at all raucous or strident, these horns have the ability to penetrate the cabs of French lorries and they seem to work indefinitely without maintenance.

The other modification was a little more complicated; basically it was the installation of Cibie 22 headlamps, because these have a little more range and the sharply cut-off dipped beam which

Left: The oil filler cap (ringed top left) needs quite a lot of strength to lock in place and should it come loose the rate of oil loss is colossal. The timing chain tensioner (bottom right) is easy to adjust and quite accessible; this is more than can be said for the distributor, hydraulic reservoirs and petrol pump, all of which are buried below the Weber carburetters.

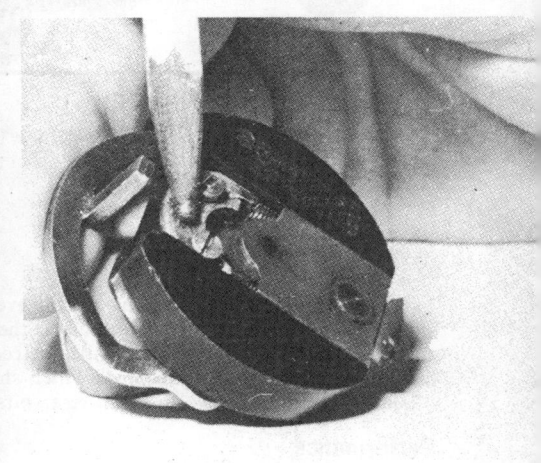

This is the governing rotor which is normally fitted to the distributor. The spring loaded bob-weight (under the pencil point) centrifuges out with increasing speed until it shorts out the h.t. at 6,500 r.p.m.

I prefer, but in the process the wiring was modified as well so that the headlights no longer come up lit—they come up switched off. So if the need for flashing is anticipated—as on a motorway—they can be left rampant and flashed instantly with the headlamp switch or with a flasher switch. Whether this arrangement is preferable is a matter of opinion but it takes only a minute or two to achieve it.

When the fixed-head coupé Elan was designed it was given different doors, boot lid and seals from those which leaked water in the earlier open cars—the current open car has acquired the coupé components. The only time that my car has ever admitted a drop of water is when the drains of the heater plenum chamber have been blocked. I think it would be fair to say that the most troublesome part of the equipment has been the electric windows; the nearside one works intermittently (i.e. on some days but not on others) and the driver's window started to do the same and then stopped altogether just before the 12,000 mile service; more powerful motors are now standard. Although I started by thinking that this was an unnecessary luxury, I now regard ordinary manual winders as an almost intolerable burden and inconvenience.

I mentioned that practically nothing was done to the car between 6,000 and 12,000 miles. It should, of course, have been serviced every 1,500 miles and the fact that it has only had 500, 1,500, 6,000 and 12,000 mile services in its whole life is something I shall now try and justify. It would be tedious to do this point by point but of the 16 checks in the 1,500 mile service some are impossible (like lubricating grease points—there aren't any); some are things you automatically check whenever you open the bonnet (e.g. oil level); some bring themselves automatically to your attention if necessary (slow running, steering, headlamp operation); and some should not need checking at such close intervals.

Similarly the 3,000 mile service contains one or two items which I have preferred to do myself if and when necessary (plugs and fan belt tension) and a number of items which I feel are better left alone. I certainly don't want the wheels changed round, the toe-in checked or altered, the headlamps re-set or the valve clearances touched at this mileage. Nor I feel is it necessary to change the seven pints of oil in the sump more often than once every 6,000 miles when 14 pints of replacement oil are added during this period. The very small amount of work which I have actually done myself (air, oil, water, battery, timing chain, fan belt and carburettor adjustment as a result of this attitude adds up to a small fraction of the time I should have spent getting the car to and from agents and it has certainly not suffered in consequence).

Lotus service is not cheap; the 12,000 check which included

There is plenty of space ahead of the radiator for the Fiamm wind horns which are supplied with air through flexible pipes from a small underbonnet compressor.

the rectification of the faulty electric window and the changing of all brake pads, cost nearly £27 of which £9 went to spares and materials. After this the brakes, which had always been much too heavy for my taste, felt much lighter but became prone to fade in heavy use. It only emerged much later that cheaper non-standard pads had been fitted (similar to those used on the Triumph Vitesse). It has now reverted to current standard pads which give lighter braking than the originals but which work in wet weather as well.

Before final performance testing, another Crypton check showed only two faults—the engine needed new plugs and the air cleaner was partly blocked. To my surprise I found that nowhere in the

Lotus Elan

handbook or service instructions does it ever tell you to renew the air cleaner element so I couldn't blame the agents who serviced the car. Another omission from the instructions concerns the steering swivels—these have plugs which should be removed at 12,000 miles to re-fill the small oil reservoirs.

Performance

Motorists are a cynical lot. A lot of people told me that if I expected my Elan to go like our road test car, I was going to be very disappointed. They were quite wrong. Bearing in mind that the road test car was the open model with 3.90 final drive ratio and mine the heavier coupé with 3.55 axle, the acceleration figures (see table) are very comparable. The high axle produces a marked improvement in both high speed fuel consumption and in maximum speed as shown by a "Maximile" figure some 3 m.p.h. higher. The true maximum has never been measured because there is no suitable venue in this country since the 70 m.p.h. limit came into force. But it has lapped the banked circuit at MIRA at a timed speed of 116.6 m.p.h. and in our experience this corresponds to a true maximum speed of about 120 m.p.h., the difference being lost on the bankings which are designed for only 90 m.p.h.

Intentionally, most of this report has been devoted to the operating and economic side of Elan ownership and not to the pleasures of driving it. The latter kind of information is to be found in our road test (*Motor* September 26, 1964). Most potential Elan owners are already convinced that this is the car they want but many of them are less sure that it is reliable, practical and versatile enough to be their only, everyday transport. Our experience of the coupé suggests that it is. Before long we should be able to carry this story up to 24,000 miles; in the meantime it seems that the worst snag about owning an Elan is what to have next to avoid anti-climax.

Second opinion

I have a peculiar love-hate relationship with Charles Bulmer's Lotus Elan. At the risk of being barred from driving the editor's transport for ever more, I must confess that my several hundred highly entertaining miles in it have been marred by some rather scary moments. Perhaps it is because the Elan's roadholding is so good that any unprovoked loss of adhesion tends to be unexpected and, due to the nature of the car and its tyres, rather sudden. Apart from having a front tyre blow-out at a speed that shall merely be recorded as high (a frightening experience, incidentally, even though the car remained more or less controllable) I have also managed to "lose" the front and the back ends on different occasions at cornering speeds that, for an Elan, seemed quite sane. Conceding that this may partly be due to Bell's incompetence, it also indicates that the Elan is by no means infallible. The trouble is that this car encourages wilful nibbling at its enormous reserves of cornering power until, if you're not careful, there are no reserves left. This is what it does to me, anyway.

All the other Elans I have driven have been low-mileage new ones so it was good to find that CHB's well kept but well used model still felt very fast, very smooth and reasonably one-piece. It is not devoid of rattles and clonks but then I don't think any Elan ever is. The only obvious clues that betrayed the car's 18,000 miles were the rather oily engine, paint peeling from the rocker covers, clattery door catches and rather tired fibre glass round the door hinges. In general, though, the feel and condition of this car has only enhanced my opinion of the Elan.

Roger Bell

Other owners' comments

Lotus owners are nothing if not enthusiastic even in the way they overflow the confines of a questionnaire form—I wish we could include all the interesting information which emerged. Of the later coupé Elans there are few complaints and these parallel my own experiences—electric window winders gave some trouble and so, in a lesser percentage, did inaccurate tachometers, the decorative strip round the front bumper and oil leaks from the cam covers. Open cars and earlier models (with mileages up to more than 40,000) suffered water leaks in wet weather, radiator leaks, wear in the track rod ends and failures of the rear wheel bearings and doughnut couplings. Nobody seemed to have had any serious mechanical breakages.

To the question: "Have you had good service?" only one owner said "no" although there were reservations about spares—for example "Supply of parts either immediate or never".

The things which people liked were just those you would expect—roadholding, performance, cornering, tractability, driving position and comfort. Handling and acceleration drew adjectives like "excellent", "superb", "brilliant"—depending on the tyres there was sometimes a little less enthusiasm about wet road behaviour. Quite a lot of owners find the brakes too heavy without assistance and have fitted servos.

The average fuel consumption of all our respondents seemed to be about 28 m.p.g. although there is considerable variation with driving methods and axle ratios—the best figure mentioned was 35 m.p.g.

Apart from the faults listed above, owners tend to dislike the rattles and vibrations from the gearlever, the oiliness and inaccessibility of the distributor, hydraulic reservoirs and petrol pump, the poor handbrake position and operation, the coarse heater control, the vulnerability of the exhaust and the lack of a through ventilation system (now fitted).

The question "Would you buy another?" was illuminating. One man said "no"—he had done 40,000 hard miles already, intended to keep it for at least another year and was then attracted by something much faster. All the rest answered with a solid "yes" and indeed, to prove it, four of them were already on their second Elans and two of them on their third. These experienced owners agreed on the great improvement in reliability and standard of finish in later cars. In fact only one owner considered the Elan to be an unreliable car and he had suffered mainly from persistent oil and water leaks.

Manufacturer's comments

We were amused and naturally concerned that the article should be written with a continuous note of incredulity that an Elan could be reliable when our own experience of over 5,000 of these cars has been that they are probably more reliable than many a family saloon.

Mr. Bulmer states that he was advised by Lotus service department that it would take three days to carry out a post-build check. The check takes three hours but we advise customers to put three days aside in case we have to rectify their handiwork.

The following faults listed on Mr. Bulmer's car have arisen on other vehicles and modifications introduced: chrome strip now has new means of location; new type gear levers now fitted with rubber integral bush; exhaust system has been raised in the light of customer complaints—the problem arose due to the slight rear end weight increase on the coupé when compared with earlier S2; on all twin cam engines leaving off the oil cap will cause loss of oil but we have always ensured a tight fit and now have a retaining wire to the cap; some intermittent operation of early electric windows was found to be caused by a faulty earth which is common to the courtesy light switch earth.

Finally, we are pleased to find that all the small faults reported on the car had not only been picked up and rectified many months ago through our normal channels but that service bulletins are in the hands of dealers on each fault. We regret the two handbook omissions pointed out to us and will rectify this with adenda slips immediately.

We now look forward to the 24,000 mile report and hope the car will continue to give good service even if we don't get a chance to look at it again.

'68 MODELS

The new car is 2ft longer overall and 8in. wider. Ventilation is improved and there are chromium-plated steel bumpers front and rear

LOTUS ELAN +2
FULL DESCRIPTION, SPECIFICATION AND CUTAWAY DRAWING

NEW 2+2 Lotus coupé, much bigger than the Elan, but using many of its mechanical components. Same general layout as the existing two-seater, but with new chassis and glassfibre body. Convertible version not available. £373 more than Elan Coupé.

PRICES					
In component form	..	..	..	..	£1,672 0s 0d
Assembled, basic	..	..	..	..	£1,554 0s 0d
Purchase Tax	..	..	..	..	£369 0s 0d
TOTAL (in G.B.)	..	..	..	..	£1,923 0s 0d

SINCE 1962 the Elan has achieved a remarkable reputation for performance, handling and often excellent fuel economy. As a strictly two-seater "fun" car, it has many outstanding qualities which could not be repeated in any other car with four seats. Many of the Elan's 5,000 buyers have married and are raising families, so there was nostalgia and a steady demand to Lotus for a "bigger Elan." The Elan +2 is a newly integrated design intended to give almost Elan characteristics while providing very generous 2+2 seating. Lotus have developed only a closed coupé version of the new car, as a convertible 2+2 shell would be difficult to engineer and probably not as popular in its intended market.

To their credit, the Lotus design team have made no attempt merely to stretch the Elan to a longer wheelbase.

The familiar Lotus twin-cam derivative of the Ford engine is unchanged. Accessibility is slightly better because of the wider bonnet lid

LOTUS ELAN +2...

Structurally the Elan + 2 is identical with the two-seater. On production cars the spare wheel will be upright to give more luggage space

Autocar copyright
J. G. HOSTLER
© Iliffe Transport Publications Ltd. 1967

The chassis and body, though recognisably Lotus and having many design similarities to the Elan, are new; even the suspensions have been re-worked while retaining the basic Elan aims. In fact, the Elan +2 is a much larger car than expected. Eyes grown familiar with the attractively tiny two-seater will be surprised at first. Considered alone as a design, it is still small by comparison with obvious competitors, and is certainly one of *the* most compact occasional four-seaters.

Compared with the Elan, the wheelbase is up by 1ft, to 8ft, while the tracks have been widened by 7in. and 6·6in. to 4ft 6in. (front) and 4ft 7in. (rear). All the extra wheelbase has gone in to giving a bigger passenger box, but to balance the overall styling, a longer nose and tail have pushed the overall length up to 14ft 1in. (Elan 12ft 1in.). The turning circle remains very compact at 28ft. Weight has increased considerably (more even than the proportionate size changes) from 14·1cwt to 18·6cwt.

Mechanical details

The Elan +2 has a rigid backbone pressed steel chassis closely related to that of the original Elan, suitably lengthened and widened to suit the new car's layout. Front and rear suspensions are also similar to the original Elan's, though few parts are interchangeable; 10in. Girling disc brakes are fitted all round, and servo assistance is standard; swept area is 334 sq. in. (compared with 298 sq. in. for the Elan).

Firestone F100 textile braced radial ply tyres are standard, but Dunlop SP41 or Goodyear G800s of the same 165-13in.

The interior cockpit is a lot more roomy, but the back seats are strictly of the "plus two children" variety. Quarterlights are fixed and the windows have electric lifts

66

67

Rear-end treatment is particularly neat with a modified Wolseley Hornet bumper and tail lamps from the Alfa Romeo Giulia Sprint GT

LOTUS ELAN +2...

size can be fitted on request. Lotus knock-off wheels, with five locating pegs and 5.5in. rims are a feature; similar wheels are extra on the 2-seat Elan.

Engine, gearbox and rear axle are all basically those on the Elan (and in the Cortina-Lotus) but the final drive ratio has been lowered a little to 3.70 to 1, and minor engine changes have raised the power output to 118 b.h.p. (net) at 6,000 r.p.m.

New 2 + 2 coupé body

The body is a one-piece glass-fibre moulding, made by Lotus themselves at their new Wymondham factory. Its layout, while similar to that of the smaller Elan, has several obvious recognition points, notably that the flush-fitting "pop-up" headlamps are farther inboard, and the nose has an increased droop. As with the Renault-engined Europa, the Elan +2's body shape was partly dictated by the choice of suitable bumpers. Like on the Europa, an Anglia bumper graces the front, while a suitably modified Wolseley Hornet rear bumper is used at the back. Press tools for bumpers would cost a lot of money—by Lotus standards—so such compromise was inevitable, even though Wilmot Breeden are having to make major changes to the basic Wolseley Hornet pressings.

Space inside the closed coupé body is generous for two full-sized front occupants, and adequate only for small children behind them. Adults would be cramped and unhappy if they sat in the rear seats for any length of time; leg room and headroom are both very restricted. Full size Aeroflow-type face level outlets are a great improvement over the tiny vents squeezed on to the Elan's facia last year.

Among many expensive appointments are the expanse of burr-walnut facia panel, electric winding door glasses, air horns, a Pye radio and—most unusually—a burglar alarm. Seats are in good quality leathercloth and there is carpet.

Development history

Lotus needed only 18 months to convert the idea of a project into a new model; their greatest difficulty was in choosing a title. At first this was to be an Elite, then an Elite II, then an Elite 2, an Elite +2, and finally the Elan +2. The new car is slipping comfortably into the Lotus scheme of things at Wymondham, where two production lines can turn out 40 Elans, 15 Europas and 20 Elan +2s a week. This is remarkable for such a small plant, where all bodies and chassis are made on the spot, and engine assembly is carried out as well.

Priced at £1,672 in kit form, the Elan +2 is £373 more expensive than the Elan 2-seater coupé, and is therefore in a completely different market. If supplied complete, its recommended price is £1,923.

SPECIFICATION

ENGINE
Cylinders	4, in line
Cooling system	Water; pump, fan and thermostat
Bore	82.6mm (3.25in.)
Stroke	72.8mm (2.86in.)
Displacement	1,558 c.c. (95.19 cu. in.)
Valve gear	Twin overhead camshafts
Compression ratio	9.5-to-1: Min. octane rating: 100
Carburettors	Two Weber 40-DCOE18
Fuel pump	AC mechanical
Oil filter	Full flow
Max. power	118 b.h.p. (net) at 6,000 r.p.m.
Max. torque	108 lb. ft (net) at 4,000 r.p.m.

TRANSMISSION
Clutch	Borg and Beck diaphragm spring, 8in. dia.
Gearbox	4-speed, all-synchromesh
Gear ratios	Top 1.0; Third 1.40; Second 2.01; First 2.97; Reverse 3.32
Final drive	Hypoid bevel, 3.70-to-1

CHASSIS and BODY
Construction	Welded steel backbone with glass fibre reinforced plastic body

SUSPENSION
Front	Independent, wishbones, coil springs, telescopic dampers
Rear	Independent, wishbones, coil springs, telescopic dampers

STEERING .. Alford and Alder rack and pinion
Wheel dia. .. 14in.

BRAKES
Make and type	Girling discs front and rear
Servo	Girling vacuum
Dimensions	F, 10in. dia.; R, 10in. dia.;
Swept area	F, 167 sq in.; R, 167 sq in. Total 334 sq. in.

WHEELS
Type	Pressed steel disc, five stud knock-on type, 5.5in. wide rim
Tyres make	Firestone
type	F100 radial-ply tubeless
size	165-13in.

EQUIPMENT
Battery	12-volt 57 amp.hr.
Generator	Lucas C40, 42 amp
Headlamps	Lucas F700, 120/90 watt (total)
Reversing lamp	Extra
Electric fuses	2
Screen wipers	Variable speed, self-parking
Screen washer	Standard, manual plunger
Interior heater	Standard, water-valve type
Heated backlight	Not available
Safety belts	Standard
Interior trim	Leathercloth seats, p.v.c. headlining
Floor covering	Carpet
Starting handle	No provision
Jack	Screw scissor type
Jacking points	Along undertray
Windscreen	Laminated
Underbody protection	Non-corroding glass fibre plastic body

MAINTENANCE
Fuel tank	13 Imp. gallons (no reserve) (58 litres)
Cooling system	14 pints (including heater) (8 litres)
Engine sump	7.5 pints (4 litres) SAE 20/50. Change oil every 3,000 miles; Change filter element every 6,000 miles
Gearbox	1.75 pints SAE 80EP. Change oil every 6,000 miles
Final drive	2 pints SAE 90EP. Change oil every 10,000 miles
Grease	2 points every 1,500 miles
Tyre pressures	F, 22; R, 22 p.s.i. (normal driving). F, 28; R, 30 p.s.i. (fast driving).

DIMENSIONS
Wheelbase	8ft 0in. (243.6cm)
Track: front	4ft 6in. (137.1 cm)
Track: rear	4ft 7in. (139.7cm)
Overall length	14ft 1in. (429cm)
Overall width	5ft 6in. (167.6cm)
Overall height (unladen)	3ft 11in. (119.3cm)
Ground clearance (laden)	6in. (15.2cm)
Turning circle	28ft 0in. (853cm)
Kerb weight	2,086 lb. (948 kg)

PERFORMANCE DATA
Top gear m.p.h. per 1,000 r.p.m. 18.0
Mean piston speed at max power 2,864 ft/min
B.h.p. per ton laden 106

THE LOTUS ELAN PLUS 2

AN entirely new model, the Elan Plus 2, has been introduced by Lotus, whose splendid modern new factory at Norwich was officially opened on 23rd August, although production of all Lotus models has been going on there for several months.

The Elan Plus 2 is the first all-Lotus machine to have more than two seats and is easily the best-looking motor car so far produced by this concern.

The well-tried "backbone" frame of the Elan has been retained, but stretched in order to give an extra 12 ins wheelbase. Similarly, the all-independent suspension is by helical springs and wishbones, front and rear, the latter incorporating the Chapman strut. Telescopic hydraulic dampers by Armstrong are employed, and 10-ins Girling disc brakes are used all round, with servo assistance, giving a swept area of 334 sq ins.

Power comes from the sturdy 4-cylinder, 2 ohc 1558 cc Lotus engine, which produces 118 bhp at 6250 rpm, with 9.5:1 compression ratio. Twin d/c type DCOE40 Webers are used, and ignition is by Lucas, a normal generator being fitted. A new gearbox, described as "semi-close ratio", is all-synchromesh and the latest Borg & Beck diaphragm clutch is used. Pressed steel, five-stud Lotus "knock-off" wheels are featured, with 165 x 13 ins radial-ply tyres.

The body is a one-piece reinforced glass-fibre unit, considerably wider than that of the two-seater Elan. Pneumatically operated retractable headlamps are installed, with rapid-action control for daylight flashing. Electrically controlled windows are standard on the exceptionally wide doors. A 13-gallon petrol tank gives a cruising range of something approaching 400 miles—a highly desirable feature.

The interior is tastefully carried out, with a full-width fascia of polished mahogany and complete instrumentation. A push-button, two-wave radio is a standard fitment, as are safety belts. Bucket front seats have been developed by Lotus competition experience and have generous fore-and-aft adjustment. The rear seats are as roomy as any contemporary 2+2, ideal for children, but accommodating two adults if necessary. Luggage space is adequate. Interior ventilation has been carefully studied and the Lotus airflow system, with its large sidevents, is extremely efficient. Heater, air horns, windscreen washers and safety glass all round are standard fittings.

On the road, the Elan Plus 2 at once impresses with the now-acknowledged superb roadholding which is a notable feature of the two-seater. The longer wheelbase seems to make no difference to the high cornering-power, and the absence of any pitching ought to make this machine an ideal fast tourer on the Continent. The car is noticeably quieter than previous Lotus models and, in spite of the necessarily increased weight as compared to the normal Elan, performance is remarkably good. We look forward to doing an extended road test of this new car, which is available on the home market at £1672 in kit form or £1923 including tax.

The Plus 2 breaks entirely new ground for the enterprising Lotus concern, and at once solves the problem of the family man who prefers something rather exclusive, with more than two seats. It is the result of many thousands of miles of rigorous testing, on what were known as the M20 prototypes.

SPECIFICATION

Car tested: Lotus Elan Plus 2, price £1923 including PT.
Engine: Four-cylinder, 2 ohc (chain-driven). 82.55 mm x 72.75 mm (1558 cc). 118 bhp at 6250 rpm. Compression ratio 9.5:1. Two twin-choke DCOE40 Weber carburetters. Lucas ignition. Four-branch Lotus exhaust manifolds.
Transmission: 4-speed all-synchromesh gearbox with central lever, ratios 10.92, 7.44, 5.18 and 3.7:1. Hypoid level final drive. Borg & Beck hydraulically operated diaphragm clutch. Hardy-Spicer prop shaft.
Suspension and brakes: Independent all-round suspension by wishbones and helical springs. Chapman strut at rear. Telescopic Armstrong dampers. Servo-assisted Girling 10-ins disc brakes. Trigger-type handbrake.
Equipment: Pneumatic retractable headlights. Electrically operated windows. Two-wave push-button radio. Safety belts. Airflow ventilation and heater (with booster). Windscreen washers, etc. 13-gallon petrol tank.
Dimensions: Overall length, 14 ft 1 in; height, 3 ft 11 ins; width, 5 ft. 6 ins; wheelbase, 8 ft 0 in; track (front), 4 ft 6 ins (rear), 4 ft 7 ins. Turning circle, 28 ft. Weight (unladen), 18¼ cwt.

Road Test: Lotus Elan Plus-Two

By John Blunsden

LET US PREFACE OUR REPORT ON THE LATEST AND LOVELIEST FROM LOTUS by making two relevant comments. First, the Elan Plus-Two is badly named, because if offers a whole lot more than simply a two-seater Elan with additional accommodation for two children. Second, there is no need to rush off to your nearest friendly Lotus dealer waving a bunch of hundred-dollar bills because he'll have no Plus-Twos in stock, nor any likelihood of any before well into '68. The Elan Plus-Two was conceived at a time when Nader was still having the swing-axles removed from his pedal car, and at the time of announcement in Britain it had not been looked at with a view to its conformity to the still-ambiguous GSA rulings. It is conceivable (but highly unlikely) that Lotus will choose to ignore the American market with this one. Our own prediction is that U.S. importers, once they've read of the car's performance and all-around salability, will pressure the factory into making the car comply. This, of course, will take time, hence our prediction of a mid-'68 initial delivery date. Meanwhile, it may be of little comfort to potential purchasers to learn that even in Britain — land of the female Minister of Transport, the seventy-mile-an-hour speed limit, and the high insurance premiums for sports cars — the entire Elan Plus-Two production for the remaining four months of 1967 was committed to orders received within five days of announcement. It's that sort of car.

The decision to go ahead with the development of a two-plus-two of the Elan was taken in late 1963, the design requirement being to use a lengthened, widened, and strengthened Elan backbone chassis

You can have the ultimate in road handling, and take the kids along for the ride

The Lotus Elan Plus-Two retains much of the similarity to its cousin, the Elan. Yet, the longer, wider appearance makes it a closer relative to a true GT, which seems the way to go.

Lotus Elan Plus-Two

Entrance to the Plus-Two, far left top, is made easier with wider doors. Bottom, rear seat gives more leg room than many. The pop-out headlights have to make it look ugly, at night only. Above, trunk space is enlarged. Right, there's extra power with Special Equipment twin-cam and Webers.

and to incorporate as many other common parts as possible.

Owing to the development of the Elan Coupe in 1964, the Plus-Two took second priority that year, but early in 1965 the first running prototype appeared, disguised by the nameplate 'Metier II'. At that point it was decided that the car in this form would offer too little, and so the decision was taken to increase the interior dimensions by five inches, and the overall width by 4½ inches. Styling changes were also ordered in the light of data obtained from a joint wind-tunnel exercise carried out with the Rover Car Company (notice the points of similarity between the Plus-Two and the Rover gas turbine car). The completely revised prototype duly appeared, and could have been productionized by the end of 1966, but the car was kept back for two reasons — the unexpectedly high demand for the two-seater Elan last year and the pending move to the completely new Lotus factory at Hethel, near Norwich, Norfolk. The wise decision was taken to hold back production until after the factory move. A side bonus from this decision, of course, was that a more extensive development program could be carried out on the prototype Plus-Twos, and certainly the first examples off the line at Hethel have gone together much better, and are much better finished than any previous Lotus product.

As an indication of this, the car we had for test carried the chassis number 0001 (and you can't get much earlier than that!), and had been on a month's solid testing immediately prior to our taking it over (we caught them on the wrong foot, crept in on a Lotus rally where the car was acting as a display piece, and whipped it away from them before they even had time to show it a grease gun!). We were told to expect the worst.

In fact the car was a good deal better than we might have expected, and the list of 'debits' was mighty small for a first car off the line, let alone one which had since been given the treatment by a load of heavy-footed journalists. It amounted to an inoperable passenger door interior handle, weak springs on the headlamps causing them to flutter in the raised position, too fierce a clutch (this is being changed), a poor handbrake, an inevitably rather loose and slightly clattery engine (the car had covered nearly 5,000 miles), and a few minor squeaks and rattles, mainly in the dashboard area and behind the rear seats.

The Elan Plus-Two looks, and is, much more of a car than the two-seater. The overall length has gone up twenty-three inches to 168, the wheelbase by twelve inches to eighty-four, the track by seven inches to fifty-four front and fifty-five rear, the width by ten inches to sixty-six, and the height by one inch to forty-seven. The technical specification remains very similar to that of the smaller Elan, although apart from the insertion of a twelve-inch section into the center part of the steel chassis backbone, and stiffening-up areas of high stress, some additional aid to rigidity is provided by a pair of channel-section steel rails bonded into the fiberglass body between the front and rear wheel arches. This way, the plastic body is able to make some contribution to overall torsional rigidity, and at the same time the occupants are offered some measure of protection in the event of an accident resulting in a sideways impact.

Apart from different wishbone lengths and appropriately different chassis mounts to produce the wider track without affecting the inclination of the spring units, the suspension is traditional Elan, although the extra weight of the Plus-Two (approximately four-hundred pounds) has meant increasing spring rates, the increase being rather greater at the front (75 to 110 pounds) than at the rear (67½ to 93 pounds). The increases of front and rear track have made slight alterations to roll centers, which almost exactly compensate for the greater wheelbase in its effect on roll axis, and with the Elan two-seater's almost equal front-rear weight distribution also maintained, it is not surprising to find the new car's basic handling characteristics very similar to that of the other Elans.

Such changes as have occurred are without exception for the better. It has been difficult enough for most people to find the limit of adhesion (at least on a dry road) of a two-seater Elan, but that's kids' stuff compared with doing so with this beauty. You just get in and steer it, and it's a fair prediction that on an average journey, involving no speed limits or other traffic, ninety percent of the back-offs will be because the driver has chickened out, not because they were necessary. We went through the whole gamut of cornering errors to try to get the car badly out of shape but failed. Over rough and wavy surfaces the suspension feels softer than on the two-seater, giving a more comfortable ride and a lower frequency of body movement. But even when the body movement gets out of phase with the next dip in the road, pulling the suspension on to full rebound or down on to the bump stops, those wheels still stick on the road like they were held there by magnets. Traction is so good with Dunlop SP radial-ply tires that it's virtually impossible to induce dry-road wheelspin, though you can easily get the rubber howling away in the turns. It could fairly be called the safest-handling production car in the world, yet there's a built-in danger aspect to that. Some drivers could well be tempted into cornering speeds which demand a higher-level of mental and physical reaction than they themselves can offer. The Elan Plus-Two may corner as true as a blade on a windmill, but the driver still has to turn the steering wheel the right amount at the right moment; therein lies this car's limit of performance.

The car is being marketed in Special Equipment form, which means it has the same 118-bhp version of the Ford twin-cam engine as fitted to the latest Lotus Cortinas (the extra power over the normal twin-cam comes from bigger exhaust valves, modified piston crowns, different jets in the twin 40 DCOE 18 Weber carbs, and a modified distributor).

The soon-to-be-changed heavy-acting clutch transmits through a four-speed, all-synchro gearbox with comparatively wide gear spacing, as used by Ford on its Corsair range (ratios 2.97, 2.01, 1.40, and 1.00 to one), and although our car had no distributor cut-out, which enabled us to see that the 1.6-liter twin-cam would rev smoothly to well over 7000 rpm, normally the ignition will cut at 6500 rpm, giving maxima of 39, 58, and 83 mph in the three lower gears with the 3.77 to 1 axle ratio. Our through-the-gears acceleration times used the 6500-rpm rev limit and gave us zero-to-thirty in 3.4 seconds, to fifty in 6.2, to sixty in 8.3, to eighty in 14.7, and one hundred in 25.0 times, which compare very closely with those obtainable from a two-seater with the close-ratio box which, like a higher final drive, is an optional item on the Plus-Two. We can quite believe the claim of a top speed of around 125 mph (considerably more than the two-seater) because 'our' car was still accelerating well at 115 mph when we ran short of straight road (even a Plus-Two refuses to take a fifty-mile-an-hour left-hander at 115-plus!).

The higher terminal speed, also the extremely low wind-noise level (you can drive at high speed with the electrically operated windows lowered without a lot of roar) speaks eloquently for the slippery body shape (drag coefficient 0.3). Lowering the compound-curvature door windows creates practically no cockpit draft, though with through-the-car ventilation you get plenty of fresh air with them both closed once the car is on the move.

The driving position is superb, with the fixed-backrest seats inclined at just the right angle for arms-out driving. A fairly high, top dashboard-line may be a slight embarassment to short drivers, but there is ample fore-and-aft seat adjustment. The rear-quarter roof panels inevitably provide small blind spots, but otherwise vision is pretty good all around. Even with the front seats well back, there is ample leg room for a couple of ten-year-olds behind, the limiting factor for a taller child probably being headroom. As at the front, the seats are divided by a central console passing through the car, above the chassis backbone. In the front compartment it conceals a slim map-tray among other things, and mates up with the now popular T-shaped dashboard, on which all the circular instruments are high-mounted. The entire surface of the dash is walnut veneer, with all the trim and padded areas finished in matt black to match the upholstery and carpets.

Luggage accommodation is reasonable in a carpeted trunk, and is due to be extended by bringing the spare wheel to a vertical position instead of lying below the trunk floor, where it currently shares a separate compartment with the tool kit. The engine hood-release arrangement is a vast improvement over that on the Elan two-seater, the lid swinging up on a support strap immediately the cockpit release is pulled. The front compartment is pretty full, but with the exception of the distributor and fuel pump hidden below the Webers, most items requiring routine attention are fairly easily accessible.

In Britain, the Elan Plus-Two is being marketed at approximately twenty percent above the price of the two-seater Coupe, but the extra price includes a good deal of additional equipment in the standard specification, including a radio. For the family man there can be no question which is the better buy, and even those without children may consider the extra looks, performance, and refinement of the larger car worthwhile. Potential buyers in the United States may have to exercise patience, but it will almost certainly be patience well rewarded. As we mentioned earlier, the first Plus-Twos have been coming off the line looking pretty good, but you can bet that six months from now they'll be a lot better still. Fundamentally this is a great car; it now needs a period of production development to give it that long-life-without-visible-or-audible-deterioration element which most of the older-established members of the motor industry manage to build into their prestige products. And if we were Colin Chapman, we'd start off with a memo 'To whom it may concern', reading: "Either take the surge-effect out of those drive-line doughnuts, or look for a suitable alternative...for ALL Elans!" ∎

LOTUS ELAN S/E

We've never driven a car that is more sheer fun to drive

COLIN CHAPMAN'S fame derives mainly from his racing Lotus designs but his production Elan is every bit as much a testimony to his genius as any of his successful racing cars. The basic design of the Elan is now five years old and though it has undergone the usual refinement it has had no fundamental changes during the time—and it is still one of the most advanced cars of our time.

On paper and in fact, the Elan does almost everything most of the world's car builders cannot quite do yet. It's a featherweight—1580 lb for this latest Special Equipment convertible—and yet it rides well, runs quietly, offers luxurious accommodation for two moderate-size people, and has a rigid body structure. It has an inline 4-cyl engine but is devoid of the usual vibration periods associated with them.

The basis for the Elan is a "backbone" steel frame with forks at each end for the mechanical masses. The frame weighs just 75 lb; a separate fiberglass body mounts to the frame at 14 points, and is a staunch structure on its own using steel reinforcements around the door jambs and windshield pillars.

For the powertrain, suspension and brakes Chapman has made the greatest possible use of components available from Ford of England and other suppliers. The engine is a Cosworth-designed derivation of the well known Ford 116E 4-cyl unit: it has a dohc head, a bore increase to give it 1558 cc and two Weber 40-mm dual-throat carburetors. The standard Elan engine produces 105 bhp @ 5500 rpm,

LOTUS ELAN S/E
AT A GLANCE

Price as tested	$5610
Engine	4 cyl inline, dohc, 1558 cc, 115 bhp
Curb weight, lb	1580
Top speed, mph	119
Acceleration, 0-¼ mi, sec	16.4
Average fuel consumption, mpg	24

Summary: Unique combination of performance, small size, roadholding and refinement ... some signs of temperament and assembly defects ... great fun to drive ... rather high price.

LOTUS ELAN S/E

compared with 78 bhp @ 5200 rpm for the 1500-cc Cortina GT; and all this gain is realized at no increase in noise level and a *decrease* in mechanical vibration! Our test car was the S/E version, which is further hotted up by means of greater valve lift, carburetor calibration and a smoother exhaust system to give 115 bhp @ 6000 rpm. The S/E package also includes stiffer rear shocks, a numerically lower final-drive ratio, power brakes, knockoff wheels, radial tires, trim items and inertia-reel seat belts; the package adds $540 to the $5070 base price of the Elan convertible.

The gearbox is also from Ford of England. Compared with the box in the standard Elan we tested in 1963, its ratios are spaced wider in the S/E to offset the 3.55:1 final drive's effect on low-speed performance (the 1963 car had a 3.9:1, but the standard car now has a 3.70). The final drive unit is a standard Ford differential in Lotus' own aluminum case, and although the gearset is from a car (the Cortina) with less torque we must say that the entire drivetrain lived through considerable abuse without any kind of deterioration in our test. Metalastic rubber couplings at each end of the halfshafts serve the U-joint function, as well as allowing the necessary small changes in halfshaft length.

Front suspension is by unequal-length A-arms and coil springs; steering is rack-and-pinion. Rear suspension is not so ordinary: it is Chapman's adaptation of the MacPherson-strut idea to the rear end and is called Chapman Strut. Wide-base A-arms combine with a sloping strut incorporating both shock and coil spring to provide the necessary loca-tion; the strut anchors to a high tower to provide generous suspension travel. There are no anti-roll bars in the suspension, and Chapman's race-car suspension philosophy—soft springing, good damping and precise geometry—prevails to combine a remarkable ride with equally remarkable roadholding.

Brakes are Girling solid discs all around, of 9.5-in. diameter at front and 10.0-in. at the rear. The rear brakes are mounted well inboard of the wheels for good cooling but are not categorically "inboard" because they're at the outer ends of the halfshafts. Wheels are 13-in. carrying 5.20- or 165-13 tires.

The sheer innocence of the Elan's appearance—especially when it is painted refrigerator white like our test car—can be most entertaining, for it's great fun to go storming off from traffic lights just to show those guys in the big-inch machinery how fast a little job like this can be. With proper use of the gearbox it is a strong-willed car; without it one can get bogged down at low engine speeds. Mechanically smooth though the engine is, it seems to be over-carbureted. There's a noticeable flat spot just as the throttle is opened up, and those flexible couplings mentioned earlier take the stumble and amplify it into a buck-bucking motion for the whole car. The idle gets erratic when the engine is warm.

In our acceleration tests the Elan needed several runs before its plugs were clean enough for the car to do its best. Once perking well, however, it beats our 1963 test car through the standing ¼ mile, and to 60 mph, by ½ second and puts on a solid 12 mph of extra top speed, all in spite

Top framework is ultra-simple but it goes up and down easily and occupies little space when folded; top is noisy at speed.

Hood opens without hinges; spring wasn't strong enough to keep it fully open on test car. Padded wheel is welcome.

Inertia-reel seat belts are part of the S/E package.

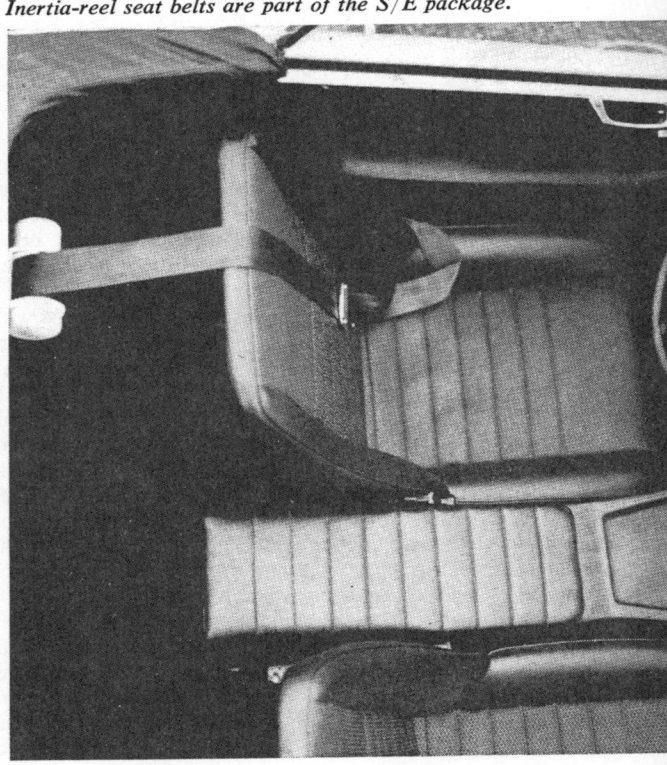

of an increase of 65 lb in weight. All things considered, however, the prospective buyer might be wise to try the standard version; the considerable low-speed temperament of the S/E may get on some drivers' nerves.

The Ford gearbox is quiet, its synchromesh infallible. Shift linkage is notchy, but throws are delightfully short and the lever is in exactly the right place. There is no gear whine and no noise from the final drive—remarkable for an aluminum case.

Steering and handling are above reproach. Fingertip efforts on the nice leather-rim wheel (S/E item) get one anywhere he wants to go, and the rack-and-pinion gear combines with the S/E's light weight and radial tires to provide what must be the present ultimate in light, precise control. Adequate spring travel and relatively soft spring rates allow the worst bumps to be taken with a trace of bump-steer but (unless the passengers are very heavy) no bottoming or bouncing off course. The absolute cornering power is as high as that of any road car we've driven; as with many light cars it's fairly easy to break the front tires loose by a quick twitch, but this is possible because of the light steering, not because of a lack of adhesion. Understeer, then, is the prevailing characteristic with the normal (18/22 psi) tire pressures if one gets overexuberant —but up to tire breakaway the Elan's response is pretty much neutral. On the other hand, there's usually plenty of torque available for snapping out the rear end. In all we've never driven a car that is more sheer fun to drive on a winding road—or around a leisurely city corner.

76

ROAD TEST
LOTUS ELAN S/E

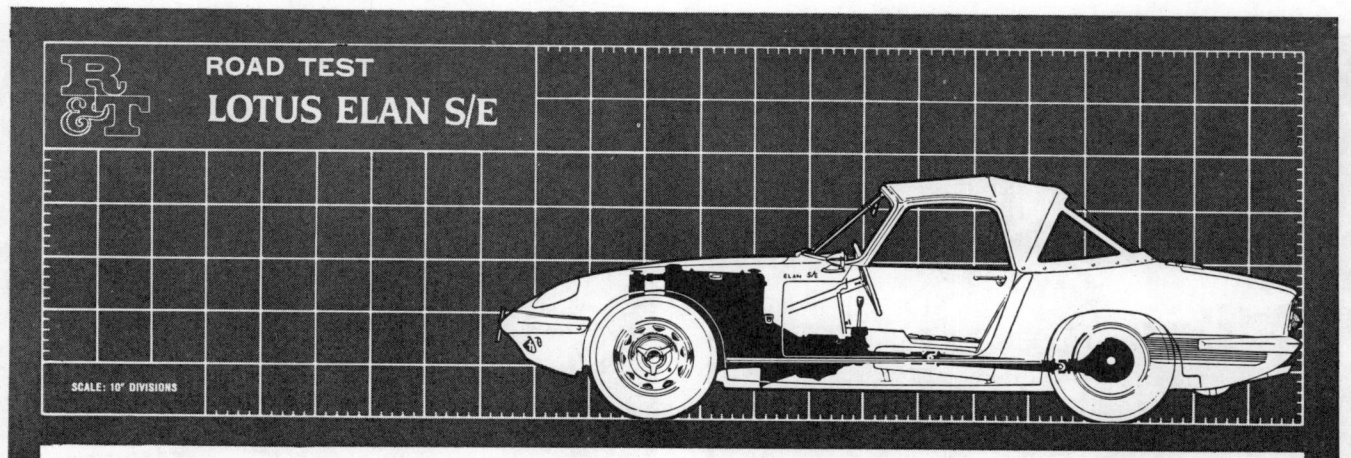

SCALE: 10" DIVISIONS

PRICE
Basic list.................$5610
As tested................$5610

ENGINE
Type...........4 cyl inline, dohc
Bore x stroke, mm.....82.6 x 72.8
Equivalent in........3.25 x 2.86
Displacement, cc/cu in..1558/95.2
Compression ratio...........9.5:1
Bhp @ rpm............115 @ 6000
Equivalent mph............106
Torque @ rpm, lb-ft..108 @ 4000
Equivalent mph............72
Carburetion..2 Weber 40 DCOE 18
Type fuel required.......premium

DRIVE TRAIN
Clutch diameter, in...........8.0
Gear ratios: 4th (1.00).....3.55:1
3rd (1.40)................5.11:1
2nd (2.01)................7.33:1
1st (2.97)................10.6:1
Synchromesh..............on all 4
Final drive ratio...........3.55:1
Optional ratio..............3.77:1

CHASSIS & BODY
Body/frame: steel backbone with separate fiberglass body.
Brake type: Girling disc; 9.5-in. front, 10.0-in. rear.
Swept area, sq in..........358
Wheels...steel knock-off, 13 x 4.5
Tires.......Dunlop SP41 145-13
Steering type......rack & pinion
Overall ratio.............n.a.
Turns, lock-to-lock........2.7
Turning circle, ft..........29.5
Front suspension: independent with unequal-length A-arms, coil springs, tube shocks.
Rear suspension: independent with lower A-arms, Chapman struts, coil springs, tube shocks.

OPTIONAL EQUIPMENT
Included in "as tested" price: none.
Other: radio, tonneau cover.

ACCOMMODATION
Seating capacity, persons........2
Seat width, front.......2 x 15.5
Head room, front...........39.0
Seat back adjustment, deg......0
Driver comfort rating (scale of 100):
Driver 69 in. tall............85
Driver 72 in. tall............55
Driver 75 in. tall............45

INSTRUMENTATION
Instruments: 140-mph speedometer, 8000-rpm tachometer, oil pressure, water temperature, fuel level.
Warning lights: directional signals, generator, handbrake.

MAINTENANCE
Crankcase capacity, qt........4.2
Change interval, mi.......3000
Filter change interval, mi.....6000
Chassis lube interval, mi.....1500
Tire pressures, psi.........18/22

MISCELLANEOUS
Body styles available: convertible as tested, coupe.
Warranty period, mo/mi...6/6000

GENERAL
Curb weight, lb............1580
Test weight.................1955
Weight distribution (with driver), front/rear, @....47/53
Wheelbase, in..............84.0
Track, front/rear......47.1/48.4
Overall length............145.0
Width.....................56.0
Height....................45.2
Frontal area, sq ft........14.1
Ground clearance, in.........6.0
Overhang, front/rear....26.9/34.1
Usable trunk space, cu ft....4.8
Fuel tank capacity, gal......12.0

CALCULATED DATA
Lb/hp (test wt)..............17.0
Mph/1000 rpm (4th gear)....18.0
Engine revs/mi (60 mph)....3330
Piston travel, ft/mi.........1590
Rpm @ 2500 ft/min.........5230
Equivalent mph............93
Cu ft/ton mi................91.1
R&T wear index.............52.9
Brake swept area sq in/ton...366

ROAD TEST RESULTS

ACCELERATION
Time to distance, sec:
0-100 ft...................3.8
0-250 ft...................5.9
0-500 ft...................9.0
0-750 ft..................11.4
0-1000 ft.................13.8
0-1320 ft (¼ mi)..........16.4
Speed at end of ¼ mi, mph....86

Time to speed, sec:
0-30 mph..................2.9
0-40 mph..................4.4
0-50 mph..................6.3
0-60 mph..................8.0
0-70 mph.................10.8
0-80 mph.................14.1
0-100 mph................27.3
Passing exposure time, sec:
To pass car going 50 mph....5.5

FUEL CONSUMPTION
Normal driving, mpg.......21-27
Cruising range, mi......250-325

SPEEDS IN GEARS
4th gear (6800 rpm), mph.....119
3rd (7000).................89
2nd (7000).................63
1st (7000).................42

BRAKES
Panic stop from 80 mph:
Deceleration, % g..........87
Control..............excellent
Fade test: percent of increase in pedal effort required to maintain 50%-g deceleration rate in six stops from 60 mph........none
Parking brake: hold 30% grade: no
Overall brake rating.....very good

SPEEDOMETER ERROR
30 mph indicated......actual 30.2
40 mph....................39.5
60 mph....................58.4
80 mph....................76.2
100 mph...................92.5
Odometer, 10.0 mi....actual 10.04

ACCELERATION & COASTING

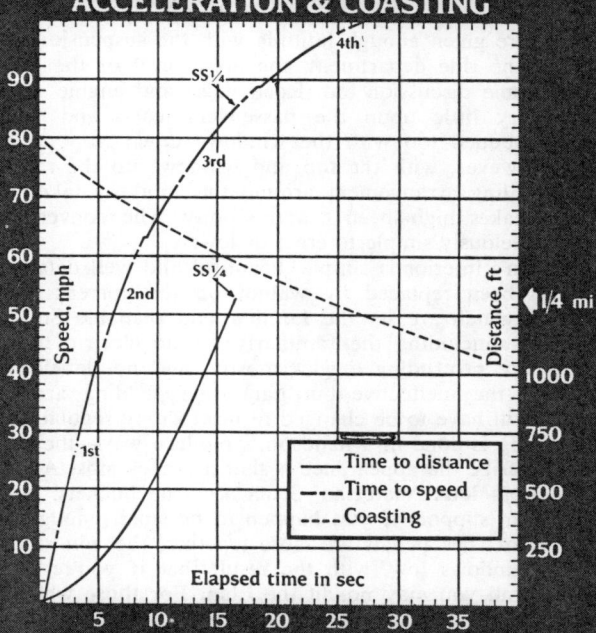

77

LOTUS ELAN S/E

Trim strip came loose when we cruised the Elan at 100 mph.

License location on fiberglass bumper needs improvement.

Though the S/E has stiffer rear shocks than the standard Elan—for straight-line stability at high speeds—its ride is still outstandingly soft for a sports car. In fact, it lends further credence to a growing belief among the R&T staff that car weight has little to do with ride, provided the designers are given enough latitude with the suspension.

Still in the ride department, the noise level of the Elan deserves some discussion too. Road noise and engine noise intrude very little upon the passengers' ears, and wind noise is subdued too with the windows down (top up or down). However, with the top and windows up the rather offhand sealing arrangement around the windows takes its toll and makes high-speed running noisy. The convertible top is marvelously simple to erect or lower.

The Elan's interior is simple, beautiful and well detailed. Teak has been replaced by walnut on the current Elan dash, into which are set the familiar and readable Smiths instruments (including the familiarly erratic electric tach). Switches are protruding toggles mostly, and not labeled—these, and the ineffective but handsome padding around the dash, will have to be changed to meet safety regulations. Upholstering is done in a handsome, modern way—the best way to describe the appearance is that it makes most American interiors look Victorian. Seats are true buckets, with much lateral support if you happen to be small enough to fit into them. The pedals are close together, the windshield and side windows low, with the result that if you're over 5 ft 9 in. tall you may not fit the Elan. For those who do fit, its excellent driving position and good ride more than make up for its lack of space around the pedals and it can be a supremely comfortable car. There is no seatback adjustment, but the seat track is both curved and sloping; nobody particularly missed being able to adjust the rake. Ventilation is good, but the heater is primitive.

Trunk space is a mere 4.8 cu ft, so if two people take a weekend trip they'd best plan on packing their stuff in "soft." The battery, on the left side of the trunk, should be partitioned off in view of this, but it isn't. Otherwise, trunk finish is as it should be for bare packing, with carpeting throughout; the spare tire and tool kit live below the trunk floor. Standard equipment in the trunk is a "touring kit" consisting of a shop manual and a supply of strategic spare parts—a wise item for a relatively rare car.

Which brings up the question of reliability. Our test car needed expert attention for tuning, and it had a curious electrical problem in that its headlights wouldn't stay lit for long if the engine were running at any speed above idle, and the trim strip between front bumper and upper nose came loose at 100 mph. Also, it had a warped front wheel and considerably out-of-round tires as delivered to us. From British reports we find that the tuning and electrical problems are common, and that the trim-strip fastening has been rectified. The Elan obviously isn't a car to "drive and forget," but then it doesn't appeal to the sort of person who just wants trouble-free transportation anyway.

In conclusion, the Elan still stands in a class by itself among sports cars. It's a unique combination of sheer guts, small size, roadholding and refinement—at a pretty stiff price, to be sure. It has the kind of behavior that can be enjoyed all the time, not just brute performance.

Supplement to Road Test No. 38/64 ● **Lotus Elan coupé SE**

Better than best

Turn the wheel softly . . . and the Elan goes where you wish, immediately.

Improved performance with no loss of economy, smoothness or flexibility

SUPERLATIVES are best avoided in road tests: they are too arbitrary and subjective and have a nasty habit of being made to look foolish by the passage of time. Nevertheless we are tempted to describe the Lotus Elan as the best all-round sports car—bar none—available today. There are other cars that can perform rather better (above about 70 m.p.h.) but they cost a lot more and generally need engines of three or more times the capacity of the Elan's to make them do so. On the other hand only one or two road-going cars that we have driven since the Elan was first introduced have as good handling characteristics or better roadholding—unless perhaps the Elan +2 or the Europa/47.

The Special Equipment version is the same as the ordinary Elan only more so: it succeeds in being better than best. The main advantages of the SE version compared with the standard model are the Special Equipment engine which develops 118 (net) b.h.p. at 6,250 r.p.m.—up by 3 b.h.p. since its introduction in January 1966—compared to the 105 b.h.p. at 6,000 r.p.m. of the standard engine, while maximum torque is up to 112 lb.ft. at 4,000 r.p.m. from the (standard) 108 lb.ft. Other differences which characterize the SE model are the fitment of the higher 3.55:1 final drive ratio (compared to 3.77:1 for the standard car), servo-assistance for the brakes, knock-on wheels, a leather-rimmed steering wheel and some other small improvements. At a basic cost in kit form of £1,486 the SE is £133 more than the standard car—the price went up £44 from the beginning of this year—and the new total is £1,830 including tax when bought assembled.

When 13 b.h.p. is added to the output of a 1½-litre engine which in standard form gives the Elan performance worthy of a 2½/3-litre unit—through light weight, low rolling resistance and a small drag factor—the improvement is likely to be significant rather than spectacular. In wet conditions, for example, and keeping to the 6,500 r.p.m. red-line limit (there is no centrifugal cut-out on SE engines) the standing start acceleration times all the way up to 100 m.p.h. were about a second quicker than those of the standard car we tested in September 1964. With an Elan we would normally be quite prepared to attempt a maximum speed run in excess of 120 m.p.h. on MIRA's track which is banked for a "hands off" 85 m.p.h. or so, but in the wet and slippery conditions which prevailed during our test session we chickened out. We therefore have no maximile or maximum speed figures to record, but would expect both to be slightly better than for the Elan +2, giving a maximum speed not far short of 125 m.p.h., when the engine would, of course, be over-revving to nearly 7,000 r.p.m.

But the significant feature of the SE engine is not so much the way it goes but how it goes—with an astonishing combination of flexibility, quietness and smoothness. It will pull cleanly from a little over 1,000 r.p.m. in top and accelerate rapidly and unobtrusively up to the 30 or 40 m.p.h. legal limits in built-up areas without turning policemen's heads or creating a boy-racer impression. When considering these virtues it is as well to remember that 118 b.h.p. from 1,558 c.c. means 76 b.h.p./litre—a specific output which few production engines can equal. Moreover, oil consumption was a moderate 300 or so miles per pint, despite the tendency for the engine to puff out smoke when changing gear, and the 25.1 m.p.g. overall fuel consumption was virtually the same as in our road test of the standard car.

Although the maximum speeds of 40, 58.5 and 84 m.p.h. (at 6,500 r.p.m.) are not quite as high as for our staff (standard) Elan which has the older-type close-ratio gearbox, the current "close-ratio Ford Corsair 2000E" gears are quite acceptable and the 3.55:1 final drive ratio allows effortless cruising at above 100

● ●

Summary of Motor Road Test No. 38/64 Lotus Elan

(open version)

Performance and economy
Performance little short of phenomenal, not only through the gears but for tractability and lack of temperament. Maximum speed 111.9 m.p.h. (soft-top car with 3.90:1 final drive); 0–50 m.p.h. 6.8s.; overall fuel consumption 25.5 m.p.g.

Transmission
Rubber doughnuts responsible for slight surging; clutch bites very quickly, almost too abruptly; little on which to fault transmission in noise or design.

Handling and brakes
Best of both worlds with sure-footed stability on all surfaces yet a ride comparable to better saloons. On fast corners handling neutral up to a limit which most people will never approach; always recoverable from quite high attitude angles with quick movements of high-geared steering.

Comfort and controls
Seat adjustment adequate for people up to 6 ft. 4 in.; rattle-free, draught-proof and waterproof hood; rather hot in summer with the hood up.

Fittings and furniture
Surprising capacity for luggage and oddments; easily cleaned interior.

PRICE: £1,486 in kit form plus £344 2s 4d purchase tax equals £1,830 2s 4d assembled.

79

Comf. accom. for two. Seat adjustment is ample for the tallest driver.

"... an astonishing combination of flexibility, quietness and smoothness..."

m.p.h. However, overdrive or a five-speed box—preferably the latter—would still benefit a car of this kind. On our test car the rubber-mounted anti-sizzle gearlever slipped round on its base several times for want of the right type of spanner to tighten the nut fully. And the kangaroo surging from the rubber drive shaft couplings can also be irritating if the rather sudden clutch is not released smoothly.

The Elan does not so much understeer or oversteer as just steer—you turn the wheel and round the corner she goes. It would be tedious to repeat the praise of Elan handling which we have written in the past (see road test No. 29/67 of the Elan +2) but it is worth relating that for our test of the SE model these virtues paid off in an unusual manner, for our period of tenure included the day in December when snow brought the South of England to a standstill for a few hours. Under these conditions the independent rear suspension and the flexibility of the engine at low r.p.m. made it easy to start off and change gear without wheelspin, while the general controllability allowed one to bowl along at 45 m.p.h. or more in perfect safety when other cars were creeping about at 20. For the same reasons, about a mile of snow-bound grass verge was negotiated to circumnavigate a traffic jam without any loss of traction—and more surprisingly, without grounding. But we were less enthusiastic about the servo brakes as they were rather non-progressive and there was some free play in the system.

Minor faults, such as a tendency to mist up (despite the extractor vents fitted to current cars); fresh air from the facia vents that was not very fresh; scattered controls—the wiper switch is on the far side of the gearlever; a very non-sporting pull-out hand brake; and feeble headlights do not prevent the Elan SE from being a very fine motorcar.

M

Performance

Performance tests carried out by *Motor's* staff at the Motor Industry Research Association proving ground, Lindley.

Test Data: World copyright reserved; no unauthorized reproduction in whole or in part.

Conditions
Weather: Wet, light wind.
(Temperature 42°–45°F. Barometer 29.1in. Hg.)
Surface: Wet concrete and tarmacadam.
Fuel: Super premium 101 octane (RM) 5-star rating.

Maximum speeds
		m.p.h.
Direct top gear		117.5
3rd gear	at 6,500 r.p.m.	84.0
2nd gear		58.5
1st gear		40.0

Acceleration times
m.p.h.	sec.
0–30	2.7
0–40	3.9
0–50	5.8
0–60	8.1
0–70	10.6
0–80	13.8
0–90	18.4
0–100	23.3

Standing quarter mile 16.1

	top sec.	3rd sec.
20–40	7.7	4.8
30–50	7.6	4.8
40–60	7.2	4.7
50–70	7.5	4.5
60–80	7.5	5.4
70–90	8.0	—
80–100	8.0	

Fuel consumption
Touring (consumption midway between 30 m.p.h. and maximum less 5% allowance for acceleration) .... 27.4 m.p.g.
Overall .... 25.1 m.p.g.
(=11.3 litres/100 km.)
Total test figure .... 1,021 miles
Tank capacity (maker's figure) ..... 10 gal.

M.P.H.	M.P.G.
30	63.3
40	46.5
50	44.7
60	40.2
70	29.8
80	27.1
90	25.3
100	22.7

Specification

Engine
Cylinders	4
Bore and stroke	82.55 mm. x 72.75 mm.
Cubic capacity	1,558 c.c.
Valves	Twin overhead camshaft
Compression ratio	9.5:1
Carburetters	Twin Weber 40 DCOE 18
Fuel pump	AC mechanical
Oil filter	full flow
Max. power (net)	118 b.h.p. at 6,250 r.p.m.
Max. torque (net)	112 lb.ft. at 4,000 r.p.m.

Transmission
Clutch	Borg and Beck s.d.p. diaphragm, 8 in.
Top gear (s/m)	1.0
3rd gear (s/m)	1.40
2nd gear (s/m)	2.01
1st gear (s/m)	2.97
Reverse	3.32
Final drive	3.55:1
M.p.h. at 1,000 r.p.m. in:—	
Top gear	18.1
3rd gear	12.9
2nd gear	9.0
1st gear	6.1

ELAN

Exhilarating, satisfying

OUR visit to Lotus would have been incomplete without an opportunity to reacquaint ourselves with the most successful Lotus road car yet, the Elan. I was offered the wheel of either a standard off-the-shelf car or of Lotus Sales Director Graham Arnold's personal and rather special Elan, and I chose the latter.

Graham's car is a Special Equipment coupé finished in non-standard black—even the normally yellow and green Lotus bonnet badge has a black background—and with red upholstery. At different times various tweaks have been applied to the engine, which is carefully balanced and now has steel rods, special cams and a power output of around 135 bhp. Other creature comforts included stereo tape recorder, expensive radio and Maserati horns.

The Elan layout, with its deep backbone forked at each end to carry engine and front and rear suspension, will be familiar to most readers. The rounded body shape of the Elan, with its pop-up headlights, is neat and pleasing, if not as attractive as either the Elite or the newer Elan Plus 2. From its introduction in October 1962—since when around 5500 have been built—the Elan has grown up considerably, both in detail design and finish, while retaining its basic specification unchanged. Latest cars boast features like airflow ventilation and electric windows, and the finish of the painted fibreglass body is very good. Kit form prices are £1353 for the standard coupé or drophead, and £1486 for the Special Equipment versions.

The Elan is a small car, but the narrow doors, with their lack of conventional window-winding mechanism, allow the simple but very comfortable seats to be reasonably wide, despite the bulky backbone. Of course the driving position is first class—one relaxes with the wheel at arm's length and all the controls within easy reach in their logical positions; instrumentation is comprehensive, and the pleasing 14 ins diameter wheel has a leather rim.

The unfamiliar driver is reminded as soon as he gets under way of the presence of Rotoflex couplings in the driveshafts, which can render lowspeed progress rather jerky until one is used to them, but a delicate touch on throttle and clutch sorts this out. In fact, all operations required in driving an Elan are delicate ones: the powerful servo-assisted brakes are very light, and a fine touch of the steering wheel is very necessary; and it seems one only has to lean lightly on the wheel—almost subconsciously, like leaning a motorcycle—to sweep through a fast curve.

With only 14 very smoothly shaped cwt to move around, the "cooking" (105 bhp) and normal SE (115 bhp) Elans are very brisk performers, and Graham Arnold's car, with a further 20 bhp over the SE, was tremendously quick. There was no opportunity to take any figures, nor to check the accuracy of the speedometer or rev-counter, but there was no doubt that the car certainly had an impressive performance. The engine seemed to want to go on and on revving, and the little car rocketed up to an indicated 70 in second and 100 in third with an almost disdainful effortlessness. The engine felt rather lumpy at low revs thanks to the special cams, but was still perfectly tractable, and once the revs began to build up it felt silky-smooth up to 7000 rpm.

The roadholding and handling of the Lotus Elan have become a standard by which others are judged, and the car is certainly very controllable and mighty forgiving. Even rushing into a sharp corner fast, piling on lock and brakes, fails to upset it; once the brakes are off and the foot is on the throttle, round it goes, understeering slightly but still completely controllable. Tweaking it into a tight hairpin, deliberately trying to provoke oversteer, still fails to produce fireworks; the tail will hang out a little, but the driver remains in complete command. The Chapman formula of very stiff chassis and fairly soft suspension works as well in the comfort department as it does in the roadholding, and for a sports car with a 7 ft wheelbase the Elan is amazingly free from pitching and bouncing.

More and more Elans are apparently being sold to professional people in their thirties and forties, showing that the car appeals not only because it is a fast sports car which is exhilarating and satisfying to drive fast, but also because as a dispassionate mode of transport it is conveniently fast and safe. Its unruffleable roadholding, controllability and feeling of undramatic safety make it a very good bet for long, hurried journeys on crowded roads of varying quality.

ROAD TEST by John Bolster

Plus roadholding, plus performance

THE Lotus Elan is a very special kind of sports car which is close to the ideal of many enthusiasts. Early examples were a bit basic, giving the driver and his passenger a pronounced vibromassage treatment through the seat of the pants at high cruising speeds. But gradually the little two-seater has become more refined, though it lacks passenger and luggage space.

The new Elan Plus 2 is wider and much longer, with occasional rear seats. It marks a considerable step forward in Colin Chapman's design technique, combining greatly improved looks with a phenomenally low drag coefficient. Though it is a real sports car, it provides practical transportation for a couple and their two children. The styling of the interior is most attractive, suggesting a luxurious GT with racing overtones.

In spite of the increased wheelbase and track, the chassis greatly resembles that of the smaller Elan. It has a central sheet-steel backbone upon which the glass-fibre body sits like a saddle. At the front there are wishbones, helical springs and telescopic dampers, with an anti-roll bar. The steering is by rack and pinion. Behind, Chapman struts are used with wide-based tubular wishbones, the rear brake discs being inboard of the bearing housings. Rubber doughnut universal joints are used at both ends of the driveshafts. The knock-on disc wheels carry radial ply tyres.

The engine is based on a five-bearing Ford cylinder block with a Lotus light-alloy head, the inclined valves being opened by two chain-driven overhead camshafts. Two large twin-choke horizontal Weber carburetters ensure that the cylinders are adequately filled. The engine is carried well forward and the Cortina four-speed gearbox has a short, central remote-control gearlever.

It goes without saying that the driving position is just right and the view excellent. The seats locate one as they should and the separate round instruments include such essentials as an oil pressure gauge and an ammeter. The headlights are normally retracted, but a control knob causes them to erect themselves. If the lights have been previously switched on, the headlamps are lit as they rise, but in daylight they come up flashing angrily, which is great fun.

The engine is much smoother and quieter than of yore and it is also astonishingly flexible. Compared with earlier Elans, this refined car is in a different class altogether. The increase in weight may add fractions of a second to the acceleration times, but the low wind resistance allows the speed to go on building up until the engine is running

ELAN PLUS 2

out of revs. There is no doubt, however, that a car of this calibre deserves a five-speed gearbox, for a geared-up fifth speed would make all the difference at high cruising speeds.

The suspension is exactly right, giving an absolutely level ride which is harder than that of the average saloon but fairly soft for a sports car. This Lotus is extremely easy to drive, with light, accurate steering, formidable roadholding, and a most forgiving nature—insurance companies should give special cheap premium rates for such a fundamentally safe car as this. The roadholding certainly is phenomenal, with no tricks to learn, and the cornering speed is prodigiously high. On wet roads, it is not so much the cornering speed which is notable as the complete controllability at the point of loss of adhesion. The message from the tyres comes through to the driver's hands, and steering round a corner is more a process of thought than a conscious physical action. The driver really does become a part of his car.

The brakes, with servo-assisted discs all round, are extremely powerful and very even, the front wheels locking first if the low pedal pressure is momentarily forgotten. The front discs are shrouded by the wheels but these are well pierced for ventilation, and the rear discs are out in the airstream. The parking brake, operated by an umbrella handle, is a poor thing.

At 120 mph the Plus 2 is just as easy to drive as at lower speeds, there being no tendency for the steering to become uncomfortably light, as happens with some other cars. It is, on the other hand, difficult at first to drive slowly with that perfect smoothness to which most of us aspire. This is due to the winding up and unwinding of the rubber universal joints, an effect which can be mitigated by careful throttle and clutch manipulation. At moderate speeds strong side winds have little effect, but nearer the maximum some deflection of the front of the car takes place.

There is a remarkable absence of road noise on all normal surfaces. The fresh air ventilators have a large capacity, their power and direction being easy to control, but the heater is not very potent. Curved side windows blend with the shape of the body and are raised and lowered electrically, a convenient arrangement which was very much appreciated. The spare wheel is carried beneath the floor of the luggage boot, which is of useful size though not particularly deep.

Of criticisms I have very few. I did have a little bother with the mounting of the final drive unit, but this was no doubt a fault applying to one particular car or the result of previous rough driving. The speedometer needle was unsteady and the rev counter was a shameless liar. Grant us better instruments, please, Mr Chapman, for these are unworthy of your superb car!

The Lotus Elan Plus 2 brings Lotus motoring to a much wider circle of prospective owners. For the man who wants a road car which handles exactly like a grand prix racer, this is the perfect answer.

SPECIFICATION AND PERFORMANCE DATA

Car tested: Lotus Elan Plus 2 two/four-seater coupé, price £2197 including PT.
Engine: Four cylinders, 82.55 mm x 72.7 mm (1558 cc). Inclined valves operated by twin chain-driven overhead camshafts. Compression ratio 9.5:1. 118 bhp at 6250 rpm. Two Weber twin-choke 40DCOE carburetters. Lucas coil and distributor
Transmission: Borg & Beck clutch. Four-speed all-synchromesh gearbox with central remote control, ratios 1.0, 1.4, 2.01 and 2.97:1. Hypoid final drive, ratio 3.77:1. Open half shafts with Rotoflex universal joints.
Chassis: Central sheet-steel backbone. Independent front suspension by wishbones, helical springs with telescopic dampers and torsional anti-roll bar. Rack and pinion steering. Independent rear suspension by lower wishbones and Chapman struts. Servo-assisted Girling disc brakes. Centre-locking ventilated disc wheels fitted 165-13 ins radial ply tyres.
Equipment: 12-volt lighting and starting. Speedometer. Rev counter. Ammeter. Oil pressure, water temperature and fuel gauges. Heating, demisting and ventilation system. Two-speed windscreen wipers and washers. Electrically operated windows. Flashing direction indicators. Reversing light. Cigar lighter. Radio (extra).
Dimensions: Wheelbase, 7 ft 11.75 ins. Track (front), 4 ft 6 ins; (rear) 4 ft 7 ins. Overall length, 14 ft 0.5 in. Width, 5 ft 3.5 ins. Weight, 17 cwt.
Performance: Maximum speed, 122 mph. Speeds in gears: third, 86 mph; second, 62 mph; first, 40 mph. Standing quarter-mile, 16.4 s. Acceleration: 0-30 mph, 3.2 s; 0-50 mph, 6.4 s; 0-60 mph, 8.4 s; 0-80 mph, 14.6 s; 0-100 mph, 24.2 s.
Fuel consumption: 25 to 31 mpg.

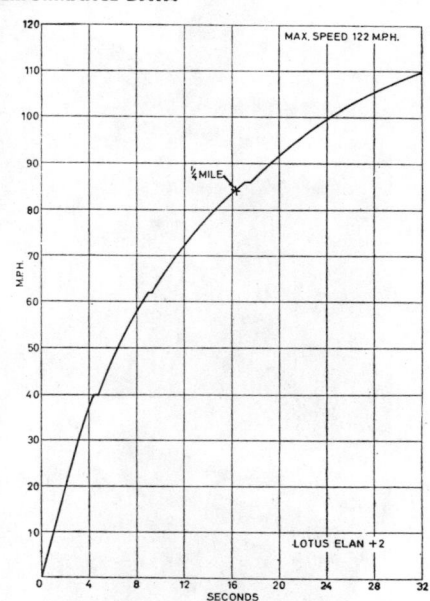

ELATION IS AN ELAN

The dictionary describes "elan" as vivacity and dash. Bill Tuckey decides the right word for the Lotus Elan is "nervous".

IF you drive a Lotus Elan long enough and fast enough you start to get some idea why Colin Chapman's Grand Prix cars have the reputation of being very fast but very nervous.

But "nervous" in its metaphorical sense. For the Elan is an aware, sensitive sort of car — not "nervous" like twitchy. The open-wheeler drivers will tell you that you drive any Lotus with fingertips and pants' seat; a Brabham you can chuck about a bit. The Elan is not for chucking about. But here, four years after our first test of an Elan, in April, 1964, we repeat what we said then: "You point it at a line and say Go There and it does. In an Elan, understeer and oversteer are dirty words."

This is the first test in Australia of a Special Equipment Elan, which Lotus Cars introduced in Britain midway through 1966. This car, an ochre yellow fixed head coupe, was imported by and is being raced by Wollongong (NSW) journalist-commentator Kevin Wolfe, who previously suffered the affliction of racing a Honda with some success. He is still a little stricken dumb by the transition from Sochiro's Song of ten-grand on the Seiko tach to the appetite for road distance that is built into every Elan, but he'll recover.

In Australia the SE costs $5290 against $4990 for the normal car. For the extra brass you get the Special Equipment engine, developing 118 bhp at 6250 rpm (up by 3 bhp since it first hit the market) instead of 105 bhp at 6000 rpm in the cooking version; similarly, torque is up to 112 lb/ft from 108. Other SE changes include the 3.55 to 1 final drive instead of the lower 3.77 in the

SPORTS CAR WORLD ROAD TEST

Doors are thickly padded with the handles recessed. The armrest makes for a very comfortable driving position. Air vent on the side of the turret is not just for show and provides a steady stream of air to the rear screen. Knock-on wheels are standard. Controls for electric windows are located on the dash and work well.

standard car, knock-on wheels instead of bolt-ons (although the knock-ons are an extra-cost option for the standard unit), servo assistance on the all-disc braking system and a smaller, leather rimmed steering wheel bearing the signature of Colin Chapman, which just HAS to up the resale value by dollars. Like all fixed-head Elan coupes, electric windows and extractor fresh air vents are standard. One other item of interest in the test car was that it sported one of the BRM-assembled twin-cam engines.

The engine tricks give the SE a specific output of 76 bhp per litre. This is astonishing for a normal non-cantankerous production engine. What was equally incredible was the fuel consumption — 26.5 mpg after a breathtakingly-fast run through hill and dale country with the speedo shooting from 80 to 100 and back again most of the time.

Elans have improved a lot in those four years. The first car — a soft-top roadster — had pronounced leapings-about from the rubber doughnuts used as drive shaft couplings, bad scuttle shake, odd creaks and groans from the glassfibre shell, and an unnerving graunch from the doors when they didn't quite hit the zero-torque locks on closing. The rubber coupling surge is still there, and you tend to cushion it a lot by hanging the clutch a little, which is not easy, for the clutch is fairly sharp in takeup. But the body is now very taut and quiet.

The history of the car can easily be traced, for Chapman hasn't been making road cars that long. His stark little Seven had begun to catch on and his sports-racing lightweights were really raking in the silverware when in his new factory at Cheshunt he started planning the Elite. It took a long time to get it into producion, but when it emerged, blinking, into the sunlight in 1957 the world saw one of the most beautiful and radical GT cars of all time.

The Elite died three years ago, but its impact remains. It was never a great success as a road car, for it was temperamental, hard to service, costly to repair and noisy to ride in. But the stressed monocoque body-chassis unit had a ridiculously low drag factor and hid a wildly-sophisticated suspension system of Chapman struts and wide-based equal length wishbones, plus the all-aluminium sohc FWE Climax of 1216 ccs and 85 bhp in its Special Equipment form (this also rated a ZF gearbox, but the last and hottest version was the Super 95, using Webers instead of SUs to give 95 bhp).

But near the end of the 50s Chapman formed up a proper design department which churned around some ideas for an Elite replacement, searching for something cheaper and better than the several-piece Elite moulding which, incidentally, formed the engine and suspension mountings in the same undertray moulding. They arrived at a one-piece glass-fibre shell, but to get enough stiffness Chapman came up with an X-shaped central steel backbone, with each end forking out

The boot lid has been changed and the rear styling altered slightly. New type muffler looks ugly and tends to scrape on the ground especially over gutters and rough roads so care is needed.

The bonnet is held on by a spring at the front and two clips at the rear and is easily removed for access to the engine. Distributor and master cylinders are hidden under the 40 mm Webers and the rather elaborate air cleaner system. The battery is mounted in the boot due to lack of space up front but is still very hard to check.

to carry the running gear. This was essentially a box girder form that took most of the loads, with the body being only partly stressed.

The Elan took a long time to draw, mainly because Lotus was trying to compromise between the expensive hand-built processes in the Elite and the cheaper production systems to be used in the Elan, for which a much larger build was planned. The wheelbase and overall length turned out shorter than the Elite's, and the body not as pretty — this mainly because the new overhead cam Ford engine was taller than the Climax. But the new engine, with the head conversion designed by Harry Mundy and gas flow work by the motor cycle firm of JAP, had real development potential. It also had an excellent Cortina gearbox that needed only some more sensible Lotus ratios.

They used pressed steel wishbones at the front with coil-damper units instead of the expensive but delightful Elite units, and A-arms and spring-damper units at rear because the driveshafts, unlike the Elite's, no longer acted as a locating medium because Chapman used Mini-Imp Metallastik doughnuts to replace splines.

The car was good right from the start, and reasonably trouble free. What's more, it could be sold in kit form to dodge British sales tax. Later modifications included stroking the engine to 1600 cc and in 1964 an S2 version with tidied-up dash and a few exterior changes. The SE followed in 1966 and last year the Plus Two, a bigger wider car built on the same principles.

The SE itself corrected a few of the minor malfunctions that appeared with the first S2 coupes — such as weak electric window mechanism and moving the window switches from the doors to the dash. It also sports a running change in all the Elans — the wider-ratio gearbox from the Ford Corsair 2000E.

And if ever a car deserved a five-speed gearbox, this is it. There's nothing wrong with the spacing of the ratios — 41, 59 and 81 mph are excellent figures, particularly with a smooth, flexible engine that will pull strongly from 1500 rpm — but there is so much sheer torque available everywhere that it seems a pity not to use it.

SPECIFICATIONS

PRICE:	$5290
OPTIONS:	nil
MAKE	Lotus Elan S/E
TEST MILEAGE:	183 miles

PERFORMANCE

Top speed (fastest run)	122 mph
Top speed (average)	120.4 mph
Speeds in gears:	Equivalent rpm
First	41 mph at 6750 rpm
Second	59 mph at 6750 rpm
Third	81 mph at 6750 rpm
Fourth	120 mph at 6750 rpm

ACCELERATION:
(through the gears)—

0-30 mph	3.6 secs
0-40 mph	4.5 secs
0-50 mph	6.6 secs
0-60 mph	8.7 secs
0-70 mph	12.2 secs
0-80 mph	15.2 secs
0-90 mph	20.3 secs
0-100 mph	25.0 secs

(in gears)	3rd gear	4th gear
30-50 mph	4.6 secs	7.8 secs
40-60 mph	5.2 secs	7.5 secs
50-70 mph	5.1 secs	7.2 secs
60-80 mph	4.2 secs	8.0 secs
70-90 mph		8.7 secs
80-100 mph		8.3 secs

Standing quarter mile:	
Fastest run	16.3 secs
Average of all runs	16.4 secs
Fuel consumption:	
Overall for test	26.5 mpg
Normal cruising	28-30 mpg

CALCULATED DATA

Mph per 1000 rpm in top gear	18.1 mph
Piston speed at max bhp	2930 ft/min
Power to weight ratio	174.7 bhp/ton

ENGINE:

Cylinders	four in line
Bore and stroke	82.55 mm by 72.75 mm
Cubic capacity	1558 cc
Compression ratio	9.5 to 1
Valves	twin overhead camshaft
Carburettors	twin Weber 40 DCOE 18
Power	118 bhp at 6250 rpm
Torque	112 lb/ft at 4000 rpm

TRANSMISSION:

Type	four-speed all syncro
Clutch	8 in. dia Borg and Beck s.d.p.
Overall ratios:	
1st	10.62
2nd	7.14
3rd	4.97
4th	3.55
Final drive	3.55 to 1

CHASSIS AND RUNNING GEAR:

Construction, backbone chassis, glass fibre mono body	
Suspension front	coils, wishbones, a/r bar
Suspension rear	A-arms, coil/damper struts
Shock absorbers	telescopic
Steering type	rack and pinion
Turns lock to lock	2.6
Turning circle	30 ft
Brakes (type)	disc/disc
Dimensions	9.5 in. dia/10 in. dia

DIMENSIONS:

Wheelbase	7 ft 0 in.
Track front	3 ft 11.1 in.
Track rear	4 ft 0.4 in.
Length	12 ft 1.3 in.
Width	4 ft 8 in.
Height	3 ft 9 in.
Fuel tank capacity	10 gals
Tyres (size)	5.20-13

The SE is a superb car; it's one of the finest open-road goers we've ever tried, and has so much to give the expert driver that every day becomes a new day for exploring its incredible levels of adhesion and superb braking. But it has the faults that one expects in a small-volume car — particularly a sports car — without the considerable fail-safe quality control exerted by a big maker. The interior ergonomics are of the casual sort — unlabelled switches for which you have to grope, a wiper switch hidden behind the gearlever, a choke feet away from the ignition switch . . . much of the switchgear (mainly the two steering column stalks) are still patently Triumph Herald. The horn is feeble and the double bonnet locks don't work properly, while the interior still mists up despite the extractor vents in the rear quarters.

The car was also poorly pre-delivered to Wolfe. There was no sign of the inertia-reel belts specified in the catalogue, there were loose bolts and nuts all over the engine, with a number of oil leaks, the window frame binding was unglued, and there were one or two small leaks. Also, the jack bundled the first time it was used; the standard equipment tools, incidentally, are three spanners, a cheap screwdriver, a small wrench, one plug spanner and a wheel nut hammer, all loose in a hessian sack. The boot hasn't got any larger, and still takes only soft luggage, although there is space behind the seats and a lockable glovebox, plus a small odds-and-ends tray on the central tunnel.

The test car was neatly trimmed in black, with well-fitted black woven carpet. A padded, quilted cover runs over the central tunnel, which acts as an arm rest. The door armrests are moulded along the full width of the door, with a small handle pointing downward from below the window sill. The seats are magnificent. Raked steeply backward, they have dimpled centres and high sides, and just lock the body into place. There is no reclining adjustment — but you don't need it for a moment. And even a 6 ft 6 in. driver has bags of leg and arm room behind that neat small wheel.

A short lever with a round knob (the S2 had a long, flat-topped knob) sprouts from the parcels tray near the foot of the dash. Some switches have pictorial labels, some not. There are two controls for the headlights — a knob which brings up the lights out of hiding, flashing for overtaking, and a toggle switch which brings in parkers (without changing the flasher trick) and then high beam. The lights are OK up to 90 mph, but not much chop over that. There are two-speed wipers, a two-speed heater fan for the good heater, a toggle switch for the three interior lights and the toggles for the electric windows (which seal very well, incidentally).

The tachometer (redlined from 6500 to 8000) and speedometer are quite steady apart from odd, seemingly unconnected oscillations now and then. The other dials are for fuel, oil pressure and water temperature. Under the bonnet there isn't much working room, and the distributor is still buried right under those big 40 DCOE 18 Webers, with the plugs equally buried in the well between the two cam covers, right where any moisture or condensation is sure to short them out. The battery is in the boot, and is damnably hard to check and fill.

But fire up this spectacular little car and all is forgiven. This great engine will do anything you ask and hauls hard right up to the 6750 rpm mark where the distributor cut-out came in, making everything go fluffy and causing a sharp attack of driver conscience. After a head-reeling, breath-catching, thunderous rush through mountain country, blasting up to 105 on every short straight, using 5000 to 6500 and nothing else, mashing down the speed with those wonderful discs, we pulled up the car at the edge of the road to check a funny thumping noise (it was a clumsy factory-made fibreglass air scoop for the differential; it had come loose) and we then realised that the engine was ticking over quietly at 700 rpm, 90 degrees steady on the temp gauge and 20 psi of oil pressure that went straight to 40 and stayed there when we moved off. And that never changed all the time we drove the car, even when cruising for mile after mile at a steady 100 mph.

For the tyro, an Elan would probably be quite frightening to drive. Strong winds upset it, and the relatively large suspension movements — which contribute to an excellent ride that is as good as most sports sedans — make the little car pitch and wallow a lot when the suspension gets caught out of step. The roll angles of the rear suspension can be felt working through the seat of the pants, and it takes a while to learn that, like a good horse, you don't use a hard pair of hands on the Elan. You drive it with a flick and a touch and a lean and a whisper and if you ever arrive at the point where you need opposite lock you are probably off the road.

The handling is neutral all the way up to the start of positive final oversteer, but that occurs at very rarified limits that should seldom be met on the public road. But fairly strong understeer can appear — and did appear on the Firestone radials we were using, which weren't very confident on braking — when the car arrives at a corner a little too quickly or you start braking late across the apex of a curve.

It needs — and likes — all the power you can put to it on exits from corners, and tends to get a little oopsy if you try tracking through on a trailing throttle — which only stupid and witless people do with cars anyway. The throttle is beautifully set up; not so sensitive nor so dead that you can't add or subtract exactly 200 rpm when you want to. The brake pedal is the same way; you can calculate to a pound the loading needed to produce the right result and mostly a little dab'll do ya. On the other hand the clutch is sharpish, but we found on our acceleration runs that a 5000 rpm take-off produced enough wheelspin for good early bite. Any less, and it bogged down and went away ugga-ugga with much windings up from the doughnuts. How they manage racing starts with sticky rubber I'll never know.

The gearbox is very fast and accurate, although it has a snicky sound and feel through the gate. If the clutch is not fully home it is easy to touch the edge of the gear as you go in, and it is sometimes hard to pull out of reverse.

But it's still my kind of car. For this car you would invent excuses to go Interstate for the weekend, to drive 600 miles at the drop of a spanner, to go see an old auntie in Bourke whom you haven't bothered about for 15 years. This car makes driving down to the corner shop an exciting adventure — and if any advertising copywriter pinches that we'll sue . . .   #

LOTUSE

Photos by Spencer Smith

NOBODY makes the perfect car. We might as well agree on that for a start. The motor machine which suits me down to the ground is something which would almost certainly fall short of *your* requirements by a large margin, because everyone is different and despite the efforts of a succession of governments (no politics, please) to produce a standard British adult, the nation as a whole has so far managed to resist it with success.

All of which has very little to do with the Elan Plus Two except to serve as an introduction to the mysterious fact that, although we must accept that no-one makes the perfect car, Colin Chapman and Lotus nearly always seem to come very close to it. Apart from matters of mere personal preference, the Elan Plus Two has its faults. The astonishing thing is that they are all such minor ones—this is a car which you have to think about hard before deciding what it is that you don't like, and if there is anything, it will probably turn out to be the colour. It is, we would have thought, an outstandingly handsome machine by any standards; compare it with what you like and it's still a very fast car—and who else could expect to get more than 120 miles an hour from a mere 1600 c.c.? It is well-equipped and has all the right sort of things inside and outside. Its handling and roadholding—well, that's another story. Both reach such a very high standard that it is something of a waste of time trying to find something to compare them with.

It must be hard for the people at Lotus to produce a new model, because they have continuously set such very high standards. The Elan Plus Two, the latest model so far as home production is concerned, lives up to all expectations and even manages to exceed some of them—particularly where cornering power is concerned. It also enters, or at least starts to enter, a slightly new field for the marque since, as our editorial bird put it, the Elan Plus Two is not a 'Vroom' car. It is quiet, comfortable and rather refined high-speed transport, and enables yer former Elan motorist to enjoy Lotusing even after he has produced his Standard British Family.

To make a Plus Two, you take an Elan, lengthen it by a couple of feet, widen it by nearly a foot, give it wider wheels and an extra pair of seats and move the retractable headlights from wings to bonnet. More or less. In doing so, you increase the overall weight to around 17 cwt. (not only by adding the seats—the chassis gets beefed up a bit, too) which means that acceleration from 0-60 in 9.4 secs. and a top whack of 123 m.p.h. are pretty remarkable achievements from the 118 b.h.p. and 1600 c.c. provided by the good old twin-cam engine.

Whether it's a 'Vroom' car or not, it is still more than capable of rubbing dust in the nose of the vast majority of four-wheeled vehicles one encounters on the roads, and what's more can do so with such a reserve in hand that the whole process can be enjoyed without risk or loss of dignity. If you don't believe us, hop into your whatitsname and try hanging onto an Elan Plus Two the next time you see one. Long straight or slow corners, you'll be wishing you had another litre under the bonnet before you've covered a mile. After two miles, you can stop worrying since it is unlikely that you will still be able to see the other chap . . .

The mechanical specification is basically the same as that of the Elan; it is, of course, a bigger car, and visibility is possibly not quite so good. To make up for the extra 3½ cwt. or so you have to lug around, all Elan Plus Twos are fitted as standard with the 118 b.h.p. special equipment version of the Lotus Twin-Cam engine, which is an optional fitting for the two-seater Elan. Briefly, this has redesigned pistons, larger exhaust valves, a different distributor, re-jetted Webers and a different camshaft profile. Compression ratio is 9.5 to 1 and maximum power is developed at 6,250 r.p.m., with maximum torque (112 lb. ft.) at four-six. This engine is coupled by a light diaphragm-spring clutch to the Corsair

ELAN +2 ROAD TEST

2000E gearbox, a 3·7 final drive giving 17·8 m.p.h. per 1,000 r.p.m. in top. Stopping is taken care of by 10 in. Girling discs all round, with a servo to take some of the push out of the pedal. Suspension is independent (coil-spring and wishbones) at both front and rear; standard equipment is 5½J wheels, compared with the 4½s fitted to the normal Elan.

Most cars that stick down on the road as well as this one have lost something when it comes to passenger comfort. Not so the Elan Plus Two. The suspension is, in accordance with Chapman trains of thought, relatively soft but extremely well-damped, so that there is no body roll, an almost complete absence of pitching and no nasty shocks to The Person. It is just about ideal, in fact: ploughed fields are probably different, but over widely varied terrain there was never any need to reduce speed because of surface deficiencies—you just keep your boot stuffed well in and the suspension takes care of the rest. At high speed—even up to maximum—the car runs as straight and true as an arrow, and you can take both hands off at 120 m.p.h. (in the line of duty) and if this gives your passenger a heart-attack there is absolutely no need for it. Opinions varied about the comfort of the fixed-back front seats. Of the four members of our staff who drove the car, two found them comfortable and two didn't, and the only points about which we all agreed were that there is ample adjustment (our six-footer, who is kept in a special box and only got out for such things) fore and aft and really good lateral location, provided by the hump of the backbone chassis. The back seats are really only suitable for kids on journeys of any length; we did manage to accommodate adults for short journeys but leg-room is very restricted if the front seats are well back and they all seemed to be heartily grateful that the journey was no longer. Having made something of a meal out of criticising the Elan on the point not too long ago, we were pleased to find plenty of room for the left foot other than on the clutch pedal.

Internal fixtures and fittings were up to scratch, with full instrumentation, all hand controls well placed and easily identified with minimum practice; we thought the finish, inside and outside, come to that, was extremely good. A major discomfort (seeing that it rained a lot during the test period) was a water leak which deposited a steady trickle on the driver's right shin; a major discomfort, but only a minor criticism since Lotus have assured us with their hands on their corporate heart that this was a defect on the individual car. A more important criticism was that relating to the handbrake, which was impressively, almost magnificently, ineffective—so much so that on two occasions the car set off on its own initiative down different house-drives while in the hands of separate drivers (we're not that daft) while when shown our test hills it merely laughed.

There is plenty of space for the assorted oddments that collect in the cockpit of any car and, as smokers, we appreciated the very good ventilation which is on 'Aeroflow' lines, with swivelling side vents. This has a useful and beneficial effect on visibility, although in rain and traffic conditions we were rather pleased to have a heated rear window. Side windows are, of course, electrically-operated, and when closed the Elan Plus Two is an extremely quiet car at high cruising speeds; unlike the Elan drophead, there is very little wind noise, and virtually no exhaust noise. If you simply sit in the car, it is merely a rather good-looking GT coupé, and to appreciate it to the full it is necessary to sample the Lotus way of life and drive the thing hard and fast. This is when it comes to life—on the open road, with a wide throttle opening. Driving in town, on small pedal movements, isn't difficult with the remarkably flexible engine but needs concentration and care with the pedals if you are not to be embarrassed and discomforted by the dreaded flexible-coupling surge, which requires a good deal of softly-softly work with both feet and if you get careless you feel remarkably like a learner-driver with a tankful of kangaroo-juice. It is not, in fact, the easiest car in the world to drive smoothly when travelling slowly.

Turn the wick up a bit, however, and it ceases to be a bother. If you want to, you can engage top gear at well under 30 and pull smoothly away, but this isn't really what Lotus motoring is all about. Traction at the driving end is outstanding, of course, and wheelspin requires phenomenal brutality even on wet surfaces. The acceleration is all the more remarkable because of the relative silence of the whole performance (it's not a 'Vroom' car, you see) and only the fast-approaching horizon gives you a clue about the 0-60 in 9·4, 0-90 in 20·8 acceleration you're getting. The engine is dead smooth all the way up, and previous examples we have driven from Lotus have been capable of producing their seven thousand in the gears any time you like. This particular car, however, was fitted with the dreaded cut-out which stops the heavy-footed from over-revving by simply putting the fire out at the point of safety. Unfortunately, these things aren't as precise as they might be and instead of doing its stuff at six-five, where the red mark is, it chimed in at only six-three to our great embarrassment when getting performance figures. In other words, good though our figures are, we would be the first to admit that they could be better. Speeds in the gears are 40, 60 and 85 m.p.h. and the change, as on all that range of Ford boxes, well-nigh faultless, with strong synchromesh on all four and a short, precise gearlever—a shade notchy on our very low-mileage example, but clearly capable of smoothing out with a few more miles under its belt.

Of course, with any Lotus you should expect high performance. You can also confidently assume that its roadholding will reach a very high standard—we did, but we still weren't quite prepared for the uncanny standards reached by this car. After all, the Elan sticks down better than most, but the Plus Two, with wider track and fatter tyres, does it so much better. So far as we could discover there is, to all practical intents and purposes, no limit to the cornering speed of the car although obviously duty demanded that we should keep on trying until we found one. The feeling is one of going round every bend at half speed—until you happen to peer at the speedo and find out different. In most cases, the driver will chicken out and back off long before he needs to, which argues a very wide margin of safety indeed.

Needless to say, we did manage to find a limit. This point is reached only at cornering speeds relative to the cornering radius which would be laughably suicidal on public roads, but even when we got to breakaway point it surprised us. With such high cornering power, a sudden departure into the nearest hedge before the driver even had time to realise he's gorn and lorst it seemed quite on the cards—but it didn't happen like that. All that does happen is a gentle and perfectly controllable tail slide, with nothing vicious about it at all. You simply apply opposite lock in the approved text-book fashion and whoops, you're back in a straight line again. So good is its cornering behaviour that we spent some time playing around and taking liberties (don't tell her husband, please). We chucked it into a bend at what, if there was any justice, should have been within *that* much of a spin into the background and braked hard. What happened, you ask with bated breath. You may well ask—the damn thing simply stopped, that's what happened, and prize bananas we all felt for expecting anything else. Then we tried getting the tail out and keeping it sideways, with very much less success. The car's adhesion was well up to that one, thank you, and even full boot didn't help. We came away with rather worn tyres, a frustrated look on our faces, and a strong feeling that this would be the most difficult car in the world to get into trouble with.

This sort of road behaviour, combined with the kind of performance you get from the Lotus, obviously makes for a very rapid covering of ground. On one particular journey of 40 miles we found it possible to maintain an average of over 60 m.p.h. without actually exceeding Castle's limit (honest, word of honour!) simply because it is so rarely necessary to drop below a steady 70. And when traffic forces you to do so, the lively acceleration gets you back up there before lesser cars have even thought about acceleration.

Despite using all the performance, with a pretty free hand with the gearlever, the fuel consumption is extremely good when you relate it to the sort of performance you've got on hand. We did get it down to 24 m.p.g., including performance testing: this covered some really hard driving, though, and we reckon a more representative figure for the average owner will be a lot nearer 30 m.p.g.

One could go on about the Elan Plus Two for ever—mostly in complimentary, very complimentary, vain. But as we said at the outset, it has its faults, none of them irremediable, but some very annoying on an expensive high-performance specialist car. For a start, there's that surge, wind-up—call it what you like: under any name it's damned annoying, and almost spoils the car for us. Then there's a very shallow boot, which probably has a respectable cubic capacity if you happen to be one of the people to whom cubic feet is capable of meaning anything in terms of space. But it is very shallow, and if you shove in a large suitcase you might not get the lid shut. Screen wipers— two-speed, naturally, but with only a very small difference in speed between fast and slow and with neither speed capable of clearing the screen properly in heavy rain or where there is much spray from traffic. Of the three snags, this one is possibly the greatest, since it effectively reduces your cruising speed by a colossal amount under such conditions.

Having had our beef, we must now say, in fairness, that Lotus have announced the S2 version of the car since our road-test, and although we have yet to drive the latest model it is to be hoped that it deals with at least most of our points of criticism. Whether they have or not, it remains to be said that in all general ways the Elan Plus Two does nothing but enhance the Lotus reputation for race-proved touring cars of high performance and impeccable road manners. Dear Santa . . .

SPECIFICATION AND PERFORMANCE DATA
LOTUS ELAN PLUS TWO

Engine: Four cylinders, 82·55 mm. x 72·7 mm.; 1,558 c.c.; com-ratio 9·5 to 1; twin 40 DCOE Webers; 118 b.h.p. at 6,250 r.p.m.

Transmission: Ford all-synchromesh gearbox; diaphragm-spring clutch; final drive ratio 3·77 to 1; 17·8 m.p.h./ 1,000 r.p.m.

Suspension: Independent front and rear by coil springs and wishbones (Chapman strut at rear). 165 x 13 tyres on 5½J wheels.

Brakes: Front and rear, Girling 10 in. discs, with vacuum servo assistance.

PERFORMANCE
Maximum speed: 123 m.p.h.
Mean of two ways: 123 m.p.h.

Speeds in gears—
First   40 m.p.h.
Second 60 m.p.h.
Third   85 m.p.h.

ACCELERATION
0-30   2·3 secs.
0-40   4·1 secs.
0-50   6·7 secs.
0-60   9·4 secs.
0-70   12·1 secs.
0-80   16·0 secs.
0-90   20·8 secs.

Manufacturers: Lotus Cars Ltd., Hethel, Norwich, Norfolk.
Price: component form, £1,718; fully-built, £2,197; extra for heated rear windscreen £19 3s. 4d.

USED CAR TEST

289: 1965 Lotus Elan

PERFORMANCE CHECK

(Figures in brackets are those of the original Road Test, published 21 August, 1964)

0 to 30 mph	4.8 sec	(3.3)
0 to 40 mph	6.3 sec	(4.7)
0 to 50 mph	8.0 sec	(6.6)
0 to 60 mph	10.5 sec	(8.7)
0 to 70 mph	13.9 sec	(11.5)
0 to 80 mph	17.4 sec	(15.1)
0 to 90 mph	23.4 sec	(20.4)
0 to 100 mph	28.6 sec	(26.8)

Standing ¼ mile **16.7** sec (16.4)

In top gear:

10 to 30 mph	sec	( )
20 to 40 mph	6.4 sec	(6.4)
30 to 50 mph	5.8 sec	(6.0)
40 to 60 mph	5.7 sec	(6.7)
50 to 70 mph	6.2 sec	(6.7)
60 to 80 mph	6.2 sec	(7.2)
70 to 90 mph	6.2 sec	(9.0)
80 to 100 mph	9.5 sec	(10.3)

Standing Km **31.1** sec (—)

PRICES

Car for sale at Edgware at	£895
Typical trade advertised price for same age and model in average condition	£850
Total cost of car when new (component form, less tax)	£1,179
Depreciation over 4 years	£284
Annual depreciation as proportion of cost new	10 per cent

DATA

Date first registered	27 August 1965
Number of owners	2
Tax expires	31 May 1969
M.O.T.	3 October 1969
Fuel consumption	28-32 m.p.g.
Oil consumption	Negligible
Mileometer reading	45,675

TYRES

Size: 145HR13, Dunlop SP Sport on all wheels. Approx. cost per replacement cover £7 6s 6d. Depth of original tread 9mm; remaining tread depth. 4mm all round.

TOOLS

Original kit largely complete, but no plug spanner; jack and wheel nut hammer with car. No handbook.

CAR FOR SALE AT:

London Sports Car Centre, Gemini House, Edgware, Middlesex. Tel: 01-952 0109.

EVEN in kit form, without purchase tax, the cheapest Lotus Elan available new costs £1,353, so there is good reason for taking a look at the used car market to see how prices are now and to compare the value offered by secondhand Elans. The one which we picked for test is a 1965 car with detachable hardtop and in very good all-round condition, particularly mechanically. The price asked is on the high side, but reflects the strong demand which apparently exists for good Elans.

We were at once impressed by the car's splendid performance, still up to the original Road Test standard in spite of more than 45,000 miles on the speedometer. Accelerating hard through the gears, 100 mph is reached from rest in 26.6 sec. This is almost identical with our original Road Test figure taken in the year before this car was made. At 90 mph, there is a wonderful surge of acceleration still in hand if the throttle is opened, accompanied by a purposeful exhaust roar. The engine has two twin-choke Weber carburettors and develops 105 bhp, giving a wonderful power-weight ratio. As well as still being in top tune, the engine uses very little oil, starts well and is easily able to give 30 mpg even when driven hard.

In driving snow and spray on M1 we had a lot of trouble with moisture causing tracking inside the distributor cap, occurring on any attempt to do more than about 60 mph. The distributor is terribly inaccessible, buried away beneath the carburettors, and is unprotected from spray coming past the side of the radiator. However, after thoroughly drying out and leaving the distributor open overnight, the trouble did not recur. Two small points which spoilt the pleasure of an otherwise excellent little sports car were excessive wind noise and a windscreen washer which ceased working during the test. With the amount of salt used on the roads today, an efficient washer is almost essential for such a low car. Wind noise is caused by the poor joint where the top of the hardtop meets the windscreen, and it is recommended that masking tape be used to make an effective seal on these early models.

Slight clutch judder occurs, particularly when reversing, and there is the characteristic Lotus snatch through the rubber-doughnut universal joints, noticeable occasionally under part-throttle acceleration at low speeds. The Ford gearbox remains extremely precise and quick to use, admirably suiting the car; the lever can be whipped through, the ratios are well spaced. Second gear gives well over 60 mph, and third can be held beyond 80 mph, actual maximum being 92. In top gear the maximum speed is simply a case of what the owner dares, as the

The bodywork is still in very good condition and unaffected by the blast of salt spray. We did find it very difficult to reach the distributor, which is buried under the bodies of the twin Webers. A clean interior marred by only a few inevitable scuff marks

rev counter is already in the red at 6,500 rpm before 110 mph is reached, yet the engine sounds still happy to rev much higher. The ignition governor did not seem to be working.

Beautifully accurate steering, and a good lock, remain much as with the model when new, except that a little more reaction seemed to be felt on rough surfaces. In a straight line at speed, the car feels a little "darty", as though tending to wander off course a bit, but the steering holds the car in check perfectly and there is little need to correct. The steering is also extremely light in spite of being high geared, and almost any other car at first seems rather dead and unresponsive after driving the Elan. Of course it is the fabulous cornering that really helps to make it the car it is, sitting down snugly and following exactly the line the driver chooses. It proved also an amusingly easy car to control on snow and ice.

At speed, the suspension swallows up undulations surprisingly well giving a very refined ride; but poor surfaces bring quite a lot of reaction, especially at low speeds, when the ride is quite lively and bumpy. The dampers remain very efficient.

Before taking the car away we were warned about the rather dead brakes of pre-servo Elans, but in fact reference to our earlier test, in which an Elan without servo gave a 0.96g stop with 95 lb pedal load, leads us to suspect that the brakes require attention. Heavy pedal loads are needed, and response is never as good as it should be. The handbrake, with umbrella-handle control concealed under the facia, is very effective, particularly in view of having disc brakes at the rear wheels.

Having corrosion-resistant glass fibre bodywork, and making extensive use of relatively inexpensive Ford components, a Lotus Elan should make a good choice for a used sports car. The example tried has lasted very well, and in addition to providing excitingly fast motoring, should prove economical to run.

CONDITION SUMMARY
Bodywork

Finished in bright red, the glass fibre bodywork is in very sound and undamaged condition, and cleans up very well (no more than a 10-minute job, incidentally, for such a small and smooth-shaped car). What little chrome there is has no rust, and the bumpers are plated glass fibre. Underbody examination showed a little rust on the metal parts of the structure and the exhaust system is in good shape. The black interior has reasonable marks of use—some kick marks on the side trim and a little wear on the carpets, underneath rubber mats. The white lining of the hardtop has become slightly discoloured by tobacco smoke. The polished wood facia is unmarked and still lends an air of quality to the interior. The hood, complete with quarter tonneau covers, is in the boot and in quite good condition.

Equipment

Only the screenwasher is not working; it became progressively less effective during the test until finally it would not work at all. Instruments and lighting are all in good condition, including the pop-up headlamps which still work efficiently and were not affected by a night of severe frost and thick layer of ice all over the car. Side windows tend to bow out at speed, and one of the locking catches has broken. The standard equipment heater works satisfactorily but is rather inadequate in very cold weather, even for such a small car. Teleflex inertia reel seat belts are fitted, as later became standard.

Accessories

A Motorola-type radio, with push buttons and Rootes label on the tuning dial, is included with the car. Occasionally it works well, but there is an intermittent fault and it is often "on strike".

About the Elan

THE LOTUS ELAN first shown in autumn 1962 was Type 26 in Colin Chapman's long list of designs but only the second true road car; it replaced the Elite and carried on in ever-growing production to this day. The original Elan was a two-seater tourer, with build-it-yourself hob, a separate steel chassis frame with strong backbone running between the seats and "tuning" fork extremities surrounding the engine and transmission. The glass fibre body was well equipped by any standards with reasonable accommodation and sensible boot.

Production did not begin until early 1963 by which time the 1,500 c.c. engine had been enlarged to 1,588 c.c. by enlarging the cylinder bore, and virtually no production cars with the 1,499 c.c. engine were sold; thus the original car became the Lotus Elan 1600.

Almost immediately the car became popular for production sports car racing and Lotus began to develop racing extras. The gear ratios were already ultra close (the box was also used in the Cortina-Lotus) but extras which may have found their way onto used Elans include special wheels, drive shafts, and—obviously—tuned engines.

After only a couple of years—Earls Court 1964—the Elan became the S2 with worthwhile improvements to the body. Restyled rear lamps and a full width "treewood" facia. A detachable hardtop which had become available on the Elan 1600 was continued. Only a year later the Tourer was supplemented by the Elan Coupé, which gave sleek good looks and remaining weatherproof to the sports car design together with electric window winding mechanism.

Only four months later, Lotus sprung another surprise when they released a special equipment version of Tourer and Coupé at the 1966 Racing Car Show. To the already fine basic specification a more powerful engine (115 bhp instead of 105 bhp), a higher gearing, servo-assisted brakes and knock-off wheels were offered.

In Summer 1966 came three changes when the S2 Tourer was replaced by the drop head coupé Elan. Really the Series 3 Elan was the coupé which was mechanically unchanged but used the basis of the coupé with a fold-away head, windows with frames all round, and electrically operated glasses.

Elan variants then stabilized until August 1968 when the Series 4 cars were announced. This included most of the now compulsory safety features for the US market plus 155-13in. SP Sport tyres (SPs were optional previously), rocker switches on the facia and detailed styling changes including squared-off wheel arch cut outs. At the time a twin Stromberg carburettered engine was standard only for the USA (as an anti-pollution measure) but this has now been standardized on Elans.

Testing the Lotus Elan +2

AN OPEN LETTER

SPORTS CAR WORLD ROAD TEST

Dear Pete and Leo:

IT was with great reluctance that we took your latest toy, the Lotus Elan +2, back to your sales boys last week, but you've got to admit we did get a helluva shine on that paint after having it covered in dust for a few days.

Y'know, this +2 has just got to be the best Elan ever, taking all into account. Being able to get another couple into the back for evenings out on the town really meant something. Each time we've had an Elan from you, we've been called "the stingy ones" by neighbors because we couldn't give anyone a lift into town.

This is an important point. If Elan owners are anything like us (when we're in one) we want to share the pleasure with everyone possible. Now, if you were going steady, the only person who can share the ride is your bird. If she's not hep to the virtues or vices of a car, then you've virtually wasted the ride. She may as well ride in the bus for all the kick she's going to get out of it. But what an ego-boost it is to take your middle-aged neighbor into the city with the early morning sun just starting to get warm and the peak hour traffic still a half hour away — meaning a nice, quick trip right through.

When we first took delivery of our test Elan +2, it looked an obviously bigger car. Once inside, it feels simply enormous. The car has spread in every direction of the compass, and is actually one foot longer, has a track seven in. wider which adds a whopping 10 in. to the body width. Our tape gave us a figure of exactly 23 in. extra length when you take the overhang into account. So we were right. It is simply a much bigger Elan than ever before.

However, fellas, you forgot to mention the extra weight, which adds up to around 3¾ cwt more than an Elan Coupe. And we ran figures, and ran figures, and ... well, we just HAD to call it a day because we were running out of fuel miles from any service station. But, yes, we should have checked the specifications BEFORE we set out, shouldn't we?

The suspension is independent all round with coils and wishbones at the front and a rear layout similar to the Elite with a single lower wishbone and a Chapman coil spring and damper strut. Those rubber universal joints were a source of worry, though. Lotus really should do something about them. It's virtually impossible to drive the car smoothly, which is cause for embarrassment for people who do try to give passengers the smoothest possible ride.

When you back off the throttle, the car lurches — while the same thing happens on gear changes and getting the car off the line. This is, of course, an inherent fault. We all know that. The rubber universal cushions are doing their job of damping the drive take-up to the rear wheels — but mightn't they be doing a far better job than is required? Which is a statement you can't put down to very many cars these days.

Like all Lotus products (you tell us which one you can't) you can drive the machine hard and drive it properly. No need to go pussy-footing it around the place wondering where the missile

By Thomas B. Floyd ● Photos by Gavin Shaw

The car could vaguely be called similar to this and not unlike that, but overall it is unmistakeably Lotus. Air vents extract air from behind side windows. Trunk is very spacious and well lined.

TO THE GEOGHEGANS

Power plant of the Lotus Elan +2 is the highly successful 1558 cc (95.1 ci) unit, producing 118 bhp at 6250 rpm, and 112 lb/ft at 4000 rpm. Accessibility is good and engine is quiet and willing — like all Lotus'.

Interior is very spacious, and rear seats will hold two small children comfortably for long journeys, or two adults for short hops. Steering is light, precise, and wheel twirls 2.7 turns lock to lock.

95

will aim itself next, or what will happen if an emergency arises. The Triumph Herald steering is light, most precise with slightly over 2.5 turns 1 to 1, and once you know where all the controls are and have gauged the extra width of the car properly, you can whip through traffic without any fuss and without even raising a damp forehead.

The only problem is that people look. Not only because you're driving an Elan +2 (half of 'em wouldn't know what sort of gear it was, anyway) but the car emits an exhaust note just a shade too sharp to be entirely comfortable around town. Run the rpm up a little over normal driving and the heads are beginning to swivel looking for the local Jochen Rindt (we may as well be right up in the times) playing with his new Lotus in the main street. Although the car sits well in a straight line and taking a series of corners is a breeze, a cross-wind will affect it. A gentle, wafting wind is easy to handle, but a gusty side-basher keeps you on your toes. This could be attributed to the excellent air penetration in the front as the Elite was prone to similar fads and fancies, too.

One thing everyone commented on was the ride. The too-good-to-be-true handling hasn't made the ride any worse. In fact the +2 is the best riding of the Elan group — but not quite up to the mark attained by the Europa. The mid-engined Lotus is going to be hard to beat in a lot of respects.

The new facia is nice. It's a mass of timber and the various instruments and switches are well laid out. It was too hot during our test to even attempt the heater business, but if it works as well as the fresh-air ventilation system with its variable-direction nozzles on each end of the facia, then you're certainly not going to freeze during winter in the +2. The electric windows are a labor saving device, work well and are "cool gear" for in-traffic poseurs. Besides, I suppose, it does away with finding an out of the way spot for the window winding crank on the door interior.

The pop-up headlights admittedly have aero-dynamic virtues, and work quite fast, however, if you're going to be doing some high-speed highway work, put the lights up before you start. They take just under 2.5 secs to raise and start flashing (of their own accord — and won't stop until you either lower them or turn on the headlights) which sums up to almost 200 yds at speeds over the ton. We have a "thing" about lights on the +2.

A roving Cooper with two law enforcement agents aboard gave us a defect for the number plate lights being out. We're only dropping this in Leo (Pete was horsing around in a Mustang somewhere when we picked the car up) so that when the boys in blue call on you to see if it's fixed, you can tell 'em we said we thought it was rather petty of them as the majority of drivers wouldn't check the number plate light in five years, and we figure they were peeved because we hosed them off at the three-lane traffic lights on top of Spit hill. Besides, isn't this something they could gain much goodwill from by issuing a warning in the interests of road safety?

The women's comment on the +2 was the "lovely color" — almost a royal blue — and the carefully-fitted upholstery and carpets. We had some moments of consternation when we thought the inertia reel seat belts weren't working. But the advice there is to strap them on and try a panic stop. Somehow, they only work properly when the whole car is smoking to a halt. Something to do with the balance weights or such jazz in the reel system — which is carefully hidden in the upholstery behind the front seats.

In all, you can't but help favor the +2. It's roomy, comfortable, quiet inside, and very easy to get in or out. All you need do is write a cheque for $5995, plus a $90 assembly charge, and it's yours for life.

Oh, one more thing, Messrs Geoghegan. One day we must sit down and have you teach us how to work that damned radio. Somehow we drove right past the Horsepower Hotel that Wednesday night trying to tune into the Great Race progress score. And that's something that's never happened before!   #

Specifications

MAKE	Lotus Elan + 2
ROAD TEST MILEAGE	160
PRICE	$5995 + $90 assembly
OPTIONS	Nil

Performance

SPEEDS IN GEARS		EQUIVALENT RPM
First	37 mph	6000 rpm
Second	57 mph	6000 rpm
Third	78 mph	6000 rpm
Fourth	105 mph	6000 rpm

ACCELERATION THROUGH THE GEARS

0-30 mph	3.9 secs
0-40 mph	5.6 secs
0-50 mph	7.4 secs
0-60 mph	9.1 secs
0-70 mph	12.8 secs

ACCELERATION IN GEARS

	2nd gear	3rd gear	4th gear
30-50 mph	3.2 secs		
40-60 mph	3.0 secs	5.3 secs	
50-70 mph		6.1 secs	7.8 secs
60-80 mph			8.5 secs

STANDING QUARTER MILE

Fastest run	16.4 secs
Average of all runs	16.5 secs

HARDIE FERODO TEST CIRCUIT (1⅛ mile)

Fastest lap	57 secs
Average of all laps	58 secs

ENGINE

Cylinders	4
Bore and stroke	82.55 mm x 72.7 mm
Cubic capacity	1558
Compression ratio	9.5:1
Valves	overhead
Carburettor/s	Weber
Power	118 bhp at 6250
Torque	112 lb/ft at 4000 revs

TRANSMISSION

Type	four speed semi close ratio
Clutch	single plate
Gear lever location	on floor
Overall ratios: 1st	2.97
2nd	2.01
3rd	1.40
4th	1.00
Final drive	3.77 to 1

CHASSIS AND RUNNING GEAR

Construction	steel backbone
Suspension front	independent
Suspension rear	independent
Shock absorbers	telescopic
Steering type	rack and pinion
Turns, lock to lock	2.7
Turning circle	28 ft
Brakes; type	disc, power assisted
Dimensions	10 in.

DIMENSIONS

Wheelbase	96 in.
Track front	54 in.
Track rear	55 in.
Fuel tank capacity	13 gls
Tyres; size	165 x 13
Ground clearance	6½ in.
Length	14 ft ¾ in.
Width	5 ft 6½ in.
Height	3 ft 11 in.
Make on test car	Firestone F100
Weight (kerb)	2086 lb

2000 Miles by ELAN +2

LOTUS.—Colin Chapman never would explain where the name Lotus originated. The Elan +2 is seen beside an advertisement for a useful French product on the way to Italy.

ALTHOUGH the Lotus Elan +2 has been in production for quite a time now, the opportunity to drive one had somehow been missed for too long, so a proposed visit to Turin and Modena was made the excuse for borrowing NAH 120F from Lotus Sales Director Graham Arnold. The Elan +2 follows the general plan of the Elan, having a back-bone chassis, all-independent suspension, twin-cam Lotus-Ford engine and fibreglass body. When the chubby-looking Lotus Elan appeared Colin Chapman said that Lotus had designed it as a "fun-machine", and he was absolutely right, as anyone who has driven an Elan will agree. The advent of the larger and more sophisticated Elan +2 was not heralded with any such statement for by this time Lotus were heading towards being respected motor manufacturers rather than "special" builders. Had Chapman made a statement to accompany the +2 it would have probably been to the effect that they had built a serious production car for serious motoring, rather than a "car for fun". From the styling of the body to the interior of the cockpit the Elan +2 is much more of a production motor car than a "kit-form car" as the Elan is. It retains all the desirable features of the Elan, such as lively acceleration, superb suspension characteristics, the ability to change direction suddenly, an absolute thirst for corners and a feeling of control that a lot of other makes could well try and emulate. Although the +2 is longer, wider and heavier than an Elan the difference in performance provided by the 1,600-c.c. twin-cam Lotus-Ford engine is not noticeable, although it is inferior to the Elan on twisty roads when the driver is enjoying driving. In return the +2 is a much more civilised car and I could almost visualise living in one, whereas the cramped and spartan cockpit of the ordinary Elan began to get irksome after a week at the wheel.

The car I borrowed had already covered 19,887 miles so it was well into the "used-car" category, but it gave very little feeling of this either in its manner of going or appearance, except for the Smiths fuel tank contents gauge and the radiator temperature gauge dying on me soon after arriving in France. Basically a standard Elan +2 it was being used as a pre-production test vehicle, having 5½J magnesium wheels, special seats with built-in head-rests, and experimental dust-shields on the rear suspension to keep road dirt off the rear brakes. Also, it was black in colour with a silver section to the rear of the doors as a styling experiment. Lotus thought the black and silver layout was a failure, but I received many favourable comments about it in Italy, while the magnesium wheels were admired everywhere. My instructions were fairly simple, "use 7,000 r.p.m. all you like to blow-off 'foreign rubbish', cruise at anything up to 6,700 r.p.m. in top, have fun and bring it back when you've finished with it".

After being spoilt by 4.2-litres of engine with enormous torque and a surplus of b.h.p. no matter what gear you are in or what r.p.m. the engine is doing, the buzzing little Lotus engine seemed all wrong and I had to learn a small-car technique all over again. You do not let the clutch in at 600 r.p.m., or rather, you can but you stall the

ALLOY.—The new alloy wheels in prototype form on the borrowed Elan +2 are to become standard equipment on the "S" model. Holes in the centre of the wheel locate on pins on the hub and the wheel is retained by a single tapered nut.

A LOTUS.—The shape of the Elan +2 is very distinctive and pleasing, the concealed headlamps presenting a smooth contour to the nose, even though they have their shortcomings.

engine. If you are not to be left behind in town traffic-races you must always be in the right gear with 3,500 or more on the tachometer. This was brought home forcibly when I tried a rolling-start drag-race with a Triumph Spitfire and got left behind, hiccoughing along with no torque available in third gear. In the E-type Jaguar such a situation would have been dealt with simply and easily by giving full throttle at 1,500 r.p.m. in third gear. It did not take long to get back into "fizzer-habits", stirring on the short stubby gear-lever all the time and keeping the twin-cam engine turning over rapidly. After the lolloping way the E-type makes sudden changes of direction, such as round a bus or taxi, the Elan +2 was a revelation, the steering being beautifully light, high-geared and responsive. Out on the open road the r.p.m. went up and up and 6,500 r.p.m. in top was child's play; unfortunately at 5,100 r.p.m. a serious wind buffeting round the windscreen began and the door window frames flapped horribly, so much so that after the novelty of keeping the car cruising at 6,500 r.p.m. had worn off, the buffeting became irksome and unless in a particular hurry I kept cruising to 5,000 r.p.m., around the 80-m.p.h. mark. The twin-cam engine is so smooth at maximum r.p.m., or near maximum, that you could drive it virtually flat-out on the *Autostrada* and you did not feel you were straining anything, but the smallness and lightness of the car did not make 100 m.p.h. continuous cruising a relaxed business. Once you have learned to enjoy the seven-league-boot stride of a big effortless engine in a great "iron" motor car, the apparent pandemonium in a small fibre-glass machine is hard to live with.

On the journey across France, mostly on minor roads avoiding trunk routes and big towns, the Elan +2 really came into its own and Lotus ownership began to grow on me, just as the original Elan had done on similar going. I could now see the whole point of Lotus motoring, as it wafted along in the 75-85-m.p.h. speed range on indifferent surfaces and round corners in a most delightful manner. You could sense the suspension working away keeping the wheels on the ground in a superb fashion, and the light steering was effortless to flick the car from lock-to-lock on slow or fast bends alike, and with two people on board and full luggage in the boot and behind the seats we had no bother with grounding. My passenger, who joined me on the *Autostrada* sections of the journey, was a bit anti-Lotus, refusing to take the car very seriously, especially bearing in mind its high cost, but after an hour or two of French-road motoring he became very appreciative of the real Lotus character, which is road-holding, ride and handling. It does not encourage sloppy driving, or lazy driving, for bad clutch foot work, or wrong r.p.m. can cause "wind-up" on the rubber doughnuts in the drive-shafts, and you surge back and forth as you accelerate. It likes to be driven precisely and keenly, and then it repays with a charm and character that can only be Lotus and you realise why Lotus have been Grand Prix champions for three years.

If you design and build anything that is different or good you will always find plenty of sceptics, most of whom have never even driven the car in question. When I was a Porsche owner I was always being told how bad they were, especially by people who had never driven one, or at best drove a very early and well-worn model. When I borrowed an Elan for a trip to Sicily the "dismal jimmies" all said it would fall apart. When I started my 100,000 miles of European motoring with the E-type Jaguar, they said I'd spend all my time picking up the bits that would fall off. Even in Modena anti-Lotus people said I'd never get back to England in an Elan +2. Fortunately the "dismal jimmies" have always been proved wrong and they were wrong again on my 2,000-mile trip to Italy and back, and what's more I enjoyed it.

After this trip I was able to evaluate the Elan +2 from my own personal viewpoint, which is principally that of long journeys about Europe, and living in a car. The latest seats with built-in head-rests I found comfortable and they fitted me ideally, so that I could relax back and rest my head on the long straights, but my passenger found he was the wrong proportions and the headrest was in the wrong place for him. The idea of building a head- or neck-rest as part of the seat is admirable, but to be of any use it must be made adjustable in a vertical plane. For the first few hours I found the seat itself comfortable, but after ten hours' non-stop driving I had seat pains, and in Europe driving from 9 a.m. to 7 p.m. is quite normal practice. The heating and ventilation of the cockpit was excellent, you could have hot air on your feet and legs from the heater and fresh air on your face and hands from the adjustable air vents on the instrument panel, a first-class arrangement. The electrically-operated windows were amazingly quiet and efficient, but I found them tiresome when I inadvertently got out and left a window open. With a normal mechanical winder it only takes a moment to open the door and shut the window. In the Elan +2 you have to reach across to the centre of the instrument panel to operate the electric switch and then you cannot see when the window is fully shut! If you have a tidy and orderly mind the situation never arises, you shut the windows before getting out! It is called an Elan +2 because there are two small seats behind the main ones, but even if you do not know anyone small enough to get in them it makes a very useful luggage compartment to supplement the luggage boot in the tail of the car. I give Lotus full marks for using one key for all the locks and the ignition, for some manufacturers go so far as to have three different keys, ignition, doors and luggage boot, a ridiculous arrangement. However, the boot handle on the Lotus is diminutive and caused annoyance, to say nothing of pains in finger and thumb every time I operated it. The boot itself is adequate in size but under the neat carpeting it seemed ironical to find plywood floor boards on a fibre-glass car. The spare wheel and tools live under these wooden floor boards and there is a lot of extra space that can be used for squashable items of luggage.

A special feature on the Elan and continued on the Elan +2 is that of the vacuum-operated "pop-up" headlights. This is something that I have never liked and will never learn to live with, especially motoring in Europe where light-flashing is used intelligently and not as a demonstration of bad-temper as in England. In daylight the Lotus lamps are folded away, presenting a smooth contour to the air-flow, all very admirable, and at night they hinge upwards operated by suction. A pull-out knob on the instrument panel causes them to rise, and if the main lighting switch is in the "off" position or "sidelamps" position the headlamps rise up flashing, and continue to flash until recessed again or the lights' switch is put to the "headlamp" position. In this position a normal dipping system is operated by a steering-column stalk. The lamps take just over one second to rise up, which is fine in the showroom, but quite useless at 100 m.p.h. when you see the lorry ahead of you start to wander out into the middle of the road, or

Continued on page 123

LOTUS ELEMENT.—The Elan +2 showed up extremely well on French by-ways, either on long rippled straights such as this one or in winding hill-country.

SCG ROAD TEST

"LOTUS — THE WORLD CHAMPION CAR — AGAIN." That's what it says on the rear window sticker, which is semi-transparent so you can read it correctly in the rear view mirror. "Lotus World Constructor's Champions (F1) 1963, 1965, 1968." Let me tell you: anyone who drives a Lotus knows that, and knows what Formula One means, and knows that Colin Chapman may be the foremost race-car designer in the world, and they're damn proud of the heritage. They'd better be, because they're paying for a large share of that heritage. Maybe a couple of thousand dollars worth.

Colin Chapman is a brilliant automotive engineer. He has enough imagination to stay ahead in the game, and enough restraint to keep from progressing overboard with a plethora of radical innovations than can shackle a designer into man-years of development. Mr. Chapman *is* the designer, we might emphasize, and not just a talented managerial wizard who has a lot of outstanding engineers working for him. As a matter of fact, after spending a week with his latest production Lotus, the Elan +2, we suspect that he'd better try to hire some outstanding engineers to handle detail work before this car makes him look like an engineer with a "loco-motive." Worse yet, there's always the chance that a non-technically oriented person might not appreciate the inspired, race-bred concept of the Elan, and suspect that the Championships were won by the *drivers* of Lotuses.

The concept of this car is excellent, but the execution... well, it doesn't need an execution because it slowly committed suicide, if you can call daily failures slow.

The most outstanding feature of the car is probably the frame/body structure, partly because it is so difficult to tell where one ends and the other begins. What you might call the "frame" is a sheet metal structure running down the center of the car branching out at front and rear to meet the suspension components and provide rigid points on which to hang the engine and differential. By itself, however, it probably doesn't have enough strength to support its own weight, much less contribute to vehicle torsional stiffness, so it is firmly fastened to a truly monocoque, all-fiberglass body shell which produces a surprisingly light and rigid structure. Lotus can do this because of its low volume (and high price), but as manufacturing techniques improve and costs come down, we get closer to the day when *all* auto structures will be made of a plastic of some sort.

The early production model we drove was actually a couple of hundred pounds lighter than the owner's manual claimed, but when we saw the hood buckle inward from the weight of L.A. smog, it appeared that more fiberglass was going to be needed. The surface finish was excellent, though, considering that it must have been painted in latex to keep from cracking with all the panel-flexing at various pressure points. But from a styling standpoint it's a real show-stopper, looking like it really belongs to that six-grand price tag. Until a two-cent hinge pin worked its way out of the trunk lid.

LOTUSLAND REVISITED
The Lotus Elan +2: A thing of beauty is a joy, however...

PHOTOS/PAT BROLLIER, GERRY STILES

The interior of the car was superb — in the beginning. Seating position, seat structure and steering wheel are right out of a real honest-to-gosh racing GT, and for being so low, it was quite easy to swing in and out of because of the super-long door and monocoque body with its beam in the middle, not in the rocker panels. All told, everything is real comfy — up front — while the "+2" seats are no more than you could expect in such a low, sleek machine. (Federal Transportation Law No. 3,492,821: No child over 4'10" in height shall be forced to ride in the back seat of a "+2" designated automobile.)

Once we got under way, all was roses until (Oh, no! Get me a line to England!) we discovered we had another corrugated windshield. The last was on the new Triumph GT-6+ and we'll hazard a guess that they both use the same supplier. This time, however, we knew the proper corrective measures. Take a large bottle of red-eye, empty it as fast as possible, and park in front of a large, flashing neon sign. Don't drive it, just sit there and enjoy the out-of-sync psychedelia through the windshield.

Oh yes. You can add to the effect by trying to listen to the $200 Pye AM/FM radio. After we found the knobs and screwed them back on, we discovered why American sound systems are so popular. You can take this Pye and shove it in your eye.

Now that we're red-eyed and Pye-eyed, let's try driving again. The clutch deserves some practice to avoid chatter on startup, and you need a good ear for shifts to avoid ugly lunges between gears. In reverse — resign yourself — the clutch would chatter if Colin himself tried to engage it in ballet slippers. Speaking of slippers, if you're a full-size man with full-size feet in full-size shoes, you're going to find that you don't have to heel-and-toe. No sir, in this car the pedals are so close together that you can *toe*-and-toe. In more than one exciting instance we got a neutral response to our braking efforts because the right foot was still partly on the accelerator. With a little practice sharpening your aim — and your shoe soles — you can hit them individually, and *then* you can start having fun.

Ever wonder what it would be like to ride in a slot car? Buy a Lotus. A lot of cars have quick steering, are nimble and very responsive, but in this car it is simply a joy to turn a corner. You out there... yes, you! How would you like to be the Graham Hill of Mountain View Drive? Your heaviest work made light, your twistiest road made straight, your Porcha-driving neighbor made late. Good old Colin does it again. He takes the same materials, the same basic components, and the same tires, blesses the mess, and produces a car that breathes. Being light helps a lot — it's one of the lightest sports cars we've tested — but there has to be more than that to superb handling. In normal quick driving, we got the feeling that brakes were unnecessary — that you could avoid any hazard by being able to go around it, over it, or under it without losing control.

But brakes it has, and they are faultless. For some odd reason the split hydraulic system has a separate vacuum booster for each circuit, but whatever Lotus did, they did right. The brakes stop the car quickly, stably, and repeatedly without a hint of fade, not even stinking. Perhaps having 4-wheel discs with swept area equal to a Detroit car twice its weight has something to do with it. Our electronic recorder showed a best stop of 0.9 g, second only to Citroen so far, and exactly what the Lotus manual predicted.

99

LOTUSLAND REVISITED

They were also pretty close on the lateral acceleration capability, claiming 0.8 g, while we got 0.80 g in a right turn and 0.82 g to the left, with the car being exceptionally stable yet controllable — a fact that had already been manifested in its street manners.

We now return you to the sad facts of reliability. As a general check on a test car's condition of tune, we usually give it a run on an Autoscan chassis dyno in the neighborhood, this time, fortunately, relying on the Humble Car Care Center in Encino, California. Well, sir, the car ran like a bear, producing 95 of its advertised 118 horsepower at the road, with only a slight spark-plug breakup. However . . . probably due to the lack of cooling air . . . one small part overheated. The clutch slave-cylinder hydraulic line runs near the exhaust pipe, and when we tried to drive away —spish— it melted like a piece of licorice and sprayed its life blood all over the ground. Frantic calls revealed that a replacement part might be hibernating in Frisco, but hours and the presses roll on, so the proud Humble mechanics grafted in a piece of brake hose which may still be there today.

During this encounter another conundrum struck us, to wit: If a car like this fails on the road, how do you get it to civilization? Both bumpers are bolted to the fiberglass body, which probably wouldn't take the tow load if you hooked onto them, which you can't, because they are flush with the body. The closest anchor points are the lower control arms, but you aren't going to wrap a chain around those flimsy things on a car *I* drive. Know anyone with a trailer?

We could have used one again the next night when the power windows failed. That alone wasn't so bad, since the ventilation system is passable with the windows all up, but before long we were able to catch the eye of a policeman who wanted to know why the taillights didn't work and who the car was stolen from. After a warm discussion on Lotuses he offered his flashlight to help look for the fuse box which could only be found on the schematic — along with a wiring diagram on the anti-theft switch which we never *did* find. It *was* a fuse and we got everything working again, but not before analyzing all the wires that fell out where the kick panel got tired and sagged. A short in there might have caused the trouble in the first place. And the upholstery might not have sagged if it weren't for a vibration at freeway speeds that rattled the dash and even managed to cause the one-piece body to squeak.

The acceleration runs weren't all that impressive at 16.9 seconds and 82.6 mph in the quarter — until you realize that this car has about the same displacement as a Volkswagen and might be able to get the same gas mileage. Our car got an average over 28 mpg, which is damn good considering the amount of revs needed to keep it going at low speeds where its torque isn't. At that, a person could afford to go to the optional 3.77 rear axle and close-ratio box and get even better acceleration at a negligible cost in fuel.

One other possible cause for good mileage could be the very smooth body, which we found to have a total of 95 pounds of drag at freeway speed, including rolling friction. Since this is the first car we have made aerodynamic measurements on, we have nothing in its class to compare it to, but keep tuned. Aerodynamic lift seems to be negligible also, but remember, with driver the car still weighs about 2000 pounds, and 100 pounds lift at the front reduces cornering power by ten percent.

All considered, the Elan +2 is an excellently designed and engineered car, but the bugs we shook out of our "early production" version shouldn't have happened to a prototype, and we can't really say that more care is built into the 50th or the 500th car. Only your dollar vote will convince manufacturers not to adopt the "Stingray Strategy" of making a car in quantities just smaller than demand, so that every one is guaranteed sold — and to hell with quality.

Lotus isn't that bad — yet. As a matter of fact, as long as you keep all the pieces on (whoops, we just discovered some broken lines in the engine room — apparently part of the smog control device) . . . as long as you keep all the pieces on, it's a pleasure to drive just for the sake of driving, and you can be as proud of it as a fine precision camera or watch. But you'd better remember to treat it as such. The "Master" seems to have designed it right to the hairline, and if you *cross* that line, every piece will probably go at once. One man's million-dollar reputation rides on every Lotus, and if you can drive one without knowing who the guy is that signed the pretty, leather steering wheel, you deserve to have problems.

LOTUS ELAN +2

PRICE
- Base .... $5995 (POE West Coast)
- As tested $6195
- Options .... AM/FM radio

ENGINE
- Type .... In-line 4, water cooled, iron block, aluminum head
- Displacement .... 95.1 cu. in. (1558 cc)
- Horsepower .... 118 hp at 5800 rpm
- Torque .... 108 lbs./ft. @ 4000 rpm
- Bore & stroke .... 3.24 in. x 2.86 in. (82.5 mm x 72.7 mm)
- Compression ratio .... 9.5 to 1
- Valve actuation .... Dual ohc
- Induction system .. Two 175 CD-2 Strombergs
- Exhaust system ... Cast iron headers, 4 into 2
- Electrical system .... 12 volt gen., point distributor
- Fuel .... Premium
- Recommended redline .... 6500 rpm

DRIVE TRAIN
- Clutch .... Dry disc, hydraulic
- Transmission   Gear Ratio   Overall Ratio
  - 1st Synchro ..... 2.97 .... 10.54
  - 2nd Synchro ..... 2.01 .... 7.14
  - 3rd Synchro ..... 1.40 .... 4.97
  - 4th Synchro ..... 1.00 .... 3.55
- Differential .... Hypoid, 3.55

CHASSIS
- Frame .... Steel backbone, front engine, rear drive
- Front suspension ...... Unequal A-arms, coil springs, anti-roll bar, tube shocks
- Rear suspension .... Lower control arm, upper Chapman strut with coil springs, tube shocks
- Steering .... Rack and pinion, 2.75 turns, turning circle 28 feet
- Brakes .... Split hydraulic, power assist, 10-in. discs front and rear, swept area 362 sq. in.
- Wheels .... Steel disc, 13-in. dia., 5½-in. wide
- Tires .... Dunlop Sports Radials, 165 HR 13, pressures F/R — 22/22 (rec.) 30/30 (test)

BODY
- Type ..... Fiberglass, 2 door, 2+2 passenger
- Seats .... Front buckets — adjustable, rear bench
- Windows .... 2 power, no vents
- Luggage space .... Rear trunk, 9.5 cu. ft.
- Instruments ..... 140 mph speedo, 8000 rpm tach, oil, amp, temp, fuel gauges — hazard, park, brake fail, demister indicator lights

WEIGHTS AND MEASURES
- Weight .... 1870 lbs. (curb), 2110 lbs. (test)
- Distribution F/R 48%/52%
- Wheelbase .... 96 in.
- Track F/R .... 54 in./55 in.
- Height .... 47 in.
- Width .... 66.2 in.
- Length .... 168.7 in.
- Ground clearance .... 6.5 in.
- Oil capacity .... 4.5 qt.
- Fuel capacity .... 15.6 gal.
- Coolant capacity .... 8.4 qt.

MISCELLANEOUS
- Weight/power ratio (curb/advertised) ... 15.0 (test/dyno) 22.2
- Advertised hp/cu. in. 1.24
- Speed per 1000 rpm (top gear) .... 19.2 mph
- Warranty .... 6 mos.

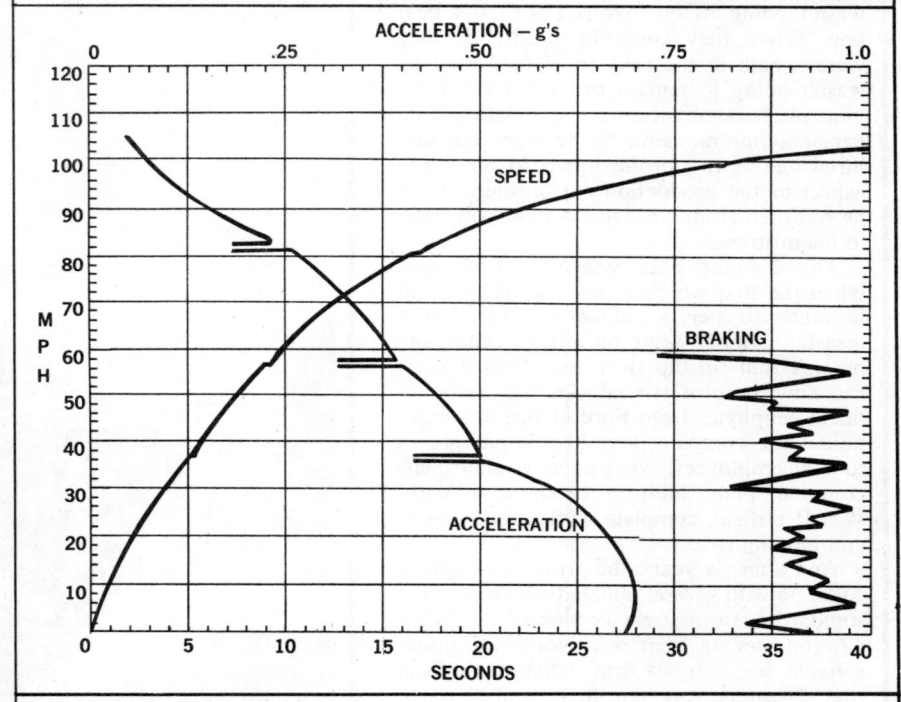

PERFORMANCE
- Acceleration .... 0-30 (3.5 sec.) 0-60 (9.5 sec.) 0-100 (31.2 sec.) 0-quarter mile (16.9 sec., 82.6 mph)
- Top speed .... 115 mph (actual) at 6000 rpm ((power limited)
- Braking .... Distance from 60 mph — 134 ft. (0.90 g av.)
  Number of stops to fade — Not attainable
  Stability — Excellent
  Maximum pitch angle — 2.2°
- Handling .... Max. lateral — 0.80 g right, 0.82 g left
  Skid pad understeer — 4.3°
  Maximum roll angle — 3.9°
  Reaction to throttle, full — oversteer; off — less understeer
- Dynamometer .... Road horsepower — 95 @ 4000 rpm
  Condition of tune — Slight plug foul
- Speedometer 30.0 40.0 50.0 60.0 70.0 80.0 90.0 100.0
  Actual 28.0 37.0 47.0 57.0 67.0 76.0 85.5 95.5
- Mileage .... Average — 28 mpg
  Miles on car — 900 to 1850

Aerodynamic forces at 100 mph:
- Drag .... 225 lbs. (includes tire drag)
- Lift F/R .... 110 lbs./ 45 lbs.

TEST EXPLANATIONS
Fade test is successive max. g. stops from 60 mph each minute until wheels cannot be locked. Understeer is front minus rear tire slip angle at max. lateral on 200 ft. dia. Digitek skidpad. Autoscan chassis dynamometer supplied by Humble Oil.

LOTUS E[

Viewpoint: David Phipps

At best, it's a distant cousin to the petit 2-seater Elan—and the extra two seats are specifically tailored for very little people—but it's still living proof that racing can improve the breed.

It's a good Lotus, but not a great Lotus. It's progression rather than innovation. Not that progression isn't a trait with the company, but this is a new car—by today's standards—and whenever Lotus makes a new car one has learned to expect trend-setting inventiveness. In this respect the Elan +2 is singularly plain.

The title doesn't suggest anything more; it is simply what will happen to a Sprite-sized Lotus Elan S4 if you stretch it a couple of feet, make it appropriately wider and heavier and stick lots of extra goodies inside and out. "Kaboomy—" (as Bob Brown once said to me at Monaco) the Lotus Elan +2.

Look at it this way. From 1958 (and probably even earlier) to 1963 (and probably even later), Colin Chapman found out enough about the production of automobiles as opposed to racing cars, to know that he wasn't going to be involved with the next one. While they could be profitable, they were a pain in the neck to oversee, and he wasn't going to remain distracted from the vital pleasure of messing about with racing cars another moment. So he went out and hired one or two professionals to run every aspect of the production car business. Then he returned from what had become his wife, to his mistress.

The 2-seater Elan was almost on sale when the first whiz kid arrived. He was an absolute disaster, a helluva swinger, but a disaster. Shortly after he left the company he was sent up the river for about a year. But now the professionals—mostly self-confident neophytes from Ford of Britain—have pulled the company together. It has grown to 600 employees, working at a giant self-contained plant, built on the site of a World War II airfield, complete with a road-course and landing strip.

And after six years, the professionals have come up with several updated versions of the standard Elan, a street version of the Lotus 47, and now an Elan +2. Not at all unreasonable for a small firm. Chapman's Elan (the 2-seater) was the first saddle-broken Lotus. Not homogenized of course, but domesticated to the point where in five years of production and in various forms, the Elan captured for Lotus a very handsome share of the enthusiast market in Europe and sold between 200 and 300 cars annually in this country.

In the meantime, Chapman's racing cars have won him the World Championship twice, his company has gone public and made him a pound sterling millionaire, and the man spends more of his time flitting over the Norfolk countryside and the Continent in a Piper Navajo than he ever does in any automobile. At age 40 the boy-wonder has found the good life. These days, Chapman has as much to do with the production lines at Lotus as he does with the shop foreman's wife. Which brings us back to the +2.

The price of a pair of jump seats and perhaps a slightly more sophisticated aura is $1140—the difference between the S4 Elan

102

AN PLUS 2

Coupe ($4855) and the +2 ($5995), both in basic trim, and both p.o.e. N.Y. This gets it pretty close to the 911 and 912 set, which is probably where the car belongs.

In the first place, it looks a lot more automobile than the 2-seater, which isn't exactly surprising because it's 23 inches longer, 10.25 inches wider and an inch higher. The wheelbase is a foot longer, the track has been widened 6.5 and 7.5 inches front and rear respectively. In expanding, it has also put on 400 pounds, which means spring rates have gone up considerably at the expense of ride comfort and certain aspects of handling on sub-normal surfaces. At best it's a distant cousin to the petit Elan, although the basic thought remains unaltered. The backbone chassis is common to both cars, the independent suspension—double wishbones at the front and Chapman struts at the rear—and the 1600 cc double overhead cam Lotus-Ford engine. The +2 version of the twincam is listed with slightly more horsepower, but this is probably negated by the increase in weight. The transmission is 4-speed Ford, whereas both Porsche and Alfa Romeo have 5 speeds (standard on the Alfa, semi-optional on the Porsche). One important addition and difference is a boxed steel side member below the doors. These are intended to provide protection in the event of side impact—although the unreinforced 2-seater Elan has a surprisingly good record in this respect—but they incidentally also increase torsional rigidity.

On the outside things are appropriately different. The overall design is extremely stylish, as sophisticated as the 2-seater is cute, and the general standard of exterior finish is far higher than anyone would have dared to expect from Lotus a few years ago.

Under closer scrutiny, however, things are far from perfect. The door latches are hardly in keeping with the car's $6000 price tag. The doors are sometimes difficult to open, and for six-footers getting in requires the usual sport car contortions. But once you're there the legroom is ample and the cockpit area is contoured to provide an excellent driving position. The seats are spartan-padded and the fixed backrests recline rather more than the majority of cars, but then that's the Lotus-pioneered driving position, isn't it?

The rear seats are specifically tailored for very little people only, and even *they* are likely to experience mild claustrophobia with the high sill line and the absence of rear quarter windows.

In view of Lotus' racing image you might have expected the instrument panel to be boldly padded in Grand Prix-black leatherette, but the new wave of market research wizards must have felt it necessary to make their presence felt somewhere along the line, so they opted for Jaguar-traditional, simulated paste-on walnut—ordered by the trainload. In compensation, they prescribed a very racy, small diameter steering wheel, complete with an A.B.C. Chapman auto-

PHOTOGRAPHY: DAVID PHIPPS

graph engraved on the lower spoke, and a very full complement of instruments.

Electric windows, first introduced on the Elan in 1966, are a break with traditional simplicity and help to accentuate just how far Lotus has come since the first Elan was introduced. On the other hand, it's fairly obvious that most of the other interior fittings are from mass produced family sedans, along with the major mechanical components, of course, and there are some people who may wonder why the end product is in the same price bracket as an all-original Jaguar. There's no point in selling yourself short when there are enough people around who'll pay the top dollar. And anyway, a door handle is a door handle and hardly has much to do with the true function of an automobile —nobody complains because they use chain saw engines to run go-karts. And then too, kicking tires is one thing, driving the Elan +2 is another.

The engine starts easily enough and first gear snicks in very sweetly, but the emergency brake is hidden away in the dark recesses beneath the dash, and when you let the clutch out you're almost bound to kangaroo away like a novice because the donuts in the driveshafts tend to wind-up and unleash themselves like an angry mule. With practice and careful co-ordination of clutch and throttle you'll learn to conceal this—it'll set you aside as a real Lotus owner—but you'll have more difficulty in controlling the surge that sets in when you back off the throttle, especially in the lower gears. Whatever your feelings about this phenomenon, you will undoubtedly explain to the curious that donuts are an essential part of the car's drivetrain and that they're largely responsible for its tremendous traction—and nobody will argue with you about this. Even on wet roads it is virtually impossible to get wheelspin unless you drop the clutch at 5000 rpm in first. On dry roads wheelspin simply doesn't occur. As you may well imagine this poses some problems if you happen to want to make a fast getaway or do some friendly drag racing with Porsche owners, but for normal motor-

It's a sophisticated Lotus: bigger, heavier, and with things like jump seats and electric windows. It allows you to amuse yourself without disturbing your adrenalin.

LOTUS ELAN PLUS 2

ing you simply have to get the car rolling before sticking your foot into things. There's no doubt about it, security in adverse conditions is far more useful than smoking tires at a stop light.

Anyway, there you are, languidly reclining, arms barely bent at the elbow, a shining hood of fiberglass preceding you, the road sliding under you as quick as you fancy and a fast flat turn coming up. The Lotus Elan +2 is now in its element. Keep your foot in it as long as you dare, because the odds are you're going to quit long before the car will. Lift off and get onto the brakes hard, you can stay hard on deep into a corner with confidence. The power-assist detracts very slightly from the brake's feel, but it permits the use of pads that are unlikely to fade however hard you use them. Incline the wrists slightly and the car goes around. Except for a rather higher ratio and a lot more damping, this is race car-type steering, and if you have to use any opposite lock you know you're really trying.

Because of its extra weight, the +2 is not as agile as the 2-seater Elan when it comes to maneuvers like lanechanging, but it actually has better roadholding and corners as flat as Audrey Hepburn without any drama.

By Funny Car standards the Elan +2 doesn't make it. You have to work very hard and run the engine up to its governed limit of 6500 rpm to get a 0-60 mph time in under nine seconds. Performance gets better as the speeds get higher, but there are precious few places left where you can use the 120-mph maximum—and precious few people who would care to endure the associated noise level for very long.

At legal speeds and moderate throttle openings the +2 is reasonably quiet, but the engine starts to really howl over 5000 rpm, and after a few minutes the wind noise from 80 mph on up becomes rather like the water torture.

High speeds are also inclined to become interesting on poor surfaces when the ride becomes rather sudden, and fast night driving is not to be recommended unless you've fitted additional lights—at least the pop-up headlights don't suddenly retract themselves when you're running with a wide-open throttle, as they were inclined to do on some of the early Elans.

In daylight hours on main roads this car is living proof that the tired old adage of racing improving the breed has a spark of life in it yet.

If you admired the way a '62 Corvette handled and cornered you'll be disappointed and bored by the Elan +2. If you want a car that's easy on your passengers while you're amusing yourself—but at the same time doesn't tend to disturb your adrenalin—you'll be hard put to find anything better no matter how much you're willing to pay.—*David Phipps* •

LOTUS ELAN

(continued from page 7)

The carpeted luggage compartment at the rear has a useful size by sports-car seats, this extra accommodation being sufficient to take a baby basket.

The cockpit of the Elan has been very well thought out indeed for the enthusiast driver, and the general standard of finish is definitely more acceptable than on the Elite. The oiled teak dash panel, which is itself a structural member of the body, has a deep center section extending down to the body floor. Matching rev counter and speedometer are straight ahead of the driver, with a combined oil pressure and water temperature gauge to the right, and a fuel gauge to the left. Dual hood release catches are placed high up in the center of the panel, where they can be reached by a driver wearing a safety harness, and the control switches are arranged neatly in the center section of the dash. An open glove compartment is provided on the passenger's side.

The seats have a good range of adjustment, and the backrests are raised slightly as the seat is pushed forward. The interior is fully trimmed in Vynide, and fully carpeted, and has the general appearance of being a coachbuilt job. There is nothing spartan about the Elan, Chapman having realized that today the discerning buyer is not satified with performance alone. One feature not often seen these days, but one which has been used very successfully on a number of cars within the last few years (including the Austin A35) is the vertically sliding door window, with transparent plastic "pulls" mounted centrally close to the top edge. The engine hood is front-hinged, and is carried in nylon runners; it can be removed completely in about 10 seconds.

This, then, is Chapman's best-by-far production car to date. The Elan, with its five-bearing, high-torque and extremely smooth 20HC engine, its all-synchromesh gearbox, and rubber-cushioned final drive, its all-round independent suspension, precise steering, and powerful braking, must surely be the smoothest-running and safest handling sports car ever to have been produced by a British factory. In fact, so saleable is its specification — particulary in view of its price — that it must surely rate as *the* new sports car of 1962.

"The Race Chairman says to disqualify Car Nine!"

LOTUS ELAN COUPE

continued from page 42

Packard phaeton in a Thirties gangster movie, but which hung on like prickly pears anyway. The ride comfort was outstanding for a car of the Elan's light weight.

The engine is a smoking bear. The distributor in the test car had a cunning little gizmo that shuts off the juice whenever journalists try to rev it over 6500 (it'll turn seven), and it was breathing easily at that speed. It's understressed at 105 horsepower, and is tractable in traffic from 1000 rpm on up, although its pulling power isn't enough to pass without downshifting. Our acceleration runs, made with only one person in the car, were only two-tenths of a second worse in the quarter-mile than the mechanically-identical, but much lighter roadster. Still, 1320 ft. in less than 16 seconds is no mean accomplishment for a 95 cu. in. GT car.

The brakes, a four-wheel disc system, are powerful and easy to modulate. The tires seem small, even for a light car, and appeared to be the limiting factor in a .73 g panic stop from 80 mph. Several panic stops produced some fade, but this came in the form of a gradual increase in required pedal pressure rather than a sudden loss of braking ability.

Rack-and-pinion steering pinpoints the Elan with great precision. It's extraordinarily light and delicate, which should contribute to fatigue-free long-distance touring. Bent into a corner, we sometimes felt that there wasn't enough weight on the front wheels, but again, that may be characteristic of the tires. Road feel is direct at all times—a reversion to "seat of the pants" driving—and the turning circle is delightfully small. As a whole, the Elan is more maneuverable than anything on wheels but a Mini or a motorcycle.

The Elan gives away something in styling to several of its competitors; something in performance to others and something in luxury to all of them. Against this, the Elan has the Lotus name and all the right specifications which makes it a sports car that does everything a sports car is supposed to do. Like any one of a number of slim volumes of poetry, it is a minor classic, a definition-by-example of sophisticated engineering applied to a production car. Is this enough? Can the Elan with its limited objectives, limited production, limited dealer network and limited appeal survive? We hope so; the Elan deserves to make it.

C/D

Unequalled roadholding, performance and economy

THE latest version of the Lotus Elan is a greatly improved car. The engine is very much smoother and revs more freely, while higher gearing (lower numerical ratio) permits high cruising speeds to be used without over-revving. In order to obtain a sufficiently low first gear for rapid starts, a wide-ratio gearbox replaces the previous close-ratio component. Theoretically the car needs a five-speed box, but in practice it has so much torque in the middle ranges that it does very well with the present compromise, as the performance figures show.

The test car had two Stromberg carburetters instead of two twin-choke Webers. There is said to be a loss of about 3 bhp, but in fact the engine seemed livelier; I have certainly never driven an Elan that rushed past 7,000 rpm in top gear in the way that this one did. When I timed it at 127 mph I was suffering from floating foot, as I did not want to risk doing any damage and the rev counter was far into the red section. The rather fast speedometer very frequently went past the 130 mph mark.

Structurally the car remains the same, with a steel backbone chassis and a glass-fibre body. It is very small, and this is an enormous advantage, permitting every gap in the traffic to be exploited. With such a narrow car it hardly matters on which side the steering wheel is placed, unlike wide cars, which are awkward to use on the continent with right-hand drive. There is, in fact, all the room that two normal people need, and the driving position is just about perfect.

I have often remarked that I choose horses for courses, and so I jumped at the chance of taking an Elan to the Frankfurt Show. This meant 1,000 miles of driving in two days, with one very tough day sandwiched in the middle to blister one's feet at the Show. The roads of France, Belgium and Germany were sampled, and once again the Townsend Ferry took us across the Channel. It was one of those trips where speed was of the essence, and for such a journey there is no greater luxury than a car which will make a really high average.

The Lotus handles like a racing car—there is probably no other sports car with such controllability. Light, precise, and extremely quick, the steering at once gives

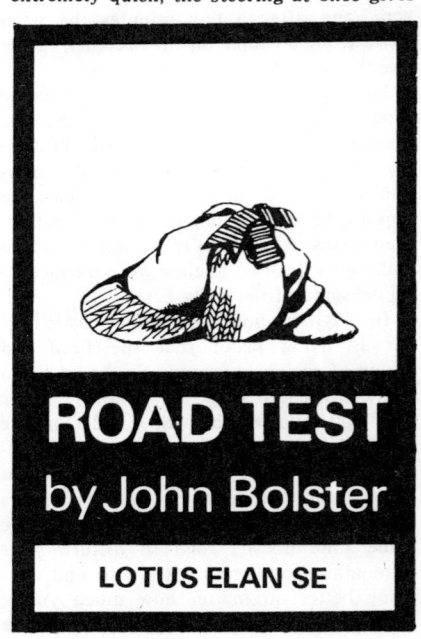

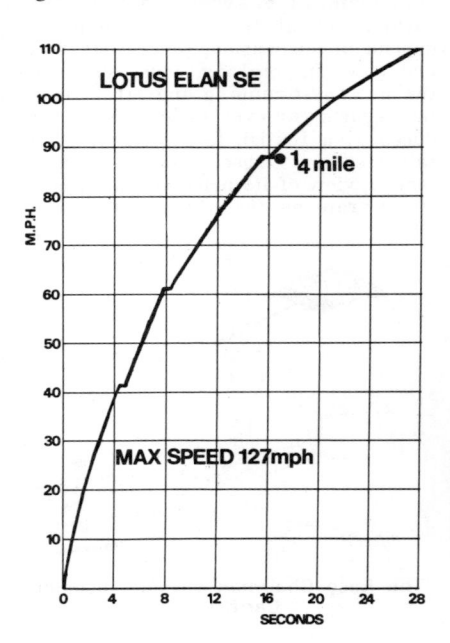

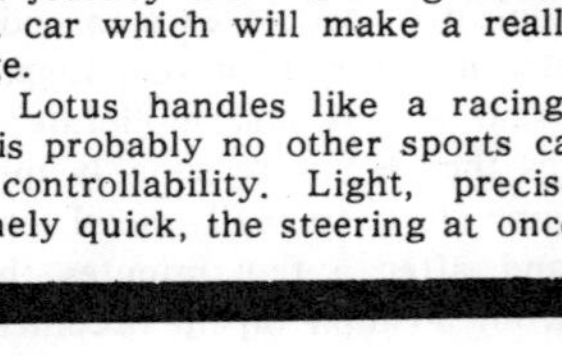

LOTUS ELAN SE

MAX SPEED 127mph

ROAD TEST
by John Bolster
LOTUS ELAN SE

the driver complete confidence, and the cornering power is always greater than seems possible. Even at high speeds the machine simply goes round corners, with no under- or oversteering, and it is only at extreme velocities that the tail can be hung out, still under complete control. The ride is fairly firm, but the seat is remarkably comfortable and in fact the result is smoother travel than most sports cars give.

There is very little road noise, though the wind roars round the windows at the highest speeds. The engine is not noisy for a car of this type, and the transmission is outstandingly quiet. One advantage of the small size is that the Elan really feels fast when it is flat out. Big GT cars, such as the Aston-Martin and the 7-litre AC, almost feel as if they are parked when travelling at 140 mph. Driving down the bumpy and fairly narrow Jabbeke road, the little Lotus seemed to be rushing along though it was only doing 120 mph or so and was quite steady. This sensation of speed is great fun and keeps the driver awake on a long journey.

Perhaps the most unexpected feature is the high-speed acceleration. With a fairly wide gap between third and top, one has to overtake on the direct drive at normal autobahn speeds. Though this seems disconcerting at first, I never found another car that could keep up with the Elan when accelerating from 100 to 120 mph, even though they were making use of their five-speed gearboxes. The brakes have been cured of their old tendency to lock the wheels and are now as progressive as they are powerful.

From the above, it might seem that the Lotus Elan is the best sports car yet, and in many respects this is true. Yet there are certain faults which persist, though they could be so easily remedied. The worst of these is the surging caused by the winding-up and unwinding of the doughnut rubber universal joints. Then there is the handbrake, which is very awkward to reach and, in the case of the test car at least, would not pass the MOT test. The ventilation system is rather inadequate and the heater would not turn off properly, persisting in turning itself on full during a heat wave. One of the electric windows ceased to operate and I think an emergency control handle should be kept in reserve.

This seems rather a formidable list of complaints, but the car is so outstanding that I forgave it these imperfections. It was an admirable trip which I shall long remember, covered at very high average speeds in remarkable ease and safety. Almost beyond belief was the fuel consumption, which has been greatly improved by the constant-vacuum carburetters. Driving hard with as much over-110 mph motoring as possible. I consistently averaged 33 mpg. I am sure that some owners will achieve 40 mpg in 70 mph England.

The Lotus Elan is a car which is appreciated all the more when it is driven fast and far. Its roadholding and steering are superb, and few drivers will be satisfied with lesser cars after experiencing this grand prix cornering. The driving position is all part of the magic, and the gearchange is as light as it is quick. On the autobahns it was great fun to bring up the retractable headlamps, already flashing angrily, which seemed to shift the sleepiest Teutons from the fast lane, though these lamps are not very powerful for night driving. To sum up, this car handles just like a very good racing car, and it flatters the skill of any reasonably competent driver.

Perhaps one day Colin Chapman will offer us a five-speed Elan with its few imperfections ironed out. That would be just about the ultimate in sports cars. Until then I am very happy with this Lotus just as it is, warts and all.

Car tested: Lotus Elan SE Coupé. Price £1,486 in kit form, £1,942 with tax.
Engine: Four cylinders, 82.55 mm x 72.75 mm, 1558 cc. Twin overhead camshafts. Compression ratio 9.5 : 1. 115 bhp at 6500 rpm. Twin Stromberg carburetters
Transmission: Single dry plate diaphragm spring clutch. 4-speed all synchromesh gearbox, ratios 1.0, 1.4, 2.01 and 2.97 : 1. Hypoid final drive, ratio 4.55 : 1.
Chassis: Central steel backbone with saddle-mounted glass-fibre body. Independent front suspension by wishbones and helical springs. Rack and pinion steering. Independent rear suspension by struts and lower wishbones. Telescopic dampers all round. Disc brakes on all four wheels with vacuum servo. Knock-on disc wheels fitted 145-13 ins radial ply tyres.
Equipment: 12-volt lighting and starting. Speedometer. Rev-counter, oil pressure, water temperature and fuel gauges. Heating, demisting and ventilation system. Windscreen wipers and washers. Flashing direction indicators. Radio (extra).
Dimensions: Wheelbase 7 ft. Track (front 3 ft 11 ins; (rear) 4 ft 0.4 ins. Overall length 12 ft 1.25 ins. Width 4 ft 8 ins. Weight 14 cwt.
Performance: Maximum speed 127 mph. Speeds in gears: third 88 mph, second 61 mph, first 41 mph. Standing quarter-mile 15.7 s. Acceleration: 0-30 mph 2.8 s. 0-50 mph 6.0 s. 0-60 mph 7.9 s. 0-80 mph 13.4 s. 0-100 mph 21.6 s. 0-110 mph 27.8 s.
Fuel consumption: 32 to 40 mpg.

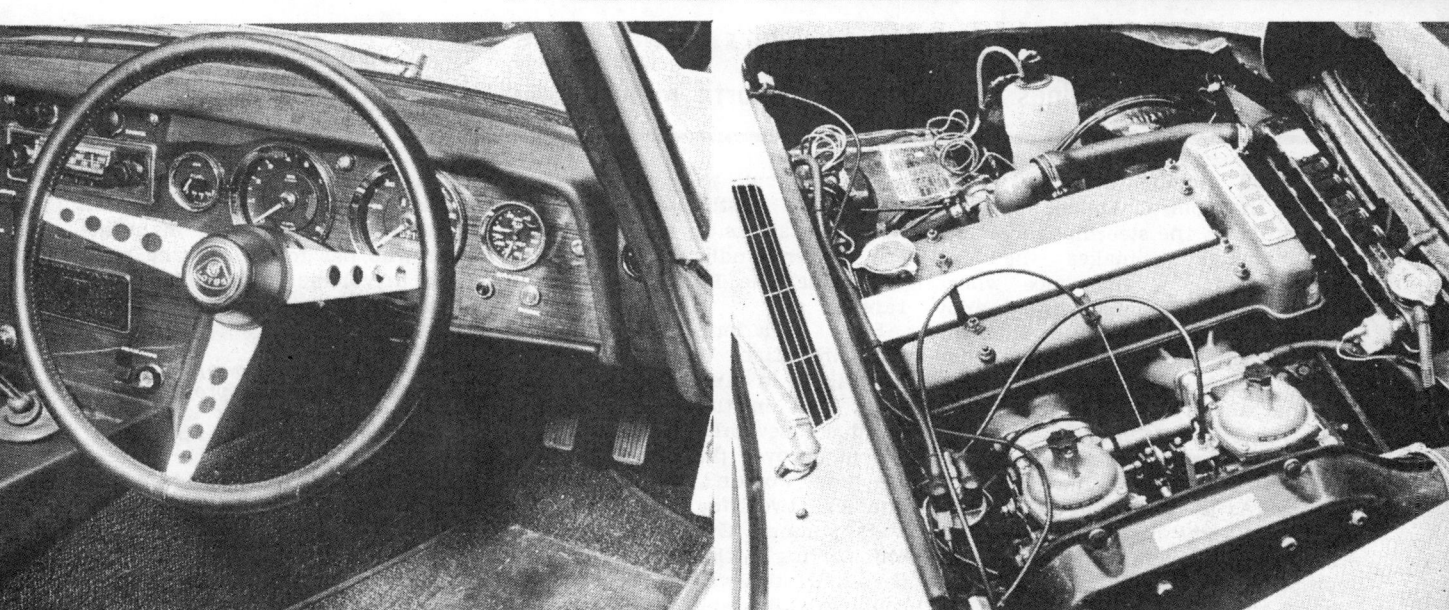

The Elan SE retains its previous compact shape (top). The driving position is ideal with all the instruments well placed on the attractive dash (left). Beneath the bonnet sits the 115 bhp twin-cam fitted with two Stromberg carbs (right).

It's the type of motoring the French have a word for; it's called...

elan wheels ROAD TEST

The Lotus Elan Plus Two is Colin Chapman's answer to the family man who clings to his flair for sportif motoring.

ABOUT the first thing you notice is the Colin Chapman signature engraved on the steering wheel, and that somehow makes the day brighter. It's a very nice wheel, slightly dished, three drilled alloy spokes, and a padded rim with fillets on the spoke joints just where your thumbs rest.

The wheel is the same as that in the S4 roadster and coupe in the Elan series, but the Plus Two is like no other Elan that has gone before. As the first four-place Elan, it has a niche in history; but it is also probably significant as the first proper car — as distinct from hand-built sports cars — to be turned out by Chapman's modernised factory. At around $6000 it is expensive, but will also be rare enough to justify that expense. About as fast as an Alfa 1750 GTV, but better-handling and not as well-made, the Plus Two breathes rarefied air.

But it is a long, long step from that first Elan. We were the first journalists in Australia to test an Elan, back in the days when you could see several shades of red in the paint over the glass-fibre, and the doors wouldn't fit and the pull-handles (two) for the bonnet always jammed. Even then it was a soul-stirring little car, mainly for the fantastic way in which one could get all usable power down on the road. It stuck like glue, and went very hard for its specific output, but you had to be a hair-shirt to own one, for each weekend could be spent rebuilding.

The Plus Two is meant as a family car, a GT for the two-child family, a civilised cross-Europe conveyance. That it falls short in sophistication is an inevitable result of coming from a small manufacturer who has to use existing parts made in volume for the big manufacturers. Without enough volume

Most handsome view of the Elan Plus Two is its slim profile. Cabin extractor vents are set into blind-spot quarter panel of turret.

Any sophistication of line is destroyed when the hydraulically operated eyes pop-up for a bug-eyed Sprite frog-look. Lights are Lucas.

The extra width of the Plus Two over the roadster is obvious from front three quarter. Shell remains fibreglass while tyres are Dunlop.

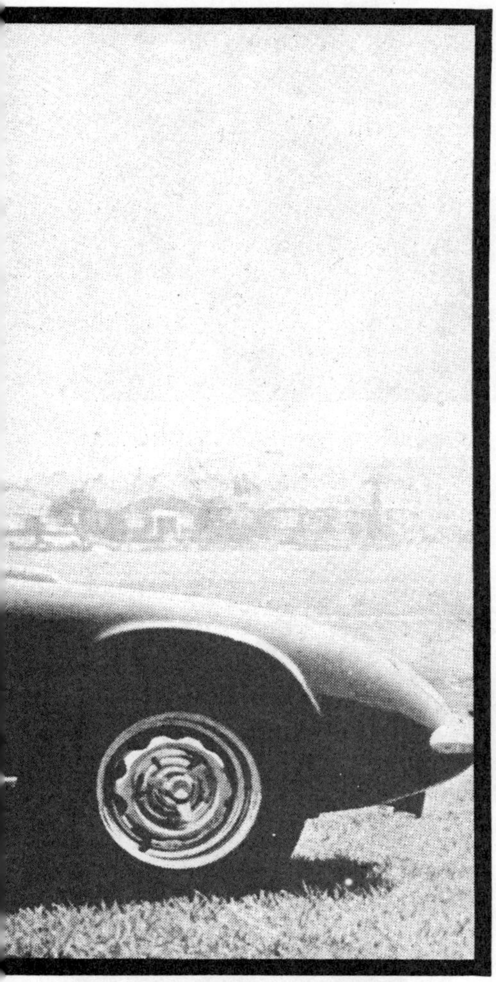

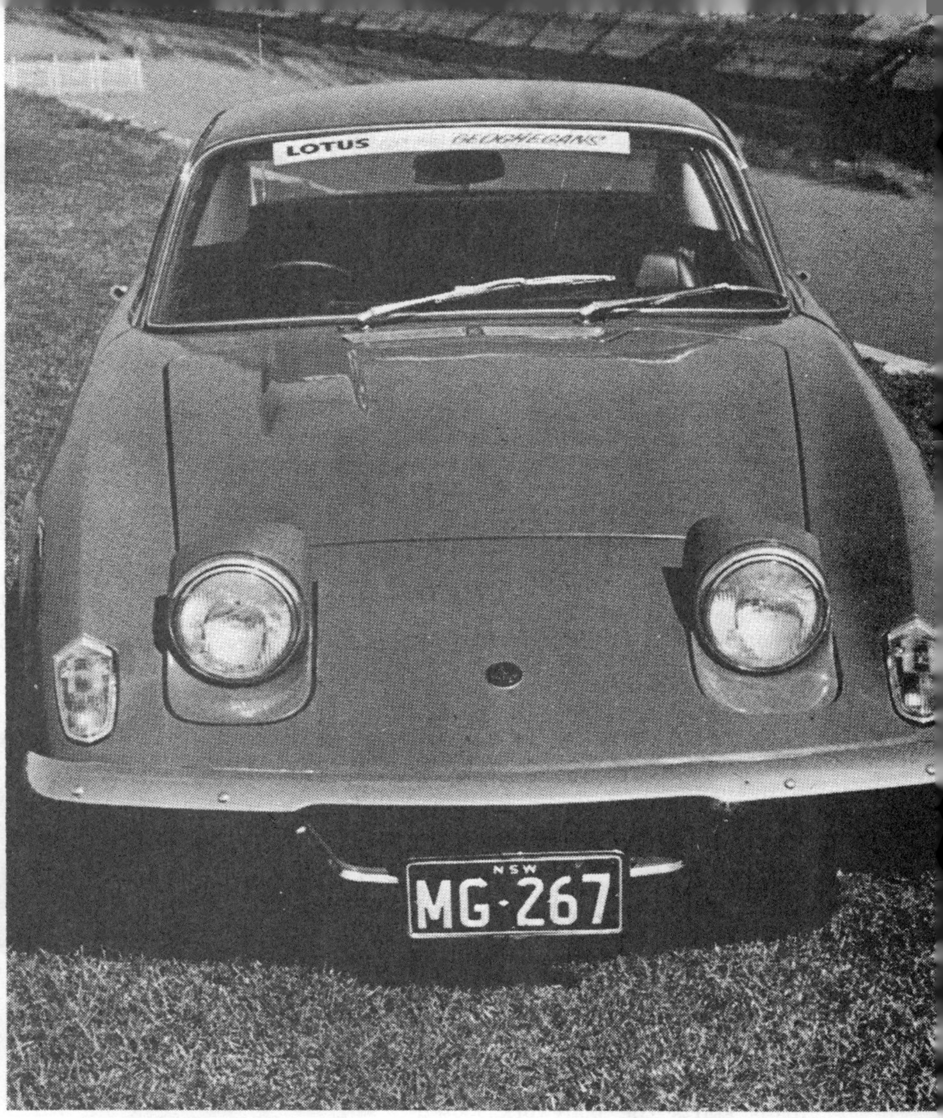
LOTUS
GEOGHEGANS'
NSW
MG-267

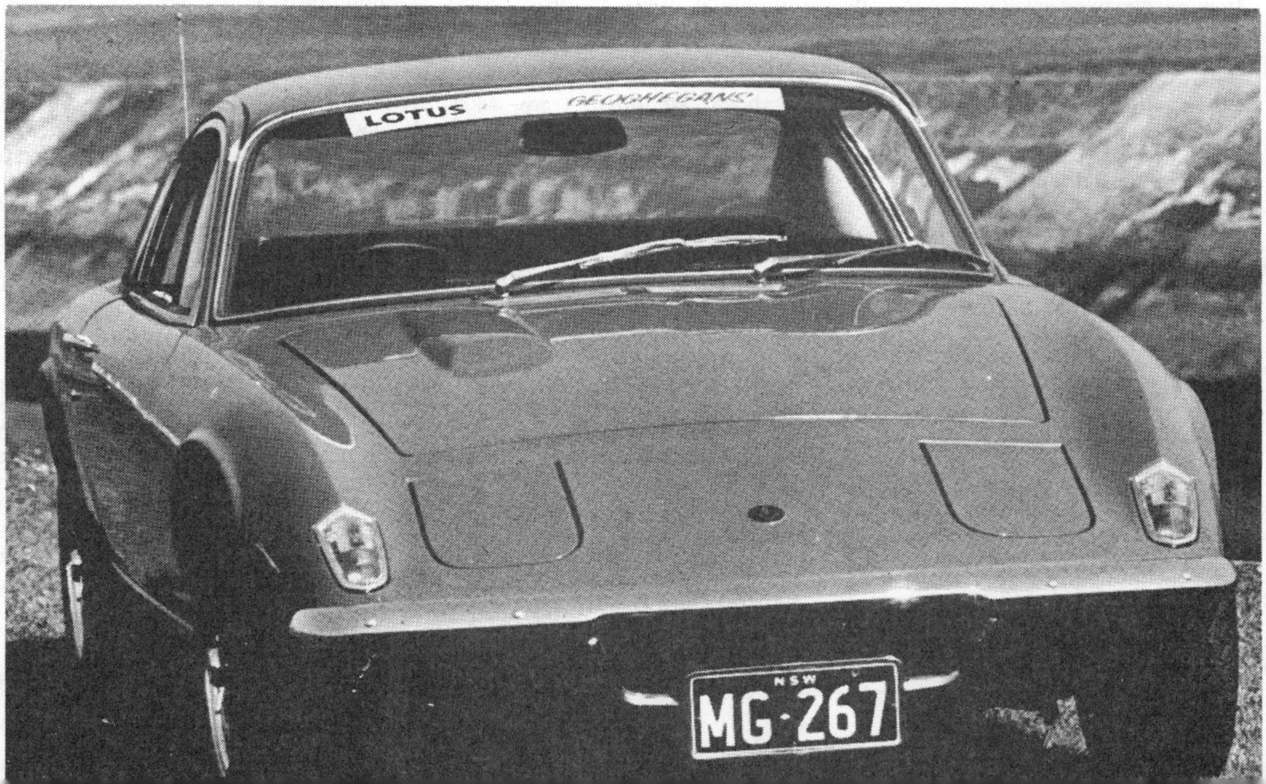
LOTUS
GEOGHEGANS'
NSW
MG-267

to demand individuality in the hardware he buys in for the product, Chapman has had to use borrowed bits, mostly Ford with some Triumph.

The interior light, trafficator stalk, cigarette lighter, wiper-washer switch, choke knob, air vents, ashtray, rear vision mirror, sun visors and handbrake are all pure Cortina. And this is where the Plus Two fails. These things are perfectly acceptable in a two-seat sports car like the Elan S4, but in a fixed-head coupe for the big-income bracket they are very non-aesthetic. They are understandable, and excusable, but this doesn't make you any more proud of your $6000 car.

It goes without saying, however, that like all Elans the Plus Two is a superb road car. It has a extraordinarily good ride for its taut handling, striding smoothly and neatly over harsh and lumpy surfaces alike. Nothing whatsoever could possibly cause the Plus Two to change its line or lose its footing in a corner. It does everything so beautifully that it becomes a very easy car to drive. Elans have always flattered their drivers. A good car won't necessarily make a good driver out of a bad one, but it can make an excellent driver out of one already good. It would be one of the best Interstate road rockets one could ever find, although past experience with all Elans has shown that continued belting over bad roads starts the bodywork loosening up.

From the outside, the overwhelming impression of the car is size. It is nearly two feet longer than the little roadster, and 10 in. wider. Once inside, you notice the extra width, but not the extra length, although the overhang does call for attention when you realise that you can't judge that downswept nose in parking and that the rear quarter-panels produce a considerable blind spot. However, where the other Elans use polyurethane-packed glass-fibre bumpers that will pock and split on impact, the Plus Two uses chromed steel.

The Plus Two uses the 118 bhp Special Equipment engine available

---

AT-A-GLANCE: superb roadholding . . . retains glass fibre's attraction for rattles . . . requires finesse in driving . . . excellent brakes . . . good economy . . . impressive performance . . . adequate comfort for four . . . radio OE.

Something new for British sports car, radio as standard. As a "family GT" the boot is adequate, with wide entry. Spare is set under floor.

Cockpit is neat and functional. Chrome toggles either side of ashtray are for the power windows. Wheel has Colin's signature.

as an option for the SE roadster and coupe. This twincam Ford is one of the most successful and reliable engines ever built, and will stand up to an incredible amount of abuse. Redlined from 6500 to 8000, it actually has a centrifugal distributor cut-out which chimes in at 6750 to stop ham-fisted testers from sawing the block in half. This simply shows up as a breaking-down in ignition, and is a handy reminder that you are getting a little too serious. The engine is quiet, with little valve gear thrash and hardly any induction noise, and is staggeringly easy on fuel. We couldn't believe our test figures, but a later run proved them out. We ran it on 100 octane, which it needs, but during our test the timing slipped, causing bad pinking under load.

The gearbox is Lotus-modified Ford, as is the clutch. There is no gearbox noise whatever, and the shift mechanism is beautifully light, sharp and fast. It is just about beyond criticism. But the test car had those Metalastik rubber doughnut joints on the driveshaft inner ends, and while they do a fine job of soaking up end-play and lateral movement in the axles, they are not beefy enough for the Plus Two. A combination of high side-loading and sudden three-quarter throttle in second gear exploded one on the test car in the middle of traffic. Later cars have an altered and improved driveshaft universal to solve this problem. Let's hope this also copes with the ever-present Lotus problem of drive train surge. Not as bad as it used to be, this is a reverse torque reaction from the rubber couplings that tends to produce a kangarooing motion, particularly when accelerating away from near-idle in the lower three gears. After a while you counter it with slight clutch slippage and better control of throttle, but it is always there to remind you. And it is not good enough for an expensive GT car.

Continued on page 112

wheels ROAD TEST

TECHNICAL DETAILS

MAKE: Lotus
MODEL: Elan Plus Two
BODY TYPE: 2+2 coupe
PRICE: $5995
OPTIONS: Dunlop SP Aquajets

COLOR: red, black trim
MILEAGE, START: 4710
FINISH: 5337
WEIGHT: 2086 lb

FUEL CONSUMPTION:
Overall .... 24.5 mpg
Cruising .... 26-28 mpg

TEST CONDITIONS:
Weather, fine, warm; surface, bitumen aggregate; load, two persons and gear; fuel, 100 octane

SPEEDOMETER ERROR:
Indicated mph: 30 40 50 60 70 80
Actual mph: 29.0 41.1 50.0 60.2 70.5 80.0

PERFORMANCE

Piston speed at max bhp .... 2900 ft/min
Top gear mph per 1000 rpm 19.1
Engine rpm at max speed .... 6250 rpm

MAXIMUM SPEEDS:
Fastest run .... 119.8 mph
Average of all runs .... 119.4 mph
Speedometer indication fastest run .... 117 mph
Maximum in gears: 1st, 40, 2nd, 58; 3rd, 88 mph.

ACCELERATION:
(through gears)
0-30 mph .... 4.25 sec
0-40 mph .... 5.75 sec
0-50 mph .... 7.30 sec
0-60 mph .... 10.15 sec
0-70 mph .... 13.30 sec
0-80 mph .... 15.95 sec
(in top gear)
20-40 mph .... 10.8 sec
30-50 mph .... 10.2 sec
40-60 mph .... 10.9 sec
50-70 mph .... 10.25 sec

STANDING QUARTER MILE:
Fastest run .... 16.4 sec
Average of all runs .... 16.7 sec

SPECIFICATIONS

ENGINE:
Cylinders .... four, in line
Bore and stroke .... 82.55 mm by 72.7 mm
Cubic capacity .... 1558 cc
Compression ratio .... 9.5 to 1
Valves .... overhead, dohc chain driven
Carburettors .... two double-choke Weber
Fuel pump .... electrical
Power at rpm .... 118 bhp at 6250 rpm
Torque at rpm .... 112 lb/ft at 4000 rpm

TRANSMISSION:
Type .... four-speed, all syncromesh
Clutch .... single dry plate
Gearlever location .... central

OVERALL RATIOS:
First 11.196
Second 7.577
Third 5.278
Fourth 3.777
Final drive .... 3.777 to 1

CHASSIS AND RUNNING GEAR:
Construction .... steel backbone, glass-fibre bodywork
Suspension, front .... independent, coils, wishbones, struts
Suspension, rear .... independent, single wishbone, coil/damper units
Shock absorbers .... tubular hydraulic
Steering, type .... rack and pinion
Turns, l to 1 .... 2.7
Turning circle .... 32 ft
Steering wheel diameter .... 15 in.
Brakes, type .... discs all round

OVERALL DIMENSIONS:
Wheelbase .... 96 in.
Track, front .... 54 in.
Track, rear .... 55 in.
Length .... 14 ft 0¾ in.
Height .... 3 ft 11 in.
Width .... 5 ft 6¼ in.
Fuel tank capacity .... 13 gal

TYRES:
Size 165-13
Make on test car .... Dunlop SP Sport Aquajet

GROUND CLEARANCE:
Registered .... 6½ in.

Acceleration through gears with change points graph:
- 1ST → 40 MPH
- 2ND → 58 MPH
- 3RD → 88 MPH
- STANDING ¼ MILE 16.7
- TOP SPEED 119.4 M.P.H.

111

But this doesn't stop the Elan Plus Two from being a gorgeous open road car. With a low drag factor, emphasised by the fact that you can sit on near-ton speeds with both windows open and hardly get a draught, it rushes smoothly and quietly up to 110 mph. The last 10 mph takes a little more road, but not that much. It is happy cruising anywhere in the 70 to 105 mph range, although there seems to be some airflow disturbance around the tail of the car because over 100 it starts to dodge about a bit in sidewinds.

The steering is excellent, short in movement and very accurate, producing results defined to the last milimetre. The car can be placed exactly where wanted, even though this dodging-about in side gusts produced a sort of over-control compensation in the steering, which may be partly due to tyres and/or pressures, for we are still building up our experience of these new Dunlops.

The Plus Two neither understeers nor oversteers to any noticeable degree. It tracks almost neutrally, and can be steered on power. The very fast winding roads we used called for a technique which is best summed up by saying that you set up the approach by snatching off the power and the car develops a slight oversteer attitude into the apex, then you belt it hard and it storms out with the outside wheel working hard. The ability of this car to produce incredibly high sideways cornering forces has to be felt to be believed. To get it unstuck demanded that you be criminally rough with the steering, at the same time adding twice the sensible power. Then, and only then, would the car start to slide.

Point to point it is well-nigh untouchable, not only for the handling but also because of the excellent brakes, although in the test car — which in retrospect is starting to show up as a bit of a dog — the servo assistance needed adjustment, for it started as a dead pedal and came in with a bang. Although there was a slight tendency to lock one wheel or another, the car generally stopped very well. Working very hard on fast give-and-take roads the brakes allowed you to run right up to the corners and to commit the car completely to what otherwise would be marginal situations. This really is a very safe fast car, by anybody's standards, except possibly those of the road safety do-gooders.

The Plus Two will carry two children up to about 12 years of age quite comfortably for long distances. An adult, however, is uncomfortable in the two shaped rear seats for even short distances. The wide central backbone divides the car down the middle. It is typical Elan construction, with the steel box-section tunnel forking out to form outriggers for the suspension. There is a deep rear parcels shelf and a reasonably good boot, operated by a neat latch in the driver's door pillar. Inside there is one glovebox (lockable), an odds-and-ends tray around the gearlever, and a peculiar quarter-inch deep flat tray under a thinly-padded, lift-up armrest covering the central divider.

We liked the seats very much, as they are typical long, reclining, Lotus seats with well-defined hip and shoulder wedges. You sit low in this car, legs, and arms well out, and you need the inertia-reel belts supplied because you have to sit up and forward to check any attacks from the right or left rear quarter. It goes without saying that the seating position and the relation to gearlever and steering wheel, is impeccable. Unfortunately Australian authorities do not recognise inertia belts in their motor vehicle standards, so future cars will use fixed belts.

Ahead of you is a dashboard faced in African cherry-wood and studded with gear that at first looks jumbled but which ergonomically is really fairly good. Central piece is an expensive, complicated and very good AM-FM radio that comes as standard equipment. At each end are the swivelling eyeballs for the through-flow ventilation system, that has its exhaust vents in the rear quarter just behind the trailing edge of each window. At the left of the radio, in front of the passenger are gauges for fuel contents and amps, balanced on the other side of the radio by dials for oil pressure and water temperature. The cigarette lighter is also on the left of the radio where the passenger can reach it, with the wiper-washer switch on the right.

Flanking the heater-demister control slides are tumbler switches for interior light, heater blower, main and panel lights. A crackle-finish central ashtray is flanked by two small chromed tabs to operate the electric windows, and below these again are the ignition switch (too far away on the left) and the pull-knob which raised the concealed headlights, both flashing for overtaking action.

The big tachometer and speedometer are neatly done in white and orange, while the bonnet release and utterly useless umbrella-head handbrake are under the dash on the right. The wipers are two speed, and do not start lifting off the screen until over 90 mph, which is too fast in the wet for any sane person anyway. We also liked the extra ashtrays in the doors and the neat flip-over door latches, but would have expected a dippable rear vision mirror. The car comes with good, piercing air horns as standard.

The standard of paintwork on the test car was very good. We could find few flaws, although the exposed spot-welded seam along the length of each door sill looks a bit untidy. Inside, the perforated black leatherette trim, as used in most BMW and Mercedes models, looks and feels excellent. The carpet fits well, and should wear well.

Last we come to the looks. Most people liked it. The droopsnout slightly wedge shape is unusual, but distinctive. To us the car is handsomer from the back than the front, but the designers have done a good job of maintaining the Lotus look while coming up with a trendy new style.

Like all Elans, the Plus Two offers that rare, distinctive something that no other car can supply, although you have to be willing to overlook some crudities and primitive touches. These do not, however, mar what is essentially a beautiful, thoroughbred car that every time you drive it reproduces a taste of honey. #

"Care for a sandwich officer?"

Motor Road Test No 15/70

Lotus Elan S4

Elan avec élan

Even more performance from latest twin-cam SE engine; roadholding very good in dry, sometimes less predictable in wet; soft top slow to furl; noisy exhaust; good ride; compact and fun

Nearly six years have passed since we tested our first Lotus Elan; in the intervening years we have tried the various model revisions and generally remained pretty faithful to our original enthusiastic assessment. Even though the competition has had six years to catch up, the Elan is still a first class all-round sports car which is hard to beat; very few are faster, very few can equal its roadholding; probably no other two seater has such a good ride. The strength of these attributes is to us great enough to outweigh some of the disadvantages—like fussiness and noise—and still bring the Elan out on top. At over £2000 (assembled) it isn't cheap but it is a very complete and compact little car with a lot of appeal.

Its performance, from a development of the original twin-cam engine using Stromberg CD carburetters in the latest SE specification, is better than ever. From rest to 70 mph in under 10 seconds is very fast and unmatched in this capacity class. Efficiency has also been increased, the overall fuel consumption of 25.4 mpg being marginally better than before despite the extra power. Perhaps the weakest department is the transmission; the overall gearing is too fussy and for long runs the noise becomes tiring. On the convertible, with less sound insulation than the coupe, the fussy feeling is accentuated by a noisy exhaust system. This and inevitable wind noise with a soft top, however good, would be enough to make us opt for the fixed head car with the highest available final drive like that on the S2 Elan we ran on the editorial fleet. For those less concerned with effortless progress than open air motoring, the convertible is still practical enough for such a compact car, with a surprising amount of general storage space.

PRICE: £1595 plus £489 13s. 6d. equals £2084 13s. 6d.

Over 24,000 miles in the staff S2, and a further test on the S3 SE two years ago, makes our total Elan mileage well over 35,000 miles. Contrary to our recent owner survey on the Plus 2, which fared poorly on reliability, we have always found the Elan fairly trouble-free.

Unlike many cars the Elan has a strong character; everyone came back with strong views after driving it. It wasn't the most popular commuter's car—it is very low in relation to other traffic and you have to be delicate with your clutch foot to avoid surge. But it was very much at home on the open road, although those who used it for long journeys found their enthusiasm waning again. If the Elan could have an overdrive—or better still a five-speed gearbox—it would still be as far ahead of its rivals as it was six years ago; as it is there are cheaper cars which offer more relaxed long-distance transport, albeit slower and less satisfying.

Performance and economy

About the only obvious change under the bonnet is Stromberg CD carburetters (instead of Webers) to cope with the American pollution laws; the power output is as good as before, and possibly more consistent from engine to engine, so the only change noticeable from the cockpit end is the starting technique. No longer are a couple of dabs on the throttle sufficient to prime the manifold with accelerator pump squirts; you now have to use the choke, but it still starts straight away and the knob can soon be pushed in—before the temperature gauge has moved off its stop—without any hesitation from the astonishingly tractable engine.

With the Webers it was necessary to feed the accelerator in gradually when taking top gear figures from 20 mph. With the Strombergs (even with the SE engine) you can floor the pedal at 20 mph and the car will pick up cleanly. This one wasn't quite

PERFORMANCE

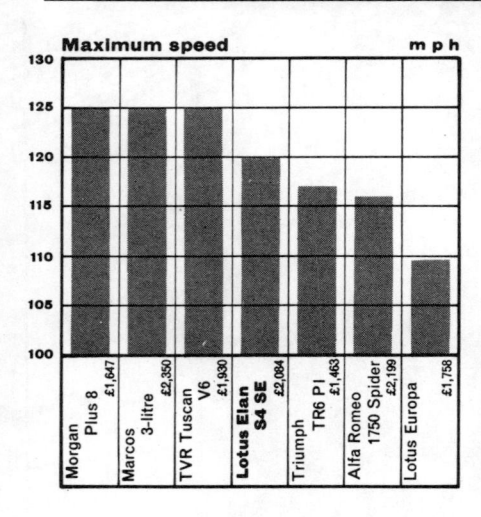

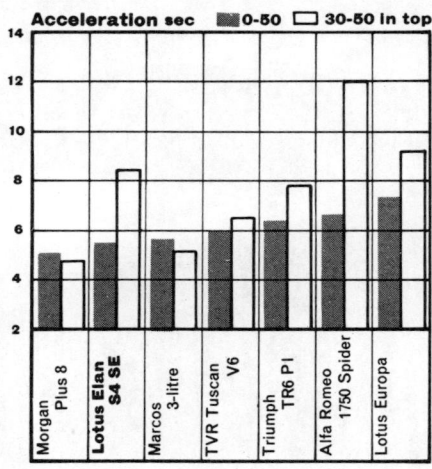

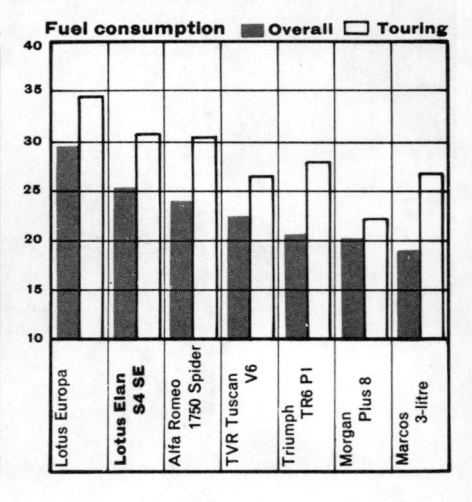

Performance tests carried out by *Motor's* staff at the Motor Industry Research Association proving ground, Lindley.
Test Data: World copyright reserved; no unauthorised reproduction in whole or in part.

Conditions
Weather: Dry, light winds 7-15mph, cold
Temperature: 25-29deg F
Barometer: 29.65-29.70in. Hg.
Surface: Dry tarmacadam
Fuel: Premium 98 octane (RM) 4 star rating

Maximum Speeds
	m.p.h.	k.p.h.
Mean of opposite runs	120	193
3rd gear	81	131
2nd gear at 6500 rpm	56	90
1st gear	38	61

"Maximile" speed: (Timed quarter mile after 1 mile accelerating from rest)
Mean 116

Acceleration Times
m p h	sec.
0-30	3.1
0-40	4.1
0-50	5.6
0-60	7.3
0-70	9.5
0-80	12.0
0-90	15.0
0-100	20.0
Standing quarter mile	15.5
Standing Kilometre	28.4

mph	Top sec.	3rd sec.
10-30	—	6.0
20-40	9.3	5.5
30-50	8.5	5.0
40-60	7.9	4.6
50-70	7.5	4.6
60-80	7.8	5.0
70-90	8.7	—
80-100	9.8	—

Fuel Consumption
Touring (consumption midway between 30 mph and maximum less 5% allowance for acceleration) .... 30.7 mpg
Overall .... 25.4 mpg
(=11.1 litres/100km)
Total test distance .... 1085 miles

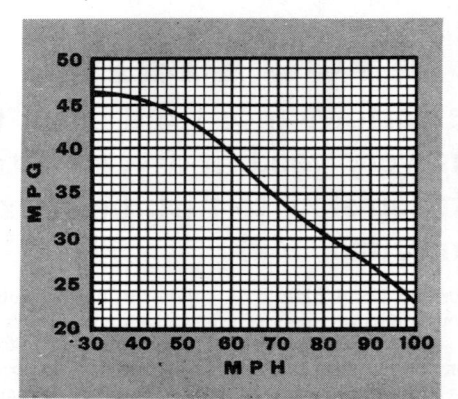

Brakes
Pedal pressure, deceleration and equivalent stopping distance from 30 mph
lb	g.	ft
25	0.31	97
50	0.64	47
75	0.87	34½
95	0.98	30½
Handbrake	0.21	143

Fade Test
20 stops at ½g deceleration at 1 min. intervals from a speed midway between 40 mph and maximum speed (=80 mph)

	lb
Pedal force beginning	35
Pedal force at 10th stop	32
Pedal force at 20th stop	38

Steering
Turning circle between kerbs: ft
Left 31
Right 32
Turns of steering wheel from lock to lock 2.6
Steering wheel deflection for 50 ft. diameter circle 0.8 turns

Clutch
Free pedal movement .... = ½in
Additional movement to disengage clutch completely .... = 3in
Maximum pedal load 36lb

Speedometer
Indicated	10	20	30	40	50	60	70
True	9	18	27	37	46	55	64
Indicated	80	90	100	110			
True	73	81	91	100			

Distance recorder 2% fast

Weight
Kerb weight (unladen with fuel for approximately 50 miles) .... 13.6 cwt
Front/rear distribution 49/51
Weight laden as tested .... 17.4 cwt

Parkability
Gap needed to clear 6ft wide obstruction in front

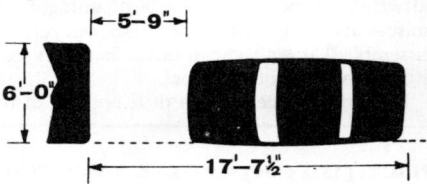

5'-9"
6'-0"
17'-7½"

as fast at the bottom end as our previous coupe, but beyond 5000 rpm it is better—not only in top and third gear but also in the upper standing start accelerations. It was slower against the stopwatch—it didn't feel it—to 30 and 40 mph but beyond 50 the gain was progressively obvious, with nearly 3½ seconds in hand to 100 mph.

Customers may not be able to record the same figures as our test car did not have the ignition cut-out which cuts the sparks at 6500; we used 7000 rpm for the best figures. In top gear it could pull 6500 rpm (113 mph) after only a mile from rest; our maximum at 6900 rpm of 120 mph is taken from observed rev counter readings round the MIRA banked circuit. On a long straight road it would probably build up to over 7000 rpm in top; with the higher final drive it should do nearer 125 mph as this would drop the revs back towards the power peak for ideal gearing.

Another change you notice from the cockpit is the absence of throaty Weber gobble as you accelerate hard from low engine speeds; there is still a noticeable amount of mechanical noise, a mixture of twin cam chain whine at low speeds with a general combustion harshness over 4500 rpm; but induction noise is more subdued. The engine itself, though, is astonishingly smooth and willing to rev. On the convertible, exhaust noise is rather obtrusive although (initially at least) not unpleasant.

Our overall fuel consumption on road test Elans has been pretty constant at 25-26 mpg; with the Strombergs consumption doesn't increase so suddenly after 50 mph and the touring consumption is some 10 per cent better than the Weber-carburetted S3. Our staff S2, with the higher final drive, usually returned nearer 30 mpg, which gives almost 280 miles per 9¼ gallon tankful. We hadn't the nerve to go much beyond 180 miles, at 25 mpg, on the test car.

Elan S4 speeding along the shores of Lake Vyrnwy; outwardly the same as the first series, S4s now have a bright sill strip and a completely different tail panel. The twin-pipe silencer is rather noisy

Americanised facia has almost flush rocker switches and large flat knobs for choke and heater. Leather-rimmed wheel is an SE addition

Bare bones of the hood are revealed with the material about to be rolled up into the tray; the sticks fold up under the furled hood. An instruction sheet is stuck to the tray. It takes some time to get the hood covered up under the bag.

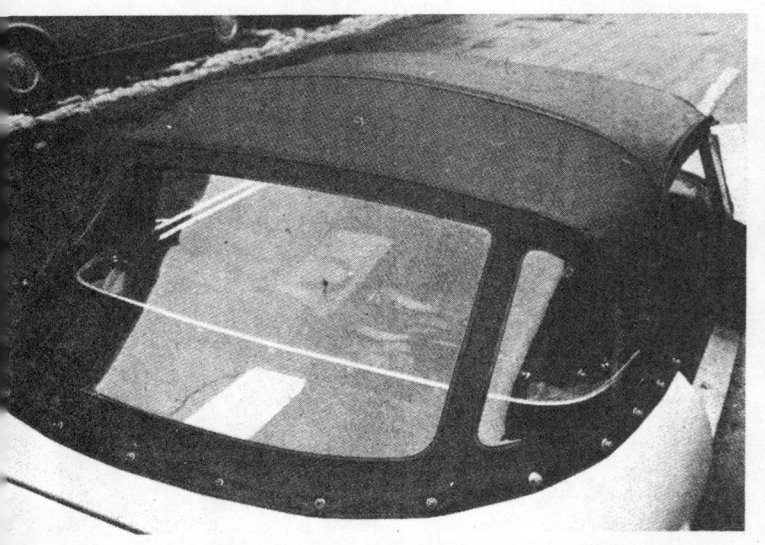

With the hood up the outline is a little different from the original type. Clear panels probably give better visibility than you get in the coupe

Space behind the seats is smaller than with the coupe to allow the hood to be folded. Seats tip forward, but are retained for American cars. Outline of backbone chassis is clearly shown

Transmission

We have already referred to the engine fussiness with the 3.77:1 final drive ratio and certainly the better insulated coupe with the 3.54:1 ratio gives much more relaxed 90 mph cruising at 4850 rpm. No doubt open-air drivers buying the convertible will find it quite acceptable as the engine noise merges with the general wind commotion at Continental cruising speeds. The gearbox has standard Cortina GT ratios which seem nice and close on the parent saloon, less so on the Lotus if you are used to a really close ratio set; most of us were quite happy with them as a compromise solution though, as they give useful speeds in the intermediate gears. The greater rev differences demand more accurate synchronization to make the changes completely surge free as the rubber driveshaft couplings are still a handicap to those unaccustomed to Elans. The twin Metalastik joints in each driveshaft absorb driveshaft plunge with wheel movement as well as cushioning transmission shocks. They also absorb the jerk of our standing starts remarkably effectively, allowing just a little wheelspin before the Dunlops grip and the car squirts away; you can do the same sort of thing on a 1 in 3 hill, too, so the ratios are well chosen for all practical road use.

With light brake and throttle pedals, we found the clutch relatively heavy although fairly progressive. As usual the gearchange movement is excellent with the delightful flick-switch feel characteristic of the first Elan; we found third gear a little noisy but this isn't usual. The final drive was quiet though.

Handling and brakes

The Elan's roadholding is still very impressive; the car has relatively soft suspension (so the grip is always good even on bumpy roads) and it therefore pays to make one's movements progressive on both throttle and steering wheel. If you do anything jerkily the car responds jerkily, so it pays to be in the right gear at the right time; progress through a corner is then smooth and positive. It pays, more than usual, to get the braking done before the corner. It isn't dangerous if you brake deep into the apex since the grip is so good; but it just isn't as comfortable. With power down in the dry the car eventually oversteers, which a premature unwinding of lock, rather than an obvious correction will remedy.

On wet roads the car is not as sure footed—still good by comparison with other cars but against its dry road performance the difference is striking. Steering feel is excellent—it goes light at the front end at quite low cornering forces, without the car going straight on—but you sometimes don't know how much adhesion is left in hand; power carelessly applied then can flick the tail quite suddenly and you have to be quite quick to catch it. On *clean* wet roads it is good; on greasy wet ones, it can be tricky. Perhaps we are being over-critical but then Lotus themselves set the standards by which we judge sports car suspensions nowadays. Apart from increasing the tyre section from 145 to 155-13 on SE models, and making the damping a little firmer, little has been changed.

The 3.1 cu.ft. pile on the right fits into the boot, while the two 0.8 cu.ft. boxes fit behind the seats. The toolkit is better than most cars offer

SPECIFICATION

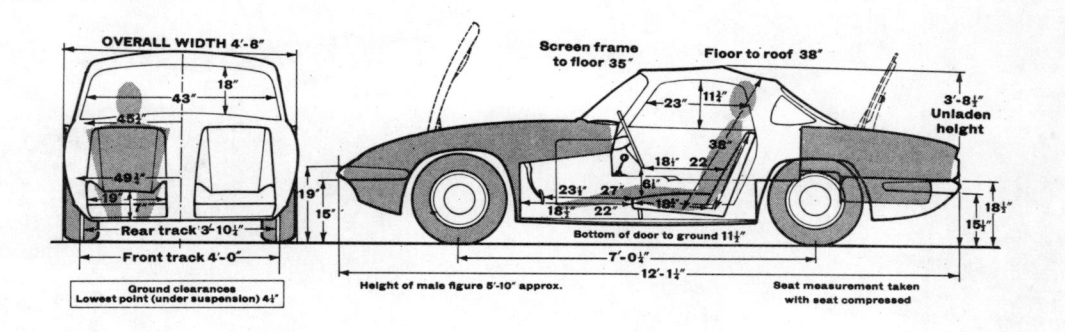

Twin overhead camshaft 1558 cc engine; all independent suspension; steel backbone chassis

Engine
Block material	Cast iron
Head material	Aluminium
Cylinders	4
Cooling system	Water; pump fan and thermostat
Bore and stroke	82.6 mm (3.25in.) 72.8 mm (2.86in.)
Cubic capacity	1,558 c.c. (95.2 cu. in.)
Main bearings	5
Valves	D.o.h.c.
Compression ratio	9.5:1
Carburetters	Twin Stromberg 175 CDS
Fuel pump	AC mechanical
Oil filter	Full flow
Max. power (net)	115 bhp at 6,250 rpm
Max. torque (net)	105 lb. ft. at 5,000 rpm

Transmission
Clutch	8in. s.d.p. diaphragm spring
Internal gear box ratios	
Top gear	1.0
3rd gear	1.40
2nd gear	2.01
1st gear	2.97
Reverse	3.32
Synchromesh	On all forward ratios
Final drive (type and ratio)	Hypoid bevel 3.77:1 (3.54 std on SE)
Mph at 1,000 rpm in:—	
Top gear	17.4
3rd gear	12.4
2nd gear	8.7
1st gear	5.9

Chassis and body
Construction	Steel backbone chassis with separate glass fibre bodywork

Brakes
Type	Girling discs
Dimensions	9.5in. dia. front; 10in. dia. rear
Friction areas:	
Front	20 sq. in. of lining operating on 159 sq. in. of disc
Rear	10.5 sq. in. of lining operating on 159 sq. in. of disc

Suspension and steering
Front	Independent wishbones and coil springs
Rear	Independent by strut and lower wishbone, coil springs
Shock absorbers:	
Front	Telescopic
Rear	
Steering type	Rack and pinion
Tyres	185 × 13 Dunlop SP Sport
Wheels	Centre lock, peg-drive steel
Rim size	4½J × 13

Coachwork and equipment
Starting handle	No
Tool kit contents	Plug spanner, screwdriver, 3 open-ended spanners
Jack	Scissor screw
Jacking points	4 under body sill
Battery	12 volt negative earth, 57 amp. hrs capacity
Number of electrical fuses	2
Headlamps	Lucas F700 120/90 watt
Indicators	Self-cancelling flashers
Reversing lamp	Yes
Screen wipers	Two-speed electric
Screen washers	Electric
Sun visors	No
Locks:	
With ignition key	Doors
With other keys	Boot
Interior heater	Fresh air
Upholstery	Leathercloth seats, pvc hood
Floor covering	Carpet
Alternative body styles	Fixed-head coupe
Maximum load	450 lb
Maximum roof rack load	None
Major extras available	Final drive

Maintenance
Fuel tank capacity	9¼ galls
Sump	7½ pints SAE 20/50
Gearbox	1½ pints SAE 80EP
Rear axle	2 pints SAE 90EP
Steering gear	Grease
Coolant	14 pints (2 drain taps)
Chassis lubrication	Every 6,000 miles to 2 points
Minimum service interval	3,000 miles
Ignition timing	9° btdc
Contact breaker gap	0.015 in.
Sparking plug gap	0.020 in.
Sparking plug type	Autolite AG22
Tappet clearance (cold)	Inlet 0.006 in. Exhaust 0.010 in.
Valve timing—	
inlet opens	26° b.t.d.c.
inlet closes	66° a.b.d.c.
exhaust opens	66° b.b.d.c.
exhaust closes	26° a.t.d.c.
Rear wheel toe-in	to 0 in.
Front wheel toe-in	1/16 to 1/16 in.
Camber angle	0° to 1°
Castor angle	2½°-3½°
King pin inclination	8½°-9½°
Tyre pressures:	
Front	18 psi; 22 psi fast driving
Rear	23 psi; 27 psi fast driving

Safety Check List
Steering Assembly
Steering box position	Ahead of front wheels
Steering column collapsible	Yes
Steering wheel boss padded	No
Steering wheel dished	Slightly

Instrument Panel
Projecting switches	Flat rockers
Sharp cowls	No
Padding	Above and below facia

Windscreen and Visibility
Screen type	Laminated
Pillars padded	Covered
Standard driving mirrors	Interior
Interior mirror framed	Yes
Interior mirror collapsible	Yes
Sun visors	Two padded

Seats and Harness
Attachment to floor	Front pivot bolted to floor
Do they tip forward?	Yes (not for N. American cars)
Headrest attachment points	No
Back of front seats	Firm
Safety Harness	Lap and diagonal
Harness anchors at back	Unnecessary

Doors
Projecting handles	No
Anti-burst latches	No
Child-proof locks	No

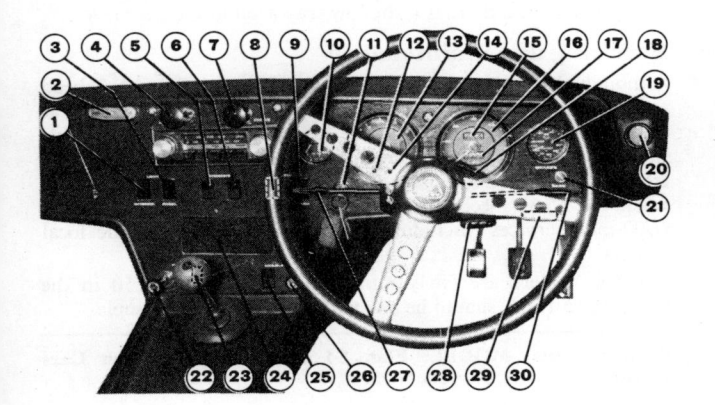

---

1 interior light. 2 map light. 3 panel lights. 4 heater temperature control. 5 and 6 window lift switches. 7 choke. 8 two-speed wipers. 9 washers. 10 fuel gauge. 11 ignition/starter. 12 main beam telltale. 13 rev counter. 14 ignition warning light. 15 trip recorder. 16 speedometer. 17 total mileage recorder. 18 indicator tell-tale. 19 oil pressure/water temperature gauge. 20 fresh air vent. 21 handbrake warning light. 22 cigar lighter. 23 heater fan. 24 ashtray. 25 lighting switch. 26 headlight lifter. 27 dipping stalk. 28 bonnet release. 29 handbrake. 30 indicator stalk

Polishing the lights with the picture taken between the flashes—it isn't possible without wiring modifications to have them up but off. Part of the SE extras are the side indicator repeaters and the 155 x 13 radials on knock-on wheels

Harder pads and a servo are fitted to the SE which makes the brakes just about the right weight, not tiringly heavy but firm enough to provide a pivot for heel and toe gearchanges. They didn't fade or suffer from two trips through the water splash. The pull-out umbrella handbrake is not very strong as an emergency system (only 0.21g) but it held the car on a 1 in 4 hill.

Comfort and controls

The first Elan particularly impressed us with its ride which is still exceptionally good for a sports car; there is a useful amount of suspension travel which allows the wheels to soak up bumps easily with little disturbance to the occupants. Despite the low overall weight of the car, the sprung to unsprung ratio is still favourable and the suspension has been carefully designed to make it soft without inducing high roll angles. Even on bad surfaces at town speeds it doesn't rattle and the substantial backbone chassis is rigid enough to prevent scuttle shake.

The seats are still comfortable hip-huggers which grip even the broadest of beams. Originally we found the lie-back attitude a bit too "racer" but times change and it now seems perfectly natural and there is enough seat adjustment for six-footers. However, people with large feet might find the pedals too close together; the clutch has been re-sited to allow a space between it and the tunnel but there is still nowhere to rest it.

It takes a very good soft top to be as quiet as a fixed head; as folding hoods go, the Elan's is quite flap free, but no one could call it quiet, even at 60-70 mph. The frame has been modified since our 1964 road test; the hood sticks now fold neatly together and hinge into the well in front of the after deck. The hood material is fixed to the bodywork at the rear and folds into the well. But even if you follow the instructions and keep it tightly rolled, it will take getting on for five minutes to wrap it away.

1 washer reservoir. 2 air horn compressor. 3 dipstick. 4 oil filler cap. 5 radiator cap. 6 air cleaner for twin Strombergs

Assembly takes a little less time with practice—around two minutes. With the hood down and the side windows up you can recapture the joys of open motoring with very little buffeting; with a scarf round the back of the neck and reasonably warm clothing it can even be pleasant on a sunny winter's day with the heater on full blast and wafting across your legs and face. The heater controls are simple but effective—a temperature control, a two-speed blower and a couple of flaps at leg level so that there is always air coming through the system. But it is easy to keep the atmosphere pleasant whatever the temperature outside and small fresh air vents give a reasonable flow at face level.

With clear panels in the rear quarters the convertible Elan has better visibility than the coupe; it is a very compact car the edges of which are easily seen, so it is easy to park and manoeuvre in crowded streets. The two-speed wipers sweep a reasonable area, although it is a compromise setting for left- and right-hand drive and the swept area is well short of the edge of the screen pillars.

Elan lights are famous for the way in which they gradually unfurl from the fully retracted position, like the eyes of a sleepy cow at dawn; unfortunately they are slow to come up which makes instant flashing impossible—the switch for this is awkward to grasp quickly, being too close to the facia. They come up flashing unless you select the headlight setting; once up and in normal use they provide a useful range.

Fittings and furniture

Unlike that of the Elan Plus 2 the facia on this car is pleasantly uncluttered with just four dials all within the sight line, although the wheel rim partly obscures the water temperature/oil pressure gauge on the right; the switches are all labelled and easy to memorize being intelligently coupled, with the washer and wiper pair nearest the wheel rim. In the centre of the facia are the two window lift switches; not quite as convenient as the original position in the door recess itself, but they now work more smoothly and faster.

Space behind the front seats is reduced to accommodate the hood mechanism but it is still large enough for a briefcase or fairly flat suitcases. The boot takes 3.1 cu.ft. of our test luggage which is enough for most people for a short term holiday. The spare wheel is housed underneath. Smaller items can go in the glove pocket, and there is a shallow tray around the gear lever.

Servicing and maintenance

Although the compact twin-cam engine stretches from bulkhead to radiator with little to spare endwise, the various ancillaries at the side are reasonably accessible—even the distributor without the bulk of the Webers to obscure it. Servicing is required pretty frequently, every 3000 miles, but since this is mostly just engine work the home mechanic might well do it himself, leaving the 6000-mile services (including two greasing points) to the local dealers.

Lotus dealers are fairly numerous, there are now 50 in the country, so there should be one within reach of most people.

MAKE: Lotus. **MODEL:** Elan S4 SE. **MAKERS:** Lotus Cars Limited, Norwich, Norfolk NOR 92W

The Plus 2S is undoubtedly the best-looking production car from Lotus.

THE FIRST LOTUS LUXURY CAR

Lotus cars have perhaps suffered in the past from a do-it-yourself image, resulting from selling kits of parts for tax reasons. The latest Plus 2S can be acquired only as a complete car, and it is finished and equipped so lavishly that it would amaze Lotus owners of a few years ago.

The performance appears to be virtually identical to that of the previous model, which one would expect as the mechanical specification is similar and the weight increase is negligible. However, the new machine has accessories as standard that are extras on most cars, even the radio being included in the slightly higher price, also two quartz-halogen foglamps. The interior is thickly carpeted, the mahogany instrument panel has enough dials and switches for an aircraft, and there are automatic courtesy lights under the bonnet and in the boot as well as in the car, with red lights in the trailing edges of the doors.

The basic construction remains the same, the central sheet steel backbone spreading out at both ends to embrace the engine in front and the hypoid differential unit behind. The suspension is independent by helical springs all round, by wishbones in front and struts behind with lower reinforced wishbones. The glassfibre body drops over the backbone like a saddle on a horse. Longer and wider than the original Elan, the body has two rear seats for children which could be used by adults if the front seats were adjusted well forward. It is not a four-seater but, as its name implies, it provides occasional seating in addition to the two normal front buckets.

The Plus 2S feels an altogether bigger car than its small sister. As the body shape is even more efficient, the extra drag is quite small, but there is more weight. The same twin-cam engine is employed for both cars, and the larger machine does not feel as fierce as a well-tuned Elan. However, it holds the road just as well and is even more stable at speed, while many people will think that the extra space is more than worth a fractional loss of performance. There can be no doubt that the Plus 2S is the best looking Lotus yet.

Like most Lotus cars, this one is comparatively low geared, and the rev counter will go well into the red in top gear. The machine will certainly exceed 120 mph, however, though it might not be advised to maintain this rate for long. The excellent Ford Cortina gearbox has the superb change for which it is noted and, compared with the earlier Plus 2 which I tested, the front wheels were much less inclined to lock during panic braking.

Steady development has made the twin-cam engine more refined and the new car has better sound damping. The exhaust tended to be audible on the overrun, but I formed the opinion that the silencer of the test car was past its best work. The ride is fairly hard, becoming very comfortable as the speed rises, and there is no pitching. The steering is light and quick—just about ideal. It is difficult to analyse the steering response, the car simply answering the wheel and fairly flying through corners at a speed which is astonishingly high.

The well-known winding-up and unwinding effect given by the rubber doughnut universal joints is far less tiresome than on the lighter Elan. The hand-brake, an umbrella handle hidden under the instrument panel, unfortunately remains rather a feeble thing. An excellent driving position, with all the pedals correctly placed, adds greatly to the pleasure of driving the car. It was sometimes necessary to use considerable force in engaging reverse.

Even at high cruising speeds, the fuel consumption remains moderate as a result of the efficient body shape. The drag is reduced by the usual Lotus disappearing headlamps, which are not very powerful by modern standards. However, the auxiliary quartz-halogen lamps which are standard can be used to extend the area of forward

The usual disappearing headlamps plus a pair of auxiliary quartz-halogen lamps are fitted as standard equipment on the £2300 Plus 2S.

visibility. Until one has covered a considerable mileage, the array of switches, all so much alike, can be somewhat disconcerting in the dark, though they are clearly labelled.

Somehow an air of quality has been built into the Plus 2S which no previous Lotus has enjoyed. Even the well-known twin-cam engine, which can seem somewhat rough in a steel saloon, becomes quite refined in this glassfibre coupe and separate chassis.

This larger Lotus is not much an exciting car as the little Elan, and one does not get the feeling that any hole in the traffic is big enough, as one does with the smaller car. It is nevertheless an altogether more practical form of transport, both for business and for family weekends. It is fundamentally a safe car because of its excellent road-holding and steering and it is surprisingly flexible if one feels like pottering along in top gear. In snow it gives much better traction than most front-engined rear-drive cars, and the handling remains impeccable. Its construction is likely to stand up much better to the dreaded salt on the roads than do most pressed-steel cars.

The Lotus, which started as a bit of a hairy special in spite of its scientific design, is now really growing up; I have even seen a Plus 2 with automatic transmission on the road. In spite of this civilised approach, the production models are still closely related to the Lotus grand prix cars, which is obvious as soon as one drives them in anger. Immense trouble is being taken to improve the quality of the cars which the public will buy, and some of those unkind jokes will soon be for retirement. The Lotus will always sell, because of its racing background, but the Plus 2S would also appeal to the man who thinks that Jochen Rindt is the name of an alcoholic beverage.

JOHN BOLSTER

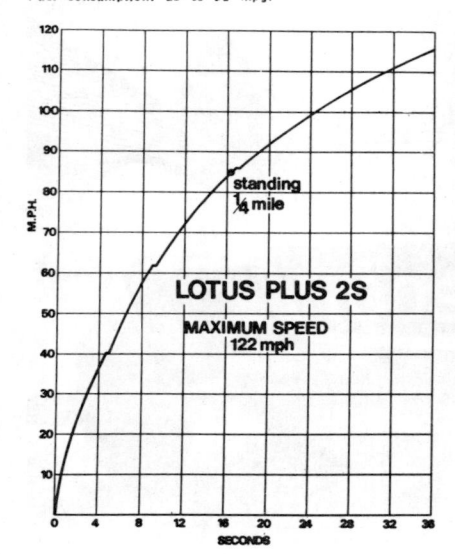

The fair-sized boot in no way detracts from the clean lines at the rear of the car.

SPECIFICATION AND PERFORMANCE DATA

Car tested: Lotus Elan Plus 2S two/four-seater coupé, price £2,376 including tax.
Engine: Four cylinders, 82.55 mm by 72.7 mm, 1558 cc. Inclined valves operated by twin chain-driven overhead camshafts. Compression ratio 9.5 to 1. 118 bhp at 6250 rpm. Two Weber twin-choke 40 DCOE carburetters. Lucas coil and distributor.
Transmission: Borg & Beck clutch. Four-speed all synchromesh gearbox with central remote control, ratios 1.0, 1.4, 2.01 and 2.97 to 1. Hypoid final drive, ratio 3.77 to 1. Open half shafts with Rotoflex universal joints.
Chassis: Central sheet-steel backbone. Independent front suspension by wishbones, helical springs with telescopic dampers, and torsional anti-roll bar. Rack and pinion steering. Independent rear suspension by lower wishbones and Chapman struts. Servo-assisted Girling disc brakes. Centre-locking light-alloy wheels fitted 165-13 in radial ply tyres.
Equipment: 12-volt lighting and starting. Speedometer. Rev. counter, Ammeter, Oil pressure, water temperature, ambient temperature and fuel gauges. Clock. Heating, demisting and ventilation system with electrically heated rear window. Two-speed windscreen wipers and washers. Electrically operated windows. Flashing direction indicators. Reversing lights. Cigar lighter. Radio. Foglamps.
Dimensions: Wheelbase 7 ft. 11.75 in. Track, front, 4 ft. 6 in.; rear, 4 ft. 7 ins. Overall length, 14 ft. 0.5 in. Weight, 17 cwt.
Performance: Maximum speed 122 mph. Speeds in gears: Third, 86 mph; Second, 62 mph; First, 40 mph. Standing quarter-mile 16.4 s. Acceleration: 0-30 mph, 3.2 s; 0-50 mph, 6.4 s; 0-60 mph, 8.4 s; 0-80 mph, 14.6 s; 0-100 mph, 24.2 s.
Fuel consumption: 25 to 31 mpg.

There is a large array of clearly marked switches on the dashboard (above). The twin-cam engine is now more refined after steady development (below).

LOTUS PLUS 2S — MAXIMUM SPEED 122 mph

ROAD TEST

LOTUS ELAN +2S

Speed in Style

LOTUS always seem in the news these days whether it be in the City columns, the introduction of a revolutionary new racing car or the comings and goings of various members of the staff. Colin Chapman and his devotees seem to have come a very long way in a short space of time from their humble workshops in Hornsey to the new open-plan offices and works at Hethel, Norfolk. Every Lotus owner—past, present or future—seems to have strong views on his car. It is either the finest handling, best engineered, most beautifully styled sports car in the world or a dreadful device which was totally unreliable and decidedly overpriced.

Recently we put almost 1,000-miles on the clock of the car that heads the range—the Lotus Elan +2S—and the only things that actually fell off were the rear view mirror which, after a shaky start, finally deposited itself in our lap, and a light-flashing knob. As it happened we were on our way to Brands Hatch, where we found a Lotus mechanic who promptly screwed the mirror back on again. Apart from that the car was totally reliable and showed itself to be a most desirable, if expensive, form of transport which seems to have benefited tremendously from continued development and improvement.

But first, what of the history of the first four-seater (just) from Colin Chapman's brilliant team? It was as far back as 1963 when Lotus decided that some time in the future it would be worthwhile to have a 2+2 in their range. Project studies were commenced and it was decided that the car should basically be an Elan derivative utilising a lengthened, widened and strengthened Elan chassis with the incorporation of as many common parts as possible.

By mid-1964 the rapid development of the Elan coupé was in full swing so there wasn't too much time spent on the 2+2 project, although a basic overall plan had been agreed. It was one misty morning in early 1965 that the directors and other senior management met in a rather clandestine manner at a North London park to view the first running prototype. Naturally the car was something of a lash-up and the glass-fibre body had been taken direct from the original aluminium styling mock-up. This secret device was called the Metier II.

At the meeting known and anticipated 2+2 models from other manufacturers were considered against the new Lotus and it was decided to increase the interior dimensions considerably to meet the car's maxim that it "must be capable of transporting two adults and two children 1,000 miles in comfort with their luggage".

In addition slight styling changes were incorporated in the revised version after considerable wind tunnel testing carried out in conjunction with the Rover Car Co. A drag coefficient of 0.3 was finally achieved but certainly not with the use of some of the rather ugly and tremendously bulbous shapes often attributed to low drag factors. In fact, the Elan +2 was, to nearly everyone, a strikingly beautiful shape, being something of a cross between the original Lotus GT car—the Elite—and the Elan coupé with touches of the Rover-BRM Le Mans car thrown in.

Another prototype was added and later came two new cars with a fully-engineered new backbone rather than the cut-and-weld-modified Elan backbones which had previously been used on the earlier prototypes. With the move to Norwich coming up and Elan coupé sales at a high level it was decided to delay introduction of the car from 1966 until August, 1967, by which time Lotus were in their new factory

Over 2,000 Plus Twos were built when Lotus decided to revise the model, call it the Plus Two S and announce it in July, 1969. There were improvements which made the car far more luxurious and well appointed, but the engineering concept remained basically unchanged apart from better rear universal rubber couplings for the drive shafts and one or two other features, including plenty of sound-deadening material. For the 1970 Motor Show further improvements included an alternator, a revised cooling system, a Philips radio and a revised and far better silencer. What with ever-rising costs plus the many improvements this has put the price up from an original £2,200, tax paid, to £2,616. Here, perhaps, is the main drawback of the Lotus, for at this price it is in direct competition with a Jaguar XJ6 4.2 or a 2+2 E-type which is only a hundred pounds dearer.

The actual test car delivered to Standard House was an ultra smart white model which was nicely run-in. Once in the driving seat one feels immediately comfortable with steering wheel and gear-lever coming easily to hand. The facia is a mass of dials and switches all neatly labelled, although their locations take a bit of learning in the dark. The speedometer and rev.-counter are directly in front of the driver, while the other smaller instruments are ranged to the left. These cater for every need, the race-bred Lotus firm obviously having rather different ideas on what the driver should know than some other manufacturers. In fact, thoughtful Lotus even provide an ambient temperature gauge so that you will know whether to put your overcoat on when you get out of the car. Also on the wooden facia is the radio, which is fitted as standard, and the various rocker switches, including those for the electric windows. Incidentally, considering this is a glass-fibre car,

COCKPIT of the Lotus Elan +2S is crammed full of instruments. Steering and gear-change are delightfully light.

the radio works very well with little interference. There is a decent-sized glove compartment, but getting the hang of the "magic" push rather than pull-to-open idea is a little difficult at first. Underneath this is, for the passenger's convenience, a map-reading light. This is not the sort of accessory that we would fit but once you have it you realise just how useful it can be. In fact, the Lotus is very strong on extra lights for, as well as illuminated boot and engine compartment, there are three ashtrays which all have little glowing lights as a safety factor. There seemed to be a few more trick lights, as well, for happily glowing away on the edge of the doors even when they were shut were red safety lights. The facia is completed by the air vents from the Lotus through flow-air system which works very effectively. If one wishes to strap oneself in, the safety belts are of the inertia reel type which are built in so that the reel itself is hidden behind the trim.

The trim and carpets are to the standard you would expect from a £2,600 motor car being conservatively black. It is interesting to note that Lotus attempt, as much as possible, to manufacture a large proportion of the car themselves and this includes the production of trim and seats. The door handles are the same as those used on several of the British Leyland range, particularly the 1100/1300s, and are undoubtedly the best for the job. These easy lift-up flaps are so much better than the usual finger-nail-braking devices so many sports cars seem to utilise. The windows are operated electrically, which is great as long as they keep working.

Before driving off we considered just how comfortable those extra two seats would be for adults. The answer is that they might be practicable for popping round to the pub but certainly not for any long-distance runs. As long as the front-seat passenger puts his seat fully forward then the person in the back will be only mildly cramped, but whoever fits in behind the driver is not going to be so happy, particularly if the driver happens to be more than about five foot six. Of course, if the driver happens to be D.S.J. then the problem would not be too bad but, even so, there is no way the Elan +2S can be considered a full four-seater. In fact, even the editorial Scimitar GTE, which is considerably more commodious, has its limitations, particularly for the passenger behind the driver.

The motive power comes from the famous race-bred Lotus Ford twin-cam in special equipment 1,600 c.c., 118 b.h.p. form. Although utilising several Ford parts, including the block, this is very much a Lotus engine these days for it can no longer be found in any of the Ford range and is built up at Hethel. It is undoubtedly a fine engine, although some owners become a little frustrated at constantly replacing cam cover gaskets and there was a stage when the engines seemed to eat exhaust valves at an alarming rate. This now seems over and, in their old age, the engines have settled down into reliable units, although for the Elan +2S the power is adequate more than sensational.

We therefore commend Lotus' announcement just a month ago that they are introducing a new big-valve version of the unit developed from the lessons learned in racing by former BRM chief engineer Tony Rudd, who is now increasingly making his presence felt at Lotus. By enlarging the size of the inlet valves and increasing the lift and duration of the camshaft Lotus have upped the power to 126 b.h.p. with no loss of flexibility. Also with the new development of the engine comes a stiffer cam cover which will be less prone to oil leaks.

The new car is called the Lotus +2S 130 and in addition to the new engine has a distinctive paint job with a silver cabin area, a strengthened differential plus new outlet drive shafts and revised drive couplings all for the addition of only £60.

Once one starts to drive the +2S the enjoyment really sets in. To drive the car fast and accurately takes a little practice as one adjusts to the precise movement of the steering and the ability to hug the road. First of all the steering is incredibly light and precise and to those used to getting a bit of muscle behind the wheel it will come as quite a surprise. However, once one settles down to the finger-tip control and sheer accuracy then there is no problem. Unlike the GT6 we tried last month, which was light but rather insensitive, one can feel everything that is going on.

Another aspect of driving the +2S is getting used to those rubber doughnut drive couplings. They have been improved tremendously since the early days but there is still a trace of surge under fierce acceleration and also under braking. I fully realise that rubber couplings of this type do have advantages over more conventional Hardy-Spicer-type universal joints and tend to act as a buffer to the transmission, but I still do not like them at all. They also have the

TWIN-CAM power from the Lotus-Ford gives 115 b.h.p. The new uprated engine with larger inlet valves produces around 126 b.h.p.

problem of being physically large.

Lotus have always been known for their excellent brakes and this model is no exception. A servo unit is fitted to assist the all-round discs, but there is still plenty of feel and the cars pull up nice and square making a mockery of those figures on the back of the Highway Code.

The all-round independent suspension with its racing-like wishbone and link lay-out gives the car superb handling, of that there is no doubt. The glory of it is that you can whip along country lanes with their twists and turns without drama, in complete safety and not working hard while drivers in lesser vehicles struggle to keep up. However, I would suggest that the ultimate road-holding is not up to the standard of the Elan, particularly in the wet. In fact, on one occasion, on what appeared to be a dry road, the tail came round alarmingly and had it not been for the quick steering I might well have spun. As I was unable to repeat the phenomenon I can only assume that I hit a patch of oil, which is a pretty old excuse, but I just was not going very quickly at the time.

High-speed cruising on the Motorways of Britain threw up very few deficiencies, for the Elan will pull close on maximum revs. in top gear and one feels that perhaps an overdrive would be a welcome addition. The top speed is somewhere close on 120 m.p.h., achieved without too much fuss or bother, although naturally one can't afford to be half-asleep at those kind of speeds. Even at a 100 m.p.h. one is completely relaxed but for a Motorway trip at high speed I would prefer the Scimitar, although, of course, the Tamworth device would be left behind on twisty roads.

A side aspect of high-speed touring with the Lotus is the inability to flash the headlights quickly. They are buried away in two

SPACIOUS BOOT for the +2S which is opened from a pull knob in the well of the driver's door.

LOTUS 2+2 TEST

pneumatically-operated pods and these have to swing lugubriously into position before they can issue the warning of impending approach. By then you might as well have used the loud air horns instead for the operation takes about five seconds and the knob of the pull switch came away in the Editor's hand before I even sat in the car. Included in the specification are also two fog and spot lamps mounted below the chrome bumper and these could be flashed instead.

Performance in the traffic lights grand prix is not to be sneered at for 0-60 m.p.h. time of just over eight seconds makes the car on a par with something like a Triumph TR6 and not much slower than a Jaguar E. Still accelerating the +2S will be up to 100 m.p.h. in around 25 sec.

My personal acquaintance with the car was unfortunately all too brief for, while the Editor was able to clock up some 800 miles, my trips in the machine were unfortunately limited to various runs within London and a drive down to Brands Hatch to see the new Formula Atlantic. Meanwhile, the chief photographer drove the car out to Epping Forest with myself tagging along behind in the Triumph GT6. We did discover that the Lotus had far superior brakes when the photographer spotted a suitable spot for pictures and almost collected the GT6 up his glass-fibre boot. The said gentleman, who is an avid MG-B GT owner of some years standing, was not at all impressed and, above all, claimed that the car smelt of glass-fibre and he would not have one as a gift. As we said, Lotus models usually promote strong feelings. Having disturbed some budding lunch-time romances in a rather remote part of the forest, the Lotus returned to London by way of some most dreadful traffic jams but showed no signs of becoming overheated.

Running an Elan +2S should not, in theory anyway, be an expensive operation for the fuel consumption worked out around the 23-24 m.p.h. mark, while this engine was not very heavy on oil, although twin-cams do usually develop a thirst to the tune of a pint per 500 miles after a year or so. Lotus dealerships are usually run by enthusiasts possibly with a competition background so service should be efficient and knowledgeable if you pick the right place. Lotus have recently instituted a new scheme where, for a small charge, urgent parts are despatched *via* a security service van rather than by the rather hit-and-miss British Rail system, particularly as all lines hardly lead to Norwich.

Despite its high price the Elan +2S is attracting something like 40 buyers a week and many of the more affluent young amongst the population see the car as a definite alternative to a Jaguar XJ6. One lesson we learned from the road-test is that Lotus have undoubtedly more than got the hang of making luxury cars which are a far cry from those first Lotus 6s and 7s Colin Chapman built not so many years ago.

"The 130"

As mentioned earlier, Lotus have just announced a new version of the Plus 2S called the "130" and as we closed for Press we were able to borrow one of the first of the new cars for a quick Sunday afternoon's drive to assess briefly the improvements. Our refresher drive served not only to remind us what a good car the Elan Plus 2S is, but also to show that those extra 10 b.h.p., plus the other improvements, are excellent value at an additional £60. In fact, we anticipate sales of the normal Plus 2S falling considerably as the pepped-up version catches on.

Just as the publicity material said, the larger inlet valves and slight camshaft alteration has in no way adversely affected the engine with regard to tractability and, if anything, made the car easier to drive. Also noticeable was the great improvement in the rotoflex couplings in the rear-drive train and the dreaded surge is now almost completely eliminated. We gather that these new couplings, developed for the 130, will be used on the ordinary Plus 2S types as well in the near future. Incidentally, our only complaint about the 130 was the fact that the driving rear view mirror was just about to fall off!

A quick blast up the Motorway showed that performance was considerably improved and the car ran right round to 7,000 r.p.m. in top, which can only be described as impressive. This was achieved with such a lack of fuss and wind noise, one imagined that we were only a fraction over the legal limit. With this new version it appears Lotus have got very close to the ultimate that can be expected from the Plus 2S. With Tony Rudd working energetically to ensure new standards of quality and reliability for the Norwich concern their future seems bright.—A. R. M.

2000 MILES BY ELAN +2—continued from page 98

the VW that is flat-out at 68 m.p.h. puts his winker on and hopefully starts to try and overtake the Fiat that is doing 65 m.p.h. In such moments you want instant full-beam headlamps, you cannot wait for one second or even half-a-second. The Lotus Elan and Elan +2 have a lot of endearing features which I like very much, but the "pop-up" headlamps is not one of them. If I became a Lotus owner I would either fix the lamps in the up position or fit a pair of spot-lights to use for flashing. A strident Maserati or Fiamm horn is all very well, but in the modern hermetically sealed saloon you don't hear them until they are very close. Lotus must have a good reason for retaining their Vacuum Operated Headlamp System, but apart from anything else page 30 of the Owner's Handbook puts me off. It is headed Fault Diagnosis, and covers the following: Headlamps do not lift at all, lift slowly, lift halfway, lift unevenly, lift but drop immediately, only one lifts up, one stays up, both waver vertically, will not stop flashing, no flashing, no main beam, no dipped beam, no light at all. Definitely not my favourite part of the Lotus Elan +2.

The mechanical specification of the Elan +2 is exactly what you would expect with the racing associations of Lotus. The chassis is a backbone affair fabricated from steel pressings, with a very deep centre section which forks towards the front to embrace the engine and gearbox. Fork suspension is independent by double wishbones with interspersed coil-spring/damper units, rear suspension is by a wide-base lower wishbone and combined coil-spring and damper strut unit in one with the hub carrier. Disc brakes are fitted to all four wheels, the rear ones being inboard of the hub carriers, and a brake servo is fitted. The engine is a four-cylinder Ford-based unit, with Lotus aluminium cylinder head with two overhead camshafts driven by a roller-chain, and carburation is by two double-choke horizontal Weber carburetters fed by an air box and long flexible trunking from a filter in the nose of the car. The gearbox is a Ford four-speed and reverse with short central gear-lever, and rack-and-pinion steering gear is used. The body is of glass-fibre and is of coupé form with external luggage compartment at the rear, the driver's and passenger's seats are adjustable fore and aft but have fixed backs, and there are two small children's seats behind the main seats. Between the front seats is a flat box suitable only for paperwork and on the passenger's side of the instrument panel is a lockable glove compartment. In spite of being a low car the long doors give a wide opening and make entry easy, and the driver is confronted by large speedometer and r.p.m. indicator, gauges for fuel contents, oil pressure, water temperature and ammeter are spread about the centre of the panel, and under the dash is a rather ineffective "umbrella handle" type handbrake. Pressed steel "knock-on" type wheels are standard with 165×13-inch. tyres, but alloy wheels are shortly to be introduced as standard on the "S"-type Elan +2. In spite of giving the appearance of being a small car it has an overall length of 14 ft., due mostly to the long tapering nose.

Elan enthusiasts tend to look sideways at the Elan +2 and mutter about more weight, more roll, more frontal area and so on, but there is no question about the fact that the Elan +2 is a much more civilised car and has put Lotus into the manufacturer category and got them away from the "kit-car" image, and whereas the sight of an Elan would evoke the feeling "there is one of those funny little Lotus cars", the Elan +2 evokes a feeling of "Oh look, a Lotus".—D. S. J.

Road & Track Owner Survey

LOTUS ELAN

"This is certainly not a car that can be bought and forgotten."

ADVOCATES OF CONSUMERISM, those thin-lipped devotees of prudent materialism, will find scant comfort here. The findings of this survey of Lotus Elan owners are simultaneously a sharp stick in the eye of watchful protectionism and a triumph of the human spirit—proof, if you will, that money isn't everything.

In numbers, the survey is one of the smallest in our series. There were 77 valid responses, fewer than the 100 we try to have as a minimum. But, on the basis of replies per total ownership, this is the best. There are only a few thousand Elans in the U.S., while the Fiats, Volvos and Mustangs number in the hundreds of thousands. We have a small picture, but it's very clear.

There is a blur on models and types. The Elan itself is confusing. From the original 1964 model, convertible only with haul-up windows, there came in quick and confusing succession a coupe, another convertible with electric windows, the Series 2, 3 and 4, the SE option which soon became standard equipment, and the Super Safety model for the U.S. market. We retreated to using model year only, so the survey consists of 29% early cars ('64 and '65), 62% middle-aged ('66 and '67) and 9% newish ('68, '69 and '70). Ten percent of the responses involved cars with more than 60,000 miles, the record going to a 1965 Elan with 72,000 on the clock. The average owner drives his Lotus 10,000 miles annually.

The Owners

AT A GUESS, Elan owners are younger and more enthusiast than even the average sports car owner. Only 44% of the cars were bought new, and one-third of the cars are in one-car families. MGB and Porsche owners told us they bought used cars only 31% and 13% of the time, respectively. The Elan owner most likely is a bachelor who'd rather have a used Lotus than a new MG, or a family man with an Elan, new or used, in place of a Porsche or a BMW.

To back this up, another record. Surprisingly, 80% of the Elans are in daily use, bearing out the single-car figure. But there were record numbers of several uses. Fully 11% of the cars are used for racing! That's not just high, it's twice as high as the results of the MG and Datsun tests, in our surveys the only cars with a significant number of owners who race. All the people who used to drive their racing cars on road and track have bought Lotuses. And 22% of the Elan owners drive in rallies (about average for sports cars); 36% run slaloms, twice the average. Between one third and half are being used for one or more forms of sports.

Reasons For Buying

THIS IS THE first hint of the promised heartwarming conclusion. There was no contest. A full 36% wanted performance, 22% wanted handling, 13% bought because of the Lotus' engineering, 7% listed "fun to drive" and another 7% simply "wanted a Lotus." From there, the figures are too small to be measured, although it's gratifying to see a reply like "because of R&T's report."

There was no mention of practical virtues, such as economical fuel consumption and fiberglass bodywork that won't rust.

Service And Maintenance

ONCE THE CONTRACT is signed, the trouble begins. For this section, we create two new categories. Added to the spaces for good, fair and poor dealer service are answers for No Dealer, and Very Poor dealers.

But when the dealer is good, he is very good. Only 24% made it, the worst showing we've seen so far, but there are a few places whose customers love them. Three owners made it a point to recommend Bob Challman, Manhattan Beach, Calif. (a longtime Lotus racer, and friend, and the man who loans us test Lotuses the distributor claims not to have). Bill Young, Montrose, Calif., got two plugs from customers. His own racing Elan was the terror of C Production not long ago. An obvious moral here. Quoting one owner, "Don't let anybody except a qualified racing mechanic touch your Lotus."

A total of 39%, a plurality if not a majority, do not have or use a dealer. Two reasons were cited. For 28%, there was no choice. They live where there are no dealers within driving distance. And 11% said they left the dealer in disgust.

Twenty-three percent of the owners do some or all of the work, although this probably reflects the competition-mindedness of Elan owners as much as it does the service available to them.

The concern for maintenance was general, though. A normal 25% follow the factory's schedule, and only a handful (4%) do less. Those who follow the schedule most of the time tallied 36%. Another new entry, with 24%, was owners who do all the factory directs and more. (The reason for this was not devotion alone, as we'll see when the proper time comes.)

Best Features

NARY A DISAPPOINTED customer, in this sense. The favorite best feature was handling, with 47%. Next came performance, defined as handling plus braking and power, with 44%. We might as well consider the two as one, and that comes to 91%. Remember, that's what attracted most buyers to the car in the first place, with handling and performance the favorites there as well. Desire for a pure sports car, fun to drive, and engineering also figured in the reasons bought, and can also be considered as fitting the performance category. They wanted a car that did certain things, and the Elan does them.

For the record, 6% said the design was the best feature, 3% said driving comfort, and 2% listed the ride.

Worst Features

NO CLASS WAS especially large here, simply because there are 22 items in the worst features list. Fragility comes first, with 13%, then 12% for many small repair and service items, 10% each for expense and scarcity of parts and poor paint and bodywork quality, and 7% for lack of reliability. The full list is too long to be given, but it covers just about everything you can think of, except that nobody mentioned fuel consumption or price of the car itself.

Grouped in categories, service and maintenance account for 29% of the worst features, quality control for 30%, and operations, in which fall fragility and lack of reliability, for 41%.

Trouble Spots

OH, WOW, ANOTHER record here, with 35 items having given at least one owner a bad time. There is something of this in any car: with enough samples, one of everything is likely to go wrong. But this is a small sample.

And some of the things went wrong in different ways. The Elan has hidden headlights, actuated by engine vacuum. There are reports of lights that stuck open, lights that stuck shut,

---

SUMMARY: LOTUS ELAN OWNER SURVEY

New or Used?
Bought New.......44%
Bought Used......56%

About Driving Habits
Drivers who said they drive "moderately"...11%
Drivers who said they drive "hard".........62%
Drivers who said they drive "very hard".....17%

Would they buy another?
Yes................85%
No.................15%

Mileages Driven less than
5000 mi a year.....18%
Driven 5–15,000....70%
Driven more than
   15,000..........12%

Problem Areas
Reported by more than 10% of owners:

Radiator Leaks	Overheating
Starter	Weather Leaks
Ring Gear	Electrical
Oil Leaks	Generator
Instruments	Body Parts

Reported by 5–10% of owners:

Freeze Plugs	Tuning
Water Pump	Valve Gear
Flexible Couplings	Clutch
Headlights	Differential
Transmission	Engine Mounts
Wheel Bearings	Wheel Balance

Five Best Features
Handling
Performance
Design
Driving Comfort
Ride

Five Worst Features
Fragility
Number of Repair and
   Service Items
Expense and
   Scarcity of Parts
Poor Quality Control
Lack of Reliability

How Owners feel About Lotus Service
Rated "good".....24%
Rated "fair".......19%
Rated "poor"......14%
No Dealer.........39%

LOTUS ELAN

and lights that sink softly into their nests during long uphill pulls. Some hood latches jammed, and some released at speed. If there were two ways for a component to break, it did both.

In fairness, the worst trouble area was the instruments and they are Lotus' fault only at one remove. Still, just that the factory doesn't make them is no excuse for always buying them. But back to Lotus, and we find 44%, yes, another record, had instrument failure or malfunction.

Pure lack of quality control surely caused the leaking radiators suffered by 24%.

In this category, but with enough entries of its own to qualify for mention, is overheating. So many owners passed along their cures that we'd be remiss not to keep up the work. If your Elan runs hot, change to a cooler thermostat, fit four blades instead of two to the fan, swap the electric fan for the viscous drive fan on the Lotus Cortina, move the air cleaner from the inside of the airstream and the front license plate from the outside, and trade the stock radiator for one from a Triumph Herald. We're told some or all of these work, in most cases.

Not much to say about the oil leaks, except to quote the stoic who said, "Of course. It's English, isn't it?"

The starter problem must be infuriating. It's really two problems. In some cars, the Bendix drive chews itself to pieces, while in others the ring gear shifts on the flywheel and tears the Bendix drive to pieces. Sorry, no cure here. There was a wistful notation from the owner of a '66 that the factory has since cured this. Apparently not so. The owner of a '67 said, "it's ridiculous that after five years they still haven't found a starter motor that will mesh with the ring gear."

There were two cars with no trouble spots. One had 22,000 miles on it, enough for major breakage but not a full test. The other, with 54,000 miles, has been serviced from infancy by Bill Young.

Component Life

ANOTHER RACING-RELATED area. The purely competition answers, as in spark plugs every 300 miles and tires every 500, won't count, except to other racers. Better to pick the medians, and say you can expect to replace tires every 25,000 miles, plugs every 10,000 and brake pads at 11,000. And remember to allow for driving habits. Shock absorber life went from 10,000 to 50,000, and the flexible rear axle couplings from 14,000 to 44,000. Plan on lots of maintenance, in other words.

Buy Another?

CHEER UP, sports car fans! Pretend that you don't know a loaded question when you hear it.

Now then, protector of helpless consumers, we have before us a car that sells for a high price, and isn't suited to family life. Dealers are rare, and good ones rarer still. Parts are scarce and expensive. The manufacturer can't seem to correct the simplest defects. How do you suppose the owners feel now?

They love the car. A full 85% would buy another. The Elan is the most troublesome car we've surveyed, yet its owner loyalty ranks with cars that all but repair themselves. What Lotus and Mercedes-Benz have in common is that they do what the owners want them to do, and if it costs money, spend it.

AUTOTEST

LOTUS ELAN SPRINT (1,588 c.c.)

AT-A-GLANCE: New version of Elan with up-rated engine, strengthened final drive and stiffer drive-shaft "doughnuts". More performance, slightly less economy, smoother but firmer ride. All other qualities every bit as good as before.

MANUFACTURER
Lotus Cars Ltd., Norwich, Norfolk.

PRICES
Component form	£1,706
Seat belts (approx.)	£10
Total (in G.B.)	£1,716

(Not available as factory-built car and therefore exempt from purchase tax)

PERFORMANCE SUMMARY
Mean maximum speed	118 mph
Standing start ¼-mile	15.0 sec
0-60 mph	7.0 sec
30-70 mph through gears	6.6 sec
Typical fuel consumption	26 mpg
Miles per tankful	240

Above: The two-tone colour scheme and side lettering identifies the Elan Sprint from all other Elans. Production cars will not have the bonnet bulge. Below: Cornering power is superb with very little roll and plenty of grip

NEXT YEAR it will be 10 years since the Lotus Elan first came on the scene as something of a revolution in small sports cars. Never before was so much performance allied to such superb handling in such a compact and manoeuvrable package. Along the way it has been improved and developed, appearing as the Elan Coupé S/E in 1967, the Elan S4 two years later and now the Elan Sprint.

This latest version incorporates major modifications to the engine and drive line and has a distinctive colour scheme to make it stand out from all the other Elans. In this form, which is the only kind of Elan now made, it is easily the best Lotus we have ever tested.

With the possibility of legal action under the Trades Descriptions Act ever present, most manufacturers are becoming much more honest in their engine power claims. The 115 bhp (net) which has been quoted for the Elan since 1967 was always a very optimistic figure so that against it the Elan Sprint's output of 126 bhp (net) does not look so impressive. Suffice it to say that, in fact, there is a 25 per cent increase in true power output.

The engine for the Elan Sprint is the same "Big Valve" unit which powers the Lotus Plus 2S 130, this other Lotus being the subject of a full Autotest a few weeks ago. It is a development of the well-proved Lotus-Ford twin-cam with larger valves and twin Weber DCOE carburettors once again (these were relinquished on the Elan S4 in favour of Strombergs to meet American anti-pollution requirements). The Webers do not need the rather ugly bonnet bulge necessary for clearance with the Strombergs, but it was there on the test car because it had been converted from an S4. Production Elan Sprints will be without it.

To cope with the extra power passing through the drive line, the differential and drive shafts have been strengthened and much stiffer Rotoflex "doughnut" joints are used. These effectively eliminate the unpleasant surge so characteristic of all earlier Elans and make the Sprint a much smoother car to drive.

The rest of the mechanical specification remains the same as before, with the important exception of the exhaust system, which is now much quieter. It still produces a purposeful growl, but that rude rasp on the overrun has been eliminated.

Starting has always been immediate and completely without temperament on Ford twin-cams fitted with Webers, and the big-valve engine is just as good in this respect. Two prods on the accelerator are enough to provide rich mixture for a cold start and the engine then seems ready to run evenly and develop all its power without hesitation or flat spots. It is smooth all the way to its power peak at 6,500 rpm, but above that it begins to rumble and sound harsh. There is a red sector on the rev counter from 6,500 to 8,000 rpm and we only entered this briefly when desperately trying for maximum acceleration.

Lotus launched the Elan Sprint with a great blaze of publicity about its performance, and their advertising quotes a 0 to 60 mph time of only 6.2sec. We were therefore very disappointed in barely being able to break 8sec the first time we took the test car to MIRA and attached our fifth-wheel speedometer. Using the car's instrument, which was subject to the usual inertia swing on its needle and a steady error of at least 5 per cent, we came closer to 7sec, but nowhere near the claimed 6.2sec. At this point we would normally have checked the obvious things, like whether the throttle butterflies were opening fully, but the bonnet had jammed shut and we were forced to return the car to the factory for investigation.

When retested some two weeks later it proved substantially quicker and returned a true 0 to 60 mph time of 7sec. This was in a laden condition with two testers and some 50lb of gear on board, so that with the driver alone and nothing in the boot it is conceivable that a time around 6½sec might just be possible.

127

ACCELERATION

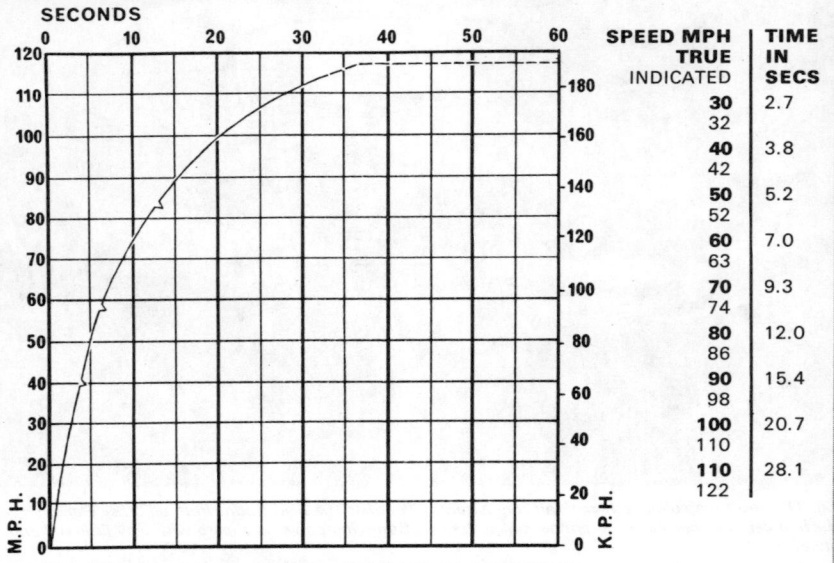

SPEED MPH TRUE / INDICATED	TIME IN SECS
30 / 32	2.7
40 / 42	3.8
50 / 52	5.2
60 / 63	7.0
70 / 74	9.3
80 / 86	12.0
90 / 98	15.4
100 / 110	20.7
110 / 122	28.1

SPEED RANGE, GEAR RATIOS AND TIME IN SECONDS

mph	Top (3.77)	3rd (5.26)	2nd (7.57)	1st (11.20)
10-30	—	6.4	3.8	2.5
20-40	9.3	5.1	3.0	2.2
30-50	7.7	4.3	2.9	—
40-60	7.2	4.3	3.2	—
50-70	7.2	4.5	—	—
60-80	7.8	4.8	—	—
70-90	8.4	6.3	—	—
80-100	9.2	—	—	—
90-110	12.5	—	—	—

Standing ¼-mile 15.0 sec 89 mph
Standing kilometre 28.1 sec 110 mph
Test distance 1,450 miles
Mileage recorder 2 per cent over-reading

PERFORMANCE
MAXIMUM SPEEDS

Gear	mph	kph	rpm
Top (mean)	118	190	6,800
(best)	118	190	6,800
3rd	83	133	6,800
2nd	59	95	6,800
1st	40	64	6,800

BRAKES

(from 70 mph in neutral)
Pedal load for 0.5g stops in lb

1	35		6	40
2	35		7	40
3	35		8	40
4	35-40		9	40
5	40		10	40

RESPONSE (from 30 mph in neutral)

Load	g	Distance
20lb	0.24	126ft
40lb	0.48	63ft
60lb	0.75	40ft
80lb	0.92	33ft
100lb	1.0	30.1ft
Handbrake	0.30	100ft

Max. Gradient 1 in 4

CLUTCH
Pedal 35lb and 4.5 in.

MOTORWAY CRUISING
Indicated speed at 70 mph . . . . 74 mph
Engine (rpm at 70 mph) . . . . 4,020 rpm
(mean piston speed) . . . . 1,900 ft/min.
Fuel (mpg at 70 mph) . . . . 33 mpg
Passing (50-70 mph) . . . . 4.1 sec

COMPARISONS

MAXIMUM SPEED MPH
Morgan Plus 8	(£1,700)	124
Marcos 3-litre	(£2,514)	120
Triumph TR6	(£1,582)	119
Lotus Elan Sprint	**(£1,706)***	**118**
VW-Porsche 914	(£2,201)	102

*Component form without tax

0-60 MPH, SEC
Morgan Plus 8	6.7
Lotus Elan Sprint	**7.0**
Marcos 3-litre	7.5
Triumph TR6	8.2
VW-Porsche 914	14.8

STANDING ¼-MILE, SEC
Lotus Elan Sprint	**15.0**
Morgan Plus 8	15.1
Marcos 3-litre	15.9
Triumph TR6	16.3
VW-Porsche 914	19.9

OVERALL MPG
Lotus Elan Sprint	**25.5**
Marcos 3-litre	22.3
VW-Porsche 914	20.5
Triumph TR6	19.8
Morgan Plus 8	18.3

GEARING (with 155 HR-13in. tyres)
Top . . . . 17.4 mph per 1,000 rpm
3rd . . . . 12.2 mph per 1,000 rpm
2nd . . . . 8.7 mph per 1,000 rpm
1st . . . . 5.9 mph per 1,000 rpm

TEST CONDITIONS:
Weather: Cloudy. Wind: 10-20 mph. Temperature: 12 deg. C. (54 deg. F). Barometer 29.7 in. hg. Humidity: 70 per cent. Surfaces: Dry concrete and asphalt.

WEIGHT:
Kerb weight 14.2 cwt (1,580 lb—719 kg) (with oil, water and half full fuel tank.) Distribution, per cent F, 47.5; R, 52.5. Laden as tested: 18.1 cwt (2,025 lb—920 kg).

TURNING CIRCLES:
Between kerbs L, 30ft 8in.; R, 32ft 6in. Between Walls L, 32ft 1in.; R, 34ft 1in. Steering wheel turns, lock to lock 2.6.

Figures taken at 4,500 miles by our own staff at the Motor Industry Research Association proving ground at Nuneaton.

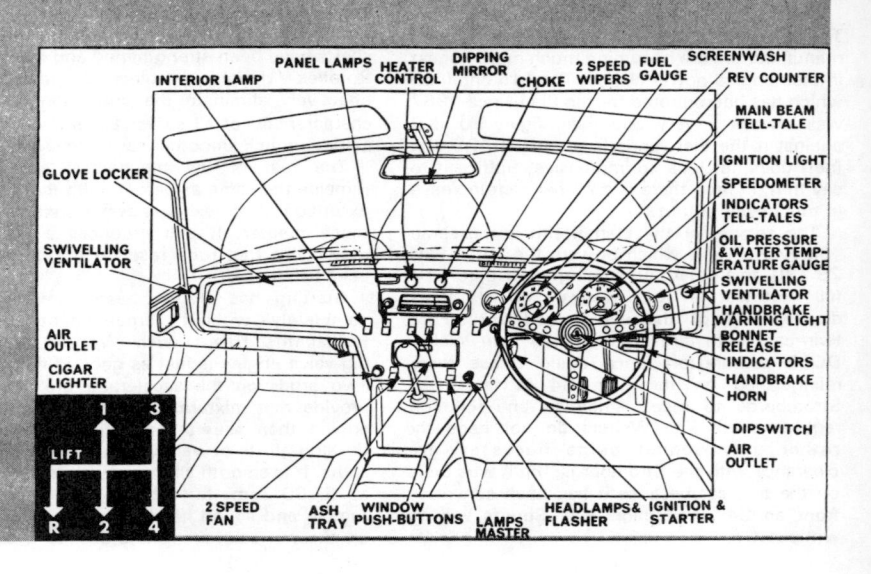

LOTUS ELAN SPRINT (1,588 c.c.)

CONSUMPTION

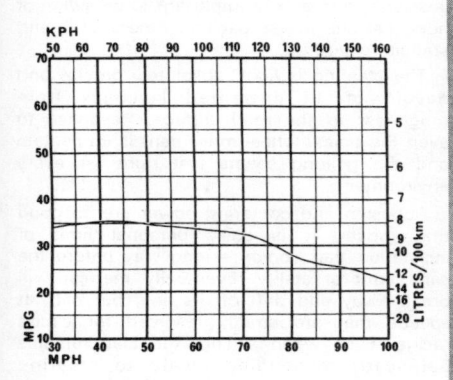

FUEL
(At constant speeds—mpg)

Speed	mpg
30 mph	34.2
40 mph	35.1
50 mph	34.8
60 mph	33.9
70 mph	33.0
80 mph	27.6
90 mph	25.2
100 mph	22.5

Typical mpg 26 (10.8 litres/100km)
Calculated (DIN) mpg . 30 (9.4 litres/100km)
Overall mpg 25.5 (11.1 litres/100km)
Grade of fuel . . . Super premium, 5-star (min. 101 RM)

OIL
Miles per pint (SAE 20W/50) 1,000

SPECIFICATION — FRONT ENGINE, REAR-WHEEL DRIVE

ENGINE
- Cylinders . . . 4, in line
- Main bearings . 5
- Cooling system . Water; pump, thermostat and fan
- Bore 82.6mm (3.25in.)
- Stroke 72.8mm (2.86in.)
- Displacement . 1,588 c.c. (95.2 cu. in.)
- Valve gear . . . Twin overhead camshafts, chain drive
- Compression ratio 10.3-to-1. Min. octane rating: 100 RM
- Carburettors . 2 Weber 40 DCOE 31
- Fuel pump . . AC mechanical
- Oil filter . . . Full-flow renewable element
- Max. power . . 126 bhp (net) at 6,500 rpm
- Max. torque . . 113 lb.ft (net) at 5,500 rpm

TRANSMISSION
- Clutch . . . . Borg and Beck diaphragm spring, 8in. dia
- Gearbox . . . . Ford 4-speed all-synchromesh
- Gear ratios . . Top 1.0
  - Third 1.40
  - Second 2.01
  - First 2.97
  - Reverse 3.32
- Final drive . . . Hypoid bevel, 3.77 to 1

CHASSIS and BODY
- Construction . . Welded steel backbone chassis, glass fibre body

SUSPENSION
- Front . . . . . Independent, coil springs, wishbones, telescopic dampers
- Rear . . . . . Independent, coil springs, wishbones, telescopic dampers

STEERING
- Type . . . . . Alford and Alder rack and pinion
- Wheel dia. . . 14 in.

BRAKES
- Make and type . Girling discs front and rear
- Servo . . . . . Girling vacuum
- Dimensions . . F 9.5 in. dia., R 10 in. dia.
- Swept area . . F 139 sq. in., R 159 sq. in.
  - Total 298 sq. in. (329 sq. in. ton laden).

WHEELS
- Type . . . . Pressed steel, centre lock. 4.5 in. wide rim
- Tyres—make . Dunlop
  - —type . . SP Sport, radial ply tubed
  - —size . . 155 HR-13 in.

EQUIPMENT
- Battery . . . 12 Volt 57 Ah
- Alternator . . Lucas 17ACR 35 amp a.c.
- Headlamps . . Lucas F700, 20/90 watt (total)
- Reversing lamp . Standard
- Electric fuses . 2
- Screen wipers . 2-speed
- Screen washer . Standard electric
- Interior heater . Water-valve type
- Heated backlight Extra
- Safety belts . Standard
- Interior trim . Pvc seats, pvc headlining
- Floor covering . Carpet
- Jack . . . . Screw, scissor type
- Jacking points . Anywhere under sills
- Windscreen . Laminated
- Underbody protection . Non-corroding plastic body

MAINTENANCE
- Fuel tank . . 9.25 Imp. gallons (42 litres) (no reserve)
- Cooling system . 14 pints (including heater)
- engine sump . 7.5 pints (4 litres) SAE 20W/50. Change oil every 3,000 miles. Change filter element every 6,000 miles
- Gearbox . . . 1.75 pints SAE 80EP. Change oil every 6,000 miles
- Final drive . . 2 pints SAE 90EP. Change oil every 12,000 miles
- Grease . . . 2 points every 6,000 miles, 3 more every 12,000 miles
- Tyre pressures . F 18; R 23 psi (normal driving) F 24; R 29 psi (fast driving)

PERFORMANCE DATA
- Top gear mph per 1,000 rpm 17.4
- Mean piston speed at max. power . . 3,100 ft/min
- Bhp per ton laden 140

STANDARD GARAGE 16ft x 8ft 6in.
OVERALL LENGTH 12'1·25"
OVERALL WIDTH 4'8"
OVERALL HEIGHT 3'10"
GROUND CLEARANCE 6"
WHEELBASE 7'0"
FRONT TRACK 3'11"
REAR TRACK 4'0·4"

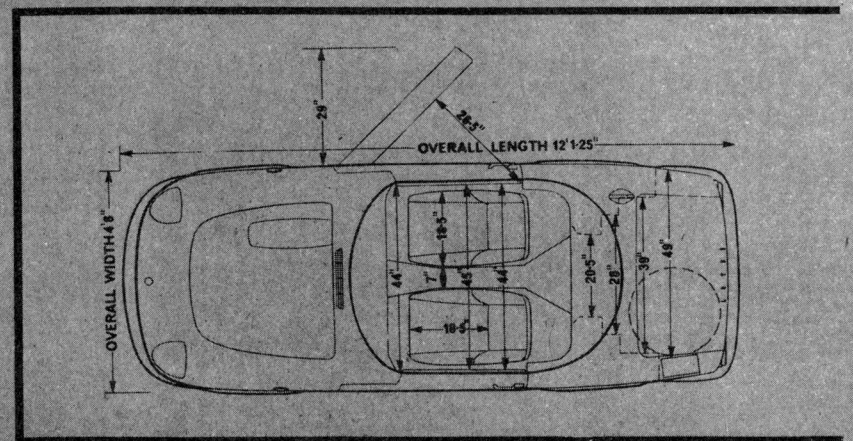

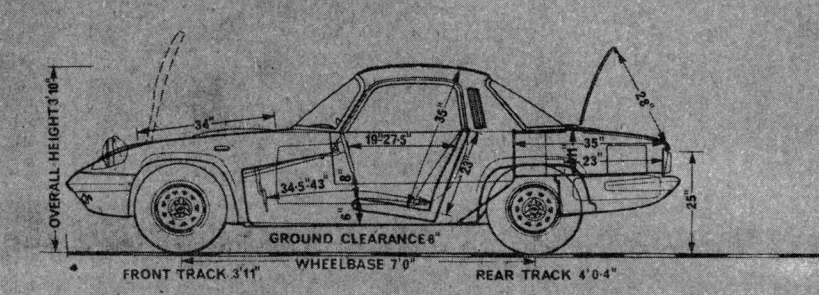

SCALE 0.3in. to 1ft.
Cushions uncompressed

AUTOTEST
LOTUS ELAN SPRINT

Compared with the Elan S4 we tested on 9 October 1969, the Elan Sprint is a lot quicker. The earlier car took 7.8sec to reach 60 mph and 23.3sec to attain 100 mph. The Elan Sprint took 7.0 and 20.7sec respectively and was much more flexible, surprisingly so at low speeds, in addition. From 20 to 40 mph in top, for example (although few Elan drivers are ever likely to potter such an eager car in this way), takes only 9.3sec compared with 14.7sec in the S4.

This good bottom end pick-up is partly the result of quite low overall gearing; the Sprint retains the same 3.77-to-1 final drive ratio as the S4 although it could easily pull a much higher one. The name Sprint is therefore an apt one as the car is obviously geared for the ultimate in acceleration. The top speed is set entirely by the rev limit on the engine, the rev counter needle flicking round to the red line in top with the greatest of ease.

While in other countries devoid of our overall 70 mph speed limit such gearing would be a decided handicap, it works very well here, giving the Sprint an incredible ability to overtake instantly and enabling motorway cruising to be maintained at a reasonable 4,000 rpm.

Speeds in the gears at the red line show on the speedometer as about 40, 60 and nearly 90 mph, which makes nicely progressive spacing in relation to the 118 mph top speed. If there is a gap in the gearbox ratios at all, it comes between second and third, but it never really shows up with such a broad overlap of torque between each gear. The shift on this Elan seemed stiffer and more notchy than usual, largely as a result of the ultra-short lever although there has been no modification to it.

Despite what you might expect, the extra performance has not really been obtained at the expense of fuel economy. For the bulk of our test, driving hard, we recorded 26 mpg overall, which was the same as with the last Elan we tested on Webers. During the retest, with slightly more performance available, the consumption fell to 23.3 mpg. At a steady 70 mph the Elan Sprint managed 33 mpg compared with 36 mpg for the S4 (on Strombergs) and 34.5 mpg for the S/E (on Webers).

Making the drive-shaft couplings stiffer in torsion has made them a lot stiffer also in bending and this increases the spring rate at each rear wheel, with very noticeable effects on the ride quality. In the past we have praised the Elan for its absorbent ability to deal with bumps and rough roads, but the ride now is no better than the average for the class and no better really than, say, an MGB.

If this aspect is disappointing, the steering, handling and roadholding are all every bit as delightful as before and in a totally different class from all other road cars. We know of no other car which can be tossed at a corner with such abandon at such incredible speeds and just simply steer round precisely and without drama. One finds oneself taking bends a full 20 or 30 mph faster than one previously thought possible, so it is extra important to be aware of how fast one is approaching other traffic and stationary hazards.

The steering is light, absolutely precise and devoid of all unwanted kickback from roughness in the road surface. Response to even the tiniest wheel movement is immediate and the gearing seems just right for every environment.

Adhesion and cornering power are so good that mostly it is one's personal limit of inclination that comes a long way before the car's limit of ability. Eventually the car will break away and drift off its line, but only at speeds that are strictly reserved for circuit racing. Even when sliding, the Elan remains balanced, responding nicely to steering correction with no unwanted tail wag.

On ordinary roads it is a satisfying and absolute sort of car, which can be hustled through narrow lanes or threaded through heavy traffic with an agility impossible for anything larger. It feels like a ballet slipper or hand-made riding boot that one pulls on and is immediately at-one with.

A lot of this feeling stems from a well-moulded driving seat and the small steering wheel set nicely at arm's length. Big drivers tend to be cramped because the cockpit is narrow, but most of our test staff fitted in well enough. Getting in and out is hampered by doors which only open about 40 deg.

The Elan's one-piece wooden facia is well laid out, with the two main instruments in front of the driver and the switches all in the centre. Everything is clearly labelled and is mostly worked by rocker switches. The pop-up headlamps are vacuum-operated and come up flashing on main beam unless the ordinary lighting switch has been put on first.

Heating and ventilation are rather lacking for a modern car, with just a simple water-valve temperature control, manual trapdoors on the central tunnel for distribution and butterfly flaps on the tiny fresh-air outlets. There are extractors on the rear quarter panels which seemed effective enough.

Side windows in the doors are actuated electrically, but only when the ignition is switched on. Wipers have two speeds and there are electric washers.

With static seat belts properly fastened it is impossible to reach the handbrake tucked away under the right of the facia and this could not hold the car on the 1-in-3 test hill. It managed all right on the 1-in-4.

Boot space on the Elan is small, but there is room behind the seats for additional luggage. The test car leaked in this area and had soggy wet carpets. There is very little space inside for oddments other than in the small facia locker. A shallow tray around the gearlever just about takes a packet of cigarettes or a bar of chocolate, but the heat from the transmission soaks through.

As we said at the beginning, this is by far the best Lotus we have tested. In most respects it has been sensibly improved and it is still just about the fastest way of getting from A to B other than by motorcycle. It offers a tremendous amount of fun for the enthusiastic driver with great big safety margins in hand. It is a civilized, docile little car which lives up well to the new name for it. Never was a sports car more a sports car than this one. □

Above: There is a one-piece wooden facia with well-separated switches and good positioning of the instruments. Although the wheel looks large here, it is only 14in. dia.

Left: The boot is small and shallow, but there is more room behind the seats. The spare wheel is under the floor and the tool roll lies on top

LOTUS 130S
big valve, big value

Elan 130S bodywork is in the so-what category. Little changed apart from detail dress-up gear it hides big news in engine refinements.

Tuned for the Trans-European autoroutes where it can flex its 130 mph muscles, the Plus Two Elan 130S "Big Valve" fizzed out as a deep-freeze fireball. Intrepid correspondent Harold Dvoretsky reports on the sad saga of AVF 500J...

TO BE a motor-noter you have to have a masochistic/sadistic streak — a sort of love-hate relationship with some of the cars you drive.

Imagine if you can, 25 degrees below zero (that's real cold man). You are stuck on a snowy jura pass with a lush-looking 120 mph-Plus GT worth upwards of $4000 before you've paid purchase tax.

You freeze for the next two hours while help comes to tow you six miles to get under cover. And the ignominy of it all is that a rather wrecked Renault R4 van is doing the towing... and your Australian ex-secretary who you've been trying to impress, keeps looking longingly at the Deux Chevals which potter by, their occupants warm and snug in the inelegance of a ridiculous French design.

Examination shows your original thoughts are right. Those very expensive looking double choke Webers have frozen jets and the lines to them are also frozen. Someone has dished you up some fuel and a lot of water moisture. In that temperature with the ambient temperature gauge showing the maker's name, despite a scale down to minus 15 deg. C everything was frozen solid.

Little you can do about until things thaw out next day, the man from the "snow garage" tells you. But what neither he, nor you, know is there's also a hairline crack in your distributor. This has also let in moisture which has now frozen, splitting the cap.

By this stage, the circulation in your fingers has stopped for the umpteenth time. You would have liked to examine the distributor but it is buried beneath those expensive carbs and a few minutes in that temperature and your fingers are frozen.

Your leather driving shoes have soaked up melting snow underfoot and now have gone from soggy to freezing so the soles are like boards. You charter, at great expense, the only Taxi in town, which actually doubles as the local ambulance — one of those Citroen Safari affairs.

Two hours later as you start to thaw out in Geneva — 35 miles away, you have nothing but sadistic thoughts for that car on the mountain.

But it doesn't end there. For the next five days you watch a precious time schedule being eaten away while you first get the car down the mountain and through two lots of

131

LOTUS 130S

customs before it once again fires on all four.

At great expense the development engineer brings you a new distributor cap from the English factory — only to find it's the one that fits the model just replaced. Instead of getting an available 7000 rpm you are lucky to break 6200 rpm before the cutout comes in.

Almost 2000 miles later you arrive back in UK disheartened, dispirited and annoyed. The car is eventually returned to you for performance testing. You would really like to hate the bleeding thing — but you can't.

Despite this week of extended agony and frustration, I still have more than just a sneaking likeness and admiration of the Lotus Plus 2S 130 — the car at the root of it all.

Up to the legal (British) limit of 70 mph it's darn near perfect and behaves like the race-bred thoroughbred it is. After that, and up to its maximum of 114 mph which it gets to in around 45 seconds, I have some reservations. But it's one of the best compromises I've ever met.

If you think of 30 mph coming up in under four seconds, 50 in six seconds, 90 mph in 15 seconds and the ton in under 22 secs and think of a car handling like a formula racing car that it was bred from, then you probably (like me) are prepared to make a few concessions.

The Plus Two was of course originally conceived by Colin Chapman for the man who rose from the kit-car Lotus Seven through to the two seater Lotus Elite.

By this stage our young man had convinced his Lotus Seven bird he was on the way up. She married him and he bought the better weather-protected Lotus Elan.

But the sound of little feet meant that he needed more room. The Plus Two was the answer. The rear "seats" hold two kids admirably or, with the rear squab folded down, help give the 130S one of the biggest GT sports car luggage holding capacities in the business.

The new 2S 130, under ex-BRM man, Tony Rudd as development engineer, has had the breathing of the 1558 cc Twin Cam four cylinder opened up and the valves increased in size to help give a remarkable 25 percent increase in the power potential.

Despite this increase, the unit is even more flexible and you can potter around down to around 1250 rpm in top and find flexibility right up the scale to a maximum of 124 mph.

All this is with a 3.77 final drive ratio and four speed gear box.

To be pedantic, I'd like a five speed box and a 3.55 to lower top end revs at higher speeds. But the 3.77 is a fair compromise.

Up the scale, the 25 percent power increase has resulted in better performance figures — and for town running, the flexibility is what is wanted.

In this new version the rubber doughnut couplings have been strengthened so you don't get that horrible driveline surge that was apt to get you down in town running with the old model.

Tony Rudd tells me the production doughnuts will be tougher still, so the little bit of surging left should be eradicated. The drive-shafts have been strengthened to take the extra torque.

The 130S has lost none of its wonderful precise handling characteristics which make it a delight to get through traffic and overtake as the opportunity arises.

Steering from the rack and pinion is very direct at 2.6 turns lock to lock. There's no freeplay at all, which means for the first few minutes you might be inclined to overdo it. But given a few miles and any owner will be delighted.

It is the nearest you will ever come to driving a formula car. Once you learn gentleness is needed and brute force unnecessary, you can outcorner, outmanoeuvre anything on the road.

The brakes are almost perfect. The servo is powerful and extremely progressive so that you have to be a heavy footed clot to do the wrong thing.

The steering position behind the leather bound steering wheel will suit most drivers between five foot nothing and six foot three. The doors open wide and though the car is extremely low it is very easy to gain access.

The stubby gearlever is just where you want it and visibility is excellent, even for tall drivers.

I dislike that spade grip handbrake beneath the dashboard. The instrument layout could be better (and Tony Rudd tells me it is being improved) the tacho and speedometer are vaguely numbered and could be better, and the multitude of switchery from lights to electric window winders drives you mad.

The heater (when the car is motoring) was good and the ventilation seemed adequate.

I was late getting across the channel on a wintery Saturday night and landed at Calais as a big freeze set across Europe. Before I hit the motorway some 70 miles away it was snowing hard. At first the extremely direct steering coupled with a high cross wind had me going very carefully indeed. But the Lotus handles well.

"Big Valve" Lotus Twin Cam shows obvious BRM influences in Cam-cover design following Tony Rudd's transfer to Lotus. Simple engine breathing lifted power output 25 percent.

COLOR PAGE: Elan Plus Two 130S gets power boost for better small family highway cruising. It will straddle the autostradas at better than 125 mph, though wind-cheating shape is often noisy, and front headlights spoil aerodynamics when popped up.

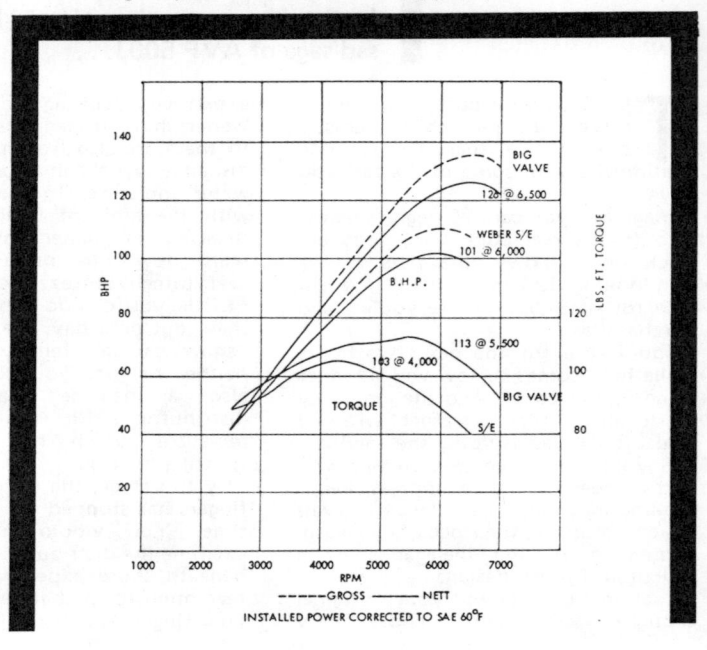

132

even if it does get thrown out of line from bumpy French roads and the wind.

Once on the motorway, I was prepared for anything. Luckily the weather, though very cold, was clear. I left Calais just before 7 pm and was around Paris by 9.30 pm — almost 170 miles, which in those conditions was a very fair time.

My original intention was to go down the motorway to near the Macon off-point (from where I would go cross-country to Geneva and the motor show).

Macon South came up just at midnight — I'd travelled 250 miles from Paris in around two and a half hours.

Only once was I troubled — a warning of things to come. Suddenly, just as it would do to me barely 15 hours later, the power cut out. My immediate reaction was fuel starvation so I pumped the Webers. There was no response. I then lifted off and the engine spluttered into life again as the jets unfroze. The ambient temperature gauge (put in by Colin Chapman to even up the dash layout) was showing just below the minus 15C.

I guessed frozen jets.

But the next 60 miles to Geneva went in no time. Just after 2.30 am I pulled up at my Geneva Hotel with 560 miles from Calais behind me in a little more than 7.5 hours. Considering the early conditions with those snowy and icy roads of Northern France, it was quite an average at more than 70 mph.

Fuel consumption overall from the slow-filling 13-gallon tank worked out at 25 mpg which though not as good as the original car can't really be faulted when you consider the performance (and it was Tony Rudd who reminded me that the power output from this refined DOHC of 126/BHP (Din) is not far below that of the first of the 1.5-litre Formula One cars back in the sixties — we have progressed).

The new DOHC unit delivers 126 bhp at 6500 rpm and peak torque comes in with 113 ft/lbs at 5500 rpm. The rev limit is 6800 though if you buy a standard Lotus rotor arm you can go to 7000 rpm for the odd occasion.

And you can match the old Jaguar E-type (six cylinder) to 60 mph or over the flying quarter.

For the rest, here's how the timing goes:

0-30 mph in 4 secs, to 40 in 4.5 secs to 50 in 5.5 secs, to 70 in 10 secs to 80 in 12.5 secs to 90 in 14.5 secs and to 100 mph in 21.5 secs.

From 20-40 mph in third takes 5 secs in top 11 secs; 30-50 in third is 5 secs in top 9 secs; 40-60 in third is 8 secs and top also 5 secs; 60-80 mph 8 secs in top and 80-100 mph in top takes 7 secs. Price ex-factory is $A4096 plus purchase tax.

BRIEF TEST

LOTUS PLUS 2S 130

At the beginning of this year Lotus introduced the "Big Valve" version of their famous twin ohc 1588 cc engine, claimed to have much better torque all the way up the speed range and 25 per cent more maximum power than the previous Special Equipment engine. The output is now quoted as 126 bhp (net) against 101 bhp before.

Neither our previous test of the Elan Sprint (w/e March 6, 1971) nor this one of the Plus 2S 130 throws any doubt on the output now claimed. In both cases the performance is startling. For a 1600 cc engine to accelerate a 17cwt. 2 + 2 coupe to 60 mph in 7.7sec and to 100 mph in 23sec is astonishing—to retain such refinement and quietness in the process makes it almost incredible. Looking back, however, to our original test of the newly introduced Plus 2 (September 2, 1967) it is only too clear that that car didn't have anything like a standard engine so that a comparison of the two shows very much smaller gains than would have been expected.

However, leaving aside this comparative aspect, the latest version of this engine is truly remarkable. The higher the specific power which it is persuaded to give, the smoother and more flexible it seems to get; 80 bhp/litre is more than enough to excuse a stepped power curve but in fact the engine works hard, as the figures show, from about 1500 rpm as well as continuing very smoothly to its 6800 rpm rev limit. This limit was reached in top gear at 121 mph, the figure we have quoted for maximum speed, after about $1\frac{1}{4}$ miles acceleration from rest so there is little doubt that an appreciably higher speed could have been attained by over-revving—probably about 125 mph—or higher still with the optional 3.55 final drive ratio.

Like most engines with multiple Weber carburetters, this one starts from cold with a few strokes of the throttle to activate the accelerator pumps; the choke seems to be redundant. It pulls smoothly from cold straight away and prolonged periods in London traffic don't upset it as long as the electric fan works. But on several occasions the fan failed to cut in for some reason—presumably the fault of the thermostatic switch—and then it boiled, vigorously.

One other difference which we noted between the latest engine and its predecessors is its much greater thirst at low speeds—below about 60 mph or 3000 rpm the steady speed fuel consumption curve is an entirely different shape. Whereas the original Plus 2 did about 63 mpg at a steady 30 mph, this one did only 33 mpg; a similar effect was noted with the Elan Sprint. Since Lotus owners don't use this part of the range much—we certainly didn't—the overall effect is much less dramatic (about $3\frac{1}{2}$ mpg) and would be smaller still in open road driving. The Plus 2 still does nearly 30 mpg at a steady 70 mph and over 22 at 100. The 13-gallon tank gives a refuelling range of around 250 miles with hard driving, or nearer 300 miles at a touring pace. This tank, however, behaved in a most curious way in that the fuel level rose into the filler neck long before the tank was actually full. On several occasions garages assumed that it was completely full and yet in fact it proved able to accept no less than another four gallons before it finally overflowed.

Perhaps the transmission isn't quite as sporting as the rest of the car. The gearbox is quiet and has sensibly spaced ratios

Motor Brief Test No. 34/71 Lotus Elan +2 130

Make: Lotus. **Model:** Elan +2 130. **Makers:** Lotus Cars Ltd., Norwich, Norfolk Nor. 92W. **Price:** £2100 plus £526.88 purchase tax equals £2626.88.

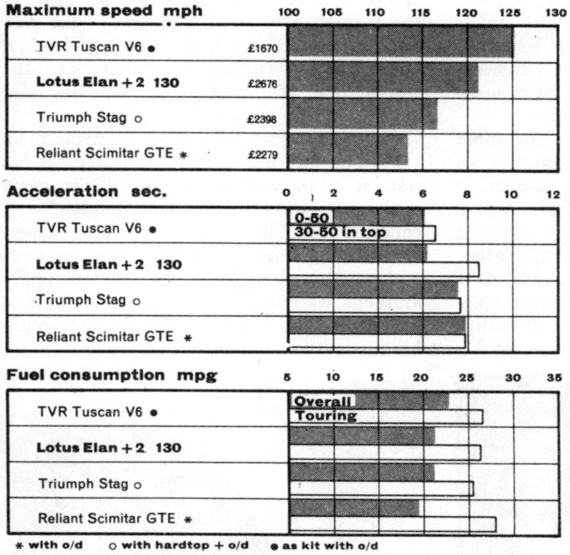

Maximum speed mph

		100 105 110 115 120 125 130
TVR Tuscan V6 ●	£1670	
Lotus Elan +2 130	£2676	
Triumph Stag ○	£2398	
Reliant Scimitar GTE *	£2279	

Acceleration sec. 0 2 4 6 8 10 12

TVR Tuscan V6 ●	0-50 / 30-50 in top
Lotus Elan +2 130	
Triumph Stag ○	
Reliant Scimitar GTE *	

Fuel consumption mpg 5 10 15 20 25 30 35

TVR Tuscan V6 ●	Overall / Touring
Lotus Elan +2 130	
Triumph Stag ○	
Reliant Scimitar GTE *	

* with o/d   ○ with hardtop + o/d   ● as kit with o/d

Performance tests carried out by *Motor's* staff at the Motor Industry Research Association proving ground, Lindley.
Test Data: World copyright reserved; no authorised reproduction in whole or in part.

Conditions
Weather: Dry, dull, no wind
Temperature: 52-65°F
Barometer: 29.5in. Hg.
Surface: Dry tarmacadam
Fuel: Super Premium 101 octane (RM) 5 Star rating

Maximum Speeds
		mph	kph
Top gear	}	121	195
3rd gear	} at 6,800 rpm	86	138
2nd gear	}	60	96
1st gear	}	41	66

"Maximile" speed: (Timed quarter mile after 1 mile accelerating from rest)
Mean 117.4
Best 118.5

Acceleration Times
mph	sec.
0-30	3.2
0-40	4.3
0-50	6.1
0-60	7.7
0-70	10.7
0-80	13.6
0-90	17.6
0-100	23.0
Standing quarter mile	15.9
Standing kilometre	29.5

	Top sec.	3rd sec.
10-30	—	6.4
20-40	9.2	5.7
30-50	8.5	5.1
40-60	7.8	4.9
50-70	8.2	5.1
60-80	8.8	5.5
70-90	8.9	—
80-100	9.8	—

Fuel Consumption
Touring (consumption midway between 30 mph and maximum less 5% allowance for acceleration) .... 26.1 mpg

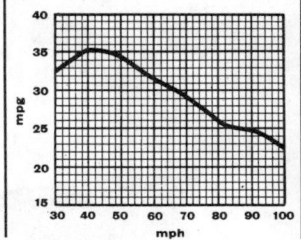

Overall .... 21.0 mpg
(=12.3 litres/100km)
Total test distance ...... 1,392 miles

Speedometer
Indicated	10	20	30	40	50
True	10	20	30	40	50
Indicated	60	70	80	90	100
True	60	69½	79	88	98

Distance recorder 4% fast

Weight
Kerb weight (unladen but with fuel for approximately 50 miles) ... 17.2 cwt.
Front/rear distribution 47½/52½
Weight laden as tested .... 20.9 cwt.

Engine
Block material .... Cast iron
Head material .... Aluminium alloy
Cylinders .... 4 in line
Cooling system ..... Water pump and thermostatically controlled electric fan
Bore and stroke 82.55mm. (3.25in.) 72.75mm. (2.864in.)
Cubic capacity · 1558 cc (95.1 cu.in.)
Main bearings .... Five
Valves .... Operated by twin overhead camshafts
Compression ratio 10.3:1
Carburetters . Twin Weber 40 DCOE
Fuel pump .... AC mechanical
Oil Filter .... Full flow, removable paper element
Max. power (net) 126 bhp at 6,500 rpm
Max. torque (net) 113 lb.ft. at 5,500 rpm

Transmission
Clutch   Borg and Beck 8½in. s.d.p. diaphragm
Internal gear box ratios
Top gear 1.000
3rd gear 1.396
2nd gear 2.009
1st gear 2.972
Reverse 3.324
Synchromesh . On all forward gears
Final drive Hypoid bevel, 3.77:1 ratio
Mph at 1000 rpm in:—
  top gear 17.85
  third gear 12.6
  second gear 8.9
  first gear 6.0

Chassis and body
Construction   Steel backbone chassis, glass fibre plastic body

Brakes
Type .... Girling discs all round
Dimensions . 10in. dia. front and rear

Suspension and steering
Front   Independent by unequal length double wishbones, coil springs, telescopic dampers and anti-roll bar
Rear   Independent by MacPherson type struts, coil springs and lower wishbones
Shock absorbers:
  Front: } Telescopic
  Rear: }
Steering type ... Rack and pinion
Tyres .. Dunlop SP Sport, 165-13in.
Wheels ... Pressed steel knock-on
Rim size 5½J

---

well suited to the very wide torque band. But this Lotus, although ideally geared for acceleration and for speed-limited countries, might be less at home maintaining a cruising speed of 110 mph on a continental motorway since this represents no less than 6200 rpm. For this a much higher final drive ratio, higher even than the optional 3.55, would be desirable or else a five speed box with overdrive top. This particular gearbox was rather stiffer and more notchy than is usual with Ford boxes and although the new drive couplings are supposed to be less flexible, this modification has not entirely eliminated acceleration surge as it has on the smaller Elan Sprint.

Our 1967 memories of Plus 2 roadholding were not spoiled by re-acquaintance. Straight away one revels in steering which is high geared yet so light that you can throw it round even the sharpest corners at very high g without straining at the wheel. Yet it has all the feel you could want and is positive—positive almost to a fault because quite a lot of joggle is fed back from the front wheels through the rigid linkage and on very rough roads the wheel kicks quite hard.

It is a beautifully blanced car—very precise, very responsive and rolling so little that you automatically drive it very much nearer to its limits than you would lesser cars, even though these limits themselves are exceptionally high. It shows the same cornering characteristics as the Elan—you get the best results by accelerating quite

All the information is there, but the array of dials and switches is cluttered and confusing

strongly round corners and if you have to lift off there is pronounced tuck-in.

The Plus 2 is quite sensitive to tyre pressures. Recommended pressures are quite low but the only disadvantage of this is that it is possible to make the tyres squeal if you try very hard. If you raise them much the ride, normally very comfortable, becomes excessively harsh at low speeds; also unless the recommended front/rear pressure differential is maintained (or even increased) a tendency to twitchiness in the high speed handling is accentuated.

Our test car seemed to be a little more bump-sensitive than previous examples we remember and side winds also deflected it noticeably. We suspect that the car may be a little over-damped now because the ride is at its best at high speeds becoming rather bumpy at low speeds with quite a lot of road noise and harshness and even some body shake. It is very much better with a full load.

We didn't try the back seat ride because these seats are quite unsuitable for adults unless they are very small; there is neither adequate headroom nor legroom—they are essentially for children. The front seats, on the other hand, are good as they usually are in a Lotus. You sit very low down inside behind a high scuttle which hides most of the bonnet. The blank quarters in the rear are not noticed much in ordinary driving, not even in town, but they can be troublesome at angled T junctions and also when reversing in confined spaces.

There is a good flow of air from the facia vents but this was partially negated on the test car by the inability to turn off the warm air supply from the heater completely—a common trouble with water-valve types. Most of our remarks about comfort, controls and equipment in the 1967 test still apply although we must mention again that a new exhaust system and better soundproofing has made it much quieter.

It is, of course, a very fully equipped car with electrically operated windows, fog and spot lights below the bumpers, reclining seats, built-in safety belts, air horns and illuminated bonnet and boot compartments. This is one of the reasons why the facia board presents such an enormous array of instruments and switches that the heart of the strange driver sinks as soon as he looks at it. Fortunately, all the controls are clearly labelled but it never becomes easy to hit the right one without prior scrutiny, nor even to remember where all the dials are. Some controls, like the wiper/washer switches, would be better transferred to the steering column on a fast car like this. And our least favourite control is the under-facia pull-out handbrake which you have to lean right forward to use.

Nevertheless, detailed criticisms cannot alter the fact that this is an outstanding car for sheer driving pleasure and, together with the Elan Sprint, the best Lotus yet. ■

Not much spare space in the engine compartment, above; in contrast the interior is roomy—for two people—and the seats comfortable; the car's dimensions are compact, and the new two-tone colour scheme makes it even more attractive than before, below

ROAD IMPRESSIONS

LOTUS ELAN SPRINT

THE LOTUS twin-cam engine has been a great unit over the past 10 years but now with the introduction of four valves per cylinder, belt-drive and the rest of it the twin-cam seemed to be on its way out. But Lotus, who originally commissioned this overhead-cam layout based on the Ford Cortina motor, recently gave the engine a new lease of life when it was updated to the "130 Big Valve" specification. A few months ago we reported what a difference this had made to the Elan +2S which, though not short of urge, welcomed a few more brake horse-power. The two-seater Elan, which also became available with the 130-b.h.p. engine at the same time, was undoubtedly a startling performer in original trim and now with the "Big Valve" motor is little short of shattering.

We were able to try the Lotus Elan Sprint recently over a fairly extensive mileage and since then we gather, although not directly from Lotus who no longer have a p.r. department, that all other Elan models are discontinued, so you have to have the Sprint whether you like it or not. Actually there is no question of that, for not only is the engine a great advance but such improvements as a strengthened final drive, stiffer drive-shaft doughnuts and a very much better and quieter exhaust system, all help to make the Elan a better car for a very reasonable increase in cost.

When the Sprint Elan was introduced back in February the price was quoted at £1,686 and has since found its way up to £1,716. This is, of course, in component form which is the only way an Elan Sprint is offered and compares with the £1,700 for a Morgan +8 which, if anything, has fractionally more straight-line performance, while something like a Triumph TR6 retails at £1,582. Our road-test car was an open version but, strangely, if you prefer a coupé it runs £10 cheaper.

We collected our road-test Elan Sprint at the Pub Lotus near Regents Park and immediately set off in this Gold Leaf-Team Lotus-liveried machine northwards and fast. It would probably be best not to give any details of the average speeds of the journey mostly on the Motorway, but suffice it to say it is within the bounds of possibility that we could have reached Sheffield a couple of hours later!

The Elan is remarkably comfortable for, once snuggled into its cockpit, nearly everything comes to hand easily and naturally. All the controls are delightfully light and need to be treated rather more delicately than those of something like a Vauxhall Ventora. The back axle has a low 3.77-to-1 final drive for maximum acceleration and sprinting, but it is sufficiently high enough to allow the car to cruise at 115 m.p.h. at just on the 6,500 r.p.m. red line on the rev.-counter. The noise level in the open version, with the hood up, is remarkably low and obviously would be much less in a coupé. The car also makes much less noise outside the car and that rasping growl on the over-run has been eliminated.

Naturally the Elan Sprint will win just about any traffic lights grand prix and Lotus claim a 0-60 m.p.h. figure of 6.2 sec., which is faster than any other car currently available. A Lamborghini Miura's time is around 6.7 sec., while a good "E"-type will record 7.4 sec. In fact, the Lotus claim is probably optimistic on the normal run of the mill car but a high 6-sec. figure would be possible. Even so, this should set you up pretty well at Santa Pod. Our Elan Sprint topped the 100 m.p.h. mark in just over 21 sec., which is fast in anyone's language, but most impressive of all was the way it picked up speed from 25-30 m.p.h. and whipped past those queues of slow-moving vehicles behind which, in any normal car, you would be stranded for ages.

The gearbox is delightful as one snicks through the gears with the short purposeful lever. By red-lining the rev.-counter one would change at 40, 60, 88 m.p.h., but, unless you are going all out to burn off the Jensen Interceptor alongside, this is hardly necessary, thanks to the broad overlap of torque between each gear.

It should be pointed out that driving an Elan quickly and safely is not something one can do without practice or skill. The tremendously responsive steering and handling requires similar qualities from the driver and the speeds achieved round corners and on the straight are deceptively fast. This, therefore, calls for a lot of concentration on the driver's part. Once mastered, however, the Elan is the nearest thing to a single-seater racing car one is likely to be able to drive comfortably on the road. To master the car and explore its tremendous handling potential along that delightfully twisty piece of road one knows so well is close on perfection for the sporting motorist. One could write the most flowery prose to describe the sensation, but suffice it to say that the Lotus reputation in this field is unparalleled.

When I visited Lotus some months ago I spent quite a while discussing the relative merits of Rotoflex couplings and sliding spline and universal joints in the rear drive-shafts with Tony Rudd, the firm's Director of Engineering. Rudd had been dubious of the Rotoflex or doughnut coupling before he joined Lotus and agreed that the diabolical surge they caused had to be cured. To this end various experiments were tried when he joined the firm, one of which was the use of the more conventional u/js. However, for some reason, concerned with the elasticity of the doughnuts, the handling undoubtedly deteriorated considerably using the metal joints. So Rudd did quite a lot of research on Rotoflex couplings and after a couple of improvements has now come up with one that almost entirely eliminates the wind-up. These are naturally somewhat more rigid and perhaps, because of this, the ride seems to be a little harder than on the earlier and exceptionally smooth-riding Elans. Personally I hadn't really noticed this until it was pointed out by a colleague who owned a couple of Elans.

We continue to receive letters from readers who are disgruntled with their Lotus Elans, the most recent one and quite a few earlier ones, plagued mainly with engine troubles. With the Elan Sprint we feel sure that the great majority of problems experienced with the engines, like burned-out exhaust valves and incessantly leaking cam cover gaskets, are eliminated.

Some of the other faults readers have complained about possibly stem from the original build of cars from the component form by amateurs. However, the fact still exists that Lotus models, and Elans in particular, do not have a particularly good reputation for long-term reliability. Thus we were hoping that our fresh and smart-looking road-test car would show the improvements that Tony Rudd has been working hard to introduce. Sad to say that, though everything important performed its tasks without problem, a couple of little things let the car down. The first may be an inherent design fault for the heater control had the most strange knack of turning itself on and roasting the occupants. For maximum heat a knob on the dashboard just above the radio had, in theory, to be pulled out. In practice this infernal device had the uncanny habit of pushing itself out of the dashboard and turning the heat full on every five minutes. Attempts to twist or turn it into a locked position failed completely and I was almost forced to drive the Lotus in my underwear!

The other problem concerned the pop-up headlamps which are vacuum-operated and after a session of flashing on the M1 they became decidedly droopy but later managed to restore themselves to their former glory.

Considering the performance, the petrol consumption was very light at around 26 m.p.g., but the engine liked Castrol GTX and consumed almost three pints in the course of 1,000 miles.

The Lotus Elan Sprint is a fine sports car that will provide invigorating, entertaining and dynamic transport for its owner. This latest Sprint version undoubtedly moves the Elan even further up the desirability scale.—A. R. M.

THE LOTUS ELAN Sprint in the paddock at Mallory Park race circuit.

Elan Sprint: The Latest Lotus Position
Camelot Revisited/By John Christy

MT Road Test

Anthony Colin Bruce Chapman has gone and done it again. Taking his Lotus firmly in hand he has tilted against the windmills of Ecology and Safety and beaten them in single combat where the armies of the titans have gone down to abject defeat. Put less flamboyantly, Mr. Chapman has taken what has to have been one of the best sports car *designs* in the world and made it into one of the very best sports *cars* in the world. He has improved the power, the performance, the handling and the quality all in one fell swoop and at the same time has met all current safety and emissions standards, a feat which, if Lotus Group Car Companies Ltd. had a greater influence in the market place, should have the collective management eyes of the majors dark with panic.

We have, in the past, tended to superlatives when describing the performance, security and handling of the genus Lotus. If we were over-enthusiastic, perhaps we might be forgiven for the fact that the Elan Sprint had yet to be built. The interesting point about all this improvement is not how much the specifications have been changed but how little. Dimensionally the Elan Sprint is exactly the same as the previous S4 and all the Elans that have gone before, which is to say that it is a very small car indeed, having roughly the same accommodation as such surrogates as the Triumph Spitfire and MG Midget — which is where the comparison abruptly ends. In fact, about all it means is that if you are built along the lines of Wilt Chamberlain and must have a Lotus you bring more money and ask the man for an Elan + 2 Sprint.

The biggest change of all is in the engine. It is referred to in Lotus literature as the "Big Valve" engine, a designation that is repeated for posterity in the casting of the cam cover. It's not a put-on nor any sort of flakery either. The head as well as the cam cover is completely new. The result of the combined efforts of Brian Hart and Tony Rudd, formerly of BRM, the new head has intake valves giving approximately 25 percent more area and carries cams that have both more duration and more lift. All this is fed by a pair of Zenith-Stromberg 175 CD-2 carburetors. An appreciation of their size may be gathered from the fact that they are essentially the same as those used on the Triumph TR-250, a 2.5-liter six. At first look all this would shout "overcarburetion" in loud, ringing tones and smacks of the old "if some is good, more is better and too much is just enough" school of modification. Not so. Mess'rs Hart and Rudd have done their work well. Everything works in perfect harmony and the new engine pulls like a tractor from the bottom end while at the same time retaining the high-revving response associated with the Lotus Twin Cam. It's an amazing piece of work and, in a sense, feels as much like a six and it does a four-banger. It starts pulling way down *here* and just keeps on pulling all the way up *there* with the "up there" part being 6500 rpm at which point a cutout in the distributor pulls the plug and there isn't any more at all. We took the car to the Times Grand Prix, last of the season's Can-Am series, and let it *idle* around in the crowded garage area in low gear. It didn't stumble or miss a beat. Yet when we got in the clear we just booted it and it took off as though we had been running all that time at full noise.

Sharp-eyed readers or those with good memories will spot an anomaly in the spec tables. In spite of an increase to 113 net horsepower as opposed to the 103 net bhp of the previous S4, the actual acceleration times of the Sprint are not all that much better statistically than those of the S4. However, this can be explained (if not excused) on several counts. First, at the time we ran the S4 our "gray box" with its strip chart recorder and electronic measuring equipment was in the process of being built and was not operable, proving that stop-watch thumbs can be over-enthusiastic or at least inaccurate to a degree. Second, the claimed net torque of the new engine in Federalized form is roughly the same as before although response and power are better. And finally, the improved stern hamper is such that there is no wind-up of drive components on a standing start with the result that there is considerably more wheelspin which can be felt and heard. It also shows up on the g-force trace of the strip-chart as a series of spikes that rise and fall and rise again before the tires get a true bite and the speed trace starts its rise. The lag between the first spike of the g-force trace and the start of the speed trace is over eight tenths of a second. Mounting low-hysteresis flat-tread bias-ply or bias-belted tires in place of the 155HR x 13 radials ⟫⟫⟫

Elan Sprint

would probably eliminate the lag altogether. Combined with the elimination of a similar but shorter lag on the 1 - 2 shift, the potential acceleration times of the Sprint would seem to be as much as a full second shorter all the way up the line. Marvelous things these recorders, they explain a lot. Make good lie detectors, too. You can't goof a shift or a turn that doesn't show up indelibly on the graph.

The business of the rear end mentioned earlier brings us to the next piece of improvement. Elans, both of the two-seat and +2 persuasion have all had Metalastik or Rotoflex biscuits as U-joints used in the half shafts of the rear end and the center section has also been heavily rubber-mounted. In the past this has led to a phenomenon known as the Kangaroo hop (or Lotus two-step) when the car was driven by one of the unshriven or even by one familiar with the car if he let his attention lag while accelerating through the gears. You either paid attention to what you were doing and did it with precise decisiveness or you could find yourself going down the pike in a series of embarrassing rabbit jumps. No longer.

The rear end has been more solidly located and the rubber biscuits are of a harder rating (higher hysteresis). This has taken away all the feeling that each clutch application resulted in winding up the rubber bands before forward motion could begin. Other than wheelspin on hard application, the car moves out with a solid rush, grabbing a new linear bite with each succeeding shift, much more like the Europa than earlier Elans.

The quality control, already much improved with the later series of cars from the new Hethel plant now approaches the Teutonic. Nothing, but nothing, rattles, jiggles or vibrates. Nothing comes adrift and no knobs, switches or ancillaries come off in your hand. The windshield was clear and distortion-free (somebody at Hethel must have been listening to Paul Van Valkenburgh). The top, though a bit of a bother to put up and down, was tight; it did not drum and all the snaps went where they were supposed to go. Most important of all it was totally weather-proof, a point we had proven to us when we were blessed with the heaviest rain and hail storm to hit Los Angeles Anno Domine 1971. In defense of the operation of the top, it was built with lightness in mind, a fetish *chez* Chapman. That it accomplished that part and served its purpose as well speaks loudly in its favor and makes bearable the slight inconvenience of having to get out of the car to put it up. As for the finish, it couldn't be faulted. It looks as though the body was done in a vacuum mold with the color being a bonded gelcoat, it's that smooth. But we are given to understand that it is an actual lay-up and painted in the normal manner. If so, some of the finishers of so-called luxury cars could stand to take a quick course at Hethel.

But it's when you get the Sprint out on the road that it all comes together. In a word, it's a Lotus with all of the good qualities the name implies and, now, without the host of petty annoyances and objections that applied in former years. In fact the only fly in our particular jar of Lotus balm was that the brakes developed a minor squeal when cold. It wasn't loud — at least not very — but it was there, and really only annoying because everything else seemed so *right*. The Lotus Sprint is a car that does *exactly* as it is bidden — instantly. If it does something wrong it is the driver, not the car that has done the misdeed. The feeling of security is such that you have to make visual checks of the surrounding traffic and of the instruments to keep from being

The reason Lotus cars handle like race cars is that they are designed like race cars with little or no compromise for boulevard ride although they achieve smoother characteristics than most sports, GT or economy cars. Front suspension, (top) is a fairly normal-looking, though very light, unequal-length A-arm with race car-like coil-shock unit springing and a moderately stiff roll bar and excellent anti-dive geometry. The fully independent rear end is where the biggest improvement (other than the engine) lies. Rubber-and-steel Rotoflex U-joints are stiffer than before and the center section is more firmly mounted. Shafts are also stronger.

highly illegal. What feels like a comfortable cruising speed in the Sprint would, according to the instruments and the other traffic fading rapidly in the rear-view mirror, seem like a flat-out blind in almost anything else. On more than one occasion we found ourselves entering one of those two-lane-going-into-one interchange ramps figuring on dropping into the line of other traffic as the squeeze came up. In every case we were at the head of the line before the two lanes became one. In no case was it reckless barreling either; we just started in last and with what seemed a sort of time warp ended up first. The shocking thing about it was that it was done with such utter smoothness, security and safety. The only danger is that, having gotten used to the Sprint, one might try the same thing under similar circumstances with another car. We did with one of our mini-rod Q-ships and only then did the fact of Lotus road-holding really sink in. What had seemed normal operating procedure with the Sprint was an effort in the better-than-average mini-rod.

This also brings up another point about Lotus cars. About 75 percent of the mental horsepower expended at Hethel is devoted to race cars and the rub-off on the street machinery is inevitable. These cars are designed as performance machines in the first place, not rebuilt or redesigned from the parts shelves of more mundane sedans. As a result everything about the operation of the car has a race car feel to it. The steering, at 2.7 turns lock-to-lock, is so precise that the term loses meaning when applied to almost any other tiller device you care to name including those attached to the most exotic of machines priced at double, triple and quadruple the bottom line of the Lotus sticker. The operation of the gearbox feels more like the action of an electrical switch than moving a collection of mechanical bits. Each gate drops in with a sort of hard "click" rather than the soft slither associated with the better gearboxes on other cars. It's so quick and precise that you can wind up with a sore hand from trying to push the lever further into the gate until you get used to it. Braking is cut from the same mold, the only limitation seeming to come from the tires which, as pointed out in our remarks on acceleration, are on the small side for the capabilities of the car. While the brakes are incredibly strong, being capable of pulling the car to 3-second, 120-foot stops from 60 and less than 27 feet from 30 mph in under a second, it was all too easy to lock them up inadvertently. The difference between a full-lock panic stop and a controlled stop from 60 was more than a second and upwards of 25 feet greater for the panic stop.

The too-small tires also showed up on the 200-foot circle. While it would

continued on page 161

LOTUS ELAN SPRINT

Engine	In-line 4 DOHC
Bore & Stroke—ins.	3.24 x 2.86
Displacement—cu. in	95.1 (1558cc)
HP @ RPM	113 @ 6500
Torque: lbs.-ft. @ rpm	104 @ 4500
Compression Ratio/Fuel	9.5/1—Premium
Carburetion	2 Zenith-Stromberg CDE 175
Transmission	4-Speed manual, all synchro
Final Drive Ratio	3.77/1 (3.55/1 opt.)
Steering Type	Rack and pinion
Turning Diameter (curb-to-curb ft.)	33
Wheel Turns (lock-to-lock)	2.7
Tire Size	155 HR x 13
Brakes	4-Wheel disc (Girling)
Front Suspension	Unequal-length A-arms, coil springs, tube shocks, sway bar
Rear Suspension	Independent with lower control arm, Chapman strut, concentric coil-shock
Body/Frame Construction	Steel backbone, subframes, bonded fiberglass body
Wheelbase—ins	84.0
Overall Length—ins.	145.0
Width—ins.	56.0
Height—ins.	45.5
Front Track—ins.	47.1
Rear Track—ins.	47.06
Curb Weight—lbs.	1,530
Fuel Capacity—gals.	11
Oil Capacity—qts.	4.5

PERFORMANCE

Acceleration	
0-30 mph	3.2
0-45 mph	5.5
0-60 mph	9.4
0-75 mph	13.2
Standing Start ¼-mile	
Mph	83.79
Elapsed time	16.833
Passing speeds	
40-60 mph	5.6
50-70 mph	5.5
Speeds in gears *	
1st ... mph @ rpm	38 @ 6500
2nd ... mph @ rpm	57 @ 6500
3rd ... mph @ rpm	78 @ 6500
4th ... mph @ rpm	113.1 @ 6500
Mph per 1000 rpm (in top gear)	17.4
Stopping distances	
From 30 mph	26 ft. (0.9 sec.)
From 60 mph	120 ft. (3.0 secs.)
Gas mileage range	26-29 mpg

Speedometer error

Car speed	30	45	50	60	70	80
True speed	30	45	49	59	69	78

* Speeds in gears are at shift points (limited by the length of track) and do not represent maximum speeds.

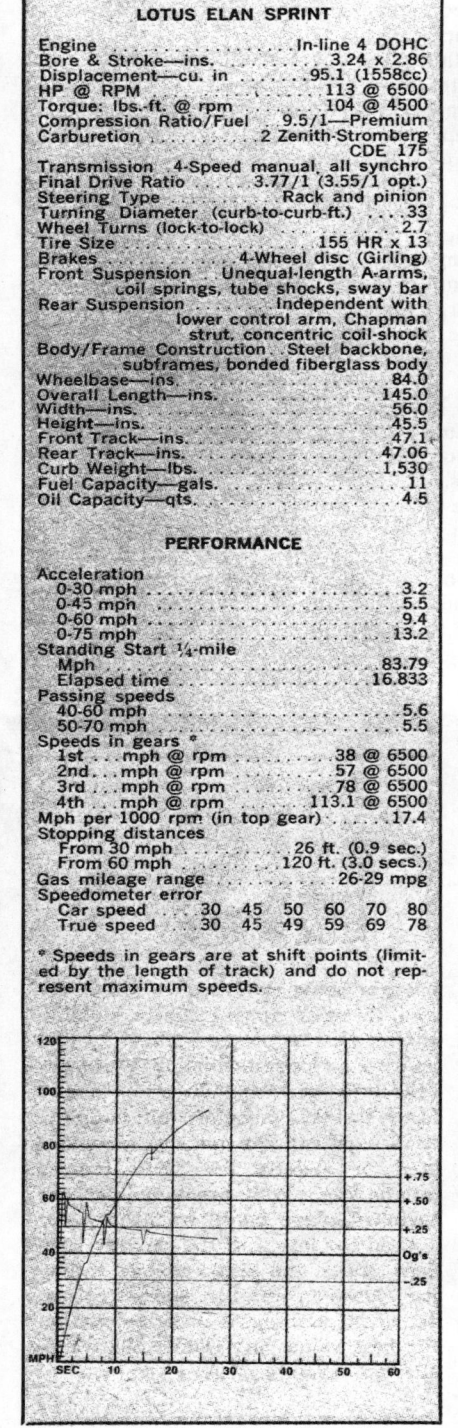

The Sprint engine is readily recognized by the redesigned (and stronger) valve cover. To drive the point home the words BIG VALVE are cast into the front chain cover. Plug wires and ignition are tidily hidden in the cam valley. Below right: The styling remains essentially the same. Recognition points are gold bumpers, Sprint badges.

141

LOTUS ELAN SPRINT

COLIN CHAPMAN'S SECRET has been cunningly and carefully concealed for many years. Ever since that first, fantastic Elite coupe and the bizarre yet irreplaceable Seven, racing and sports car enthusiasts have known that Chapman is more than merely a clever and successful racing car designer-builder and canny businessman. But we haven't been exactly sure what else Chapman is, how road-going Lotus models endear themselves to us almost against our will and theirs.

Now ALL can be Revealed. We have before us the Lotus Elan Sprint, the latest Elan and the best, by any objective or subjective measurement one would make. And yet . . . and yet, well, that's part of the secret.

In the technical sense, the Sprint is improved from one end to the other, literally. The engine is known as the Big Valve because it has (you guessed?) bigger intake valves which, with revised porting, combustion chambers and camshaft timing, result in a sizable power increase. Exactly how much depends on which figures one cares to accept. In England, with Weber carburetors, the Big Valve is rated at 126 bhp—a gain of 25%, the factory said, while quietly admitting that the 115-bhp rating of the S/E was a gross figure and the earlier engine actually produced only 101 net. The U.S. Big Valve, with Stromberg-Zenith carburetors and devilishly intricate dual manifolding, is rated at 113 bhp net. The Sprint is heavier than the earlier model and faster as well, so we are willing to accept the figure.

In back, surely in response to complaints about part-throttle and clutch-engaging surge caused by the flexing rubber doughnuts that serve as U-joints in the Elan's rear suspension, are doughnuts made of less supple material. And the differential mounting has been revised and made stronger. Some Lotus mechanics say that the doughnuts weren't the flaw; the differential moved about under torque. In any case, both are changed and the surge has disappeared.

At the extreme end there's a new, larger muffler. Also in response to complaints? We did say the Series 4 Elan's exhaust was too rorty. Would we could take that back. The new one muffles more than a sports car should be muffled. And it looks as if it could drag on a steep driveway, although there was no actual contact during the test.

That's nearly the only visible change. The Elan wasn't an especially striking or modish style when new, so nine years later it's as quietly and tastefully attractive as ever. The Sprint is differentiated from the earlier Elans only by having gold-colored bumpers.

But that matters little. The Big Valve engine is the important change, and the Big Valve engine works. In contrast to so many other makers, Lotus has neither surrendered performance nor kept power by increasing displacement. The Sprint at least equals the time-to-speed figures recorded in our three previous Elan tests and is the quickest over the standing quarter-mile by nearly half a second.

Marvelous. The Sprint started easily when cold and its only sign of temperament was erratic idle speed, which went from 800 to 1200 rpm depending on temperature and whim. No flat spots, no surge (although the test car was built in 1971 and didn't have the NO_x controls required for 1972), no evidence that the emissions laws hampered the engine at all.

Everything else is much as before. The gearshift is still precise, positive and too confounded stiff; the ratios are nigh perfect for the sort of driving the Elan is supposed to do. The brakes are discs, of course. And the test car stopped from 80 mph in the shortest distance recorded by a road car since R&T began measuring stopping distance. So much for the brakes.

The handling is close to being as good as the brakes, but one must venture into subjectivity to prove it. The Elan's tires are a bit on the small side, as tires are sized currently,

The best Elan yet, and still one of the best cars in the world for the enthusiast

LOTUS ELAN SPRINT

and the factory recommends pressures lower than most, presumably in the interest of ride comfort. So the lateral grip isn't especially high and there are several less sporting cars with higher figures. It can be improved, however, simply by raising tire pressures and the owner can benefit from up to about 10 psi over the recommended pressures.

But handling is much more than just cornering power. The Elan steering is light, sure and completely accurate. No lost motion, no false readings. The car is stable up to breakaway and just as stable before, during and past that point. The Elan can be driven—not just steered or aimed, but driven—in attitudes and at speeds through maneuvers that are plainly impossible for ordinary cars, large tires or no. During all this, the Elan is on your side. Your mother will trip you as you step onto the stage to accept the Nobel Prize before an Elan will do anything that wasn't intended or expected.

There is of course a price for all this good fun. The Elan is very small, with room for two people and a duffel bag.

The noise level is quite high at freeway speeds, even with the top up. The R&T noise measurement test is a new one, but we expect the Elan cockpit din will be a high point in this category for some time.

While we are inside, the wood dashboard is attractive, although the various switches seem to have been located at random. Confusing at night. The seats are narrow, with fixed back angle and padding that didn't conform to most of the staff. There are some improvements in habitability. Putting the top up and down still involves myriad little snaps of the typical English roadster variety, but they all fit and the result is adequate weather protection, which is not typically English roadster or convertible.

Elan headlights used to be held up by engine vacuum, and at high speed or climbing grades, they sometimes sank back down into their homes. But now the engine vacuum holds the lights *down* and they come out at the bidding of springs. So while it's surprising to see them emergent in the morning after an overnight sit, it's nice to know that they no longer disappear at the worst possible time.

The program of improving Lotus quality seems to be successful. During earlier Elan tests, weather strips worked loose, throttle cables pulled free, vital bolts needed daily tightening, etc. Our Sprint was well finished inside and out and needed no repairs or corrections during the test period.

Sounds like a paragon of everything you ever wanted, eh? It isn't, not quite. The Elan is small, cramped and noisy, and it demands a lot from its driver. And even if you are prepared to tolerate these, the Elan Sprint is just about impossible to drive smoothly. Each carburetor has two throttle valves and the entire linkage is loaded by seven (by actual count) return springs. The main spring looks adequate to control the screen door on the vault at the First National Bank.

Pushing against all these springs is work. A survey of cars in the parking lot showed an average of 6 lb pressure required to open the throttles, but the springs on the Elan needed 20 lb. Whether you're stomping those 113 horses into action or merely moving away from rest in traffic, you must try to tread lightly on the clutch, steer lightly with the left hand and use maximum strength with right foot on the gas and right hand on the gear lever. Unbalanced, in a word, and hard to do with any precision.

This point has been belabored at length because the required effort produces a paradox: The engine is perfectly smooth, the drive train has been revised to eliminate the surging that made the Elan so hard to drive smoothly be-

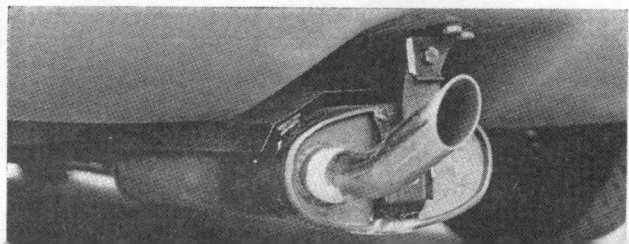

LOTUS ELAN SPRINT

fore, and all those throttle springs make it just as tricky as ever.

Finally, the secret. The Lotus-owning member of our staff says the Elan Sprint is not perfect because Colin Chapman secretly doesn't want it to be perfect. He speculates that Chapman knows a sports car owner doesn't want a perfect car, because a perfect sports car wouldn't be as much fun, wouldn't need its owner or the attention he lavishes on it.

The Engineering Editor says Balderdash! Chapman merely has the bad habit, says the Eng. Ed., of starting with a good idea and releasing it before it's perfected.

In either case, the imperfections can be fixed. Not by Chapman, nor a factory of mythical elves, but by the buyer. He can lighten the throttle return springs, shift the seat padding so it fits him and him only, install a smaller muffler; in short, either fix Chapman's mistakes or cooperate in Chapman's technique. When that is done, owner and car should live happily ever after.

ROAD TEST
LOTUS ELAN SPRINT

SCALE: 10" DIVISIONS

PRICE
List price, west coast......$5593
Price as tested, west coast...$5843
Price as tested includes standard equipment (electric window lifts, radial tires), dealer prep, AM-FM stereo radio and stereo tape player ($250)

IMPORTER
British Motor Car Distributors, Ltd.
19100 Susana Rd.
Compton, Calif. 90221

ENGINE
Type................dohc inline 4
Bore x stroke, mm....82.5 x 72.8
  Equivalent in.......3.25 x 2.86
Displacement, cc/cu in..1558/95.1
Compression ratio............9.5:1
Bhp @ rpm, net......113 @ 6500
  Equivalent mph..............113
Torque @ rpm, lb-ft..108 @ 4000
  Equivalent mph...............70
Carburetion: two Zenith-Stromberg 175 CD
Fuel requirement........premium
Emissions, gram/mile (1972):
  Hydrocarbons..............2.76
  Carbon Monoxide..........22.30
  Nitrogen Oxides............1.84

DRIVE TRAIN
Transmission.....4-speed manual
Gear ratios: 4th (1.00).....3.77:1
  3rd (1.40).................5.26:1
  2nd (2.01)................7.58:1
  1st (2.97)...............11.20:1
Final drive ratio...........3.77:1

CHASSIS & BODY
Layout.....front engine/rear drive
Body/frame....separate fiberglass body, steel backbone frame
Brake system....9.5-in. disc front, 10.5-in. disc rear
  Swept area, sq in..........304
Wheels......steel disc, knockoff, 13 x 4½J
Tires..........Dunlop SP155-13
Steering type.......rack & pinion
  Turns, lock-to-lock..........2.7
  Turning circle, ft..........29.5
Front suspension: unequal-length A-arms, coil springs, tube shocks, anti-roll bar
Rear suspension: Chapman struts with lower A-arms, coil springs, tube shocks

ACCOMMODATION
Seating capacity, persons.......2
Seat width.............2 x 17.5
Head room...................36.0
Seat back adjustment, degrees...0

INSTRUMENTATION
Instruments: 140-mph speedometer, 8000-rpm tach, 99,999 odometer, 999.9 trip odo, oil pressure, coolant temp, fuel level
Warning lights: handbrake, brake fluid level, generator, high beam, directionals, hazard

MAINTENANCE
Service intervals, mi:
  Oil change................3000
  Filter change.............6000
  Chassis lube..............3000
  Tuneup....................6000
Warranty, mo/mi........6/10,000

GENERAL
Curb weight, lb.............1640
Test weight.................2005
Weight distribution (with driver), front/rear, %....47/53
Wheelbase, in................84.0
Track, front/rear......47.1/48.4
Length.....................145.0
Width.......................56.0
Height......................45.2
Ground clearance.............6.0
Overhang, front/rear....26.9/34.1
Usable trunk space, cu ft....5.3
Fuel capacity, U.S. gal.....12.0

CALCULATED DATA
Lb/bhp (test weight).........17.7
Mph/1000 rpm (4th gear)....17.4
Engine revs/mi (60 mph)....3450
Piston travel, ft/mi........1645
R&T steering index..........0.80
Brake swept area, sq in/ton..289

RELIABILITY
From R&T Owner Surveys the average number of trouble areas for all models surveyed is 11. As owners of earlier-model Lotus reported 22 trouble areas, we expect the reliability of the Lotus Elan Sprint to be far below average.

ROAD TEST RESULTS

ACCELERATION
Time to distance, sec:
  0-100 ft....................3.5
  0-500 ft....................8.7
  0-1320 ft (¼ mi).........16.0
Speed at end of ¼-mi, mph....82
Time to speed, sec:
  0-30 mph....................2.9
  0-40 mph....................4.4
  0-50 mph....................5.9
  0-60 mph....................8.4
  0-70 mph...................11.4
  0-80 mph...................15.3
  0-100 mph..................26.5

FUEL ECONOMY
Normal driving, mpg........22.0
Cruising range, mi (1-gal res.)..240

SPEEDS IN GEARS
4th gear (6500 rpm).........112
3rd (6500)...................79
2nd (6500)...................56
1st (6500)...................38

BRAKES
Minimum stopping distances, ft:
  From 60 mph..............124
  From 80 mph..............247
Control in panic stop....very good
Pedal effort for 0.5g stop, lb....45
Fade: percent increase in pedal effort to maintain 0.5g deceleration in 6 stops from 60 mph...11
Parking: hold 30% grade?......no
Overall brake rating.....excellent

HANDLING
Speed on 100-ft radius, mph..32.9
Lateral acceleration, g......0.720

INTERIOR NOISE
All noise readings in dbA:
  Idle in neutral..............60
  Maximum, 1st gear..........87
  Constant 30 mph............70
    50 mph...................79
    70 mph...................89
    90 mph...................96

SPEEDOMETER ERROR
30 mph indicated is actually...29.5
  50 mph....................49.0
  60 mph....................59.0
  70 mph....................68.5
  80 mph....................77.0
Odometer, 10.0 mi...........9.8

ACCELERATION

(graph showing Speed, mph and Distance, ft vs Elapsed time in sec, with curves for 1st, 2nd, 3rd, 4th gears, SS¼ markers, ¼ mi indicator; Time to distance (dashed) and Time to speed (solid))

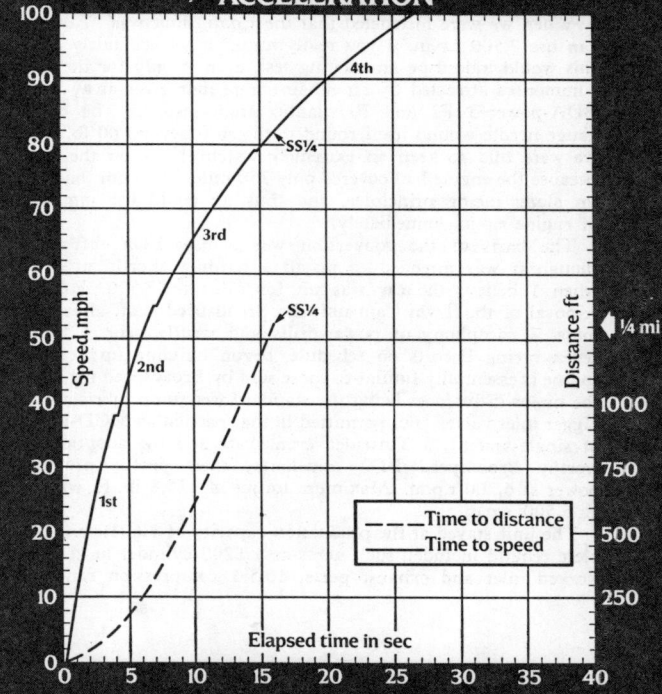

TUNING TOPICS

AN ELAN WITH A DIFFERENCE

—170 bhp Broadspeed BDA under the bonnet

A FEW issues ago I looked into the possibilities of further developing the Elan for road and track use, concluding with some brief impressions of a 2-litre Twin Cam-engined example of the *marque*, as raced by David Brodie. Shortly after publication of that article we were told that a Mr. David Pannel had asked the Broadspeed concern to convert a new Elan road car to a specification that sounded far more like a racing machine than a public highway conveyance. The intended power output was to materialise as very little less than that racer we tested. Actually, a total of 170 b.h.p. was to be gently extracted from the Ford Cosworth 16-valve engine that was substituted for the normal 118 b.h.p., Twin Cam unit.

Nobody short of an experienced competitive driver would be likely to describe the production Elan as anything less than downright exciting anyway. As it emerges from Hethel the Sprint will run from 0-60 m.p.h. in approximately seven seconds and cover nearly 120 m.p.h., thus any effective conversion, especially one employing a BDA transplant, should certainly result in entertaining transport.

In fact the converted Elan emerged as a very hot piece of machinery indeed. We picked the car up at the close of a Brands Hatch club race meeting and were immediately reminded that this was no ordinary docile sports car by the injunction "slide the clutch out slowly, keep the revs above 3,000 and I bet you stall it!" As it was wet, and the only way out of the car park was uphill, it seemed extremely likely that it would shudder to an ungainly halt—especially as that high first gear will comfortably allow over 50 m.p.h. with little thought to how the driver covers the first 10 m.p.h. of his forward progress!

When we were instructed that the r.p.m. limit was "7,000, but you can use 7,500 r.p.m. if you really must" it seemed fairly certain that this would indeed be an exciting test, even if only for the number of summonses attracted by an exhaust note that gives away little to the BDA-powered F2 and F/Atlantic single-seaters. The oil pressure gauge needle wound itself round to the stop beyond 60 lb. per sq. in.; we were told to keep an extremely watchful eye on the sump level because the engine had covered only 350 miles. The unit had been built up along racing principles, and thus we could use our full quota of engine r.p.m. immediately.

The basis of the conversion was a new Elan soft-top Sprint, though it was intended to install a hardtop shortly after our test, when I believe the car was up for sale at £2,500. Following the removal of the Twin Cam unit the Broadspeed staff, already working midst a cacophony of power-drills and muffled curses to complete seven racing Escorts on schedule, begun building up a BDA. The engine is essentially similar to those sold by Broadspeed for F/Atlantic, the major differences being the standard wet sump lubrication system, bigger inlet valves (not permitted in that particular MCD-backed class of single-seater), a Tuftrided crankshaft and the adoption of roadworthy Broadspeed BD2 camshafts; their profile provides peak power at 6,200 r.p.m. Maximum torque of 125.8 lb. ft. will be found at 5,500 r.p.m.

The unit stayed at the production capacity of 1,601 c.c., but a complete rebuild included such items as a £200 cylinder head with hand-worked inlet and exhaust ports, 10.5:1 compression ratio, eight of those new inlet valves and a pair of the £62 BD2 camshafts. That is the trouble with BDAs, there are so many parts to modify with double overhead camshafts and 16 valves popping up and down! All new reciprocating components were balanced, lightened where appropriate and shot peened, which includes a lighter flywheel.

Exterior modifications to go with the new engine include re-jetted and choked Weber 45 DCOE carburetters, internally polished inlet manifold, and tubular steel exhaust manifolding leading into a single large bore tailpipe. A reshaped crossmember is necessary to clear the Cosworth-based engine's sump, while the water radiator is moved slightly further forward and a Serck oil-cooler added.

The transmission changes are pretty radical too. The gearbox was completely rebuilt to utilise needle roller bearings and new ratios to give those impressive gear speeds. The end result is pretty similar to a four-speed Group 2 touring car gearbox, with beautifully chosen ratios for someone in a real hurry. The independent rear-end retained the standard 3.77-to-1 final drive and incorporated a Salisbury limited slip differential.

An equally comprehensive conversion programme was followed to make the car stop and handle in keeping with its racing heritage. To begin with the rack and pinion steering received new steering arms and a new home on the crossmember to cut out bump steer. The four standard coil springs were replaced by shorter springs giving a ride height reduced by an inch, whilst Bilstein gas-filled shock-absorbers do an able job of keeping some of the production vehicle's excellent riding qualities. Excellent ride characteristics by sporting standards that is, Citroën drivers probably wouldn't recognise that this Elan had any shock-absorbers at all. Anti-fade disc pads and revised brake balance to increase the proportion of effort applied to the front wheels.

THE DIFFERENCE.—Nestling snugly in the engine compartment of the Elan is a tuned 170-b.h.p. Broadspeed BDA engine which replaces the regular Twin Cam.

NO! J.W. has not just run over an unfortunate cyclist. The Elan-BDA pictured with the fifth wheel timing device rigged up. Unfortunately during the test runs the car suffered from a cam seizing in its carrier and so we were not able to obtain what surely would have been some of our most impressive acceleration figures ever.

From an onlooker's viewpoint there's no mistaking this Broadspeed job as a sheep in wolf's clothing; it's a wolf, and frankly its orange paintwork, obese wheel-arches and matching Minilites leave nobody in any doubt as to its intended purpose.

For the record, it is worth recording that the specially made up glassfibre air dam (*not* the one used on the same company's Capris) and 195 GP Goodyears are extremely effective in allowing straight forward progress, though I must confess that the "wing" only seems to make a difference under motorway crosswind conditions.

The step-up in size from 40 to 45 DCOEs makes the usual prompt dab, dab, and start routine even faster than usual, but they soon belch forth protest if you try and accelerate hard from less than 2,000 r.p.m. in third or fourth. Because it was wet when we picked the car up, the hood was raised, but after it tried to blow clear of the windscreen three times the following day, we lowered the PVC and left the car in a garage overnight. In turn this meant that we enjoyed the car as it is meant to be enjoyed—wind in the hair and plenty of speed.

In fact the Broadspeed Elan would work quite satisfactorily around town, when the knack of dribbling in revs to 1200 r.p.m. or so had been mastered in conjunction with slow clutch release. The water temperature would rise to 90-degrees under these circumstances, but the electric fan would reduce the coolant heat level to 85-degrees given a long jam to do its work in. Despite those wide wheels, the Lotus steering seemed as light as ever whilst the gear-change was phenomenally efficient, but I found the clutch rather heavy when dragging through London from east to west.

Under wet conditions the Elan is not at its best, though the handling and braking still provide generous margins of safety. Obviously, if the car is provoked by a flat-out throttle opening in low gear during the negotiation of a tight curve, then the driver will be presented with no grip at one end or the other, always the rear, providing sufficient power is applied. At first we could not imagine any driver hurling the Broadspeeded device about with abandon on a wet day, but with practice one finds that the limited slip differential will find a way to transmit some horsepower to a slippery surface. Those with problems that cannot be solved by the application of power—such as the strong understeer that almost any car will suffer if it is put into a slippery corner too fast—need not apply for compensation.

Whatever the prevalent weather the modified Elan's real party-piece is in the deadly efficient manner in which it can cover British roads. Just in the same way that I found myself unable to stay indoors when we had the RS1600, or the Lotus 7, or the Else converted Europa, or even such diverse vehicles as the AMC Javelin V8 or the beautiful BMW 3.0 CS, and the Alfa Romeo 1750 Duetto/GTV, I found there was a vague feeling of unhappiness until I had taken the Elan out for a brisk airing. In the largely pampered past six years or so that I have been lucky enough to use (mainly) spotless cars provided by other people in search of publicity for their wares, I've never enjoyed a trip more than the one I took in the Elan overnight to the country and back to town in the early morning.

It was only under such artificial conditions that I could understand why the owner of this car had sacrificed some everyday motoring manners on the altar of honest performance in all departments. The trouble at present is that such performance is frowned on and I can see why one eminent journalist once advised me, "never write about anything you enjoy—somebody, somewhere, will put a stop to whatever it is!" It is easy to see his point where any sort of road is concerned, for publicity draws crowds, and lots of people always seem to bring lots of problems with them.

As the Elan swooped along country lanes I reflected how much we miss inside an ordinary saloon. Would that it was practical for everyone to enjoy the thrills of extracting perfect unison from engine, brakes and gearbox, as is possible with this Elan. There's even enough power to set the car up accurately for almost any corner at any speed up to 90 m.p.h.; it is just over this speed that one has to change out of third gear if one is imposing the normal 6,500 limit. In the lower gears 6,500 translates as 52 and 68 m.p.h., whilst in top gear I never exceeded an indicated 120 m.p.h. with the hood down. However, this really misses the point for it is the sheer verve with which the car responds that endears it to the driver, especially on the sort of switch back represented by an 80 m.p.h. crest followed by a downhill 60 m.p.h. left-hander, 70 m.p.h. right, bumpy 110 m.p.h. straight and 30 m.p.h. downhill hairpin. To follow that sort of terrain you need the Elan's red hot needle performance package; even then you'll actually experience the joys of drifting with little need to do more than ease the steering onto corrective lock.

We took the car to our normal track for performance tests, but after 12 not very satisfactory runs a camshaft seized in its carrier, a problem that will be familiar to W.B. from his spell with the RS1600. The only other problem that presented itself was oil surge that materialised if the car was anything less than bung-full according to the dipstick. After the Elan was returned, I did idly wonder if the dipstick markings were correct, for such things have been known to happen before.

To my eyes the Elan represented a very healthy diversion for a wealthy man who wanted a sophisticated Lotus Seven, for it is unbelievably rapid in the sort of situations that a skilled driver could enjoy, whilst offering all the creature comforts when required, for even the electric windows worked throughout our tenure!—J. W.

Overall fuel consumption: 17-22 m.p.g.
Price of engine (including £500 for production RS1600 unit): £957.
Converters: Broadspeed Ltd., Banbury Road, Southam, Warks.

THE ELAN-BDA looked impressive with its fat tyres on some excellent Minilite rims and the bulging wheel arches to accommodate them.

● In a recent article on modified Cortinas, J.W. said that the lights on a Mk. 3 Cortina remained on the sidelight position only on one side and criticised the car on this point. The Ford press office naturally told us that this was because we had been using the parking light control, which was true, but did not account for a simple bulb failure of a front sidelight, which added to our reporter's confusion.

● Jaguar enthusiasts will be interested to learn that Warren Pearce is now trading under the name Lawrence Pearce from premises at 186 Cambridge Road, Kingston, Surrey (Tel.: 01-549 1992). Although his workshops are mainly filled with quality maintenance work these days (a Facel Vega and BMW 2002 were undergoing surgery when we called) Pearce is still offering a number of Jaguar performance improvement items, especially with regard to braking and suspension modifications. His current pride and joy is an XJ6 which apparently accelerates and corners in a way that pleases this former Jaguar E-type racing driver, now happily fully recovered from the serious injuries he incurred at Castle Combe in 1970.

LOTUS ELAN PLUS 2S 130

With the larger Lotus, you get a little more and a little less

ROAD & TRACK ROAD TEST

THE RELATIVE SIZE of the Lotus Elan is small. Quite small. Deliberately small, as the designers intentionally set out to make the Elan as efficiently quick, i.e. small and light, as it was possible for the car to be while carrying a maximum of two people. It was and is a valid aim. At the same time, though, the makers were aware that there are many people who either want or need a car that can carry more than two people. That car is the Elan Plus 2, the title indicating an expanded Elan with two normal seats and two occasional seats. In detail, the Plus 2 is not merely an expansion. There are no shared body parts, for instance. But in general, the styling of the Plus 2 follows the smaller Elan very closely, and the Plus 2 has the backbone frame, the independent suspension, the disc brakes, the 1600-cc twin cam engine and the drivetrain of the original car. In general, the designers took an Elan, cut it into sections and expanded them in all three dimensions. To the 2-place Elan were added 12 in. of wheelbase, 23 in. of overall length, 7.5 in. of width, 7 in. of track and one in. of height. With this, the Plus 2 gained two tiny seats, a larger trunk and 335 lb curb weight.

And customers. One must remember that even in these days of worldwide trade, virtually all cars are designed for their native countries. In England, one-car families are the rule and when the children arrive, they must fit into that one car. The Plus 2 has done very well in England and was in fact the first Lotus model to sell more than 1000 examples in its first year. The Plus 2 was introduced at a critical time, in late 1967, just when the U.S. safety and emission laws were coming into effect. The home market clamored for the Plus 2 and the U.S. laws kept it out until the various certifications and changes were done. Not surprisingly, the export version was a long time coming, and it took a while for us to get one. But by the time we did, there had been other changes as well. This Plus 2 test is of the very latest model, fitted with the same Big Valve engine, the stronger rear halfshaft doughnuts and the revised mounting of the differential earlier provided for the Elan Sprint.

The Plus 2 is at the same time both more and less than is the Elan. The "more" is in size and space. In the category of unquestioned gain, the Plus 2 has more elbow room for the two adults and more trunk space, more than the Elan and more even than a Chevrolet Camaro. The seats are higher and the entry way larger. And the rear seatback folds down, providing a handy place for loose luggage, parcels, etc.

The occasional seats, though, are just barely adequate to be called occasional; for a man of medium size they are nearly impossible. It's also difficult to get into them. The Plus 2's front seats are standard Elan seats, one-piece with fixed back. In the Plus 2 they hinge at the front and their integral headrests bump the roof before the seat has been raised more than a few inches. An adult who manages to get there will find his knees splayed around the front seat, his neck bent and his head resting against the roof. The rear seats are suitable only for children, and even a 5-year-old will be pressed for legroom. Tolerable, perhaps, for a one-car family whose head wishes to own a Lotus, but not a convincing argument when the family Chevrolet or Toyota sits availably in the driveway.

The "less" of the Plus 2 has mostly to do with performance. The Plus 2 weighs more than the standard Elan but has exactly the same engine. So it is less quick than the Elan, to a degree that reduces the larger car to mere equality with the competition or even with the peppier sporting sedans. The BMW 2002tii matches the Plus 2 in 0-60 time and beats it for the standing quarter-mile. The Plus 2 has a smaller engine, true, but that's not the point, surely, when it comes to buying a sports car. The Plus 2's body is reportedly slicker than the Elan's and should return better mpg at fast cruising speeds, but the extra weight requires more fuel at low speeds and during acceleration, for another net loss.

For the most part, the Plus 2 is an Elan, with vices

PHOTOS BY LARRY GRIFFIN

and virtues we have seen before. The Big Valve engine is a most satisfactory unit, smooth from idle to the factory's redline of 6500 rpm, and with more than a trace of the driveability problems also plaguing other makes these days. The gearshift is perfectly placed but its action infuriatingly obstructive. It holds up to abuse wonderfully well, but in normal driving the lever is quite notchy and needs considerable force. The test car had several thousand miles on it, so we can't explain this as merely new-car stiffness.

And the Plus 2 is very difficult to drive smoothly. We encountered this with the Sprint, you may recall, and we said then that the throttle was too stiff and the drivetrain too loose, no matter what the factory said about stiffer doughnuts and revised differential mountings. The Plus 2 also has the stiff throttle and it still surges under acceleration and deceleration, even after a few hundred miles of

COMPARISON DATA

	Lotus Elan +2S	Alfa Romeo 1750 GTV	Porsche 911T	Volvo 1800E
List price incl. prep.	$6735	$4822	$7475	$5060
Curb weight, lb	1975	2315	2390	2540
0–60 mph, sec.	9.8	9.9	8.5*	11.3
Standing ¼ mi, sec.	17.6	17.5	16.0*	18.2
Stopping distance from 80 mph, ft.	239	283	312	299
Brake fade, 6 stops from 60 mph, %	20	nil	nil	50
Cornering capability, g.	0.757	0.683	0.732	0.660
Interior noise @ 70 mph, dBA	79	n.t.	78	77
Fuel economy, mpg.	20.8	23.6	20.0	22.5

*estimated

LOTUS ELAN

WORLD CHAMPION CAR CONSTRUCTORS 1970 1968 1965 1963

practice. One test driver said he always felt as if the veins on his neck were bulging with the effort of treading properly on the pedals.

But ah, the handling! Pure Lotus, and just as good as the name promises it will be. The steering is light and direct, with no lost motion and just enough feedback to let the driver know what's happening. The ride is typically Elan, soft and controlled. The Plus 2 has a bit less sheer cornering power than the Sprint—the weight again—but the characteristics are virtually identical; close to neutral under most conditions, with gentle understeer revealing itself at the very edge of a very high limit. The hardest thing about driving the Plus 2 fast is learning that one does not need to force matters as one does with most cars. The Plus 2 is guided by gentle pressure, not steered by brute muscle. And the car is so well balanced that many things can be done at once, as in braking while cornering. We are reminded once again that a sports car is more than a powerful engine.

Speaking of braking, in the Sprint test we simply said that the Elan stopped from 80 mph in less distance than any other road car we've tested. That's all we said, or thought we needed to say, about the brakes. And there were a few complaints, along the lines of why didn't we throw in some superlatives while we were at it? Well, the Plus 2 is another quick stopper, with large tires for its weight and a superb job of balancing on both the car and the proportioning of braking effort between front and rear. In consequence, the Plus 2 brakes are even better than the Elan Sprint brakes. Consider the superlatives said.

In essence, the difference between the Sprint and the Plus 2 isn't a matter of inches. It's more like comfort (blush!) and convenience. The Plus 2 isn't really suited for two adults and two children. But it would do nicely as a touring car for two adults. There's the extra elbow room, the larger trunk and the space for loose stuff. The dashboard is larger and that area gets used for more instruments. One of everything, right down to a temperature gauge for ambient air in degrees Centigrade! The switches are placed more logically, the lack of exhaust noise (a boom on deceleration aside) is in keeping with the more refined nature of the car, and the coupe body (and perhaps the shape and interior padding) reduce noise to normal levels. There are a few of the oddities we've come to expect from Lotus, like a squeaky door and an ignition wire that shorted out during the test, but in general the Plus 2 was less sporting but more pleasant and practical in daily use.

With that, the Plus 2 comes into a different class. The Elan has few rivals. There aren't many sophisticated, demanding, fast and entertaining 2-place sports cars on the market, presumably because the manufacturers have learned that even buyers of sporting machinery like to have some room to stretch, stow luggage, carry children. The Plus 2 must compete with a number of good cars, from Fiat 124 Coupe to Porsche 911T, and each rival will have a lower price, perhaps, or more interior room or more power. None will exceed the Plus 2's roadability, most will accommodate children in more comfort. Probably the Plus 2 buyer will be the person Lotus had in mind at the beginning. If you simply must have a Lotus and you must take the kids along, the Plus 2 is for you.

ROAD TEST
LOTUS ELAN PLUS 2S 130

SCALE: 10" DIVISIONS

PRICE
List price, west coast........$6597
Price as tested, west coast...$6735
Price as tested includes dealer prep & minimum inland freight ($138)

IMPORTER
British Motor Car Distributors, Ltd.
19100 Susanna Rd.
Compton, Calif. 90221

ENGINE
Type....................dohc inline 4
Bore x stroke, mm......82.5 x 72.8
 Equivalent in.........3.25 x 2.86
Displacement, cc/cu in..1558/95.1
Compression ratio...............9.5:1
Bhp @ rpm, net........113 @ 6500
 Equivalent mph................122
Torque @ rpm, lb-ft...108 @ 4000
 Equivalent mph.................74
Carburetion: two Zenith-Stromberg 175 CD
Fuel requirement: premium, 98-oct
Emissions, gram/mile:
 Hydrocarbons..................2.30
 Carbon Monoxide..............19.96
 Nitrogen Oxides...............n.a.

DRIVE TRAIN
Transmission......4-speed manual
Gear ratios: 4th (1.00).......3.77:1
 3rd (1.40)..................5.26:1
 2nd (2.01)..................7.58:1
 1st (2.97).................11.20:1
Final drive ratio............3.77:1

CHASSIS & BODY
Layout.....front engine/rear drive
Body/frame........steel backbone frame, separate fiberglass body
Brake system...10-in. disc front & rear
Swept area, sq in..............334
Wheels........steel disc, knockoff, 13 x 5½J
Tires...Dunlop SP Sport 165-HR13
Steering type.........rack & pinion
Overall ratio................14.5:1
Turns, lock-to-lock.............2.6
Turning circle, ft..............36.0
Front suspension: unequal-length A-arms, coil springs, tube shocks, anti-roll bar
Rear suspension: Chapman struts with lower A-arms, coil springs, tube shocks

ACCOMMODATION
Seating capacity, persons......2+2
Seat width, front/rear....2x17.0/2x14.0
Head room, front/rear..........37.5
Seat back adjustment, degrees...0

INSTRUMENTATION
Instruments: 140-mph speedo, 8000-rpm tach, 99,999 odo, 999.9 trip odo, oil press, coolant temp, voltmeter, fuel level, clock, ambient temp
Warning lights: brake system, generator, low fuel, handbrake, rear window heat, high beam, directionals, hazard flasher

MAINTENANCE
Service intervals, mi:
 Oil change...................3000
 Filter change................6000
 Chassis lube.................3000
 Tuneup.......................6000
Warranty, mo/mi..........6/10,000

GENERAL
Curb weight, lb...............1975
Test weight...................2310
Weight distribution (with driver), front/rear, %....47/53
Wheelbase, in.................96.0
Track, front/rear.......54.0/55.0
Length.......................168.0
Width.........................63.5
Height........................47.0
Ground clearance...............6.0
Overhang, front/rear....30.0/42.0
Usable trunk space, cu ft......7.7
Fuel capacity, U.S. gal.......15.6

CALCULATED DATA
Lb/bhp (test weight).........20.4
Mph/1000 rpm (4th gear)......19.8
Engine revs/mi (60 mph)......3200
Piston travel, ft/mi..........1530
R&T steering index...........0.93
Brake swept area, sq in/ton...289

RELIABILITY
From R&T Owner Surveys the average number of trouble areas for all models surveyed is 11. As owners of earlier-model Lotus Elans reported 22 trouble areas, we expect the reliability of the Elan +2S to be far below average.

ROAD TEST RESULTS

ACCELERATION
Time to distance, sec:
 0-100 ft......................3.5
 0-500 ft......................9.3
 0-1320 ft (¼ mi).............17.6
Speed at end of ¼-mi, mph......81
Time to speed, sec:
 0-30 mph......................3.8
 0-40 mph......................5.2
 0-50 mph......................7.5
 0-60 mph......................9.8
 0-70 mph.....................13.5
 0-80 mph.....................17.4
 0-100 mph....................30.3

FUEL ECONOMY
Normal driving, mpg...........20.8
Cruising range, mi (1-gal res.).292

SPEEDS IN GEARS
4th gear (5900 rpm)...........110
3rd (6500)....................86
2nd (6500)....................62
1st (6500)....................42

HANDLING
Speed on 100-ft radius, mph...33.7
Lateral acceleration, g.....0.757

BRAKES
Minimum stopping distances, ft:
 From 60 mph..................136
 From 80 mph..................239
Control in panic stop....excellent
Pedal effort for 0.5g stop, lb...25
Fade: percent increase in pedal effort to maintain 0.5g deceleration in 6 stops from 60 mph..20
Parking: hold 30% grade?......no
Overall brake rating.....excellent

INTERIOR NOISE
All noise readings in dBA:
 Idle in neutral...............58
 Maximum, 1st gear.............85
 Constant 30 mph...............71
 50 mph........................75
 70 mph........................79
 90 mph........................82

SPEEDOMETER ERROR
30 mph indicated is actually..29.0
50 mph........................50.0
60 mph........................60.0
70 mph........................70.0
80 mph........................80.0

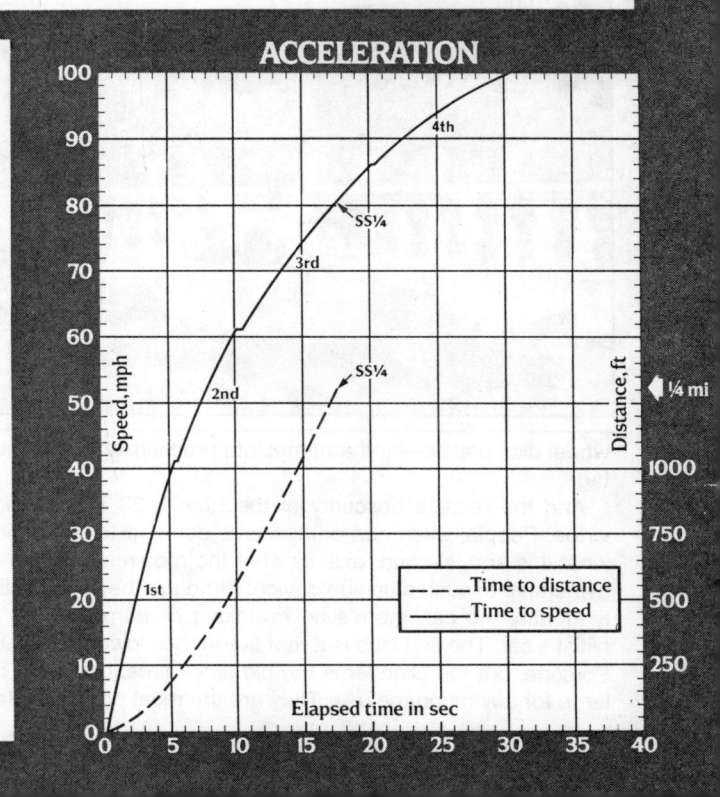

ACCELERATION

Acceleration graph showing 4th, 3rd, 2nd, 1st gear curves; SS¼ time to speed and time to distance vs. elapsed time in sec.

• The truly exclusive automobile is a vanishing breed. We're not concerned here with the sort of financial exclusivity that comes with a Ferrari or a Lamborghini or even a Stutz. Nor are we talking about the oddball cachet that comes from having a thing like an Amphicar or a King Midget. What we are lamenting are the limited production sports cars that sell for under a five digit number and are being inexorably excluded from the market by the combined forces of governmental restrictions and undeclared economic warfare. Specifically, we are talking about the Lotus Elan +2S 130, possibly one of the last examples of this type of automobile—and this type of exclusivity—to come to the United States.

The Lotus has all the proper elements: a name that is well known to the discerning, a comparative production rarity (Lotus builds only about 6000 cars of all models—Elan, Elan +2, Seven and Europa—each year), and hardware like all independent suspension, multiple overhead cam engine, and four-

Lotus Elan +2S 130

All those discomforts won't discourage those who really want a Lotus, but they will contribute to its exclusivity

wheel disc brakes—and a nameplate proclaiming racing heritage.

And the relative obscurity of the Elan +2S is a *tangible* virtue. People, even non-enthusiasts, demand to know, first, what it is and, second, exactly what the requirements are for ownership of such a unique device. Although they can't initially identify the car, there's no mistaking its purpose. It is an elitist's car. The first clue is a roof five inches lower than a 911 Porsche, but the clincher is the big black tires, obviously too large for any mundane use. They are the most prominent feature on the whole smooth profile, and no attempt has been made to cloak their function with stylish bodywork. Instead, the wheel openings completely dominate the sides of the car, and between their subtle flares and the very low hood line, little actual fender is left at all. And there, sitting inside the enormous opening, are chrome, vented wheels with a single large hex nut in the center. Business-like. Unabashedly single purpose. With such a major emphasis on the tires and wheels, the Lotus could *only* be a sports car.

The gently-sloping hood ends well below knee level and does nothing to dispel this image. At its tip is a delicate, flush-mounted bumper that surrounds an angular air inlet, undisguised as to its function. The lines of the body flow simply over the minimum volume necessary to house the chassis parts and interior package. No art critic will be offended, but the lean contours and primary attention to function are constant reminders of the car's sole purpose—driving (not to be confused with "transporting").

The interior is consistant with this theme. When the door is opened, you're sure you've stumbled into the cockpit of a Learjet. Six small gauges and two large dials as well as a gaggle of indicator lights and rocker switches guarantee control and surveillance of every system short of windshield washer fluid level. There's even an instrument for ambient air temperature—a definite plus as soon as you gain proficiency in converting Centigrade readings to more familiar Farenheit levels. And right in the middle of this array is the large leather-covered wheel, embossed with the autograph of the Lotus leader Colin Chapman. In no other car will you find such implied personal assurance that the expected will happen.

No disappointments arise from the shift linkage. A stubby lever swings in short, precise movements above the wide center tunnel, and it is no more than a hand's width from the steering wheel at all times. Deep within the footwell, the pedals encourage heel-and-toe operation, even though their effort requirements are high. Rigid lateral restraints in the seat offer the best location this side of a racing car. It's all for the driver—and the passenger is accommodated in what is left over. The two occupants are segregated by a huge intrusion from the backbone frame. All the better to let the driver concentrate on the job at hand.

For power there is an in-line-Four that delivers 113 net horsepower from 95.2 cubic inches of displacement. It was originally meant to power lowly Ford Anglias, and recently Pintos, at very moderate speeds, but there has been a transformation from those scullery maid days, in the form of an aluminum twin-cam cylinder head. In its European version, without emission controls, a 130 peak horsepower is developed, and thus the 130 delineation at the end of the model name. Although U.S. versions don't benefit from all the power, 1972 does bring the "Big Valve" configuration, a fact proudly cast in block letters on the timing chain cover. Underneath that banner one finds larger intake valves, freer-flowing passages, and more material above the combustion chamber for increased durability. There are also new camshaft profiles and recalibrated carburetors.

From the throttle response, there is no indication of family ties with the Pinto 1600 engine. Still, no other manufacturer of a $6000 car would have the gall to be so proud of such a small engine. The undersized displacement is most noticeable on the dragstrip, where a tall first gear and sticky tires limit the action to 16.8 seconds and 82.6 mph quarter-miles. While the 116 mph top speed might severely challenge less-expensive 240Zs, Porsches and most other upper-middle class sports coupes (not to mention a host of American cars)

ACCELERATION standing ¼ mile, seconds

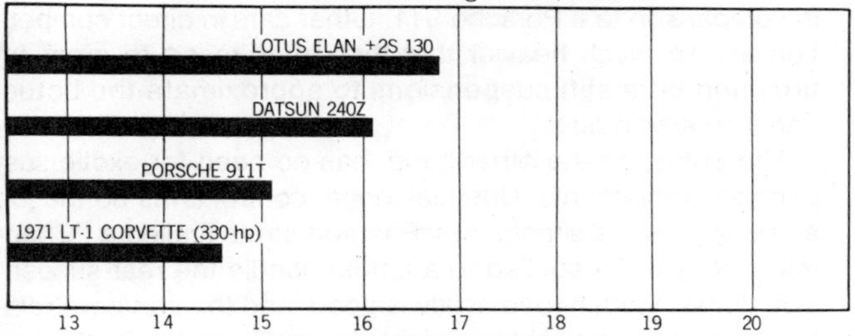

- LOTUS ELAN +2S 130
- DATSUN 240Z
- PORSCHE 911T
- 1971 LT-1 CORVETTE (330-hp)

13 14 15 16 17 18 19 20

BRAKING 70-0 mph panic stop, feet

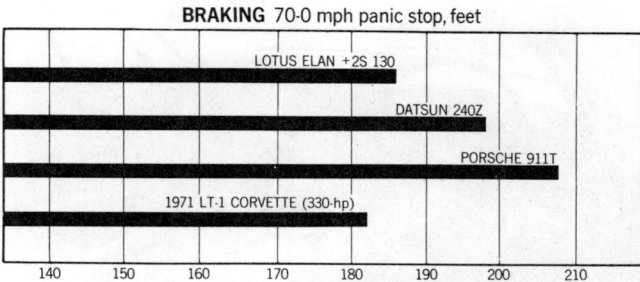

- LOTUS ELAN +2S 130
- DATSUN 240Z
- PORSCHE 911T
- 1971 LT-1 CORVETTE (330-hp)

140 150 160 170 180 190 200 210

FUEL ECONOMY RANGE mpg

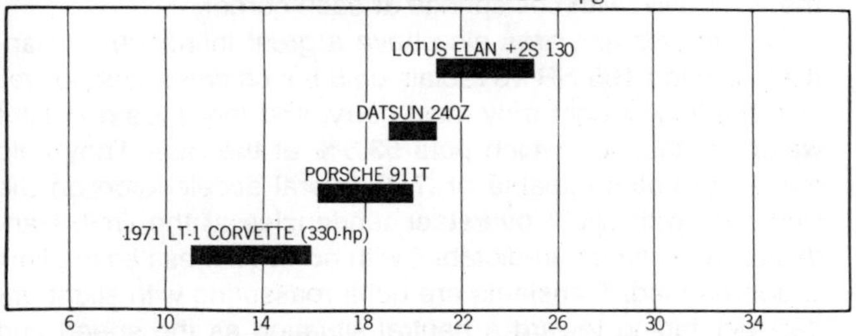

- LOTUS ELAN +2S 130
- DATSUN 240Z
- PORSCHE 911T
- 1971 LT-1 CORVETTE (330-hp)

6 10 14 18 22 26 30 34

PRICE AS TESTED dollars x 1000

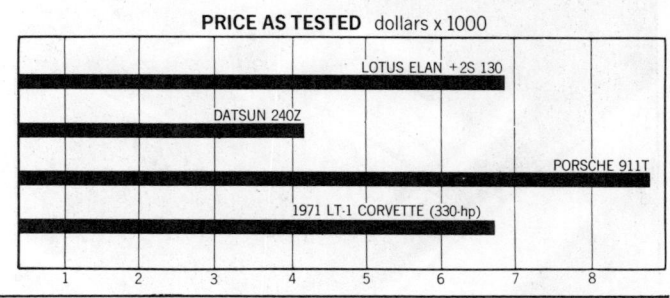

- LOTUS ELAN +2S 130
- DATSUN 240Z
- PORSCHE 911T
- 1971 LT-1 CORVETTE (330-hp)

1 2 3 4 5 6 7 8

LOTUS ELAN +2S 130

Importer: Lotus Cars
British Motor Car Distributors
1700 Van Ness Ave.
San Francisco, California

Vehicle type: Front engine, rear-wheel-drive, 2+2-passenger coupe

Price as tested: $6885.00 (Manufacturer's suggested retail price, including all options listed below, Federal excise tax, dealer preparation and delivery charges, does not include state and local taxes, license or freight charges)

Options on test car: Base Lotus Elan +2S, $6597 (West Coast); Chrome wheels, $150.00; Dealer preparation, $138.00

ENGINE
Type: 4-in-line, water-cooled, cast iron block and aluminum head, 5 main bearings
Bore x stroke . . . . 3.25 x 2.86 in, 82.5 x 72.7 mm
Displacement . . . . 95.2 cu in, 1558 cc
Compression ratio . . . . 9.5 to one
Carburetion . . . . 2 x 1-bbl Stromberg
Valve gear . . . . Chain-driven double overhead cams
Power (SAE net) . . . . 120 bhp @ 6500 rpm
Torque (SAE net) . . . . 105-lbs/ft @ 4500 rpm
Specific power output . . . . 1.26 bhp/cu in, 0.77 bhp/liter
Max recommended engine speed . . . . 6500 rpm

DRIVE TRAIN
Transmission . . . . 4-speed, all-synchro
Final drive ratio . . . . 3.77 to one

Gear	Ratio	Mph/1000 rpm	Max. test speed
I	2.97	6.0	39 mph (6500 rpm)
II	2.01	8.9	58 mph (6500 rpm)
III	1.40	12.7	82 mph (6500 rpm)
IV	1.00	17.8	116 mph (6500 rpm)

DIMENSIONS AND CAPACITIES
Wheelbase . . . . 95.8 in
Track, F/R . . . . 54.0/55.0 in
Length . . . . 168.0 in
Width . . . . 63.5 in
Height . . . . 47.0 in
Ground clearance . . . . 5.6 in
Curb weight . . . . 1970 lbs
Weight distribution, F/R 46.5/53.5%
Battery capacity . . . . 12 volts, 39 amp/hr
Alternator capacity . . . . 504 watts
Fuel capacity . . . . 15.6 gal
Oil capacity . . . . 4.5 qts
Water capacity . . . . 8.4 qts

SUSPENSION
F: Ind., unequal-length control arms, coil springs, anti-sway bar
R: Ind., Chapman strut, coil springs

STEERING
Type . . . . Rack and pinion
Turns lock-to-lock 3.1
Turning circle curb-to-curb . . . . 28.0 ft

BRAKES
F: . . . . 10.0-in solid disc, power assisted
R: . . . . 10.0-in solid disc, power assisted

WHEELS AND TIRES
Wheel size . . . . 13 x 5.5-in
Wheel type . . . . Stamped steel, center lock
Tire make and size . . . . Dunlop SP Sport 165 HR13
Tire type . . . . Tubeless radial
Test inflation pressures, F/R . . . . 28/28 psi
Tire load rating . . . . 1080 lbs per tire @ 36 psi

PERFORMANCE
Zero to	Seconds
30 mph	3.0
40 mph	4.5
50 mph	6.5
60 mph	8.8
70 mph	11.8
80 mph	15.4
90 mph	22.1
100 mph	37.5

Standing ¼-mile . . . . 16.8 sec @ 82.56 mph
Top speed (at redline) . . . . 116 mph
70-0 mph . . . . 186 ft (0.88 G)
Fuel mileage . . . . 21.0-25.0 mpg on premium fuel
Cruising range . . . . 330-390 mi

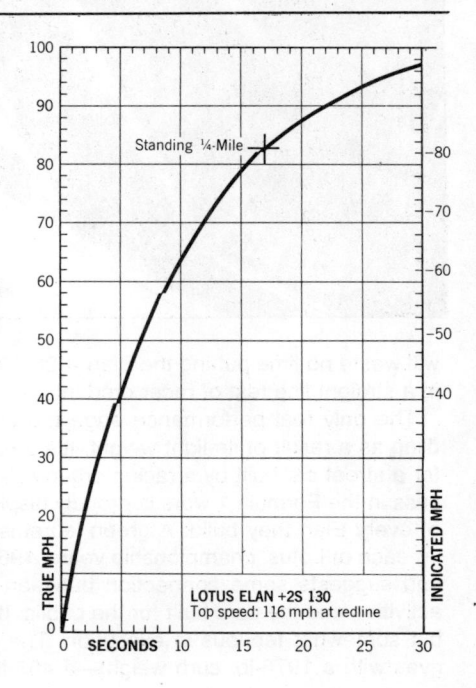

LOTUS ELAN +2S 130
Top speed: 116 mph at redline

153

As expected, the "A.B.C. Chapman" signature-model production car feels like a racer

PHOTOGRAPHY: RICK McBRIDE

will waste no time putting the Elan +2S 130 well behind them in a straight line test of racer credentials.

The only real performance edge the Lotus has is in handling as a result of its light weight. It's a natural development for a street car built by a racing organization, and Lotus' success in the Formula 1 wars is proudly displayed on the fender of every Elan they build. A green laurel is symbolic chalking up each of Lotus' championship years, 1963, '65, '68 and '70, and suggests some connection between Lotus competition activities and the cars built for the public. It's overt in concept but somewhat tenuous in execution. The Elan +2S 130 arrives with a 1970-lb. curb weight—a 455-lb. advantage even

in comparison to a Porsche 911. Other cars in direct competition are so much heavier that they must resort to great fat tires and ultra stiff suspensions to approximate the Lotus' handling advantage.

The Lotus, on the other hand, has no need for exotic suspension components. Unequal-length control arms do the job at the front while simpler MacPherson struts (called a "Chapman" strut when applied to a Lotus) handle the rear suspension duties. Rough road agility is good, and the parts are relatively simple—and light in weight. An anti-sway bar is used on the front only, with coil springs at each corner.

The wheels and tires also have a great influence on handling. Dunlop 165 HR 13 radials on 5.5-inch rims respond well with the light weight they must carry, and the +2's excellent weight distribution which puts 53.5% at the rear. They help make the Lotus capable of .75G lateral acceleration on the skid pad, with slight oversteer tendencies at the limit. Handling is at all times predictable, with no twitchiness as the limit is approached. Transients are quite reassuring with slight understeer fading toward a neutral situation as the speed and severity increase. The lack of any ponderous masses to control is obvious, and in the corners a light touch on the steering wheel will generate an immediate response. Other cars have light, fast, and responsive steering, but the Lotus Elan +2S 130 is unique in that it requires no special attention or previous experience to drive near the limit.

The situation isn't so pleasant on the freeway, however. Directional stability suffers and only an alert driver can maintain a straight line. In the centered-wheel position the car seeks its own path, and feels only vaguely dependent on steering commands. Because of the lightly-loaded front tires and additional lift from the pointy nose, high speed, long distance travel is not the Elan's strong suit.

The sticky tires also deserve considerable credit for the short (186-ft.) stopping distances from 70 mph (.88G), but they are abetted by a nonvented disc at each wheel and two independent vacuum boosters to reduce pedal effort. As might be expected from a group of slack season racers turned production car engineers, excellent modulation and directional stability are included for no additional cost, and you can feather the brakes right at the limit like a pro.

Still, there are glaring inconsistencies in the +2. For instance, no one could think for a minute that racing philosophies are responsible for the accoutrements of the Elan +2S. The list of standard equipment has it vying for the title of the Eldorado of sports cars. There are none of the overt signs of opulence to comfort your body like air conditioning—but what Cadillac has left the factory with dual Maserati air horns as standard equipment? An electrically heated back window, or a flexible map light that switches itself off when returned to the stowed position are logical aids. But how about electric window lifters or three ashtrays (even if John Player cigarettes does sponsor Lotus' Formula One effort, *that* is a bit much). Outside the car there are dual quartz-halogen driving lights and a Monza-type fuel filler. Lights in the door not only alert passing motorists that you are near their path, but separate beams also illuminate the ground beneath your feet as you exit. That feature alone should ease the $6885 price tag.

But the dollars are not the only price one must pay to own and exercise a Lotus Elan +2S 130. The driver must forfeit generous helpings of comfort just to move the car around the block. It all begins with entry. The seatback's rigid outboard edge is matched by a corresponding surface on the seat cushion. Both are covered with vinyl and the thinnest of pad-

Text continued on page 161

The latest Elan +2S is a fairly expensive coupe with a 120 mph performance.

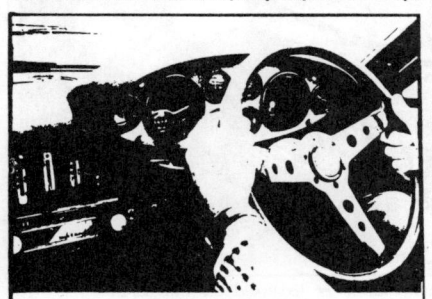

Refined Lotus Elan +2S with five speed gearbox

Road test/John Bolster

Lotus cars are changing their character. While still appealing for their performance and handling, they now have a quality and finish that attracts discerning buyers and they are both comfortable and practical for everyday use. Kit cars for impecunious enthusiasts will soon be forgotten and to drive a Lotus will never again entail being soaked, frozen and totally exposed to the elements, fun though it was.

The latest +2S is a fairly expensive coupé with a 120 mph performance and an outstandingly refined and flexible engine. Though developing 126 bhp from only 1558 cc, this twin-cam unit starts instantly from cold without the choke, warms up with no danger of stalling, and never fouls its plugs in the worst traffic blocks. With lots of torque for vivid acceleration, it is as happy at peak revs as when pottering along in top gear. It reflects the greatest credit on Tony Rudd, who has developed it to this very high standard.

In the past, Lotus cars have been well suited for England but too low-geared for the continent. Now, there is a new five-speed gearbox with an overdrive fifth speed, the direct fourth gear equalling the top gear of the four-speed model, so no performance has been lost. The fifth speed is a true overdrive on which the rev-counter cannot approach the red sector and so it is not intended to give a higher maximum speed. An ignition cut-out limits the maximum on fourth to about 120 mph and if a change is made to fifth, the car will continue at this speed at greatly reduced revs and though no further acceleration is normally possible, a little help from wind or gradient may allow the speed to mount to 125 mph or so.

The new gearbox is remarkably silent on all gears. Second, third, and fourth have the same ratios as those of the four-speed box, but first is a little lower, which improves the already excellent getaway. At present, the change is very stiff and first is extremely difficult to engage at rest. It seems as though the designers have allowed too little leverage in order to obtain the fashionable short movements. This is unfortunate but the cure should be easy, when the five-speed box will be second to none.

The performance figures speak for themselves and could have been even better with a quicker gearchange. The interior is astonishingly quiet for such a sporting car, mechanical, road, and wind noises having been very well subdued. Outside, the exhaust note is rather fruity and, though appealing to enthusiasts, might attract unwelcome attention.

Noticeably harder than before, the suspension has probably been stiffened by fitting tougher doughnut joints to the driveshafts, to reduce the well-known winding-up effect. The car has very high cornering power and can be flicked through curves with remarkably little roll. The unusually quick steering is delightfully sensitive, having an occasional suspicion of kickback over bumps, which I like.

The handling characteristic is neutral, tending towards oversteer, which makes the car very light and responsive to drive. However, it is now capable of high cruising speeds and 110 mph is a restful, all-day rate. At such velocities, a little more understeer would be appreciated for stability. In particular, the Lotus is rather sensitive to side winds, which would make the negotiation of some of the more exposed French autoroutes somewhat tiring. Below 100 mph, the car needs much less holding and runs with such delightful ease that it is advisable to watch the speedometer at first, for it is possible to underestimate the speed. In this respect, the +2 differs greatly from the Elan, which gives its occupants a considerable sensation of speed.

Like the gearchange problem, the improvement of high-speed stability should present no serious difficulty, especially to Lotus with their racing background. The retractable headlamps, which used to lack power, are now much more effective. The multitude of switches have very clear labels, though they may be confusing at first in the dark. Perhaps it would be a good idea to have the switches for the electric windows of a different shape, for these are most often used and the latest window motors are more powerful, giving quick opening if one wishes to shout the retort courteous. The eyeball ventilators pass a useful volume of cool air.

A very high standard of external finish makes the glassfibre body indistinguishable from a metal one, though the silver roof may not be to everyone's taste. The interior is most attractive, with a fine display of proper round instruments. Very comfortable front seats give good location, though the driving position is perhaps rather low for a short driver. The two separate rear bucket seats are evidently intended for children, who would be comfortable on long trips. Quite a useful boot can be opened from a hidden control on the right door pillar.

Very powerful brakes have plenty of instantaneous bite for an emergency stop. The rear discs are unusually well cooled, being mounted away from the wheels on the inner side of the bearings. The pull-out handbrake, hidden under the right side of the instrument panel, is quite effective but needs a fairly strong twist to release it.

The Lotus +2S is a good-looking, high-performance car of considerable refinement. Racing successes have brought prestige to the *marque*, which adds to pride of ownership. More luxurious and practical than any previous Lotus, it gains a new dimension in 130/5 form. With its high overdrive gear, it becomes a *grand routier*, easily capable of three-figure average speeds.

As this report indicates, there is some room for improvement, but it was courageous of Lotus to submit the five-speed car for test so soon after its introduction and we can be sure that its few imperfections will soon be ironed out. There is an increasing awareness that moderate size is even more advantageous in a fast car than one of less exalted performance, while even the wealthy are getting tired of the fuel consumption of some large-engined cars. In both these resepects, the Lotus appeals greatly, and it indicates the trend in the high-performance cars of the future.

SPECIFICATION AND PERFORMANCE DATA

Car tested: Lotus +2S 130/5 fixed-head coupé, price with extra equipment £2826.65 including tax.
Engine: Four cylinders 86.2 mm x 72.8 mm (1558 cc). Compression ratio, 10.3 to 1. 126 bhp (net) at 6500 rpm. Twin chain-driven overhead camshafts. Two twin-choke Dellorto carburetters.
Transmission: Single dry plate clutch. 5-speed all-synchromesh gearbox with central change, ratios 0.8, 1.0, 1.37, 2.0 and 3.2 to 1. Hypoid final drive, ratio 3.77 to 1.
Chassis: Steel backbone chassis with glassfibre body. Independent front suspension by wishbones, coil springs, and anti-roll bar. Rack and pinion steering. Independent rear suspension by struts and lower quadrilateral links with coil springs. Telescopic dampers all round. Servo-assisted disc brakes on all wheels. Knock-on ventilated disc wheels fitted 165-13 radial ply tyres.
Equipment: 12-volt lighting and starting with alternator. Speedometer. Rev-counter. Voltmeter. Fuel, oil pressure, water and ambient temperature gauges. Clock. Heating, demisting, and windscreen wipers and washers. Flashing direction indicators. Reversing lights. Radio (extra).
Dimensions: Wheelbase, 8ft. Track (front), 4ft 6in, (rear), 4ft 7in. Overall length, 14ft. Width, 5ft 3.5in. Weight, 17½ cwt.
Performance: Maximum speed, 120 mph (4th or 5th gear). Speeds in gears: Third, 89 mph. Second, 62 mph. First, 38 mph. Standing quarter-mile, 16.0 s. Acceleration: 0-30 mph, 2.6 s. 0-50 mph, 5.9 s. 0-60 mph, 7.3 s. 0-80 mph, 13.8 s. 0-100 mph, 24.0 s.
Fuel Consumption: 25 to 30 mpg.

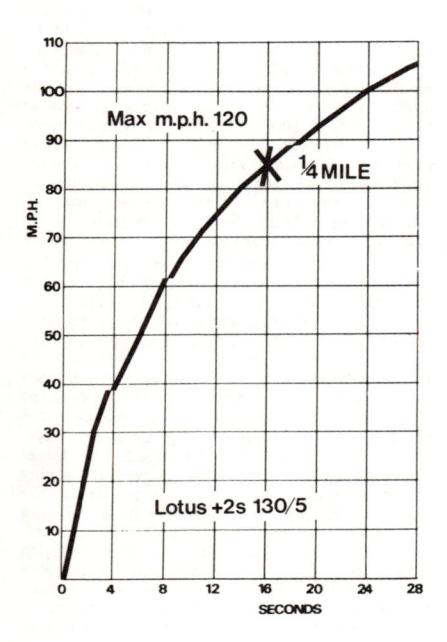

A high standard of external finish makes the glassfibre body indistinguishable from a metal one

The twin cam engine develops 126 bhp from 1558 cc

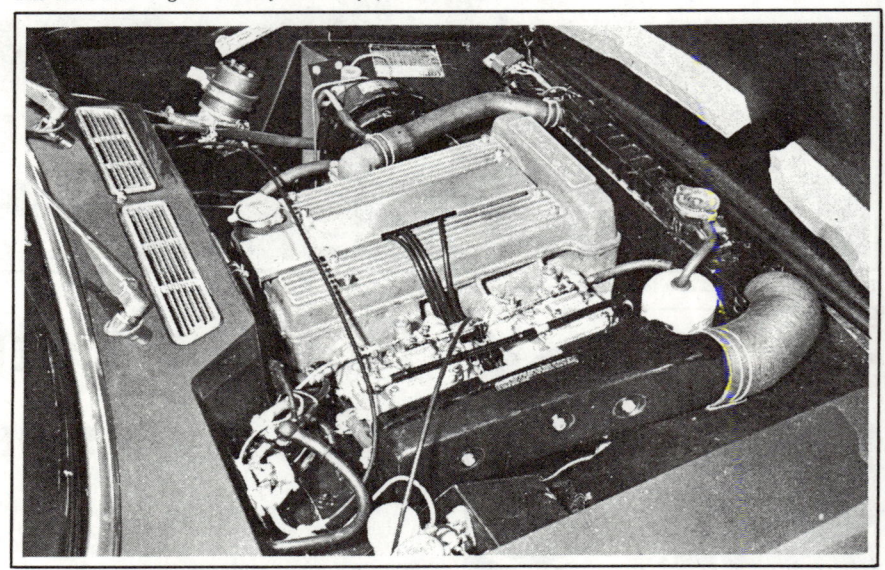

A most attractive interior with proper round instruments is featured on this Elan

LOTUS ELAN SPRINT

Lotus worshippers are addicted to cornering—each turn a challenge of man and machine

• Devout worshippers of the Lotus nameplate thrive at the very fringes of automotive enthusiasm. But like most radicals, their small number can be quickly identified. You find them devastating imaginary lap records down the rural venues regarded as imposing . . . even treacherous . . . by the more conservative. Their Elysium is much like the skier's—the down side of a mountain with an endless series of lefts and rights joined by brief linear chutes to maintain speed. Each twist unique in its curvature and camber, each a challenge to be executed at the limit of man and machine. They are addicted to the thrills of cornering and a car such as the Lotus Elan Sprint is their "works"—the utensil that provides their high.

But the Elan Sprint is no eyedropper and needle rig pressed into more serious service by its owner. Instead, the Elan is built exclusively for that narrow tunnel of pleasure it will provide. Far beneath its "ACBC" monogrammed nameplate lie the real reasons the Lotus so willingly fulfills those hooked on a generous quota of high lateral acceleration. Light weight is the key and every part emphasizes the gaunt nature of the total. Naturally with such a stringent priority there are sacrifices, but they will be rationalized into insignificance by those who understand the car's sole purpose. In truth, the Lotus Elan Sprint is the baseline from which any other manufacturer in the world will compromise to satisfy a board of directors.

Understanding that singular devotion is the key. Then you will also understand the welded steel backbone which structurally connects the mechanical pieces with the efficiency of a straight line. It stretches not an inch past the outermost chassis component and mercilessly overwhelms the interior in its path. Light weight and sufficient rigidity arrive via an interior dominated by the Holland Tunnel between driver and passenger. A hand-laid fiberglass body surrounds the steel spine like a cocoon but it must also bear a share of the structural responsibilities. Doors, decklids and even the bumpers are fiberglass and have only fiberglass connections back to the source of rigidity, the welded frame. No frivolous non-functional spoilers, flares or scoops complicate the exterior, and each opening, line or curve is optimized to function without a weight penalty. It's the lightest type of construction outside the aerospace industry and fully adequate for every situation short of barrier impacts.

With a curb weight of 1590 lbs., the Lotus Elan Sprint is a bantamweight example of unvarnished simplicity.

That uncomplicated nature extends to the suspension layout as well. Unequal length control arms define the front wheel geometry. At the rear, a "Chapman strut"—named after Lotus' chief designer who was first to apply a MacPherson strut type of mechanism to the rear of a car—defines the suspension geometry. While it does not provide the optimum camber pattern, the Chapman strut layout is very simple, compact for an independent rear suspension . . .

> **❛**
> The Elan levies excessive demands before any pleasure is delivered, but its faults won't discourage Lotus lovers—justification comes at every bend
> **❜**

and most important, light in weight. Coil springs, concentric with the strut at the rear, are used at each corner and a single front anti-sway bar is deemed enough to yield the proper roll stiffness since 53.2% of the weight is at the rear.

Such a favorable distribution can only make life easier for the tires. With the weight so allocated, each tire can generate its fair share of cornering and driving forces and bend its relatively light burden around a turn. The car's center of gravity skims down the road just inches above the pavement so that body roll is minimal and suspension geometry maintains each tire upright. Moreover, every major mass in the car lies well within its abbreviated 84 inch wheelbase (5 inches shorter than that of a 911 Porsche). Add to all that a set of tires with a load capacity well over *twice* that of the car's weight and you have the last word in production car responsiveness. Touch the steering wheel and gobs of rubber on the road will snap the light car around without even breathing hard. If you demand the limit, the Elan delivers 0.79 G on the skidpad. With less understeer, the limit would be higher (5 psi more air in the front for a starter).

But for all that cornering might, you'll pay a penalty in ride comfort. The combination of stiff springs and over-achiever tires completely destroys any indication of poise over the road. Tar strips are met with a violent heave of car . . . and occupants. Between the *con brio* dashes through corners you find that the suspension is intent on passing on to you every road irregularity you'll encounter. Moreover, the package is so bent on cornering that it refuses to follow a straight path down the road. The body willingly turns with the wind or any unstabilizing influence and the man behind the wheel must drive wide-eyed to keep from offending those in another lane.

The car's light weight also promotes an anchor overboard situation when the brakes are applied. Nonvented discs at each wheel accomplish the stopping chores in 193 feet from 70 mph (0.85 G). Here again the lightly loaded tires came into play to produce impressive results, but ideal braking effort distribution and very little weight transfer all add to the reassuring feel. Control at lockup is adequate, so that each wheel reaches its limit of adhesion with the others. Even with the overwhelming weight advantages, such braking performance speaks of extensive refinement and fine tuning.

The situation is the same with the engine. For economic reasons, Lotus begins its powerplant construction around the same cylinder block casting as in every Ford of England 1600cc application. The similarities extend very little further however, as the internal dimensions are more rpm-oriented with a larger bore and a shorter stroke. Since the rocker arm head used by Ford is not in keeping with this goal, it is replaced by a lighter aluminum casting with two chain-driven cams and enough port area to extend the horsepower peak to 6500 rpm. This year's Elan, denoted as the Sprint version, benefits from the Big Valve head and that fact is proudly cast into the aluminum cam cover. As the name implies, this distinction includes larger intake valves, but the real power gains are due to revised porting, longer duration camshafts and a revised carburetor calibration. Primarily for emissions reasons, the carburetion is two vacuum-operated 175 Strombergs but the 120 net horsepower and 1.26 *net* hp/cu. in. should duly impress any skeptical inquirer. If not, the 15.4 @ 88.4 quarter-mile will counter any illusions to a Pinto engine residing under the hood.

PHOTOGRAPHY: HUMPHREY SUTTON

But the justifiable aspersions to Colin's signature on the steering wheel must eventually surface. The World Champion laurels so proudly displayed on the fender may suffice for a few, but discerning individuals will look deeper for proof of the car's ultimate worth. Those whose eyes have not yet shifted in their heads from cornering overloads will immediately notice the Lotus Elan Sprint is not an easy car to drive. The clutch effort is excessive, decidedly so, and in conjunction with the long, narrow, stiffly sprung paddle meant to control the throttles, getting underway smoothly requires a conditioned reflex. Subtle mistakes in throttle position or just a millimeter too much clutch will not be forgiven, especially during the practice sessions. Rotoflex (heavy on the "flex") drive couplings, which take the place of normal universal joints, store up the excessive energy that would strain the driveline . . . only to unleash at their own convenience—in surges only a rubber joint can provide. The result is a jerky transition from rest that immediately segregates the novice from the veteran with his calibrated toe and ankle reflexes. And only time can insure complete comfort with the stubby shift lever. It's slightly larger than a toggle switch and has an even shorter throw. The mechanism shifts with the precision of a micrometer but the effort required to overcome the detents is so ungodly high that you must clumsily bang it from gear to gear.

All together, the demands an Elan levies before any pleasure is delivered are excessive. The bucket seats have a wide range of fore and aft adjustment but their construction is such that you operate from a bicycle seat perch—with

(Text continued on page 161
Specifications overleaf)

ACCELERATION standing ¼ mile, seconds

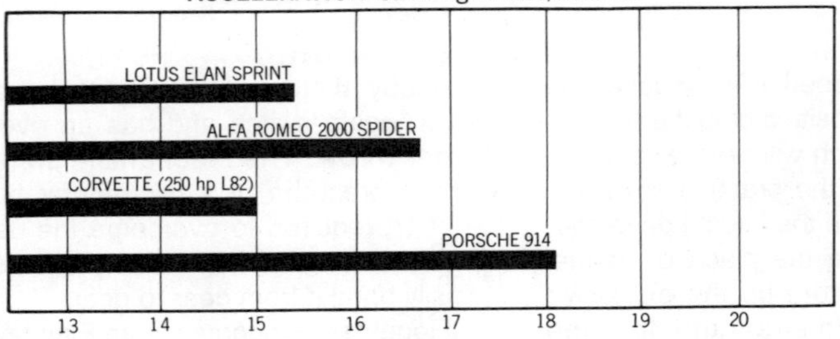

- LOTUS ELAN SPRINT
- ALFA ROMEO 2000 SPIDER
- CORVETTE (250 hp L82)
- PORSCHE 914

13 14 15 16 17 18 19 20

BRAKING 70-0 mph panic stop, feet

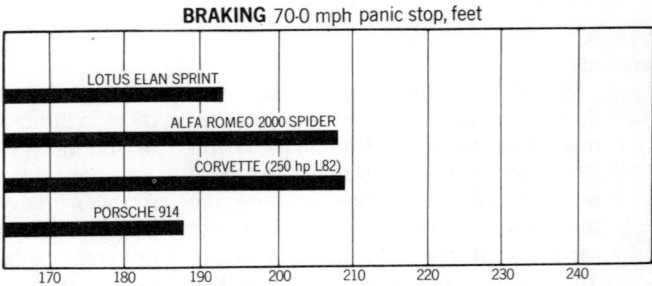

- LOTUS ELAN SPRINT
- ALFA ROMEO 2000 SPIDER
- CORVETTE (250 hp L82)
- PORSCHE 914

170 180 190 200 210 220 230 240

FUEL ECONOMY RANGE mpg

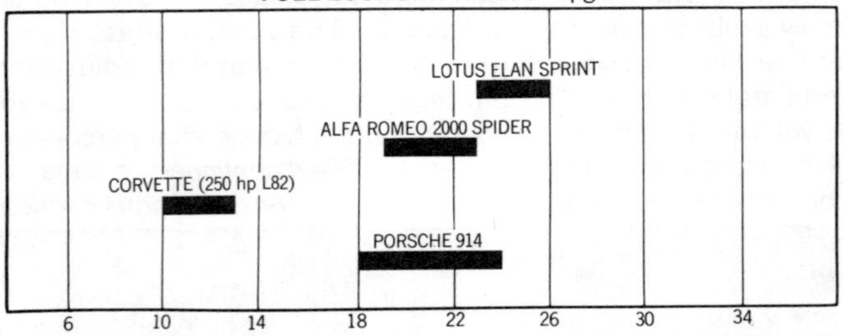

- LOTUS ELAN SPRINT
- ALFA ROMEO 2000 SPIDER
- CORVETTE (250 hp L82)
- PORSCHE 914

6 10 14 18 22 26 30 34

PRICE AS TESTED dollars x 1000

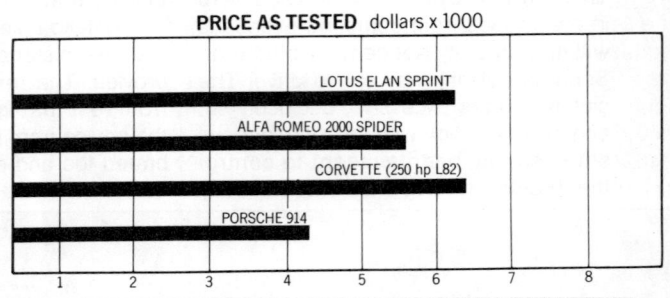

- LOTUS ELAN SPRINT
- ALFA ROMEO 2000 SPIDER
- CORVETTE (250 hp L82)
- PORSCHE 914

1 2 3 4 5 6 7 8

LOTUS ELAN SPRINT

Importer:
Lotus Cars
British Motor Car Distributors, Ltd.
1700 Van Ness Avenue
San Francisco, California

Vehicle type: Front engine, rear-wheel-drive, 2-passenger convertible

Price as tested: $6281.00
(Manufacturer's suggested retail price, including all options listed below, dealer preparation and delivery charges, does not include state and local taxes, license or freight charges)

Options on test car: Base Elan Sprint, $5693 (West Coast); Stereo AM/FM radio with tape player, $250; Dealer preparation, $138.

ENGINE
Type: Four-in-line, water-cooled, cast iron block and aluminum head, 5 main bearings
Bore x stroke . . . . 3.25 x 2.86 in., 82.5 x 72.7mm
Displacement . . . . 95.2 cu in, 1558cc
Compression ratio . . . . 9.5 to one
Carburetion . . . . 2x1-bbl Stromberg
Valve gear . . . . Chain-driven double overhead cam
Power (SAE net) . . . . 120 bhp @6500 rpm
Torque (SAE net) . . . . 105 lb-ft @ 4500 rpm
Specific power output . . . . 1.26 bhp/cu in, 0.77 bhp/liter
Max recommended engine speed . . . . 6500 rpm

DRIVE TRAIN
Transmission . . . . 4-speed, all-synchro
Final drive ratio . . . . 3.77 to one

Gear	Ratio	Mph/1000rpm	Max. test speed
I	2.97	5.9	38 mph (6500 rpm)
II	2.01	8.7	57 mph (6500 rpm)
III	1.40	12.4	80 mph (6500 rpm)
IV	1.00	17.4	100 mph (5750 rpm)

DIMENSIONS AND CAPACITIES
Wheelbase . . . . 84.0 in
Track, F/R . . . . 47.1/47.1 in
Length . . . . 145.0 in
Width . . . . 56.0 in
Height . . . . 45.5 in
Ground clearance . . . . 5.6 in
Curb weight . . . . 1590 lbs
Weight distribution, F/R 46.8/53.2%
Battery capacity . . . . 12 volts, 39 amp-hr
Generator capacity . . . . 386 watts
Fuel capacity . . . . 11.6 gal
Oil capacity . . . . 4.5 qts
Water capacity . . . . 8.4 qts

SUSPENSION
F: Ind., unequal length control arms, coil springs, anti-sway bar
R: Ind., Chapman strut, coil springs

STEERING
Type . . . . Rack and pinion
Turns lock-to-lock 2.2
Turning circle curb-to-curb . . . . 33.5 ft

BRAKES
F: . . . . 9.5-in solid disc
R: . . . . 10.0-in solid disc

WHEELS AND TIRES
Wheel size . . . . 13 x 4.5-in
Wheel type . . . . Stamped styled steel, center lock
Tire make and size . . . . Dunlop SP Sport, 155 HR 13
Tire type . . . . tubeless, radial
Test inflation pressures, F/R . . . . 18/23 psi
Tire load rating . . . . 950 lbs per tire @ 32 psi

PERFORMANCE
Zero to	Seconds
30 mph	2.0
40 mph	3.3
50 mph	4.8
60 mph	6.8
70 mph	9.2
80 mph	12.1
90 mph	16.0
100 mph	21.2

Standing ¼-mile . . . . 15.4 sec @ 88.4 mph
Top speed (at redline) . . . . 113 mph
70-0 mph . . . . 193 ft (0.85G)
Fuel mileage . . . . 23.0-26.0 mpg on premium fuel
Cruising range . . . . 270-300 mi

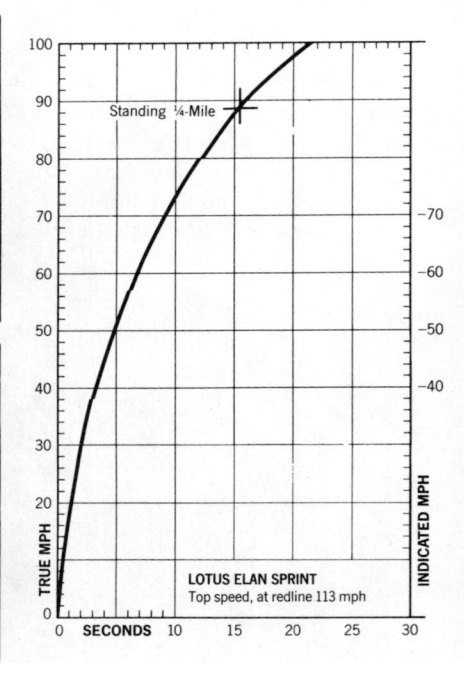

LOTUS ELAN SPRINT
Top speed, at redline 113 mph

160

LOTUS ELAN SPRINT
Continued from page 159

the bulk of both legs unsupported. Even those narrow of girth will find inadequate shoulder room and left feet ache for a resting place once clutching duties are fulfilled. During acceleration, 86 dBA worth of stereophonic noise bombards the senses, primarily from the barely adequate (and very low-hanging) muffler. And the canvas flap which serves as a top is no insulation from the 84.5 dBA din while cruising at 70 mph (Datsun 240Z: 75.5 dBA at 70). Moreover, that seemingly simple top will stoutheartedly defy attempts at erection in anything less than 15 minutes (with a crew of two and an eye on the instructions).

Inside there is some pleasure to be gained from the British Traditional teak instrument panel. The varnished finish seems too perfect for tree wood and the grain thoughtfully continues uninterrupted through the glove box door. White on black instruments relate all the necessary information to monitor critical systems save the generator's charge—a responsibility left to a lowly red light. Black rocker switches handle the electrical controls but their lack of illumination demands the Braille technique at night. Traces of high level ventilation and heater air just barely squeak through two nickle-sized openings on the dash with only a butterfly valve to direct the wispy stream. A two-speed fan is on hand to boost the flow, but a 6-71 blower couldn't raise a breeze through openings that small. Two hidden flaps reside within the footwells, but if you expect cool air swirling around your feet to give them away, you're overanticipating.

Also concealed within the depths of that overshoe-like void into which your legs are plunged, are the handbrake and ignition switch. Normally both are considered essential to the operation of a car but Lotus seems intent on dispelling that notion. Use of either necessitates unfastening the lap/shoulder belt combination and an uncomfortably long reach.

Still, none of its glaring shortcomings or even the $5693 base price will discourage the hard core aligned with the Lotus way of thinking. Their justifications will come at every curve they can execute at twice the posted rating because of Colin Chapman and his band of weight-conscious engineers. Everyone else will need a ten car garage before considering the Lotus Elan Sprint for their cornering specialist. As well as a firm apprehension of the consequences when it's used out of context. •

ELAN SPRINT
CONTINUED FROM PAGE 141

pull lateral g loadings as high as .78, it wouldn't hold them steadily, both the speed and g traces going up and down the chart like saw-teeth as the tires alternately bit and let go. However, that is not to say that the bite is not still on a very high order — it is. It's just that with a bit more rubber on the ground, lateral g's could be significantly higher, to the point of what must surely be some sort of an ultimate in a street machine. One of the interesting attributes of the Elan is that not only does it stick in such a manner that it can be driven harder through a turn than any other car you care to name except other Lotuses (especially the Europa) but it can, if the need arises, be tossed through a tight corner. Whether this is due to the extraordinarily short wheelbase (84.0 inches as opposed to 91 for the +2 and 95.7 for the Europa) or to the tires we aren't prepared to say but since there is a certain amount of built-in understeer it comes in handy when in a hurry over back roads with both fast curves and tight turns. You can drive the fast ones in total security at a shocking rate of knots and with a flick of wheel and a dab of throttle whip around the tight ones where others, including the longer wheelbase Lotuses, might well have to back off.

As far as straightaway speed goes, the version we tested with the 3.77 final drive gearing will do 113 to 114 mph at which point 6500 rpm came up on the tach (exact speed: 113.10 at 6500) and, as mentioned 6500 is it and there isn't any more due to the cutout. For more top end at a slight cost in acceleration there is a 3.55 rear end available. Since we were nowhere near running out of steam with the gearing we had at 113 mph, there is no reason to suspect that the Sprint won't pull the taller gearing all the way to peak which will give a top of 120 and change. While there are a number of cars that will exceed the 113-plus figure, we can't think of but one or two that stay with a Sprint let alone motor faster anywhere other than on a Nevada interstate. For going from point A to point B under any other conditions the new Elan Sprint has to be the quickest device you can license for the street.

There it is — the Elan Sprint: stiffer drive components, a stronger engine, heftier rear axles and top quality control. It's only the best Lotus yet. Thank you, Colin; you've proved a point. /MT

LOTUS ELAN +2S 130
Continued from page 154

ding. Since contact with these edges during entry is inevitable, getting in can be a painful experience. Once you're in, another hard edge at the front of the seat cushion makes life tough for the underside of your thighs. The seats have generous fore-and-aft adjustment, but turn out to be truly uncomfortable for long stretches due to the fact that your legs are largely unsupported. There is no justification for the Lotus' poor seating—racers above all should know better.

Fortunately, the discomfort involved is not intensified by a lack of room as in the Elan Sprint. The +2S's extra width and length over a standard Elan allow plenty of space for those in front and also a double nest in the rear for a very occasional plus-two passenger. Extra space can never be criticized, however, especially since the seatback folds to increase interior storage volume.

The trunk is much better suited for carrying large objects. It's a very efficient volume with flat sides, square corners, and a well finished, carpet lining. The spare wheel and tire, and all jacking equipment are hidden under a false bottom. Few sports cars at any price can boast of such extravagant space.

The Sprint's weak ventilation system is improved in the Elan +2S 130, and two face-level globes allow control of air volume and direction. There are also outlets for each footwell and an air exit vent in the B-pillars. A blower boosts the flow at slow speeds but opening a window is still more efficient.

The Lotus factory has yet to utilize the latest science in sound deadening, and as a result its cars are quite noisy inside. The busy engine is the main offender, generating 60 dbA at idle, compared with a more reserved 54 dbA in a Datsun 240Z. Full throttle acceleration is no louder than the Z car (83 dbA), but the din is still present to the tune of 81 dbA while cruising at 70 where the Datsun quiets to a 76 dbA level. A larger muffler and more sound deadening material between the engine and passengers would greatly ease the situation.

All the discomforts will never bother those who convince themselves the Lotus Elan +2S 130 is the car to buy. They'll accept no substitutes for the light weight and rapid responses at a budget price. Those demanding normal levels of comfort will justify a compromise and fatter, less expensive cars will fill their garages. Exclusivity, after all, should make some demands. •

Road test/John Bolster

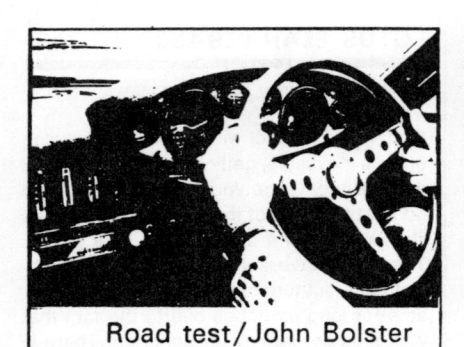

I feel ten years younger! I've just spent a week driving a *real* sports car and once again I am reminded that there is no substitute for the genuine article. Proper sports cars should be closely related to racing cars, as Ettore Bugatti once proved when he sold replicas of his Grand Prix cars for road use. Formula 1 machines are no longer two-seaters and are perhaps a little impractical; it would be difficult to go to a dinner at the Dorchester in one, for instance, though it has been done with a G.P. Bugatti. However, it is still feasible to make a sports car that handles like a racing car, provided that the designer has as much racing experience as Colin Chapman.

It is also possible to assemble quite an acceptable sort of sports car from a mixture of bits of popular cars, and even saloons can be persuaded to handle remarkably well, as their lap speeds in races prove. Nevertheless, you have only to get into a Lotus Elan and drive it on a winding road to realise that there is no comparison. Its small size is an immense advantage but it is that fantastic cornering power, combined with really quick steering, which makes it so different from anything else. You simply throw it at a corner and it goes round in complete safety at an absurd speed. It is not so much the speed as the incredible ease of the whole manoeuvre, with all four wheels sticking to the road irrespective of bumps, which is so completely satisfying to the driver.

The Elan is a superb sports car because there has been no compromise in its design, which is always fatal. It will carry two people and a small amount of luggage, and it has been built to the minimum dimensions which will endorse these things, plus a twin-cam engine. Size and weight are the two enemies in sports car design, both of which have been conquered in the Elan. As a result, it is an extremely efficient car, and will easily beat exotic machines of far greater power on roads which do not permit them to exploit their maximum speed. The Ferrari Dino is the sports car which most people desire above all others, but there are roads in England where the Elan is its master, both on acceleration and the speed through corners which its small size permits.

The Lotus Elan is ideal for England but its standard gearing is less suitable for the Continent. Under-geared, it simply rushes up to maximum revs in top, when the ignition cutout operates and restricts the speed to 120 mph or so. This is a pity as the ride and roadholding suit bad roads as well as good. Higher gearing would spoil it for England, detracting from that magnificent getaway, and it is to be hoped that the 5-speed gearbox may be made available on this model, though if one rarely goes abroad the expense would not be justified perhaps.

The original design of the Elan was sound, with its steel backbone chassis carrying a glassfibre body like a saddle. However, it is the development which has taken place over the past ten years which makes it such an effective car. I have driven many Elans during that period and have had my quota of troubles, but reliability now seems to have been achieved. The improvement in refinement has been enormous, such things as the exhaust note, especially on the overrun, having been tamed, while the irritating winding and unwinding of the rubber doughnut universal joints has been greatly reduced.

The standard of finish is very high, the appearance of the fixed head model being quite attractive and refusing to date.

Lotus Elan Sprint: Ideal for England

Perhaps the biggest single amelioration has been the adoption of Tony Rudd's Big-Valve version of the twin-cam engine. In spite of a 25 per cent power increase, the unit is also mechanically quieter than it was and nothing like so fuzzy when held near maximum revs. Indeed, the sound level inside the car is lower than would be expected, the gearbox and the hypoid final drive both being completely silent. There is very little road noise though some wind noise obtrudes at high speeds. Such mechanical noise as there is comes from a twin-cam engine obviously enjoying its work, and no enthusiast would have it otherwise.

The acceleration through the gears is really vivid while the excellent traction permits very rapid getaways. Of course, the wheels can be spun on wet roads but the adhesion is still more than satisfactory. The gearchange is not particularly tight but it is pleasantly precise in action and the top gear flexibility is quite surprising. Perhaps the most spectacular part of the performance is the top gear acceleration up hills, the car rapidly reaching 110 mph up quite considerable gradients. This is largely due to the moderate weight, which also permits the Lotus to be stopped just as easily as it can be accelerated.

Though the car is small and appears to fit one like a glove, the driving position is excellent and it is quite easy to get in and out. The heating and demisting system is effective, with an electrically heated rear window, and the side windows rise and fall electrically, though rather slowly. The inlets for cool breathing air look very small, but they pass a useful volume. In the past, the retractable headlamps of the Elan have lacked power but they are now better in this respect. However, the behaviour of some other drivers led me to believe that they were not always free of dazzle when dipped. The headlamps still come up flashing when the knob is pulled out in daylight.

Perhaps the go-faster stripes embellished with the words, "Elan Sprint," are not to

The acceleration through the gears is really vivid while the traction is excellent.

everybody's taste, but the standard of finish is very high, the appearance of the fixed-head model being quite attractive and refusing to date. The interior is exactly right, like so many things about the car, but the bonnet clips are of Heath Robinson design and the inaccessibility of the ignition distributor earns a black mark.

Fundamentally, a sports car designed without compromise and following racing practice must be more expensive than one evolved from existing saloon components. Therefore, the Elan Sprint is costly for its size, a cost which many owners have hitherto usefully reduced by taking advantage of the purchase tax concession on component cars. From April 1, VAT will be imposed and home-assembly will be at an end, the probable tax amounting to something like £450. This will make the little Lotus an expensive car for its size, and though it will still be more fun to drive than almost anything, it behoves prospective buyers to fix up a kit deal right away, if too many others have not already filled the order books.

There are those who think that the sports car is on the way out, because the modern saloon goes so well. Certainly, there is a trend in this direction and many people are buying popular coupés instead, which have a sporting look but can still be used as family transport. Yet, this is far, far away from real sports car motoring and once one has experienced the pleasure of handling a race-bred machine, nothing else will do. A really small and light two-seater, that can be flung into corners in complete safety and accelerate like the wind, is still the only thoroughbred sports car. Such a car is the Lotus Elan Sprint.

SPECIFICATION AND PERFORMANCE DATA

Car tested: Lotus Elan Sprint 2-seater fixed-head coupé, price £2471.40 including tax, or £2044.00 with tax exemption for owner assembly.
Engine: Four-cylinders 82.6 mm x 72.8 mm (1588 c.c.). Compression ratio 10.3 to 1. 126 bhp (net) at 6500 rpm. Twin chain-driven overhead camshafts. 2 Dellorto twin-choke carburetters.
Transmission: Single dry plate clutch. 4-speed all-synchromesh gearbox with central change, ratios 1.0, 1.40, 2.01, and 2.97 to 1. Hypoid final drive, ratio 3.77 to 1.
Chassis: Steel backbone chassis and glassfibre body. Independent front suspension by wishbones, coil springs with telescopic dampers, and anti-roll bar. Rack and pinion steering. Independent rear suspension by coil springs and damper struts with lower wishbones. Servo-assisted brakes all round. Centre-locking pierced disc wheels fitted 155 HR-13 radial ply tyres.
Equipment: 12-volt lighting and starting with alternator. Speedometer, Rev counter, Oil-pressure, water temperature, and fuel gauges. Heating, demisting, and ventilation system. 2-speed windscreen wipers and washers. Flashing direction indicators. Electric window winders. Reversing lights. Extra: Heated rear window. Radio.
Dimensions: Wheelbase 7 ft. 1in. Track 3 ft 11in. Overall length 12 ft 1in. Width 4 ft 8in. Weight 14.2 cwt.
Performance: Maximum speed 121 mph. Speeds in gears: Third, 88 mph. Second, 60 mph. First, 42 mph. Standing quarter-mile, 15.0 s. Acceleration: 0-30 mph, 2.5 s. 0-50 mph, 5.2 s. 0-60 mph, 6.6 s. 0-80 mph, 11.8 s. 0-100 mph, 19.8 s. 0-110 mph, 27.3 s.
Fuel consumption: 20 to 25 mpg.

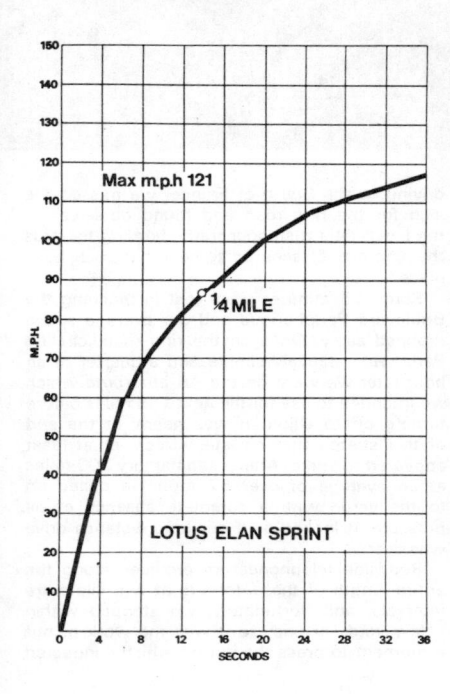

The driving position is excellent and it is quite easy to get in and out. You simply throw it at a corner and it goes round safely at an absurd speed.

Tony Rudd's big valve engine gives 25 per cent more power and is quieter.

163

Travel Talk

Non-stop to the SUN

By Michael Giles

Andover to Amalfi: 1380 miles in 30 hours

A short account of a drive made at the end of March last year from Andover in Hampshire to Naples in Italy in just under 30 hours; the relevant distance in 24 hours is the 1,190 miles from Calais to Naples, but as this included a three hour breakdown, it could have been covered in 21 hours at an average speed of over 50 miles per hour.

My navigator on this trip was my 15 year old son, obviously a non-driver, and it was his job to keep the log as well as guide us through the towns in which the signposting, particularly in France, is often confusing. The car was a Lotus Elan Plus 2S 130 and, apart from blotting its copybook on the A6 *autoroute* 100 miles south of Paris, it went well throughout the journey. When only cheap petrol was available during the Italian petrol dispute it suffered from pinking which is understandable on a 10.3-to-1 compression ratio, but while fed on the proper grade of fuel the performance was very satisfactory. The car's ability to hold its own against its Continental counterparts on fast European motorways was also gratifying and the only difficulty experienced was a susceptibility to the effect of sidewinds due, no doubt, to its very light weight.

We set off from Andover at 04.05 hours and drove the 140 miles to Ramsgate for the Channel crossing. The hovercraft took off at 07.50 hours and we were through Customs and on the road in Calais by 08.35 hours which, in view of the particularly adverse weather conditions, reflects very much to the credit of Hoverlloyd who advertise 40 minutes for the crossing alone.

In winter, or even early spring as it was when we went, the route chosen to cross the Alps dictates the approach road from France and it was decided that the Grand St. Bernard tunnel provided the most certainly negotiable route through the mountains despite the fact that one must pass through Switzerland on the way. Accordingly Pontarlier is virtually an essential point in France and two main methods of reaching this town exist. One, and the slower, is the straighter road from Arras through Rheims, Chaumont, Langres and Besancon. The faster, though roughly 50 miles longer, is from Arras via the Al *autoroute* to Paris, which is circumnavigated on the Boulevard Peripherique, and thence by the A6 to Pouilly-en-Auxois Junction, on to Dijon and then through Dole to Pontarlier. The increase in heavy goods vehicle traffic in recent years encourages the use of the *autoroute* wherever this is available. Of the 1,190 miles between Calais and Naples only 306 were not covered on motorways.

The road from Calais to Arras consists of 70 miles of rather uninteresting scenery and we were glad to join the *autoroute* for the 95 miles to the outskirts of Paris which were covered in one hour and 40 minutes. Although it is not necessary to enter Paris at all when driving to the South of France, we missed the sign for the ring road and found ourselves in the lunch time rush hour traffic hurtling towards the Champs Elysées or some other such busy place.

Some 25 minutes were lost in reaching the Boulevard Peripherique and our average speed dropped sadly. Once on the ring road, circling Paris was relatively simple and a quarter of an hour later we were on the A6 *autoroute* which we intended to use for the next 155 miles before turning off to Dijon. It was nearly at the end of this stretch that disaster struck, or at least appeared to strike. After a satisfactory 300 miles at an average of over 57 mph we pulled on to the verge with a complete absence of oil pressure; it looked as if our long distance drive was over.

Roadside telephones are provided along the entire length of the *autoroute* at two kilometre intervals, and, fortunately, we stopped within a few yards of one, so it was the work of but a moment to press the button which connected

Motorway cruising through France

been a similar amount ahead prior to our enforced halt.

Dijon was reached at 18.00 hours and Dole 35 minutes later by which time we had recovered 25 minutes on the schedule. We stopped on the road to Pontarlier to fit the headlamp lens converters as darkness was falling. Unfortunately the converters did nothing to pacify the oncoming Frenchmen but did succeed in reducing the available light and consequently our speed. Just outside the town of Pontarlier we passed through the French/Swiss customs.

Lausanne is a rather bewildering place to drive through in the dark and seems never to end, though we finally left it at 21.10 hours just 40 minutes behind our estimate. My son found it useful to border the required roads through a town on the map with a red felt pen thus making the intended route quite clear. The car is also fitted with a permanent map light and this is a very useful piece of equipment, since it saves waving a torch around. Martigny, the next check point on our list should have been reached at 21.45 hours, and we had cut the deficit to 20 minutes by the time we started looking for the Grand St Bernard tunnel; unfortunately we were still looking for it 40 minutes later having explored the whole of the north side of Lake Geneva — shown on French maps as Lac Leman — almost as far as Brig. For the rest of the journey we were unable to get back on schedule and it was not until we joined the *autostrada* that we made any inroads on the accumulated time deficit.

We had allowed one and a half hours to get from Martigny through the tunnel to Aosta but took nearly two hours and were exactly an hour behind when we joined the Italian motorway system at midnight, having covered merely 610 miles in 15¼ hours since leaving Calais, an average speed of only 39.95 mph. The approach roads to the Grand St. Bernard were windy and bordered with snow on either side, but the tunnel itself was well lit and very straightforward.

It was now Good Friday and the *autostrada* looked like Piccadilly Circus on New Year's Eve with the headlamps, winkers and brake lights from a continuous stream of vehicles which continued throughout the night. The Italians take their *festas* seriously and none more seriously than *Pasquale* when all Italy and his wife take to the road to visit the relative who lives furthest from them; it appears to be a point of honour to complete the trip in approximately half the time that it took on the last occasion and I would not willingly pick Good Froday to use the motorway again.

Much has been written about the excellent Italian *autostradas* which are very fast with remarkably good lane discipline when contrasted with normal Italian town road behaviour. However, they are predominantly two lane and the outside lane is intended strictly for overtaking. The only way to stay in the fast lane is to leave your left-hand indicator flashing all the time; if you don't the chap right in front of you will almost certainly pull out across your bows.

From Aosta to Milan is 104 miles and these were probably the most boring since they introduced us to the start of a 600 mile slog through the night and yet were so crowded that it was difficult to believe that dual carriageway driving was in operation. On this stretch, after Ivres, the Turin/Milan traffic joins the motorway and the composite result is entirely unnerving to those who are not accustomed to this sort of cut and thrust midnight driving.

The distance from Milan to Rome is roughly 335 miles though in the early hours of the morning it seems a lot longer. This stretch is completed without having to go through a toll booth and each town is merely recognised by, for example, the sign "Bologna Nord" followed by "Bologna Centro" and finally "Bologna Sud" after which you know that you are now looking for the signs marked Roma.

Florence comes and goes with its attendant signs, as does Orvieto and we noted that this town was passed at 05.40 hours after having completed exactly 1,000 miles in almost 21 hours since leaving Calais — an overall speed of a little over 47.5 mph. This was not quite as good as schedule though we had picked up to within five minutes of our intended time at Florence and we still held that margin at Orvieto. The last spurt to Naples called for 130 miles to be covered in 90 minutes and this required an average speed of just a little under 90 mph for the complete distance, which is probably fairly hopeful even under normal conditions. The closing in of fog, however, reduced our average speed to 65 mph.

It is essential on journeys such as this to ensure that you have really passed a town since you see nothing of it except the exit signposts and, in fact, the end of the motorway which reputedly terminates at Naples is roughly 16 miles outside the town. We finally arrived at 08.40 hours — 24 hours and five minutes after leaving Calais — and had covered the 1,190 miles at an average speed of roughly 49.5 mph. On our entrance into Naples we found the way barred by an enormous number of oil and petrol tankers, whose drivers had chosen the *festa* to strike. In Italy Super grade petrol is expensive costing almost 50p per gallon and it is worth noting that concessionary petrol coupons amounting to 15 litres (approximately 3.3 gallons) per day can be purchased in England and the AA office at Ramsgate was able to supply these. Obviously this amounts to a considerable economy.

We could have achieved a slightly better time without the tanker drivers' strike, and having made a final time check at Naples, we proceeded at a rather more leisurely pace to our hotel in Amalfi where we arrived at 10.00 hours after having driven 1,380 miles since leaving Andover at 04.05 hours the previous morning with stops only for the breakdown and fuel. This mileage in 29 hours and 55 minutes represents only 46.1 mph and is not particularly spectacular but included the Channel crossing and the time spent off the road at Avallon together with the constantly attendant worry of lost oil pressure. It certainly seemed a long way. However, we still felt fresh enough after a shower to walk round the town and enjoy lunch in a beach restaurant before having a couple of hours sleep in the afternoon. □

us with the area office of the Touring Club de France. It took some time, however, to explain our loss of oil pressure to a Frenchman who couldn't speak any English. Eventually we gathered that a mechanic would be sent to investigate and, after about half an hour, he arrived. After a very short time he diagnosed the trouble, though we were too ignorant of the language to understand what he was suggesting. He kept shaking his head and muttering about a *manometre*. If we had been satisfied with this we could have driven straight on since it transpired that the oil pressure gauge sensing unit was on the blink. In the event he towed us to his garage in Avallon where he confirmed that there was adequate oil pressure. He was unable to obtain a replacement unit that fitted so, after blowing ours out with an air jet, he replaced it. Surprise, surprise, the oil pressure was magically restored and we set off again at 16.40 hours — nearly three hours after stopping. We were however only one and a half hours behind our schedule, having

A break for petrol, and the Lotus catches its breath for the next stage.

165

What Car? tests/Lotus Plus 2S 130/5

Six years of sensible refinement

Lotus, a company previously synonymous with home made kit cars and racing cars are now in the luxury car market. A few years ago Lotus decided to quit the do-it-yourself market and embark on a search for quality. Now, thanks to VAT, the home-brewed bodge-ups have gone, and Lotus are producing prestige cars for wealthy advertising executives. The doors fit properly, the suspension uprights are assembled the right way up and the reliability is better than ever.

The Plus 2S 130/5, to give the Lotus which we have been driving, its full and unromantic title, is a thoroughly sophisticated car. It is thrillingly fast, with superb acceleration, faultless road-holding, quietness and comfort. And that £3390 price tag includes a fabulous engine that is docile enough to deal with the worst town traffic, and a five-speed gearbox that in practical operation is a failure.

From the outside

The Plus 2S looks like a more elegant and sophisticated version of the neat and sporty Lotus Elan, production of which has now ceased. A long, flattish bonnet curves down to the front bumper, with noticeably narrow front wings that carry only the sidelights and indicators.

The "frog-eyed" Lotus — headlamps are recessed but pop up for night driving

In the Elan tradition, Lotus have preferred pop-up headlights to attempting an aerodynamic shape around permanent headlights.

Windscreen and rear window are both large and at shallow angles. A moderate sized boot is opened by a neat pull catch in the jamb of the driver's door, avoiding the need for a separate lock. Spare wheel is stowed under the boot floor.

The bonnet tips forward to reveal a crowded engine compartment, dominated by the Big Valve camshaft covers of the twin overhead camshaft engine. Access is generally good, but the distributor is rather tucked away under the twin Delorto carburettors and their air cleaners.

The body is of glass-fibre and our model had an excellent standard of exterior finish and paintwork. The glassfibre body sits on a backbone steel chassis that runs down the centre-line of the car. Glassfibre has a number of advantages as a body material, the most obvious being that it does not rust, and that it is strong and light.

Inside story

Low sports cars are usually a problem to get in to, but the wide doors of the Plus 2S help make entry less difficult. A very sensible feature of the doors is

HOW IT COMPARES

Price	Car	cc	speed (mph)	touring (mpg)	0-60 secs	30-50 in top secs	Interior width	Boot (cu ft)	Length ins
£2413	Ford Capri RS3100	3109	125	N/A	7.6	N/A	51.0	7.8	168.0
£2464	TVR 3000M	2994	127	24.0	7.2	6.5	52.0	7.0	154.0
£2690	Datsun 240Z	2393	125	28.0	8.0	9.0*	52.3	24.0	162.7
£2899	Alfa Romeo GTV	1962	121	23.0	9.2	12.0*	50.5	6.8	161.5
£3390	Lotus Plus 2S 130/5	1558	120	27.5	7.6	9.0	52.0	8.0	168.0
£3689	Porsche 914 lhd	1971	118	24.0	9.1	10.9	54.0	13.1	156.7
£3924	Jaguar E-type	5343	140	14.5	7.0	6.0	48.7	4.8	174.5

*Fifth gear

an inset red light in each door edge that comes on every time a door is opened, regardless of whether sidelights or ignition are switched on.

Once in the car, first impression is of being in a somewhat luxuriously trimmed aircraft cockpit. Normal seating position means that the large windscreen slopes away from you and the bonnet line rapidly disappears from view in front so that an average sized driver would not see much of the front of his car unless he perched forward on his seat.

The aircraft cockpit impression comes largely from the very impressive array of neatly labelled rocker switches and rows of instrument dials, mounted on a rather cheap looking walnut veneer dashboard that was in turn held in place by large, visible, chromium plated screws. But on actually trying to use the instruments for any length of time, particularly at night, the favourable first impressions disappear. Rows of rocker switches may look good but they have always been very confusing to use. Fumbling in the dark at night for the right switch along a line of identical rockers is frustrating and can be dangerous. One feels that for appearance sake Lotus have tried to add extra, unnecessary switches; worst examples are the very silly separate rockers for windscreen wipers and washers.

The instruments, too pose problems. The driver is told all he needs to know (including ambient temperature; is it really needed?) but are arranged in a silly order with the fuel gauge being furthest from the driver. Indeed the fittings as a whole look much better than they are, to the point, even, where the light switch came away in one of our tester's hands when he tried to use it.

The neat, short gear lever sits in the middle of a padded console in exactly the correct position. In contrast, the handbrake is hidden uselessly away under the right hand side of the facia. (It would be hard, however, to suggest an alternative mounting). The console is heavily padded in Ambla of the same finish as the seats, and the floor, body sides and doors are trimmed with carpet to complete the luxurious air. The adjustable front seats themselves are extremely comfortable, well shaped to give support for the back and under the thighs.

The rear seats can by no stretch of the imagination, or the legs, be considered spacious enough to carry two adults. The "Plus 2" of the name means very strictly two children, and smallish ones at that. A further problem arises on getting into them, for the now legally required "one-hand-operation" seat belt stalks seem to have caused Lotus a problem that they certainly need to solve quickly. There is very little space for the stalks between the seats and the centre tunnel, so any attempt to tip the seats forward for access to the rear, or even simply adjust the front seats, results in the catch at the end of the stalk jamming against the seat and tearing the Ambla. On our car the covers were already badly torn on one seat and any Plus 2S owner would need to be extremely careful in moving his seats to avoid ripping them.

The heater controls, mounted in the centre of the facia, can be adjusted to give a good range of temperatures inside the driving compartment and the face level ventilators give a good supply of air. This can be augmented, if desired, by opening the electrically operated windows without any real increase in wind noise and with no buffeting draughts.

How it goes

Electrifying, sums up the performance of the Plus 2S. The Lotus will whip to 60 mph in 7.6 secs and on to 100 in 24 secs. Yet the engine is very flexible and easy to start. A dab of accelerator and it will start and settle down to an even idle without any choke in most weathers. Then, when warm, it can pull steadily in fourth from as low as 1500 rpm, with the real power coming in at 3000 rpm. Engine behaviour in town is impeccable.

Our car was fitted with the optional five-speed gearbox in which the fifth gear is, in fact, an overdrive. It is solely a cruising gear, reducing the engine speed by 1100 rpm when the car is cruising at 100 mph, and so allowing very good high speed fuel consumption for motorway travel, together with a drop in noise levels.

Unfortunately the gearbox of our car did not allow the sort of fast gear changing that a Lotus driver should expect. It was stiff and lacked the positive, precise feel of clean gate.

The car's roadholding is faultless, with virtually no roll, and corners can be taken extremely fast in the dry without loss of front or rear end grip. Under power in the lower gears the tail can be made to move out slightly but only when cornering on the limit. In the wet the car becomes a little twitchy and needs quick reactions. Using this magnificent roadholding to full advantage depends on mastering the very light and sensitive steering. With only 2.6 turns from lock to lock, it makes for virtually fingertip control.

The sound insulation absorbs much of the noise, even at high speed, only a moderate level of exhaust note and some controlled engine being present.

The facia is packed with dials, switches and warning lights. Note the fuse box (above). Worth looking at — the engine, with its smart camshaft covers (below)

The "nasty" handbrake is under the facia

Ride is generally good. In traffic the "winding-up" of the transmission "doughnuts" in the drive-shafts is apparent, as it always has been on Lotuses. Lights are a weak point, the pop-up headlights vibrating with the car body and giving very poor illumina-

Seat belt stalks tear the Ambla (above) Belts recoil neatly behind trim (below)

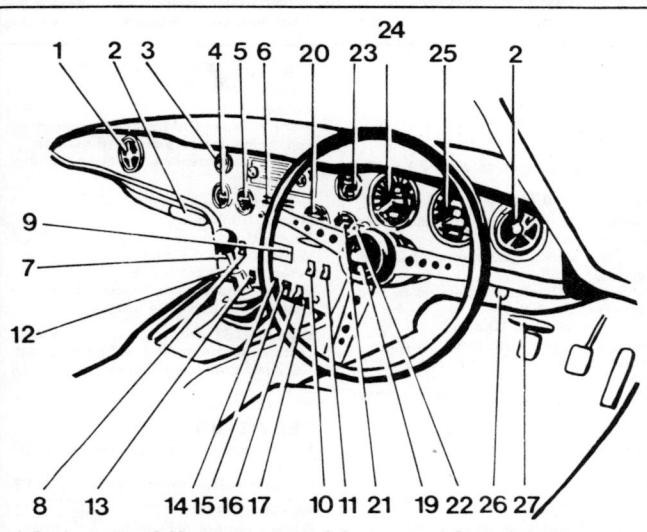

1 Fresh air vent. 2 Map reading lamp. 3 Fuel gauge. 4 Clock. 5 Ambient temp. gauge. 6 Heater and ventilation controls. 7 Rear window demist. 8 Interior and panel lamps. 9 Fuse box. 10 Wipers. 11 Washers. 12 Cigar lighter. 13 Heater blower. 14 Hazard flashers. 15 Electric window contol. 16. Fog lamps. 17 Lights. 19 Horn. 20 Voltmeter. 21 Oil pressure guage. 22 Choke. 23 Temp. gauge 24 Rev counter. 25 Speedometer. 26 Trip recorder reset. 27 Handbrake

What Car? tests/Lotus Plus 2S 130/5

The boot which is of average size, also holds the spare wheel under the floor

Spanner for the spare wheel is supplied

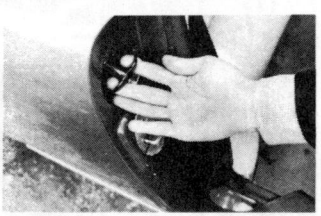

Boot catch is mounted in the door jamb

tion when dipped. Brakes are servo assisted discs all round, utterly efficient and very light.

Can I afford it?

Well, can you? At £3390 for the five-speed version — nearly double the price of the car when it was announced six years ago — it is quite expensive transport for what, in effect, are two people. Buying a sports car from the company which has produced the motor racing World Championship-winning car several times, it is automatically rated Group 7 by the insurance companies. You will have to watch your licence too, for 70 mph comes up disturbingly quickly, and that speed in fifth gear seems a real crawl.

However, once bought, the Lotus is commendably economic on petrol. The twin-cam engine, of only just over 1½ litres capacity, revs hard and willingly, but its efficiency returns a consumption of at least 25 mpg. The glassfibre body, whose sleekness also helps the petrol economy, will mean no rusting problems around the gills, but Lotus road cars have never been world famous for their lasting qualities. On the other hand, the car which we subjected to many hundreds of arduous miles never gave a moment's cause for concern; to jaundiced journalistic eyes, it was a pleasant surprise for the Lotus.

How it compares

Perhaps the Lotus's most direct opponent technically is the **Alfa Romeo Spyder** (£2949), which also boasts a five-speed gearbox and a race-bred twin-cam engine. The cheapest **Porsche** is the **914 SC**, a strict two-seater which offers nothing like the performance, comes in left hand drive only, and costs £3689.

But most of the opposition has bigger engines, like the 3-litre V6-engined **TVR 3000M** (£2464), and **Gilbern Invader** (£2668), or even the recently announced sporty version of the **Ford Capri**, the **RS3100**, which weighs in at £2413. On the other hand the purchaser may prefer the reserves of pulling power offered by the V12 **Jaguar E-type** (£3638) at the expense of the nimble road-holding and handling of the Lotus. And it really is on these last two counts that the Lotus must be judged. There is hardly any other car, more or less expensive, that compares on these two vital points.

Our verdict

It's a nice car, but its sophisticated handling and magnificent road holding will not be appreciated by all people. If you drive many miles alone, on business say, then you must get your boss to buy you one immediately. Economy, silence and comfort are good, and the real disadvantages are passenger accommodation and widespread availability of cheap servicing and repair facilities.

The smooth purposeful styling of the Lotus remains undated even after six years

Lotus Plus 2S 130/5

Price: £3390 (including tax and seat belts, but no other extras).

Manufacturer: Lotus Cars Ltd., Norwich NOR 92W, Norfolk (Wymondham 3411).

PERFORMANCE
Maximum speed: 122 mph
Maximum in 4th: 120 mph
Maximum in 3rd: 86 mph
Maximum in 2nd: 60 mph
Maximum in 1st: 34 mph
Speedometer error: 3% fast

ACCELERATION
0-30 mph: 2.8 secs
0-40 mph: 3.9 secs
0-50 mph: 5.9 secs
0-60 mph: 7.6 secs
0-70 mph: 10.3 secs
0-80 mph: 14.0 secs
0-90 mph: 18.0 secs
0-100 mph: 24.0 secs
Standing quartermile: 16 secs

FUEL CONSUMPTION
Full test: 25 mpg
Touring: 27.5 mpg
Tank holds: 13 galls
Range: 357 miles
Fuel grade: 5-star
Fuel for 15,000 miles: £210

BRAKING: 30 mph to zero: 29 ft

SPECIFICATION
Engine: Cast iron block and alloy head.
No of cylinders: 4
Bore and stroke: 86.2 mm x 72.8 mm
Capacity: 1558 cc
Valve gear: Overhead, operated by twin overhead camshafts
Compression ratio: 10.3:1
Carburation: two Delorto DHLA 40
Maximum power: 126 bhp DIN at 6500 rpm
Maximum torque: 113 lb/ft DIN at 5500 rpm
Cooling: water
Main bearings: 5

Transmission
Clutch: 8in diaphragm
Gearbox: 5-speed, all-syncromesh
Ratios: 3.2, 2.0, 1.37, 1.0 and 0.8:1
Final Drive: 3.77:1
Mph per 1000 rpm in top gear: 22.3 mph

Steering: rack and pinion
Power: No
Turns, lock to lock: 2.6
Turning circle: 36 ft.

Suspension
Front: Independent by double wishbones, coil spring/dampers and anti-roll bar
Rear: Independent by struts, coil spring/dampers

Brakes: Servo-assisted
Front: 10 ins discs
Rear: 10 ins discs
Wheels: 4.5 x 13 alloy
Tyres: Dunlop SP Sport
Body construction: steel backbone chassis and glassfibre body.

Weight: 18½ cwt
Distribution (front/rear): 47/53 per cent
NCC recommended towing weight: 14 cwt
Payload: 745 lbs

SERVICING
Recommended service interval: 6000 miles
Labour only (approximately): £5.50 to £8

PARTS COSTS
Front wing: not applicable
Front brake pads: £4.73
Windscreen (tinted): £57
Exhaust system (complete): £31.39
Clutch unit: £13.40
Replacement engine: £458
Replacement gearbox: £292

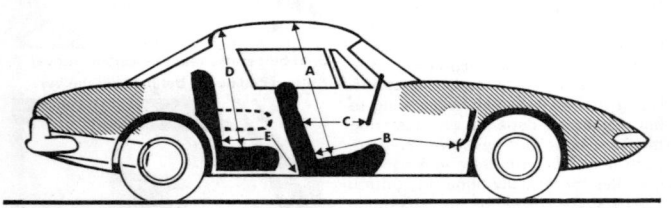

A: 39ins. B: 36½ ins. to 39½ ins. C: 22 ins to 25 ins. D: 30 ins. E: 27 ins. to 30 ins.
Length: 168 ins. Wheelbase: 96 ins. Track: 54 ins (front); 55 ins (rear). Width: 63 ins.
Height: 47 ins. Interior width: 52 ins

TRACK TEST

Lightweight Lotus Elan

'It sticks very well at the back, so well, in fact, that no matter how hard I booted it the tail didn't go far out of line'

ADDED ELAN

Willie Green once raced a Lotus Elite, but the competition version of the Elan, the 26R, was a new experience for him

Extreme functionalism characterises the 26R's cockpit

"You mean to say it held together for a dozen laps?" That was Graham Warner's reaction when he heard that my latest track test outing had been in a Lotus 26R, the lightweight competition version of the Elan. Funny, that: it wasn't the response I would have expected from the man who was instrumental in developing the 26R!

The car I tried is owned by Malcolm Ricketts, a self-confessed Lotus 'nut' who has owned Elans since 1967 and currently has seven and a half Lotuses! Besides the 26R he has two roadgoing Elans (pictured in colour on the facing page), a 26R road replica presently being built up, a Formula Junior 22, a roadgoing Elite, a racing Elite, and half of DAD10 (jointly owned with Robin Longdon). He raced the 26R regularly last season, finishing fourth in the Rolatruc HSCC Classic Sportscar Championship's 1301-3000cc GT class, a category won by Tony Thompson's similar 26R. Before I describe what Malcolm's car is like to drive, let's take a look at the background of the 26R.

Racing debut

Since the Elite has been so successful in competition, it was only natural that the Elan would be a popular racing GT car, especially as its handling and roadholding were of such a high order on the road. Although the Elan had been unveiled at Earls Court in 1962, full-scale production didn't start until well into '63, so the car that Graham Warner of the Chequered Flag got his hands on was one of the prototypes. Bearing the personal registration number LOV 1 which Warner had used on his Elite, the Elan made its racing debut at the Silverstone International Trophy meeting on May 11, 1963.

"It was a diabolical car," remembers Warner, "and it got worse and worse through the race as the handling deteriorated. We found afterwards that there was a 20 degree twist in the lower rear wishbones — it was a miracle the things didn't twist right off! I didn't like the Elan nearly as much as the Elite, and even after all the development which we subsequently did I never thought it was as strong or as predictable as the Elite." *Autosport*'s verdict on this first appearance was that 'once handling problems have been overcome, it will be a strong contender for 2-litre honours.'

With official blessing from Lotus, who were far too involved with other projects from Formula 1 to Formula Junior, Warner embarked on a development programme which in between races involved many hours of thrashing LOV 1 round Goodwood and Brands Hatch, Peter Arundell and Mike Spence helping him out with the driving. "The handling was the real problem," says Graham. "At nine-tenths it was fine, but that last tenth made it a very difficult car to drive on the limit. Jackie Stewart said that it was the most difficult sod of a car he had ever driven, because there was a sudden transition from nice steady understeer to dramatic oversteer. This was all because the chassis wasn't rigid enough."

The first changes were to remove from the steering and suspension all the rubber which had been designed into the Elan to make it a more refined road car than the harsh Elite. Metal-to-metal contact, new springs, Armstrong racing dampers, a new rear anti-roll bar and a thicker one at the front and stronger wishbones all combined to make the suspension stiffer, and the roadholding began to improve. Rose-jointing was incorporated on both rear wishbones and the top wishbones at the front to allow suspension fine tuning. Since higher cornering forces were now being fed into the chassis, strengthening was needed in parts, especially at the lower rear wishbone mountings and on the front pillars.

Power was one thing that wasn't deficient in Graham's Elan, for he fitted a Cosworth version of the Ford block/Harry Mundy-designed twin-cam head engine found in the standard Elan. By carefully balancing the engine and fitting many strengthened and lightened components, Cosworth managed to extract 145bhp at 7000rpm from a fraction under 1600cc. Cooling was a problem, so Graham's modifications included an alloy cross-flow radiator fitted with a separate header tank.

Cooked differentials

"We had all sorts of problems besides the handling in that first season," he says. "The car was always cooking its differential, so we fitted an oil cooler and a scoop to feed cool air to it, and even made a spacer to keep the boot lid open. The rubber doughnuts at the rear — straight off a Hillman Imp — gave endless trouble, so we fitted conventional universal joints. The tyres kept fouling the bodywork, and if you look at photographs of the car that year you'll see how much we had to cut away the rear wheel-arches. Generally its lightness of construction and componentry meant that the Elan was not a very raceworthy car."

The work began to pay off in race results, and one of Warner's best performances that year was to finish fourth behind a trio of Ferraris (two GTOs and a 250GT) at Goodwood. By the end of the year he was happy enough with the car to let *Autosport*'s John Bolster track test it at Brands Hatch. He was particularly impressed by how well the rear end hung on under power, and the fierce acceleration available from 145bhp in a car weighing just 13.5cwt.

The other significant Elan that year was Sir John Whitmore's Frank Costin modified example run by the Stirling Moss Automobile Racing Team (SMART). Distinctive in appearance with its Frank Costin-designed bubble hard-top, this car took Whitmore to the Elan's first race win in mid-season at Brands Hatch.

Lotus finally got round to productionising Warner's work in early 1964, the customer 26R, as the model was designated (26 was the Elan's type number, 'R' for racing), being sold in component form for £2450. A total of 52 series 1 26Rs and 43 series 2 cars would be built over the next two years, and the competition Elans mounted an onslaught on GT racing in Britain. Warner took delivery of two from the factory ("We received a pile of bits on Good Friday and were racing at Goodwood on Easter Monday — we were keen in those days!"), and they were campaigned for that season by Stewart and Warner, and occasionally Spence. The latter drove regularly for Ian Walker's 'Gold Bug' Elan team alongside Arundell, but it was Stewart who did most of the winning that year. Privateer Elans were by now flooding onto the circuits, other notable drivers being Mike Beckwith (in jazzman Chris Barber's car), John Lepp, Jackie Oliver, Sid Taylor, Malcolm Wayne and Dick Crosfield.

The 26R swept all before it in 1600cc GT racing in 1965, with Jeff Edmonds' 13 wins making him the most successful driver although John Harris and Dick Crosfield shared the latter's car to take the *Autosport* Championship. Internationally, the highlight of the year was the big Dunlop International at Zandvoort where John Hine beat Jochen Neerpasch, both of them in Elans. Geoff Breakell, Pat Fergusson, Digby Martland and Carlos Gaspar all joined the list of Elan winners in British club events. I find, as I read the written record in the Elan books, that I was even credited with an Elan win, even though I'd never driven one before I sat in Malcolm's car! I think the

169

HSCC Classic Sportscar Championship class rivals battle it out: the 26Rs of Malcolm Ricketts (left) and Tony Thompson

Warner's LOV1 follows Hedges' Midget at Zandvoort

Val Pirie in the Stirling Moss 'bubble' hard-top Elan

authors must have been mixing up their Lotuses, for I did win a couple of races in my own Elite.

The 1966 season belonged to John Miles, who won 10 races in his Willment entered car to take the *Autosport* Championship. Powered by a BRM 158bhp Phase 2 version of the Lotus twin-cam engine, his car was formidably quick. The highlight of his season was undoubtedly a race at Brands Hatch when he pipped a Sunbeam Tiger on the line with a sensational drive through the field after having to stop to have the Elan's flapping bonnet removed. This was probably the 26R's most successful year, but it was also its last at the front of the field. At the Boxing Day Brands meeting Miles appeared in the Europa-derived Lotus 47, heralding the era of the mid-engined GT racers and the end of the 26R's reign.

And what of Graham Warner's final verdict on the lightweight Elan? "There's no question that it became a better car as time went on, and it was very, very good in short races on smooth circuits. But that chassis flex was a problem on bumpy corners, and I was always slightly worried about the safety aspect since you sit outside the chassis with only glass-fibre for protection. I love the Elan as a road car — the series 4 drop-head is my favourite — but, like many other road authors must have been mixing up their Lotuses, for I did win a couple of races in my own Elite.

cars, it didn't adapt easily to competition. I certainly don't rate the 26R as highly as a racing Elite."

Malcolm Ricketts' car was originally owned by Ian Walker who beefed it up for rallying, then it became a road car, and then it was converted for racing use by D. Lamyman, from whom Malcolm bought it in 1980. He has steadily improved it by lightening it from its heavy state as a rally car, and had a good season last year, although the car was not quite as quick as Tony Thompson's class-winning 26R. His best finish in a year of 100 per cent reliability, thanks to the preparation work of Peter MacDonald Engineering, was second place overall (behind Thompson) in the FIA championship round at Donington. Over the last winter it has undergone a minor rebuild at MacDonald's north London premises, the principal work having been to fit a steel bottom end to the engine and minor suspension tuning. It was at the car's first shakedown session for the forthcoming season that Malcolm kindly invited me to try it.

Now, to be honest, I've never liked Elans on the road because they feel so fragile, but my first impression of Malcolm's car was of how rigid and strong it is. I didn't feel at all insecure in it, because everything felt so right. In fact, I can now see why I couldn't keep up with them in my Elite in 1965, even though my car, I think, had better roadholding.

The car's most amazing feature is its incredible grip, due partly to very efficiently sorted suspension. It sticks very well at the back, so well, in fact, that no matter how hard I booted it the tail didn't go far out of line, even coming out of Becketts. I soon found that Woodcote, which I expected to be a second gear corner, could be taken comfortably in third. The tendency, if anything, is towards understeer on most throttle openings, and you have to press it very hard to keep it tightly on line. If you chicken out, on the other hand, it will still tighten its line. It's so quick through the corners that there were one or two very surprised modern car drivers during my session!

Traction is terrific, with none of that driveshaft 'wind-up' which I remember on Elans, and the steering is very nice, light and precise. Because the car is so light the brakes are sensational, and I'm sure that you could out-brake practically anything, including other Elans according to Malcolm. Even though one of the modifications for racing was to alter the braking bias towards the front, you can still lock up the rear wheels when you hoof the anchors, but the car keeps going nice and straight when that happens. The feel is very progressive, inspiring great confidence.

Willing engine

The engine feels as strong as an ox and very willing — with that steel bottom end it should also last longer. Since Peter MacDonald has seen 173bhp on the dyno it must be more powerful than most of the Elans of the sixties. At my self-imposed limit of 7500rpm it felt hungry to go further, and indeed Malcolm considers it safe up to 8500rpm. The only slight problem was oil surge when I was really elbowing on, but that was due merely to the level being too low because of the cold.

The car feels strong enough to do a season without being looked at, it's very quick, it grips well, it stops superbly and it's comfortable to drive. I just wish I could think of something to criticise. Oh yes, the mirror is hopeless . . .

As a postscript, it's a shame to note that Malcolm has been officially informed by the FIA that the 26R is not eligible for the European Championship in 1985 even though Elans have been taking part for the last two years. It seems that the trouncing which the Alfa Romeo team received at Donington last year, when Tony Thompson won and Malcolm finished second, has caused the opposition to object to the Elan's eligibility on the grounds that cars were not run as the 26R until 1967, and that the only Elan which ran internationally was Graham Warner's Chequered Flag LOV 1. It seems that the objections have arisen simply because the 26Rs are quicker than all the Alfa Romeos . . .

In conclusion, I must thank Malcolm Ricketts for an opportunity which has given me a fresh esteem for the Lotus Elan.

Elans on the road

Malcolm Ricketts brought his two other roadgoing Elans to Silverstone, one a Sprint bought new in 1967 and the other a series 1/2 hybrid bought in 1981 and totally rebuilt with a view to competing in the Post-Historic Road Sports Championship.

The Sprint has covered just 31,000 miles since Malcolm built it up from a kit of parts 13 years ago — it is competely original and better than immaculate. It bears the enviable registration of ELA 111, which, with cunning placing of the number plate bolts, reads . . . yes, you've worked it out.

His other Elan, registered EUM 229D, dates from 1966, and joined the Ricketts household in fairly poor condition apart from an undamaged body. A complete rebuild by Malcolm's good friend and original race mechanic Mike Loughlin followed, and the car which emerged is perhaps the highest expression of a roadgoing Elan.

"I quickly decided that the car was just too good to race, especially after it distinguished itself by catching fire on its first appearance. I've sprinted it occasionally since then, but really it gives me the most pleasure on the road. It's my ideal road car, just how an Elan should be."

The delectable Ricketts drop-head Elan Sprint, ELA 111

With 153bhp and taut suspension, semi-race car is a joy

Besides engine work which has given it 153bhp from an all-steel version of the usual 1598cc (the standard Sprint with big-valve head produced 126bhp), the bulk of development has been to chassis and suspension, much of it following Graham Warner's route 20 years earlier. Steering rack and suspension are mounted solidly, spring rates are stiffer, dampers are new, and the rubber doughnut couplings are replaced by solid driveshafts. The car has been lightened by replacing all glass (except the windscreen) with perspex, and removing odd luxuries like the heater.

On the road the differences are immediately obvious, not only in sheer speed but in all-round tautness. With 126bhp powering just 14cwt the Sprint is a very quick car endowed with the legendary Elan handling finesse, but when you measure it against Malcolm's semi-race car you notice the surging effect of its flexible driveshafts (even though they were stronger on the Sprint) and its relatively soft springing which gives a lurchiness to the handling. The solidity of the suspension, of course, makes the semi-race car less refined in road use, but the sheer speed with which it can travel through a series of bends makes it an almost unbeatable cross-country car, with a top speed of at least 130mph.

PRACTICAL CLASSICS BUYING FEATURE

Buying an Elan

Michael Brisby says buying is a question of deciding whether you want a good one or a bad one.

There are a great many enthusiasts who have set their hearts on buying an Elan. The number of Elans which appear in advertisements proves that there are plenty to choose from, yet many of those would-be buyers will end up with a load of trouble. I will stick my neck out and try and explain how to go about buying a good one, but do bear in mind that there are almost as many Lotus experts as there were Elans built and no two advisors seem to agree!

I intend to deal with buying either an Elan or an Elan +2 in this article because, despite their rather different character the Elan +2 is basically a long wheelbase, wide track variation of the Elan formula, and if you are considering buying either car the points to look for are pretty well the same.

Now for a controversial statement: There is no such thing as a "not bad" or "average condition" Elan, they are good or bad. Even a good Elan will only stay that way if you either keep it in mothballs or work your heart out to keep it up to the mark in every respect. If you buy a tired out Elan needing an end to end rebuild at the end of the day you will be able to start motoring in Elan style with a car that is right. If you buy a Lotus which is mid-way between the two extremes — good and bad — you will probably end up doing what amounts to a total rebuild before you can feel confident about using the thing. An Elan is the sort of car where if you take any aspect of its condition for granted you are asking for trouble.

The Elan in open or fixed head form, or in 2+2 guise looks very attractive in the flesh and both the press and enthusiasts have always sung their praises, but is it the car for you? On paper the performance and economy of the Elan family is attractive and in practice the cars are still faster than the figures suggest, because the road behaviour and braking of a good one allows that dynamic performance to be used more often than any other car in their

---

Above:
*An Elan S4 Sprint and an Elan +2S 130/5 — for many Lotus fans they would be the ideal pair. Both cars belong to Dave Winter and before the letters arrive we must point out that **most** Plus 2S had a silver roof!*

Elan Buying Guide (Continued)

class. However, it must also be said that this useable performance is not blunt instrument stuff — the car is precise and fragile and demands an above average level of finesse from the driver. I'll admit it, you can be clumsy and make mistakes with an Elan and it will help you get out of trouble more than most cars but it still does not like clumsiness.

The Elans are always described as having soft suspension compared to more traditional sports cars but I would certainly not place the ride comfort in the magic carpet category. Another point to bear in mind is that while the seating and driving position are very good the noise levels and lack of elbow room and headroom may be fine for a short run but more difficult to live with, long term. You seem to either be a Lotus lover or a Lotus hater and it is worth finding out before you start spending money.

I say start spending money because below that non-rusting pretty body practically everything needs regular attention — suspension rebuilds and mechanical work crop up at rather frequent intervals and, surprise, surprise, rust is a problem which has to be kept at bay. It is not a car for taking short cuts with; cost cutting will have two effects — first it will spoil the car's appeal and a little later it will make it dangerous, and a dangerous Elan is lethal.

Right, I have probably discouraged all the dreamers and timewasters and it is time to take a look at a car. It is a seven stage process which applies to all Elans. I have chosen the order of these checks after talking to people who know the cars and the sequence reflects the importance of the checks.

1. BRAKES

With disc brakes all round the Elans have excellent, well-balanced braking performance — when everything is properly looked after. Unfortunately, we have heard some stories of cars where the brakes have been badly neglected and incorrect, cheaper, parts substituted for the correct equipment. The braking equipment is all Girling and quite conventional, but be warned that unless the previous owner has been absolutely painstaking you may well find that the handbrake does not work at all (seized linkage, wrong clearances or no pad material left), the rear brakes are not working (could be due to restriction or closure of the front-rear brake line due to careless jacking, seizure of pistons in the calipers or lack of friction material), the brakes just feel nasty (suspect that the brake balance may have been upset by seized pistons or the substitution of look-alike parts which are cheaper and incorrect).

Get the car jacked up and take the wheels off to inspect the brakes carefully and leave the wheels off while you look at the suspension.

The suspension and braking system of the (Front, above; Rear below) Elan and the Elan +2 are largely similar. They must be carefully examined and complete overhauls of the suspension are necessary at about 20,000 mile intervals. Note that on the +2s there is a steel box section behind the fibreglass sill which contains the jacking point. Since repair is expensive, check for rust.

2. SUSPENSION

Newcomers to Lotus cars may be a bit shaken to find that experts recommend that the suspension on Elans is stripped and overhauled at about 20,000 mile intervals. It is no exaggeration to say that the road-holding and handling reputation of the Elans, including the Elan +2 is legendary. This excellence is largely the result of supple suspension and low unsprung weight combined with a fairly stiff backbone chassis and for the fact that Lotus really can get independant rear suspension to work properly.

All the suspension components work hard for their living and neglect can lead to highly dangerous failures. All the suspension bushes must be in good condition and the upper and lower trunnions (at the outer ends of the front wishbones) are prone to rapid wear. The front and rear wishbones are not particularly robust and bent wishbones are not uncommon. Worn rubber bushes at the inboard end of the rear wishbones could result in rear end steering.

On the Elans, where the suspension really does work — in contrast with several less scientific sportscars — the dampers play a vital role and must be in good condition.

Before leaving the suspension I should mention the wheels and tyres. With any high-performance car the wheels and tyres must be in first-class condition and since Elans are said to be a little playful at the rear in the wet look for rather more than the legal minimum tyre tread depth.

To some eyes the Elans are fitted with very skinny wheels and tyres despite the fact that they are very light cars and renowned for their excellent road behaviour. Where wide wheels and tyres have been fitted they will impose additional loads on both the suspension and drive train and maintenance requirements will be even more frequent.

3. CHASSIS

Perhaps there is a temptation to think that because the body of the Elan is fibreglass the chassis will be equally resistant to rust — it is not. I have been told of a 14,000 miles old Sprint which had to have its rusted steel backbone replaced with a new one.

Fortunately, the most common problem areas on the chassis can be seen from the engine bay and through the wheel arches (I am assuming that most cars offered for sale are likely to have the body mounted). If the engine is installed and running have the headlamps raised — they are raised by vacuum generated by the engine — and then, with the engine stopped you can carry on with the inspection. The reason for having the lamps up is that the front crossmember of the chassis doubles as the vacuum reservoir for raising the lamps and if the lamps lower themselves over say 15 minutes the fault may be traced to the tank being porous due to rust which will mean the chassis is unsafe.

The rust starts to get a hold if drain holes at the bottom rear corners of the front suspension turrets are not kept clear and water entering through a hole behind the damper collects in the box section. The rust weakens the turrets and the walls of that vacuum tank-cum cross-member and a front end collapse is then only a matter of time.

Nobody in his right mind bought a Lotus to drive it slowly and despite the road-holding and agility of the Elans, or because of it, some people do have accidents with them. Violent contact with curbs or frontal impacts show up by producing ripples in the chassis just behind the front suspension mounting turrets, and may also be given away by bent engine mountings. The mountings can suffer from fatigue cracks around the bolt holes and cracks also occur on the top flange of the chassis close to the turrets.

The centre of the chassis is nigh on impossible to inspect with the body in place, but since the engine is a renowned oil thrower there is usually no serious rust.

At the rear there are several possible "naughties" and not all of them can be easily spotted. The tops of the combined spring and damper assemblies are mounted in rubber bushes with a steel insert bonded in — it is not unknown for this bonding to part and if that happens the possibility exists that the suspension will fold away like an unwanted deck-chair. The bracket this mounting attaches to is out-rigged from a box-section

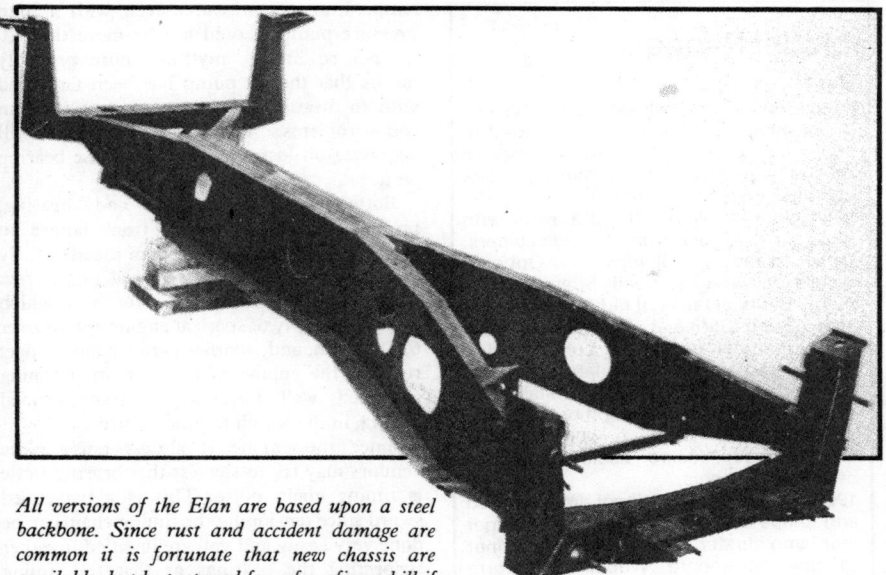

All versions of the Elan are based upon a steel backbone. Since rust and accident damage are common it is fortunate that new chassis are available, but be prepared for a four figure bill if you have a professional chassis change. Factory chassis are now galvanised and guaranteed for five years.

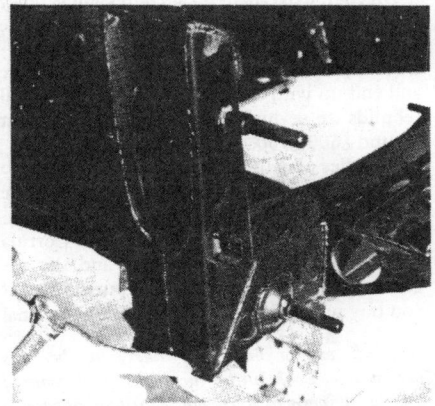

This view of the front suspension turret shows where water and mud enter behind the top wishbone — the drainhole which must be kept clear to prevent rusting is indicated. If rust has got a hold it will attack and weaken both the turret and the cross-member which also serves as a vacuum reservoir — a new chassis will be required.

At the rear the damper and spring assembly top mounting incorporates a steel sleeve which can come away from the rubber it should be bonded to with potentially dangerous results. The outrigged bracket itself may have rusted badly if the drainhole inboard of the mounting indicated has not been kept clear.

Spares

The Elan spares situation is somewhat complex. Lotus agents often get the reputation for being somewhat disinterested in obsolete cars, but the company itself is a different story. They seem to have made a real effort to make sure that owners are not left in the lurch and seem to have most areas well covered, if you ignore the engine and transmission which are more Ford than Lotus. Finding parts for the engine and gearbox is easy enough at the Ford agents provided you are looking for run of the mill bits — parts for the top end of the engine are a different matter. Turning to the less official channels it must be admitted that because Lotus parts are expensive, a number of specialists, independent of Lotus and the dealer network, have sprung up and a massive range of alternative parts and services are available. Some of those involved provide an excellent deal, sharing their intimate knowledge of the car and turning out good replacement parts. It must also be said that there are several rogues selling the wrong bits at high prices — Lotus are very concerned about this problem, particularly since in some cases the safety of the vehicle is affected.

Tread carefully, if in doubt contact Hugh Wilson, Service Manager, Lotus Cars Ltd., Wymondham, Norfolk.

turret and if the drain-hole has not been kept clear the bracket will have been weakened by rust.

The lower differential mountings deteriorate if the unit itself is not oil-tight (few are) and as they deteriorate they impose additional strains on the top mountings which secure it to the rear cross-member. These mountings are impossible to change if the bolts seize and the captive nuts rotate unless the body is removed from the chassis. The condition of the differential mountings can be assessed by inserting a tyre lever or screwdriver below the diff. and gently levering.

The rubber doughnut flexible couplings in the Elan drive-line have to transmit drive to the wheels while absorbing transmission shocks and accommodating changes in the effective distance from hub to differential during suspension movements. They lead a hard life and are prone to failure — when they go the drive shaft fails and does a great deal of damage. Performance Unlimited, Lotus specialists, manufacture an alternative driveshaft with conventional universal joints at either end with a sleeve and spline joint between them to absorb the length variations. Whether Lotus approve of this modification is not known — but the shock absorption of the original doughnut joint is lost. Drive shafts last longer if you do not attempt an *instant* 30 mph from rest.

Before completing the inspection of the chassis *do* ensure that the headlamps have remained raised. If they have dropped it is worth investigating why, just in case that cross-member which forms the vacuum tank is at fault.

Oil leaks from the differential can damage the lower mounting rubbers and impose excessive strain on the top mountings. Check for excessive movement with a tyre lever or screwdriver as shown.

Old age and weak lower differential mounting rubbers can cause the top mountings to become un-bonded or their mounting plate to crack. These mountings are often neglected and if the securing bolts round or the captive nuts turn, putting things right is a body off job.

Check that the rubber doughnuts on the drive shafts are in good condition — they need replacement at regular intervals.

Elan Buying Guide (Continued)

4. ELECTRICS

All fibreglass bodied cars are prone to electrical problems and a newcomer to Lotus motoring should be prepared for trouble. Every piece of electrical equipment has to be earthed to the chassis and most electrical faults can be traced to poor earthing — particularly on the more comprehensively equipped Elan +2. I doubt if many Lotus owners will have a word of praise for the electrically operated windows on the Series 3 and 4 Elans, and all the Elan +2's. The limited space in the doors may have dictated the adoption of a motor which was woefully inadequate.

This is how the wiring on as Lotus should look — if you find evidence of scruffy repairs to the loom be prepared to re-wire the car.

The reason for placing an inspection of the electrics so high in my list of checks is the risk of fire. Fibreglass bodywork has many advantages, but despite efforts to improve its flame resistance, fire is a very real danger and poor earths on electrical equipment are a risk. Look around the engine bay and ahead of the radiator on the nearside where the relays are sited and look for signs of partial rewiring — if you find evidence of repairs see that the joints are safe.

5. ENGINE

The Lotus Twin-Cam engine was based upon the five-bearing Ford 1500c.c. engine (the 116E from the Cortina) and is widely recognised to be a fine design. To some extent it self-destructs because it encourages very hard use, but despite this a well-maintained unit should last at least 50,000 miles between major overhauls providing nothing breaks.

Most Elan engines have had one overhaul and probably several. Despite information on the rocker covers, and from the owner regarding the state of tune and condition of the engine, take nothing for granted.

The Twin-Cam is a dirty worker which may well throw, leak or burn oil while still in good heart. Oil pressure any lower than 40 lbs per square inch at 3,000 r.p.m. (hot) spells trouble as does too high a reading. Once at working temperature oil pressure, even with a high pressure pump, should not be more than 70 lbs per sq. in. — anything more probably means that the oil pump has been tampered with to disguise or try to postpone, bottom end problems. Very high pressures will aggravate oil losses and may increase bearing wear.

Bottom end (crankshaft and bearing) problems may well result from failure to change the oil regularly or from meddling. By "meddling" I mean the removal of the rev. limiter on the distributor rotor arm which stops the supply of spark at engine speeds over 6,500 r.p.m. and, another performance dodge, running the engine with the ignition timing advanced well beyond the recommended setting, in the search for more power.

Since the engine is always noisy some vendors may try to suggest that bearing rattle is timing chain noise. This is a two-edged sword since tensioning the timing chain can be done very easily and you are justified in either suspecting the bearings or that the timing chain is stretched to the point where no more adjustment is possible — either fault costs money to put right.

An engine overhaul on a Twin Cam is fairly straightforward if you know what you are doing, but the engine does require experience — without it you may start with a worn engine and end up with a blown up one. Professional rebuilds to a high standard currently cost around £600-£700.

Supplies of cylinder heads are drying up, so go very carefully if you are told that the engine "just needs the valves done". Some Elans are running around with the Cortina 1600GT overhead valve engine and the car goes well despite disapproval of purists, but if you buy one and wish to revert to the original

Not all engine bays are likely to be this presentable. Look out for fuel leaks and beware of hybrid engines which are not what they appear to be. Average life between overhauls is 50,000 miles and it is not an engine for the unskilled to work on — a professional rebuild could cost £600 to £700.

Model Range
Elan
1963 First 22 cars built were 1500 (1498cc) — all thought to have been converted to 1588cc. Round tail lights, frameless manual windows, optional hardtop. Flick switches on panel. Short boot lid.
1964 (Nov) Series 2. Full width fascia with glove box. Larger front brake callipers. Quick release petrol filler cap. Optional centre-lock wheels (usually Special Equipment). Eliptical tail light clusters.
1965 (Sept) Series 3. Framed windows with electrical operation. Long bootlid. Fixed head versions available. Various gearbox and final drive ratios available.
1966 (Jan) Special Equipment version available with 115 b.h.p. engine, close ratio gearbox, servo assisted brakes, centre lock wheels.
1968 (June) Series 4. Wheel arches flared and shape altered. Trim changes. Larger rear lamp cluster. Power bulge on bonnet to clear Stromberg, Weber or Dellorto carburation.
1971 (Early) Series 4 Sprint. Big valve head producing 126 b.h.p. accompanied by strengthened drive train.
1973 Production ceased.

Elan +2
1967 (June) Announced with 1558cc 118 b.h.p. engine. Servo standard.
1968 (late) +2S. All factory built with upgraded trim. Bonnet power bulge.
1969 (Dec) +2S 130. Big Valve 126 b.h.p. engine. Bigger boot. Silver roof.
1972 (Oct) +2S 130/5. Five speed gearbox.
1974/5 Production ceased.

SUPER PROFILE

ROAD RACERS

Mark Hughes presents this survey of the Lotus Elan. Look no further for advice on which car to choose, how to buy and restore one, and what to pay. Photography by John Colley

THE BRIEF

The aim of the *C&S* Lotus Elan driving day at Mallory Park was to put one of Britain's most popular sports cars into perspective by examining how it evolved over its 11-year existence, and hopefully to give anyone who has toyed with buying an Elan some insight into the car's qualities and shortcomings. Three cars were selected to represent the range, and our participants drove all three in the same conditions, on a dry track and on the road, to see how they measured up against each other. It is rare that any classic car owners are happy for others to drive their cars, but in this instance the ground rules were simply that the cars should be driven hard but sympathetically. The verdicts we were seeking could be obtained only by the most thorough analysis of performance, roadholding, handling and braking on a racing circuit. Our chosen Elan owners were keen to oblige...

THE TESTERS

Taking the role of 'the expert' was Pat Thomas, one of Britain's most highly regarded Lotus specialists. His company, Kelvedon Motors of Spalding in Lincolnshire, is one of eight Lotus-appointed 'Classic Dealers', and is equipped to carry out all aspects of Lotus restoration, from engine rebuilds to bodywork renovation, but sells new and classic Lotuses as well. Above all, he is an Elan fanatic, although he admits that his first dream car was (as it was for most of us) a Jaguar E-type. But when he finally bought an E-type he was disappointed and soon replaced it with an Elan, beginning the love affair which led to setting up his own business specialising in these cars. He also has very extensive racing experience in Elans.

Our other driver, in the role of the 'the Elan novice', was Brian Herbert, a building contractor from Melton Mowbray in Leicestershire who has owned his fixed-head Sprint for three years. He is familiar with high performance cars, having owned several modern Lotuses – Eclats and Esprits – before being tempted by an Elan, but this was his first visit to Mallory Park.

THE CARS

The Elan S1, dating from 1963, is the rarest model of Elan. Only around 250 S1s were built before the S2 arrived in 1964, and it is unlikely that more than 25 per cent of these survive. Pat Thomas bought it recently because it is remarkably untouched: even the paint and the chassis are original. It is mechanically very sound rather than perfect, and the only minor alterations from original specification made by the previous owner are a smaller steering wheel (in place of the cheap wooden-rimmed wheel, which Pat has), carpets instead of rubber mats, a lid for the glovebox and a rev counter on the top of the dashboard (a crude solution by the previous owner when the proper one broke!).

The Elan Sprint, a 1972 fixed-head in Gold Leaf colours, is owned by Brian Herbert, and has received a total restoration by Pat Thomas. The car was a write-off when Brian first saw it, the car having apparently already been 'restored'. It is an illustration of how much care needs to be taken before placing work with so-called specialists that the car hadn't been given a new chassis despite several thousand pounds worth of expenditure by its previous owner. The damage occurred when part of the chassis collapsed at the front, sending the car into the path of a London taxi. Further investigation showed that many short cuts had been made, so a complete 'second restoration' was carried out. The car is now absolutely immaculate, and departs from originality in only two areas: the interior is trimmed in leather, and a five-speed Austin Maxi gearbox (as found in the Plus 2S 130/5 and a handful of late Sprints) has been fitted.

Thrown in as a 'wild card' was Pat Thomas's modified Elan Sprint, which is Pat's ideal of "the perfect roadgoing Elan". Its engine produces around 140bhp compared with the 126bhp of a standard Sprint, it features re-rated Koni shock absorbers all round (instead of Armstrongs) and uprated springs at the front, a stiffer front anti-roll bar, different track and castor settings, solid driveshafts, limited slip differential, a five-speed gearbox, a roll-over bar, flared wheelarches to accommodate wider rims and tyres and a front spoiler.

THE VERDICT

Brian Herbert: This was the first time I'd ever driven an S1 Elan, and quite honestly out there on my own I couldn't tell much difference from my Sprint! Knowing that it's a 25-year-old car, I was amazed at how well it goes. The tyres are a bit skinnier and it doesn't grip quite as well, but it doesn't feel much slower.

Pat Thomas: I think it's the low gearing which makes it feel so lively, even though there's barely 100bhp from the twin-cam on the S1. You notice on the road that you really don't need to change gear much. You can put your foot down at 1500rpm in top and away it goes.

Herbert: The five-speed gearbox conversion on my Sprint is nice for long journeys, but around the track I found that the performance was so flat in top gear that it just wasn't worth bothering with. For the entertainment value I much preferred the four-speed 'box, and the change is much nicer too.

Thomas: Yes, the old 'bullet' 'box has a much tighter change because there's no rubber in the linkage. It snicks through beautifully. The gears are very close and there's a 3.9:1 back axle, which makes it very pleasant until you want to go fast. At over 75mph, which is about 4000rpm in top, you wish you had an overdrive. Ultimately, the S1 goes very well, and its lower gearing overshadows the extra horsepower of the Sprint.

Herbert: You have to remember that there were hardly any motorways when the Elan was introduced, so cruising ability wasn't really important. If you look back at the road tests you notice that as time went by – and more motorways and better trunk roads were built – there were more complaints about buzziness in top gear. I should imagine that Lotus were almost beefing up the engine to retrieve the performance lost by making the gearing higher. First Special Equipment tune, and then the Sprint.

Thomas: I think that my modified Elan has the best compromise, with a five-speed gearbox for easy high speed, but a 4.4:1 back axle for good acceleration too. It goes beautifully from a standstill. The handling is where it really scores – it's incredibly quick through the corners, and you can balance it nicely on the throttle in a way that isn't possible with standard Elans. But all these Elans are easy to drive, and very forgiving. The thing I noticed about the S1 even more after trying the other cars is that it has so much understeer, which makes it a safe car.

Herbert: Yes, it's very tolerant. I was in a real heap with it coming into the hairpin, but it just scrubs off speed as you turn in. You can't really go wrong. Pile into a corner too quickly, the tyres start screaming, the car begins to understeer. If you think you're going too far all you do is lift off and the car points round.

Top: Fighting the understeer, Pat Thomas swings his S1 through the Mallory hairpin. Centre: Fixed-head body adds refinement to Sprint version. Bottom: Modified Elan has much more poised, neutral handling

Thomas: A lot of the fun of an Elan's handling, I think, is that you don't have to fear the car in any way. The more you get an Elan to handle better, with more built-in oversteer, the more you take it away from the original concept of a highly forgiving sports car. Plenty of people complain about the Elan's understeer, but it fits the concept of the car – after all, the average driver's natural reaction when he goes into a corner too fast is to lift his foot off the accelerator. The Elan was designed to make up for the driver's mistakes. If it was a racing car and you lifted off, you would leave the road backwards. It would be very difficult to spin any Elan – normally you would go straight off front first with your arms crossed. The later cars feel more edgy, and you have to be a better driver to get the most out of them.

Herbert: Yes, but we're talking about on the track. My Sprint may be a little more nervous at the limit, but on the road you don't know what's coming the other way and I'm never that near the edge. The big difference in normal driving is that it generally has more grip and none of the S1's understeer, so it's undoubtedly quicker through corners. The only ways in which they feel very similar is that neither of them roll much, and both feel very precise to drive.

Thomas: I think that it's surprising there isn't more contrast between them in handling. The main thing I noticed is that by the time of the Sprint the Elan had become very much more refined. It's really very quiet in the fixed-head body until you rev the engine hard: sound insulation is much better, and wind noise is quite low. There are a lot of bits and pieces on the later cars which make the S1 now look crude: its facia isn't as smart, the hood is slow to dismantle and put up, the windows only lift up, and there's more vibration.

Herbert: The performance of both cars is quite stunning. We've talked about how the gearing of the S1 makes up for its lower power, but I'm sure plenty of people don't know just how quick it is. There aren't many modern hot hatchbacks that can beat the S1's 0-60mph in around 8secs. That wasn't far short of the E-type at the time.

Thomas: It's interesting that you've mentioned the E-type, because the S1's brakes are just as bad. There's no servo, of course, on the S1, so it requires much more pedal pressure than the Sprint, but the calipers and pads are also physically smaller. When you're settled in the S1 the brakes don't feel too bad, but driving it after the Sprint it's quite alarming how poor the brakes are.

Herbert: One of the oddities of the S1 is how much more you can feel the Rotoflex couplings on the driveshafts. It's almost as if the driveshafts are connected to the wheels by elastic, giving a sort of rhythmic gentle surging forwards as the couplings twist. You also get the same effect in reverse when you lift-off. This trait teaches you to drive smoothly – accelerating firmly but not suddenly doesn't give the sensation, and must also put less stress on the drivetrain.

Thomas: You can feel that the couplings are stronger on your Sprint. If you didn't know that they were there you wouldn't notice them.

Herbert: Without doubt the modified Elan, designed as it is for out-and-out handling ability, is the most fun around the track, with a much sharper feel. It makes a fabulous road car as well because it hasn't been made any harsher. In a way, we are selling these roadgoing Elans short because they weren't designed to give of their best on the track. They have a fabulous ride as well as superb handling, and very few cars I've ever driven have achieved that compromise so well. As well as having such good performance and handling, all Elans are very easy to live with.

Thomas: It's hard to put your finger on what's so special about the Elan. It does so many things so well that it's always a joy for me to get back in one and drive. But at the same time it's forgiving enough for someone who has never driven one to feel at home straight away.

BUYER'S SPOT CHECK

Compared with steel monocoque sports cars, the Elan is relatively straightforward to inspect because of its backbone steel chassis and glass-fibre bodyshell construction, but don't think that it's free of problems. Great care needs to be taken to avoid paying too much for a car that needs expenditure on a new chassis and bodyshell restoration – there are plenty of them around.

It's a rare Elan now that doesn't have a new chassis, either a galvanised factory item (with an eight-year guarantee) or the spaceframe alternative made by Spyder. It has to be said that the factory chassis is preferable (and cheaper) because originality is having an increasing effect on values as the years go by, but there are enthusiasts who prefer the firmer handling (and harsher ride) that the more rigid Spyder chassis gives. If you find an Elan with an original chassis, the chances are that its life will be limited unless the car has been very lovingly looked after. If in doubt, the answer is always to fit a new chassis, a fairly inexpensive operation as the Lotus item costs around £400.

Your examination should begin at the front turrets, where severe corrosion can occur if the drain holes have been blocked for years. If the metal around the drain holes gives way under screwdriver pressure, the chassis is in a dangerous state – the turret could collapse in the middle of a corner. Some short-cut merchants weld new metal into the affected areas, but as the surrounding steel is weakened by years of flexing this is a stupid and potentially dangerous remedy – check for any welding ridges in the same area. Accidents or even heavily kerbing a wheel can cause distortion, which shouldn't be straightened. As all the chassis surfaces are flat, puckering is an obvious sign of misalignment. Hitting a rear wheel against a kerb can cause chassis damage around the differential, a car run on worn springs and

Specification	Elan S1 & S2	Elan S3	Elan S4	Elan Sprint
Engine	In-line four	In-line four	In-line four	In-line four
Construction	Cast iron block, alloy head	Cast iron block, alloy head	Cast iron block, alloy head	Cast iron block, alloy head
Bore/stroke	82.55 × 72.75mm	82.55 × 72.75mm	82.55 × 72.75mm	82.55 × 72.75mm
Capacity	1558cc	1558cc	1558cc	1558cc
Valve	Double ohc	Double ohc	Double ohc	Double ohc
Compression ratio	9.5:1	9.5:1	9.5:1	10.3:1
Fuel system	Twin Weber 40DCOE carburettors	Twin Weber 40DCOE carburettors	Twin Weber 40DCOE carburettors (but twin Zenith-Stromberg 175CD on some cars)	Twin Weber 40DCOE carburettors (but twin Dell'Orto DHLA40 on some cars)
Power	105bhp at 5500rpm	105bhp at 5500rpm (115bhp at 6000rpm on Special Equipment)	105bhp at 5500rpm (115bhp at 6000rpm on on Special Equipment)	126bhp at 6500rpm
Torque	108lbs ft at 4000rpm	108lbs ft at 4000rpm	108lbs ft at 4000rpm	113lbs ft at 5500rpm
Transmission	Four-speed manual	Four-speed manual	Four-speed manual	Four-speed manual
Final drive	3.90:1 (3.555 optional)	3.90:1 (3.777 on later cars and 3.555 optional)	3.777:1 (3.555 optional)	3.777:1 (3.555 optional)
Brakes	Girling discs all round (9½ins front, 10ins rear)	Girling discs all round (9½ins front, 10ins rear, servo on Special Equipment)	Girling discs all round (9½ins front, 10ins rear, servo on Special Equipment)	Girling discs all round (9½ins front, 10ins rear, servo)
Suspension front	Ind by double wishbones, coil springs, telescopic dampers, anti-roll bar	Ind by double wishbones, coil springs, telescopic dampers, anti-roll bar	Ind by double wishbones, coil springs, telescopic dampers, anti-roll bar	Ind by double wishbones, coil springs, telescopic dampers, anti-roll bar
Suspension rear	Ind by Chapman strut, triangulated lower wishbones, coil springs, telescopic dampers	Ind by Chapman strut, triangulated lower wishbones, coil springs, telescopic dampers	Ind by Chapman strut, triangulated lower wishbones, coil springs, telescopic dampers	Ind by Chapman strut, triangulated lower wishbones, coil springs, telescopic dampers
Steering	Rack and pinion	Rack and pinion	Rack and pinion	Rack and pinion
Wheels/tyres	Bolt-on 4½J steel wheels, 5.20-13 tyres (later 145 × 13 radial on S1s and all S2s)	Knock-on 4½J steel wheels, 145 × 13 tyres (155 × 13 on Special Equipment)	Knock-on 4½J steel wheels, 155 × 13 tyres	Knock-on 4½J steel wheels, 165 × 13 tyres
Body/chassis	Glass-fibre reinforced plastic body, steel box-section backbone chassis	Glass-fibre reinforced plastic body, steel box-section backbone chassis	Glass-fibre reinforced plastic body, steel box-section backbone chassis	Glass-fibre reinforced plastic body, steel box-section backbone chassis
Dimensions				
Length	12ft 1ins	12ft 1ins	12ft 1ins	12ft 1ins
Width	4ft 8ins	4ft 8ins	4ft 8ins	4ft 8ins
Height	3ft 9½ins	3ft 9½ins (3ft 10½ins fhc)	3ft 9½ins (3ft 10½ins fhc)	3ft 9½ins (3ft 10½ins fhc)
Wheelbase	7ft 0ins	7ft 0ins	7ft 0ins	7ft 0ins
Unladen weight	1410lbs (S2 1485lbs)	1530lbs	1540lbs	1540lbs

Production History

October 1962: Elan 1500 presented at Earls Court Motor Show, priced at £1499, or £1095 in kit form. Official Lotus designation is Type 26. New glass-fibre convertible body style with pop-up headlamps, separate steel backbone chassis. Ford-based twin-cam engine, all-independent suspension, Ford four-speed gearbox. Chassis nos begin 26/0001.

May 1963: 1558cc (105bhp) twin-cam replaces 1500cc unit – all cars with smaller engine recalled to have 1558cc engine installed. Optional hard-top offered.

November 1964: S2 introduced from chassis no 26/3900. New integral tail lamp treatment, larger front brake calipers, new veneer facia with lockable glovebox, smaller pedal pads, quick-release fuel filler. Knock-on steel wheels optional.

September 1965: S3 fixed-head coupé introduced, now with Type 36 designation, from chassis no 36/4510. Battery moved from cockpit to boot, boot lid extended to tail panel, electric operation for windows. Convertible continued in S2 form, with 26 prefix for chassis nos.

November 1965: Close-ratio gearbox optional on S3.

January 1966: Special Equipment package offered on S2 convertible from chassis no 26/5282. 115bhp engine, 3.55:1 final drive. Close-ratio gearbox, servo brakes and knock-on wheels standard. Repeater flashers on front wings.

June 1966: S2/S3 rationalisation completed. S3 convertible with Type 45 designation joins existing S3 fhc, having same modifications plus improved hood and framed door windows. Last S2 convertible is 26/5810, last S2 Special Equipment convertible is 26/5798. S3 convertibles start at 45/5701.

July 1966: Special Equipment also available on S3 fhc (from 36/5977). Prices now as follows: fhc and convertible £1526 (£1262 in kit form); S/E models, £1566 (£1295).

March 1968: S4 convertible (from chassis no 45/7895) and fhc (from 36/7896) introduced. Distinguished by flared, squarer wheelarches to accept wider tyres, larger rear lamps to Plus 2 style, bonnet bulge (to accommodate Zenith-Stromberg carbs on British and US market cars), perforated vinyl seat trim, rocker action for facia switches. Prices now as follows: fhc and convertible, £1665 (£1353 in kit form); S/E models, £1830 (£1486).

August 1969: Chassis nos on old system conclude at 36/9824 (fhc) and 45/9823 (convertible).

January 1970: New chassis nos start at 7001 010001 (first two figures indicate year, next two month). Suffix letters indicate body styles as follows: A, S4 fhc; C, S4 convertible; E, S4 S/E fhc; F, S4 S/E convertible.

October 1970: S4 Sprint introduced with big-valve 126bhp engine. Two-tone colour scheme available with 'Elan Sprint' wording on dividing strip. Knock-on steel disc wheels have black painted finish. Compression ratio raised to 10.3:1. Dell'Orto carbs at first, later Webers. Stronger final drive, driveshafts and Rotoflex couplings. Available only in kit form at £1686.

August 1973: Elan production discontinued after a total of 12,224 cars made.

---

dampers might have damage at the top of the front and rear chassis turrets, and broken engine mountings can cause chassis cracks where the weight of the engine bears down. A Spyder chassis can easily be spotted by its circular section crossmember in the engine bay, but if you are unsure whether the car you examine has a new chassis simply scrape away dirt or paint from a small patch to see if it is galvanised.

The bodyshell needs very careful attention as a proper respray is time-consuming and expensive. The car to beware of is the one that has received an inadequate 'flick-over' respray, because a lasting finish requires laborious stripping back to glass-fibre. Unless this has been done, gel cracks, filler and other surface imperfections will eventually show through the paint. Look very carefully against the light at the entire body surface to assess the extent of gel cracking, particularly around door handles, boot lock, fuel filler and where the bonnet is pressed down. You should also make sure that the doors, bonnet and boot lid fit properly, as the bodyshell can physically move on the chassis. Accident damage can be repaired to perfection by a skilled specialist, so any visible joins mean a sub-standard job. Look under the bonnet and interior carpets, and feel under the wheelarches, for signs. An Elan with a relatively unblemished original paint finish, such as Pat Thomas's S1 featured in colour, would be a find.

You should also check for originality of bumpers and wheels. All Elans have glass-fibre, foam-filled bumpers: Sprint bumpers are painted gold, all other models silver (although the factory put special order black bumpers on some S2s and S3s). Sprints should have black-painted steel disc wheels, but all other Elans have silver wheels.

Too many neglected Elans – and some second-rate engine rebuild people – have given the fabulous twin-cam engine a poor reputation which it doesn't deserve, so evidence of careful maintenance is important when buying. Documented service history, or better still bills for a fully rebuilt engine, are worth paying extra for, but your test drive can give you plenty of clues. Listen for any odd noises, and check that oil pressure is around 38lbs psi at 3000rpm when the engine is warm. A little puff of blue smoke from the exhaust when the engine is started is usual, but smoke on acceleration will mean severe wear to cylinder bores and piston rings, and smoke on deceleration suggests worn valve guides. A healthy twin-cam should have no oil leaks.

The most common evidence of maintenance standards is the condition of the timing chain. The adjustor is located on the inlet side of the engine, and if the threaded bolt is screwed fully home it is time for a new chain. Tension should be adjusted every 3000 miles: timing chain rattle means that it is too loose, and screeching indicates that it is too taut. Needless to say, neglect here can lead to major valve and piston damage when the timing chain snaps. People worry about the vulnerability of the water pump on the twin-cam because failure means a long job, but again trouble is always caused by poor maintenance. The vee-belt driving the pump and the dynamo should not be too tight, as excessive sideways load on the water pump spindle is usually the cause of failure.

Make sure that the cooling system contains antifreeze regardless of the time of year because its corrosion inhibiting properties are essential to the health of the all-aluminium twin-cam engine. Clogged waterways and silt deposits in the radiator cause overheating. The carburettors – twin Webers or Dell'Ortos on most models – can be trouble-spots if they have corroded, given away by lumpy performance, and ensure that they are flexibly mounted. Some strong-arm owners over-tighten the carburettors, but they are intended to be loosely mounted against the O-rings to prevent fuel frothing. Many S4s have Stromberg carburettors which need to be overhauled annually: pinking and running on are the signs of lack of attention. Strombergs have the odd trait of icing up when the temperature hovers just above freezing point, causing the throttles to stick

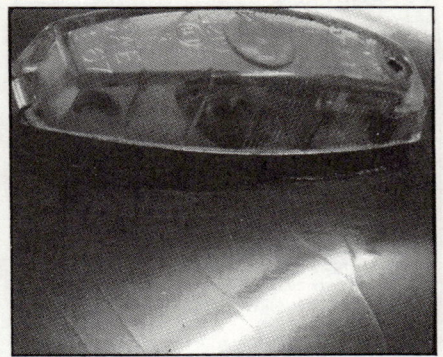

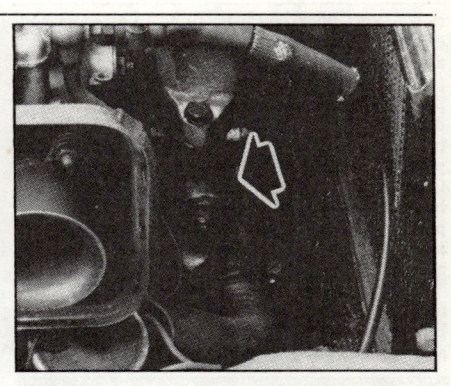

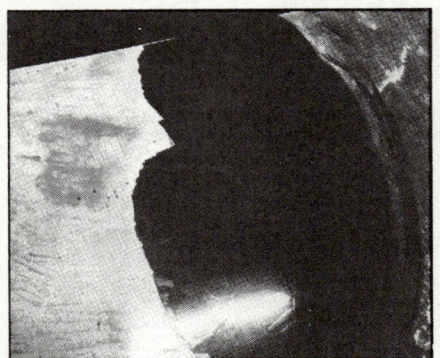

Top row, from left: gel cracks in glass-fibre; gaping holes in chassis turret; timing chain tensioner. Bottom row: perished Rotoflex; stripped glass-fibre against original paint; repairing gel cracks after grinding out and application of glass tissue

open: this is normal (!) because Lotus's attempt to provide warm air ducting didn't work very well.

Elan gearboxes are tough four-speed units of Ford origin, and very little goes wrong with them apart from the wear of hard use. Worn synchromesh will show itself by baulking the gearchange, but any serious noises will mean damaged bearings which will require a gearbox rebuild, not an expensive exercise. Some cars have been fitted with Austin Maxi or Ford Sierra five-speed units, but only three Sprints left the factory with five-speed 'boxes. The same reassuring reliability applies to the Ford differential, but again you should make sure that it doesn't hum, and that there is no clonking on power lift-off or take-up. If there is excessive vibration the differential could be touching the chassis, but adding washers to the mounting bolts can resolve this. Oil leaks should mean that the seals require renewal.

Any suspension shortcomings will need attention since there's not much point in owning an Elan that doesn't handle well, but the components are easy and fairly cheap to replace. Rubber bushes should be sound, dampers should not be soggy (owners often make false economies by living with tired dampers), and the Lotocone rubber mountings at the top of the spring/damper units should not be breaking up (as they are prone to after a few years). The Rotoflex rubber couplings on the driveshafts have met with plenty of criticism over the years because of the 'wind-up' they cause when driving hard, but they are important in cushioning the drivetrain. Their condition, with no perishing, is crucial to their efficiency, but don't be tempted by cars with solid driveshaft conversions, either by universal joint or sliding spline couplings. They can damage wheel bearings and the differential because they transmit more load. The trunnions at the bottom of each upright should be well lubricated, but a coating of grimy oil is a sign that the threads within them are worn.

The steering system, a Triumph Herald rack and pinion, should feel light and precise, any lost motion or stickiness indicating rack wear. Sometimes a new rack is taken straight off a Herald without any lock-stop modification – if the front wheels rub against the anti-roll bar on full lock, a proper rack will need to be fitted. The Elan's all-round disc brakes (those at the front also from the Herald) are very reliable, but make sure on your test drive that the car stops in a straight line without any vibration. Any pulling is usually caused by sticking pistons, which require caliper overhaul. Judder from the rear brakes may result from the driveshafts having distorted location onto the inner faces of the brake discs.

Normal advice applies to the interior of any Elan: completeness and originality of trim are an advantage, and look for tears and burns in the upholstery. All Elans were trimmed with black vinyl, so sticklers for originality would want to avoid leather or cloth no matter how neatly it has been done. All cars have a wood veneer facia (although the S1's is not as smart, and has an open cubby hole on the passenger's side) which splits very easily. Although new facias can be obtained, installation is a time-consuming job. It's amazing how many cars have trim damaged by holes cut for extra instruments and loudspeakers, so untouched originality is a plus point.

You have to be very careful when assessing an Elan because it is easy to pay an inflated price for a 'lemon'. Everyone is aware of Elan values these days, and plenty of vendors ask high prices for cars which need major restoration work: the *Price Guide* should give you clues about the condition to expect for the range of prices, from under £3000 to over £9000. You must constantly weigh up restoration costs against the purchase price. There is no substitute for examining plenty of cars before buying so that you get to know the Elan well, and the very best advice if you're buying privately is to request an inspection from a Lotus specialist once you think you have found a good car. It could be the best £50 or so that you spend!

Restoration Notes

Unless you buy near the top of the price range, a degree of restoration work will be required on your Elan. Indeed, if you're a competent and enthusiastic mechanic, the best buys are the cheapest cars which require a lot of work. Apart from engine and gearbox overhaul, and bodywork repair, Elans are simple enough for the home restorer to tackle. The other bonus is that if most of the labour is your own, your Elan can increase in value by more than you spend.

A new chassis is the most common task required, and thankfully this is inexpensive. Pulling out chassis distortions with chain equipment or welding on new sections is extremely unwise from the safety point of view, so don't even think about avoiding chassis replacement. While dismantling the car to fit a new chassis, of course, it makes sense to replace as much of the suspension, braking and steering gear as you can afford. Indeed, one specialist suggests borrowing money to do a proper job, since everything invested in the car increases its value. Almost all of an Elan's parts are available since the factory is now taking so much interest in its heritage. And, contrary to the popular view of Lotus quality, the factory parts are the best, containing minor modifications where necessary. The chassis, for example, has been strengthened by extra flitch plates at the weak points.

The greatest expense of Elan restoration is the bodywork. A proper respray can cost as much as £2000 because so much time has to be spent stripping back the paint if there is severe gel cracking. It's no good putting filler over gel cracks and then respraying as this will only be a temporary disguise. For a lasting quality finish you have to strip the car back to bare glass-fibre by laborious scraping and rubbing, and application of a water soluble stripper such as Nitromors. Gel cracks need to be ground out, any fractured glass-fibre has to be cut out and replaced with new material (this is really a job for a professional), and the whole bodyshell surface has to be treated with spray filler and carefully rubbed back with wet and dry paper. A fabulous paint finish can be achieved if enough care is taken, but any skimping will start to show through the paint within months. Repairing accident damage presents no worries as all body sections – including headlamp pods, bumpers, doors, bonnet and boot lid panels – are available from the factory.

Engine overhauls are also expensive, a really tired twin-cam costing maybe as much as £1500 to put right. Don't think you have to go to a recognised engine specialist as the eight Lotus classic dealers are all equipped to do the work. Engine blocks are the only unobtainable parts nowadays, so the expense of re-sleeving the cylinders may be necessary if the block has already been bored out to the 40 thou maximum. All the internals are easily available, and parts prices are generally not excessive (see panel). Gearboxes and differentials are easy to restore, being Ford parts, but a split axle casing would be a problem as new replacements are not available and repair would have to be carried out by a specialist in aluminium welding.

It is safe to say that no manufacturer looks after the owners of its older models better than Lotus. But for the little problem of a chassis plate, you could almost build a new Elan from scratch!

Parts Prices

Chassis	£480
Bare bodyshell (without bonnet, doors, boot lid)	£1301
Complete bodyshell	£1830
Front body section	£498
Half front body section	£272
Front wishbone (top/bottom)	£10/£15
Brake pads (front/rear)	£12/£17
Rotoflex coupling	£13
Gasket set (top/bottom)	£14/£13
Con rods (set of four)	£28
Pistons (set of four)	£58
Piston rings (set)	£33
Exhaust silencer	£24

These are Lotus recommended prices, but some specialists might offer discounts. Prices exclude VAT. Do not confuse factory parts with reproduction parts.

Maintenance Notes

The popular view that all Lotuses are unreliable is not really fair, because there are plenty of owners of well-maintained Elans who experience very little trouble with them. Like any other classic cars, there was a time when Elan prices were such that many owners couldn't afford or didn't bother with proper maintenance. The twin-cam engine isn't the bag of trouble that many people think, provided that it is regularly maintained and properly rebuilt in the first place, and it will easily clock up 80,000 miles without major attention. Irregular use, too, is often the cause of problems – it is much kinder to any car to run it frequently.

Bearing in mind the vulnerability of the Elan's chassis, it is important to keep the drain holes clear, even on a new galvanised one. It is the corrosion from inside the turrets which causes problems. If you have a car with an original chassis, it is a good idea to drill out the drain holes to ½in in diameter, and to make extra holes on the inboard sides of the front turrets.

Engine maintenance is straightforward but frequent. Oil and oil filter must be changed and timing chain tension checked every 3000 miles, and at 6000 miles plugs and points must be renewed and tappets checked and adjusted. If you're used to a modern car's lack of appetite for oil, make a point of checking the level regularly as around 450 miles per pint is normal. Keep the fan belt tensioned correctly to avoid straining the water pump.

The suspension should be kept in good shape to preserve handling quality, so dampers really need renewal every three years. Tired springs and dampers can cause chassis damage in extreme cases. The front trunnions have to be greased every 3000 miles, and the steering rack every 12,000 miles. Front brake pads last well, but rear brake pads can need replacing as often as every 3000 miles because road dirt gets thrown onto the discs.

None of this presents any cause for alarm. Don't believe the stories you hear that Lotus Elans are the most fragile cars ever made!

Price Guide

Elan prices have been appreciating fairly dramatically for the last six or seven years, certainly at a rate ahead of inflation. As the price bands covered in this section will show, Elans are now very expensive cars in the classic market and many specialists wonder whether they can go very much further. While it seems unlikely that many British buyers will be prepared to pay much more, overseas demand (particularly from Japan, where all classic Lotuses are much sought after) may well keep prices going steadily upwards. That's a pity, but it means that now is probably a good time to buy.

Under £3000: You will be lucky to be able to buy a running Elan for this money, but just occasionally a low-priced bargain is advertised privately. Without doubt, the car will need a complete restoration job: expect the chassis to be rotten, the bodywork to be faded and covered with gel cracks, the suspension to be tired and the engine in need of a rebuild. This price bracket is largely the preserve of MoT failures and crash write-offs, both of which make the best sense if you are prepared to tackle a complete restoration. If you find a drop-head Sprint, the most desirable Elan, for less than £3000, it's a bargain. Fixed-head Sprints are 10-15 per cent cheaper. There is now a premium on S1s because of their rarity and FIA historic racing eligibility.

£3000-£5000: You will only get a below-average Elan in this price range. It will do its job, but expect regular expenditure as things go wrong. The bodywork will be tatty, and although a previous owner may have been forced to fit a new chassis, little or no restoration work will have been done.

£5000-£7000: This sort of money buys a reasonable, driveable Elan, with Sprints towards the top of the band. Some restoration work should certainly have been carried out, but look for signs of sub-standard attention – it's worth looking at the very best Elans before buying to get a measure of the standards which are available. Unless the car is in extremely good, original condition, it should have a new chassis, tidy bodywork and no major mechanical shortcomings. Expect minor imperfections but better than average condition. Beware of the car advertised as 'fully restored', because it won't have been at this price.

£7000-£9000: This money should buy the very best 'honest' Elans, those which have been cherished and should need no expenditure in the foreseeable future. The paint finish should be perfect, a new chassis is essential at this money and the car should be mechanically first-class. For all but the Sprint models, this kind of car should be available at the lower end of this price range. There should be absolutely nothing wrong with an Elan for this money, you will be pleased to know.

Over £9000: The very best Elans have been known to change hands at five-figure prices, but for this you should be buying a car with so many new parts that it is almost as good as new. When you consider that the initial purchase price of a wreck, perhaps 600 hours of a professional's labour and maybe £2000-worth of new parts goes into a ground-up restoration, you can begin to understand why the best specialists are now asking – and getting – as much as £12,500 for a 'new' Elan. For the near-perfect cars, the price differential between Sprints and the other Elans tends to disappear – in fact, many people rate the S3 as superior to the Sprint.

Summary: The best buys are undoubtedly at the price extremes. Whether you are prepared for the frustrations and cost of a full restoration is your decision, but it is far better to buy a wreck and do the job properly than to buy a car in the middle ground and end up spending nearly as much on restoration in the long run. The best advice is not to buy in a hurry: almost any Elan feels good if you have never driven one before. Look at plenty of cars, get a measure of the market and obtain a second opinion from a specialist (preferably an official classic dealer) before parting with any money.

Clubs

Club Lotus: Independent from factory, quarterly *Club Lotus News*, 23 area groups, 4000 members, technical advice and printed bulletins, insurance schemes, annual national gathering at Castle Combe. Contact Graham Arnold, Club Lotus, PO Box 8, Dereham, Norfolk IP25 6AE (tel: 0362 4459)

Club Team Lotus: Run from factory, formed 1982, colour monthly *Lotus World*, 4000 members, emphasis on more recent cars and racing team, annual Ketteringham Hall open day. Contact Andrew Ferguson, Club Team Lotus, Lotus Marketing Services, Ketteringham Hall, Wymondham, Norfolk NR18 9RS (tel: 0603 811662).

Lotus Drivers' Club: Centred in Midlands, approx 700 members, concentrates on sprints and other competitions, monthly *Chicane*, 'phone-in technical advice. Contact Jenny Barton Lee, 15 Pleasant Way, Leamington Spa, Warwickshire CU32 5XA.

Specialists

Automobile Workshop, Lancaster Mews, Off Hill Rise, Richmond Hill, Richmond, Surrey (tel: 01 940 0593).

Bell & Colvill Ltd, 119-123 Croydon Road, Caterham, Surrey (tel: 0883 48013).

Daytune, Coldhams Road, Cambridge CB1 3EW (tel: 0223 211889).

Fibreglass Services, Charlton Saw Mills, Charlton, Singleton, Chichester, Sussex (tel: 0243 63320).

Kelvedon Motors, Bourne Road, Spalding, Lincs (tel: 0775 5457).

Lotus Cars (Service), Hethel, Norwich NR14 8EZ (tel: 0953 608000).

Soutar & Rhodes Ltd, Union Mills, Harrogate Road, Bradford BD2 3SP (tel: 0274 630865/632736).

Yardley Wood Service Station, 1018 Yardley Wood Road, Yardley Wood, Birmingham B14 4BW (tel: 021 474 4972).

These are the eight service dealers recognised by Lotus's 'Classic Dealer' scheme. There are many other specialists which space prevents us from listing.

Books

Lotus Elan by Ian Ward (Osprey Autohistory), £7.95. Lively historical and technical account by an Elan owner.

The Lotus Elan and Europa by John Bolster (MRP Collector's Guide), £7.95. Authoritative and gently amusing history by *Autosport's* famous Technical Editor.

Classic and Sportscar Lotus File by Mark Hughes (Newnes), £8.95. Practical buying guide to all 'first-generation' Lotuses to be published in May.

The Lotus Elan and Plus Two Buyer's Guide by Graham Arnold (Club Lotus Publication), £2.50. Basic and useful little booklet.

Lotus Elan Superprofile by Graham Arnold (Haynes), £5.95. Lots of pictures, a bit thin on words, excellent value.

Lotus: The Elite, Elan, Europa by Chris Harvey (Haynes), £14.95. Racey account, plenty of anecdote, lots of meat, accuracy suspect in places.

How to Restore Fibreglass Bodywork by Miles Wilkins (Osprey Restoration Guide), £7.95. Excellent detailed guide by leading expert in the field. Plenty of pictures and diagrams.

There are also two road test collections published by Brooklands Books at £5.95.

Acknowledgements

We are grateful to Miles Wilkins of Fibreglass Services, Pat Thomas of Kelvedon Motors and Peter Day of Daytune for their help in the compilation of this feature.